TELEGRAPHIST
AIR
GUNNER

Ken Sims dsm

J&KHP

First Published in Great Britain by
J&KH Publishing (1999)
PO Box 13, Hailsham, East Sussex, BN27 3XQ , England
E-mail: JandKHPub@aol.com

Copyright © **Ken Sims** (1999)

British Library Cataloguing-in-Publication Data. A catalogue record for
this book is available from the British Library.

ISBN   1 900511 85 1

Printed by:
XPS Ltd, Portslade

Dedicated to my dear wife Eileen
who died 23rd February, 1999,
shortly before this book was published.

CONTENTS

ACKNOWLEDGEMENTS

The Author acknowledges a major contribution from
Gordon 'Blondie' Lambert.

The Author also wishes to acknowledge contributions from
Dickie Rolph
Bill 'Nat' Gold
Vic 'Sammy' Coulter
Gordon Dixon

by

Cdr Jeff Powell DSC RN

The author is a much respected archivist and an early member of the Telegraphist Air Gunner's Association and he traces the life and work of TAGs, then Aircrewmen, from his own and others' practical experience throughout World War 2, then in the Korean War and into the relative peacetime that followed. Apart from periods as an instructor and a spell in a communications squadron, Ken spent most of his time in front line squadrons.

From the introduction of TAGs in 1922 his story reflects their feelings, complaints and successes, and includes the names and stories of a large number of his comrades as he writes of the squadrons in which they served.

I understand his rule about not mentioning the names of officer observers and pilots in his book and I enjoyed cudgelling my brain to match the crew with each of the TAGs or Aircrewmen he writes about.

Ken's encyclopaedical knowledge of Fleet Air Arm history and people was of immense value when we were putting together some of the detail needed to produce the Roll of Honour which now lies in St. Bartholomew's, the FAA Memorial Church in Yeovilton village.

I feel greatly honoured that Ken should have asked me to write the foreword to a book of his memoirs of service in the Fleet Air Arm. This book is a most valuable addition to the TAG bibliography.

The Royal Navy is reputed to be the Silent Service. I do not believe this has ever been strictly true and today's rash of stickers entreating all and sundry to Fly Navy, Dive Navy and very likely Sex Navy suggests that at least something is now being done to spread the word. However, it is some 50 years since the 2nd World War, and at that time little attempt was made to publicise the Navy's Air Branch and so the Fleet Air Arm did not enjoy particular attention. It would leap into the headlines with actions such as at Taranto or the Channel Epic but otherwise was little heard. One might read "our aircraft attacked such and such a place" and be excused for thinking this was always the R.A.F.. The Royal Navy itself contributed to this muting by banishing the term "Fleet Air Arm" which had earlier R.A.F. association and suggested a separate service. Their Lordships were anxious that the Air Branch should regard itself as an integral part of the Royal Navy. However, the Press, the Public and even the men themselves persisted with the term and after the war the name Fleet Air Arm was eventually acknowledged officially.

When I wrote the first draft of this book some 35 years ago, few naval aviators had written their stories and I deplored this fact, whilst using it as my excuse for producing my version. Since that time we have had quite a glut of such books and they were sorely needed to offer personal accounts beyond the stylised official versions of various actions. Despite all this there is still a vast body of the public who seem to think that the Fleet Air Arm remains a branch of the Royal Air Force. How do I know this ? From the many responses I have received to appeals for ex-TAGs to come forward and join our Association. "Sorry, but I was never in the Air Force" or "Try my brother, I believe he flew in Stirlings at one point". And so on. Clearly we still need to press the point that the Fleet Air Arm is part of the Royal Navy.

Two books of recent publication have indeed been written by TAGs about TAGs. So is there any point in my pursuing the same theme ? Perhaps not, but some people who have cast an eye over my scripts feel they should be seen and I believe I can cover a lot of ground that was not in either of these other books, good as they were. Perhaps my version can be considered as complementary to the total story.

If the Fleet Air Air has been limited in its presentation, accounts of its supporting personnel have been almost nil. Ground crew are often referred to in that general term because it is difficult to present them in a more exciting light. Notwithstanding that some have carried out the most hazardous tasks in appalling conditions. If some of this comes across in the following pages as occurring to TAGs, please remember that the ordinary air mechanic suffered this as his regular duty all of the time.

The pilots necessarily enjoy the major acclaim with only passing reference to the back seat crew of Observer and T.A.G.. Though the name Telegraphist Air Gunner gives a fair description of the job, the public at large barely knew of their existence. It was often necessary to amplify what this meant to a disbelieving listener. Sailors flying...? Pull the other leg!

There was one regrettable drawback that would detract from the story I had to tell. With our aircraft carriers Illustrious and Formidable being put out of action, many Fleet

Air Arm personnel and squadrons were forced to operate from shore bases. I was one of these and hence had little sea time, at least during the war years. Hardly much of a story line for a TAG !! My problem was eventually overcome by obtaining some excellent supporting stories from Gordon Lambert to whom I am indeed indebted. He spent time aboard the Eagle and later in the Indefatigable, taking in along the way attacks on the Tirpitz, attacks on Sumatra and also in the Pacific. I am glad to say that Gordon has managed to include many expressions that are peculiar to the lower deck.

In my own account, it may be that I was lucky enough to have taken part in a wide range of experiences, though in each episode bear in mind that there were others who could say they had done much the same thing. For all that, I did not take part in any major operation such as at Matapan, the sinking of Bismarck, attacks on Tirpitz, attacks on Sumatra or attacks on Japan. Nor in sub-hunts from Escort Carriers, in the Atlantic or on Arctic convoys, but there were many TAGs who did and to them I doff my cap in appreciation. My war was easy by comparison.

Included are many names of my colleagues. I could have added more but it would be overdone if the reader cannot associate an episode with those mentioned. My apologies to any who feel they have been overlooked or ignored. Clearly I cannot list everyone.

In any of the regular books on naval subjects it is recognised practice to indicate by name the ship's Captain when mentioning a ship. This is normal courtesy. In like manner it would be proper to refer to Commanding Officers of Squadrons or more specifically to pilots by rank and name when discussing any action in which they were involved. I have been sorely tempted to do this. Here and there it has been a struggle not to do so. However, this is a book about TAGs and not a treatise on the Fleet Air Arm however closely these are interwoven. I have been able to mention rating pilots, but it is immediately obvious that the mention by name of any one officer must open the door to all the rest and this would at once alter the whole tone of the book. So, with apologies, and assuring that this in no way implies any disrespect, such names have been avoided. Occasionally I have used a pseudonym. Perhaps this is as well for the anonymity may be welcomed where my views are open to contradiction. If these were historically wrong then I can only say that I report the situations as we saw them, for we were not always put into the picture.

If the action appears to unfold quite fast well we did compress rather a lot into 6 years of war. It didn't seem like it at the time. Along with so many others we spent a lot of time just waiting. The periods in between have been skipped as these were boring and uncomfortable. Parades and general duties were irksome to say the least. All servicemen know well what I mean. If the TAGs used their privileged position to duck out, well who could blame them ? Where rough conditions do show through in the following pages then let me hasten to add that our riggers and fitters and other supporting ground crew suffered to a degree beyond our experience. They have my admiration for keeping us flying.

I would like to offer a salute to our pilots and observers without whom we could do nothing. In fact whatever gallantries were performed the credit was always theirs. We, in the main, were privileged onlookers. Many a sortie could have been enacted without our presence and sometimes we were a damned nuisance. So a sincere thank you to all the pilots who brought me back in one piece. I'm still alive and kicking and I'm very grateful.

Fairey Swordfish

CHAPTER 1

Torpedo Attack

The moon sank swiftly behind the clouds on the horizon as our aircraft glided down into Valona harbour. What had been a brilliant silver orb lighting the sea thirty minutes before, had dwindled to a diffused glow and left us peering from the Swordfish cockpit into the darkening gloom. Those clouds were unfortunate as it had been expected that the moonlight would last at least 15 minutes longer. It was 0530 on the 13th March 1941 and this Albanian port was the major supply route for the Italian forces attacking the Greek frontier. R.A.F. reconnaissance had indicated several ships in the harbour.

The sing of the wing rigging was clearly audible in the cockpit with the engine throttled back to an eerie hum. It was a memorable moment for a Telegraphist Air Gunner about to experience his first torpedo attack. We had crossed the isthmus and were down to 1000 feet when the darkness was pierced by a stream of menacing lights flickering up to and all round us. So much for our hope of surprise. They were evidently well and truly on to our presence. The engine burst into life as we took avoiding action and I saw and heard shells come dangerously close. The gunner, looking back, sees this more clearly than the pilot and if the shots are near then the swish is audible. A fabric sided cockpit is no protection but it doesn't prevent an instinctive crouching at the first shock of being under fire.

Looking forward for a moment to see where we were heading I was amazed to see our leading aircraft showing navigation lights! With the usual trail we were in the way. Over on our starboard beam I could see the pit of a Breda gun with its crew lit up by the flashes. At this height we were close enough to reply with the rear gun - it would have been easier than just sitting there - but I didn't wish to offer them a sight of their target with my own tracer. As we ploughed steadily towards the main part of the harbour the minutes seemed an eternity. The guns were hosepiping around now from several places and further jinking was quite pointless.

Then as suddenly as it had started the firing stopped. We were down low on the water and I fancy that the Italians had at last learned that to fire across a harbour does

1

a lot of damage to one's friends across the way. At Taranto they did a fair job of bombarding their own merchant shipping. From our point of view it was entirely the wrong respite. The night was now as black as ink and our vision had been impaired by the firework display. We turned towards the jetty area and tried to pick out any shape darker than the rest.

At this moment I was jolted by the aircraft checking and there was a sudden change in the surrounding blackness. Two silvery white plumes of phosphorescence rose, one on each side of us. The aircraft undercarriage had hit the water. With great presence of mind and quick reaction my pilot dropped our tin-fish and incredibly the aircraft lifted clear. We turned away and I watched hopefully. The torpedo was going in the general direction of the jetties but there was no visible target. We saw nothing. After a couple of orbits we made our way to the harbour entrance still at no more than 100 feet. The sky seemed brighter now with dawn approaching or perhaps it was simply that the open sea was less black than the surrounding hills. On our starboard side four bright lights came on and shone up into the sky. I imagined them to be searchlights and stood by with the gun in case they turned our way. Much later I realised they were simply floodlights at some establishment around the harbour which seemed so bright because everywhere else was so dark. No doubt whoever turned them on got a good dressing down.

We expected a hot reception at the harbour entrance but slipped through unchallenged. Shortly after this everything opened up again over the harbour and we had an overall view of the pyrotechnics. Not a bad showing for a small port. Then I could see it was mostly directed at some flares which had been dropped. As we were headed out to sea I advised my pilot of what was visible to me but perhaps not to him. "Ah !",he said, "that will be the R.A.F. boys arriving in Blenheims to see what we have achieved". Not much, I thought, as apart from our own abortive effort there was no sign of any other success either. As five Swordfish had set out and there was no visible effect then I assumed that some were still flying round inside the harbour waiting for the flares to give them a sight of a target. We set course for home. This meant flying south down the coast to the island of Corfu and then inland to find the right valley up which to turn to reach the forward airfield of Paramythia which was nestled between the mountains. On the way my pilot asked if I could see any damage to the undercarriage. Normally from the cockpit this cannot be seen. It was also quite dark but I did have the light from the aldis lamp, not that it was much help. By leaning well over the side it was just possible to see the lower half of the wheel. The port side was easy enough but on the starboard side one got the full force of the slipstream. It was another twenty minutes before the new dawn gave me a sight of the starboard wheel. They both looked all right as far as I could tell and I reported accordingly.

I looked around for other Swordfish but none were in sight. Arriving over the airfield I was surprised to see four other Swordfish already on the ground. As a sixth machine had developed a fault and not taken off with us, it meant that we were last but one home. We landed comfortably and dispelled doubts about the undercarriage. Hastening to enquire the fortunes of the others it transpired that two had turned back when they lost touch with the formation. In fact I had noted their disappearance on the way there but it never occurred to me that they would not proceed independently as the target was easy enough to find. We had been using formation lights which were simply a small blue light fitted to a strut on each wing with a funnelled shroud such that they were only visible for a short distance from behind. I suspect that turning these off had resulted in the leading aircraft accidentally showing navigation lights which themselves are not readily visible from the cockpit unless reflecting from the ground or from cloud. We had climbed up through patchy cloud and the open formation made it difficult to keep in touch with the aircraft ahead. It was now clear that only three machines had reached the target area and one of these was missing.

This was our C.O. with the Senior Observer and Air Gunner Pat Beagley. They were eventually reported as PoWs. Command thus fell on the Senior Pilot who had flown the third aircraft in our attacking flight. He had claimed a hit on a large ship, the only success that first night. The Italians screamed that it was a hospital ship and some notoriety attached to the loss because Mussolini's daughter was aboard. Whether or not it was a hospital ship they could hardly complain with the ship completely without lights.

The new C.O. decided to lead a follow-up attack that night with the three unused torpedo aircraft - the sixth machine's fault having been put right. In the two aircraft which had turned back the first night were A.G.s Laurie Smith and Sid Boosey. I fear my lurid account of the attack would hardly have set their fears at rest. Amongst ourselves everything was always extreme. Either too boring for comment or enough to stand your hair on end. So I left them to await the next strike and flew back to Elevsis near Athens to rearm. This was our base for maintenance and weapons as Paramythia was used only as an advanced landing ground. At that time its existence was reputed to be unknown to the enemy. Our squadron, No. 815, was in fact based at Maleme in Crete and our six aircraft had been detached for this special series of sorties. Elevsis itself was borrowed from the Greeks by the RAF and we in turn were guests of the RAF.

At this time our small ground support party had not arrived at Elevsis and so, as the only rating aircrew to fly back, I found myself alone in the tent provided by the RAF for our accommodation. It was, I think, the longest 48 hours I have known. Clearly further attacks were to be made. Pat was already lost and when Laurie and Sid failed to appear the next day I assumed the worst for them. There was time to reflect on the circumstances that led to becoming an Air Gunner in the Fleet Air Arm.

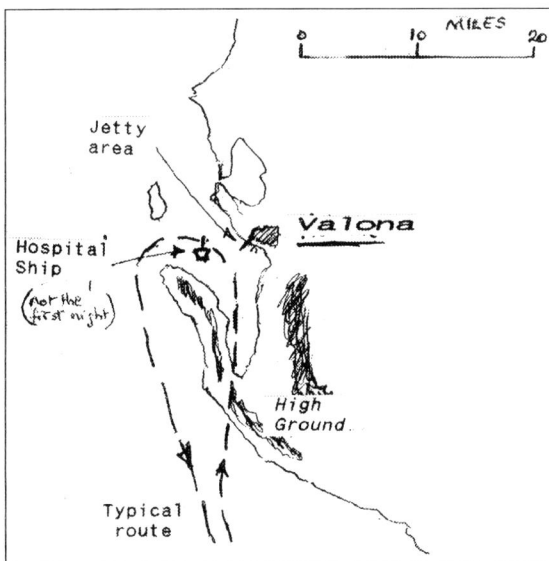

3

A view of HMS St Vincent front gate also lets us see the parade ground and ship's mast with the colonade and barrack blocks to the rear

A typical buzzer room scene at Worthy Down during SBX

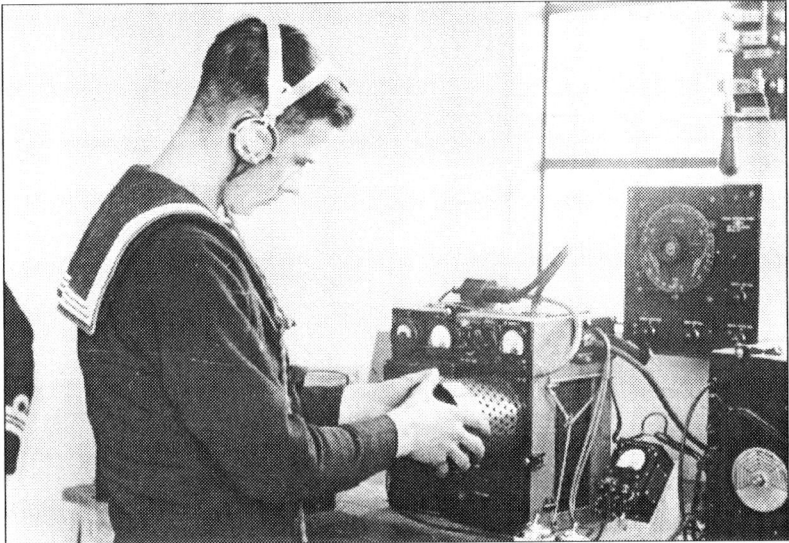

During early ground instruction. This picture lets us see the transmitter T1183 and how the coils were changed

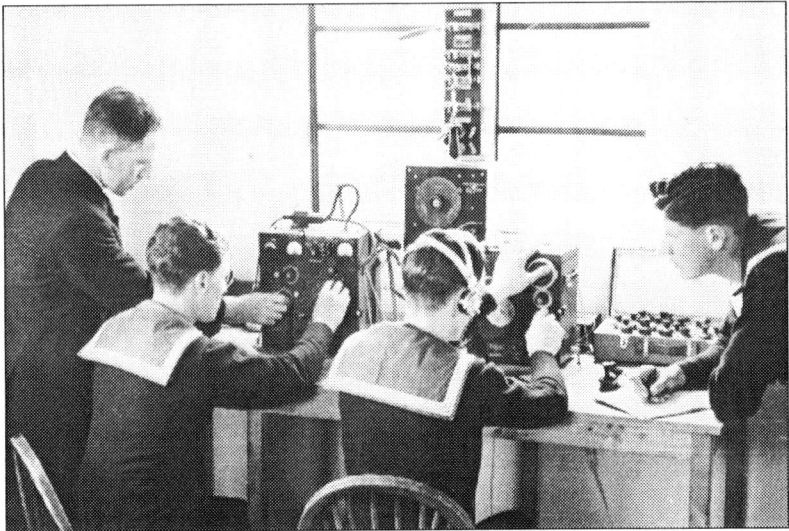

A similar scene in the instruction room but this time we may see the R1182 Geep receiver on the right-hand side (with its coils in the background)

Hawker Osprey

Blackburn Shark

Percival Proctor

6

AIR GUNNERS UNDER TRAINING, 1940

A group from 'The First 100' receiving aircraft recognition instruction.
L-R: 'Popeye' Clark; Clive Clark; J Butler; RAF Instructor; E Pousey; R Knowles;
Fred Chidlaw

Another group from 'The First 100'. This time familiarising with the Air
Lewis using the Norman Vane foresight. Both gun and sight quickly
became outdated

CHAPTER 2

"The Thrill of The Air"

Towards the middle of 1939 two office boys in a North London architectural office began to chafe at the tiresome daily routine. 17 is an age when life is opening up but one cannot explore it from the confines of an office. My colleague and chum Bill Gold and I each had our independent hobbies and outdoor pursuits but these were not enough. Ice skating for him, and camping and cycling for me, were all very well but we looked for more excitement.

We discussed the idea of joining the R.A.F. though at first this did not carry a serious tone as we realised we were too young. It was clear we had not the scholastic or background qualifications for a commission and this seemed to rule out any hope of becoming a pilot. We were not even aware of the jobs of Navigator or Observer though these too required a commission. So Wireless Operator / Air Gunner appeared our best prospect and even this might not be easy. It was peace-time and the Services were very selective. What did we care if it meant throwing away 3 years of night school study which was bringing us up to the brink of qualification for sound jobs ? As juniors we were allowed to carry out work on the drawing board and in Building Estimating but it offered little satisfaction.

However, the war clouds were gathering and I think we could feel that war was inevitable. If so, we might as well be in at the beginning doing a job of our own choosing. Our night school mathematics could prove useful perhaps. Basically though, the attraction was to travel and to fly. We would happily have participated in this only. The future was too far off to worry about.

As the younger by some months I let the idea of joining-up become something of a pipe dream but one afternoon Bill was missing from the office. Next morning he blithely informed me that he had joined the Fleet Air Arm. An advert in "Flight" proclaimed it was "The Thrill of the Air plus the Grand Life of the Sea". This was different. Why hadn't we thought of it before? I plied Bill with questions and took that afternoon off myself. It appeared that the Royal Navy had just opened up a scheme for direct-entry aircrew. I never knew of the parallel scheme for pilots and observers but sailed through the entry papers for air gunner. They were a bit perturbed at my age and pointed out that basic mans service only counted from the age of 18 but agreed that I could be accepted when I reached 17 years 6 months.

There followed the shocks for our respective parents and for our boss who was most annoyed at losing two experienced juniors without warning. Everyone signed the papers to let us go and then we waited and waited and waited. September 3rd.1939 brought the outbreak of war and much standing-to at various false alarms for air raids. As a Scout I was attached to our local Defence H.Q. as a messenger. By this time our whole Rover Crew had volunteered for one Service or another. We waited expectantly. At last the call-up arrived. September 26th.1939. I was just 17 years 6 months and two days. Bill Gold had gone a few days earlier.

From Whitehall we were sent at once to Portsmouth Barracks. I recall travelling down in the train with a fellow air gunner recruit Bob Hogg and being surprised to discover that he was a Canadian. He hadn't wasted much time getting in. Perhaps he too meant to make a career of it. Although we didn't know the difference at the time they were just taking a breather in the Barracks after the recall of all Reservists and getting them off to ships. We were just the trickle of a new intake.

Everything was fascinating. The novelty of sleeping in a hammock. Identifying badges and ranks and listening to all the naval terms. We were apt to call three badge ableseamen "Sir" and did not appreciate that continuing to wear civilian clothes for a week gave us a certain privilege. We could actually stand and gaze at classes under drill without being bawled at to "double". During the week we "signed-on", were issued with kit, and then the honeymoon was over. Several chaps protested that they desired "Hostilities Only" terms but it seemed that the wheels for such arrangements had not begun to turn and it was all or nothing at that point. The shortest term available was 7 years with 5 on the Reserve. To me this still spelled 12 years - I then had the idea that a Reservist spent every weekend at sea ! So I signed for 12 years.

Almost immediately we moved across to Gosport and the training barracks known as H.M.S.St.Vincent. Here the prime object was to teach us drill - the familiar "square bashing"-and to indoctrinate some basic naval know-how. A typical New Entries course. As the previous occupiers of St.Vincent had been Boy Entrants who had a pretty rigid set of rules largely concerned with early to bed and early to rise it seemed to us that we were regarded in much the same way. I suspect that many of the original staff remained and in age we must have appeared little different to the boys who preceded us.

All told there were about a hundred Naval Airmen 2nd Class formed into some seven or eight groups. My particular group was known as Onslow class. The names were all taken after notable Admirals - I think. I'm not sure I ever knew who he was. As the first intake of the new aircrew scheme we became known as "the first 100".

It was at St.Vincent that we met for the first time another group of entries, also Naval Airmen. These chaps would later become our pilots and observers. At a later date they would have worn the distinctive white cap ribbon denoting potential officers but it had not been introduced at that stage.

Apart from the drill we had instruction in elementary seamanship and as recognition of our objective, morse lessons. Before we left Gosport we had to achieve 10 words a minute. As a Scout I could cope with this at the outset, but surprisingly some chaps had to learn it from scratch though they were well aware that it would be necessary. There were two other features of this period. A more elaborate educational test had to be passed. This was not difficult but first time round there were a large number of failures. This called for extra coaching and a reset paper. There was a better result the second time and the Authorities breathed again. A few misfits were however weeded out. Then came the first full flying medical to ensure complete fitness. I believe even the doctors were still finding their way through the rigmarole at this early stage. The Royal Navy was training its own fliers in large numbers for the first time.

Dominating the St.Vincent parade ground was its ship's mast with ladders and rigging. A popular evening activity was to climb this mast but fortunately we were spared the boy's routine of "over the mast" before breakfast. My lasting impression of St.Vincent was the awful food eaten in a squalid mess hall. The hall wasn't filthy - we scrubbed it out daily -but it forever carried the stench of scrap food, soap and dirty water. It was always damp because we sloshed more water down before the previous lot had time to dry out. We fought for that food and argued forcibly with certain of our number who overdid their perks when duty messmen. I suppose we were fit enough to be really hungry and capable of eating anything.

An amusing recollection of the period is of Alf Pizer acting as pontoon banker whilst on the parade ground. How those cards were distributed and bet upon while actually on the march was a marvel of sleight of hand. Our hawk-eyed Petty Officer instructor never spotted that one.

One day, without explanation, we were all marched down to one of the Gosport jetties and ferried across to Portsmouth dockyard. There we were mustered in a large group alongside the historic H.M.S.Victory. To our surprise we were inspected by King George VI. He looked very pale and I suspect was already feeling the strain of the position thrust upon him. I don't think his visit had anything to do with us being the new aircrew intake; we were just a conveniently available bunch of men dressed as seamen to fill up the spaces in the dockyard. The real sailors were at sea.

We didn't get any sea-going experience at that point but we did spend many hours in boats. After our passing out parade in rifle and squad drill there was a lull as we awaited the next step. A small group of us were sent daily to a boatshed at Gosport. There we were faced with two decrepit looking cutters on blocks which might well have been there since the previous war and were full of water. We bailed them out, scraped, scrubbed and caulked them. Then repainted inside and out with a number of coats. It took us a week and most of the time we were filthy but the final result was a pleasure to see. Whether they were ever usefully employed I never knew.

We lived for the day when we would move on to the real air training. In January 1940 this day arrived. Though some of our number had failed to make the grade, of the remaining 80, half were sent to Eastleigh and half to Worthy Down. These were the Air Gunners schools. Our original classes were broken up in this distribution. At Worthy Down which was my destination we became No.13 Course.

At last we saw some real live T.A.G.s who were the Instructors and thrilled to the sight and sound of aeroplanes. We would later speak disparagingly of the Blackburn Shark trainers but at this initial view they spelled excitement. We were housed in a collection of huts built down a slope and known popularly as Goon Valley for obvious reasons. The newcomers were regarded as very green recruits indeed. Our pussers issue uniforms did nothing to dispel the impression. The Senior Course, No.11, was composed of regular Seamen and Signallers of some years experience and included a number of Leading Hands. How we envied them as they marched around in their flying boots.

The School was dominated by the impressive figure of the Training Commander and we also came under the disapproving eye of C.P.O.Tel.Bobby Maskell, one of the very first T.A.G.s and something of a legend. Much of the course was concerned with teaching us Radio Theory and we also tackled every aspect of signalling from semaphore and Naval Flags to morse Signal Lamps. Above all else was the morning Standard Buzzer Exercise or S.B.X.. Half an hour of morse reception to raise our standard to a certain 20 w.p.m.. This S.B.X. became a feature of our lives well after passing out and most TAGs could comfortably read at 25 w.p.m..There were lectures in Wireless and Visual signalling procedure plus the beginnings of a knowledge of guns. Frankly I never did see why it was necessary to know that a certain bit of metal whose purpose was obvious enough should be called a rocking-arm-trunion-catch-lever-spring or some such name and that a knowledge of all these names was vital.

Our most enjoyable moments were when the instructor T.A.G. hustled through the S.B.X. and then regaled us with stories of flying on the China Station in Baffins or Fairey 111F's. These chaps were actually trained as Telegraphists first and then later volunteered as Air Gunners. Hence Telegraphist Air Gunners. When we passed out we would only be known as Air Gunners - not having been Telegraphists first - in spite of the training we received as Wireless Operators. Not until 1942 was the term T.A.G. allowed to be used by all Air Gunner entries.

One day in March we were issued with flying clothing and at last went on our first flight as passengers with Senior Course pupils on a cross-country exercise. The first lift-off is exhilarating and I think there is always a little thrill to be felt with any take-off. Usually because we know that this is a shade crucial and success gives a sense of relief. The old Shark was pretty docile and few people suffered qualms but later, in the Percival Proctors, air sickness was quite difficult to fend off. This was not merely because of its erratic tendencies but the enclosed cockpit trapped a perpetual smell of previous sufferers misfortunes.

Each morning we were able to witness a display of aerobatic flying by a Hawker Nimrod as the Training Squadron C.O. cleared his head whilst ostensibly carrying out a weather check. Many notable names appeared in the list of pilots flying A.G.s on training. These were largely people who had obtained Pilots licences as civilians and volunteered their services as R.N.V.R. officers.The Worthy Down Wardroom must have resembled a film studio with the actors that abounded. My claim to fame is that I'm the only A.G. from 13 Course who did NOT fly with Laurence Olivier. Everyone else claims to have done so.

We had little spare time during training and less money to enjoy what leave there was. I recall that a popular outing was on Sunday afternoon for free tea and buns at the Y.M.C.A. in Winchester. In fact some very entertaining artists performed at these do's, presumably as amateurs, and if they weren't top flight then they certainly earned the enthusiastic reception they received. They put some of the ENSA artists to shame and Jolly Jack can be quite discerning in his choice of applause or otherwise. The Club's endeavour to direct our future in the field of teetotalism did not meet with the same response !

By this time most of our chaps had ventured on a tiddly-suit with bell bottoms. Ashore, a few unqualified Air Gunners aeroplane badges were sported. The Royal Navy wear red badges on their working suits and gold badges on their No.1's. A girl friend of one of our number asked why he had a red aeroplane whilst his friend wore a gold one. The reply was that he had been shot down in flames ! We nearly choked on our beer. That wasn't difficult for me either as I'd only just graduated from diffidently ordering a small brown ale and hoping they wouldn't ask my age. Of course we were all trying to grow up fast and impress. I don't suppose we knew just how fast that would have to be.

I met Gordon Dixon recently and he reminded me of a gag I got up to that had slipped my memory with the years but evidently registered with him. As a regular camper I had my own sleeping bag apart from the issued blankets. Not being a sharp riser and wishing to steal those extra beautiful minutes of shut-eye I would roll off the biscuits and under the bed after the Duty P.O.'s first "wakey-wakey" call. On his second time round a couple of scattered and trailing blankets on the bed gave me excellent cover. It worked a treat but then there was a frantic scamper to get into "Jago's" for breakfast before the doors were shut. "Jago's" was the communal eating hall named with typical Naval slang after the Admiral who introduced the idea. Before that the style had been to eat in separate messes much as one would aboard ship.

We flew almost daily throughout the summer on various exercises taking us further and further in distance from the airfield to the West but continuing to keep in touch by Wireless Telegraphy. We all came to know the Old Man of Cerne Abbas, an obvious landmark cut in a chalk hill. Radio-telephony was at this time in its infancy with limited range. Such equipment as there was went first of all to the R.A.F. fighters, certainly not into our training aircraft. Also, at this time, there was no electronic means of speaking to the pilot using the device known as inter-com which shortly thereafter appeared in all the R.A.F. bomber aircraft. In fact Fleet Air Arm aircraft such as

Swordfish utilised what were known as Gosport tubes for many years. These were very basically a speaking tube and much favoured by pilots who did not wish to be cluttered with microphones nor aggravated by background morse break-through. Yet in the training aircraft we did not even have this fundamental device. Communication with the pilot was by written note or hand signals. One day we clawed up to 17000 feet in a Hawker Osprey. Without oxygen and near frozen I could barely write the pilot a note telling him to return to base as instructed by radio. The Osprey was also a useful aircraft for camera-gun exercises as they had a suitable mounting ring.

On my first WT exercise I lost a trailing aerial - a heinous offence -because of the hand signals. No one had explained to me exactly what they were and I was simply asked if I knew the thumbs up. Well of course I did -everyone knows that ! So off we went. In the air I touched the pilot on the shoulder and circled my hand and finger. I had heard from other pupils that this meant 'can I reel out' ? Down went his thumb and I sat there glumly wondering why he had refused the request. After much waiting he rocked the wings and put his thumb up. Gleefully I reeled out and obtained a GO. To my horror as I rose up in the cockpit we came in and landed. Luckily I recovered the all important weights from out on the airfield, for the loss of which one paid dearly -which was really only as a deterrent. I didn't need telling then that thumbs down meant reel out and thumbs up - reel in. I got the lecture just the same.

Bill Gold had a narrow squeak about this time. Worthy Down is a grass airfield and actually a little hill. I saw him set off in an Osprey, go over the hump and not reappear in the air. The aircraft was a write-off on the edge of the field but Bill climbed out in one piece.

Getting ready for a flight was hard work. All accumulators for the radio and for the aircraft had to be humped each morning from the battery room where they'd been on charge overnight, carried to the aircraft and fitted. The reverse process at night. Why we didn't have some sort of trolley to assist us I don't know. We became quite experienced at humping.

About the time of Dunkirk all the aircraft were fitted with rear guns and took off and formated as a wing. We were impressed up there among it to see such a gaggle at one time but what we were supposed to be doing I never knew. I guess it was a show of strength to boost the morale of the population. Poor gullible souls. God help us if Jerry had appeared. Still, if our Swordfish were doing fighter patrols over the Dunkirk beaches why shouldn't we defend England in a Shark ? Winchester was thronged with Dunkirk veterans shortly after this. We avoided wearing our aeroplane badges as I fear the Air Force was not very popular with those men at that time. As sailors however we were the tops.

Like all Naval Shore Establishments, Worthy Down was treated as a ship - H.M.S.Kestrel. We spoke of going "ashore" into Winchester by "liberty boat" - the bus, and we were organised into watches similar to ship's routine such that every fourth day we were Duty Watch and obliged to carry out all sorts of tasks in the dog watches like peeling the next days potatoes and later in the evening clearing up the huts for rounds. Nothing remarkable in that as all new recruits will know, but with the turn in the tide of war suddenly the watches were doubled so that it came round every other day for general duties and every fourth day we had to do a four hour guard duty in the small hours around the airfield perimeter fence. Then, with the invasion scare hotting up, it became a 6 hour slog with a 2 hour dog-watch guard added in. Still we trained as normal during the day. Even for fit youngsters this was pushing us hard. I have often felt great sympathy for a certain civilian who worked in the galley and who walked from his home across the back of the airfield in the early hours of the morning. I challenged him for his pass as did two others along the road behind me. Well, they had to practice their "Halt, who goes there ?" didn't they, to relieve the monotony and we hadn't seen anyone else. It must have been hair-raising to face a succession of armed but green youngsters not quite sure of themselves. Morning after morning. At least we got to know him in the end.

There was one fiasco of an exercise in which the army were to attack the airfield. We were a machine-gun platoon for this and when called upon rushed to a certain part of the perimeter fence each carrying an air Lewis gun without cooling fins. There was no ammunition and not even the empty pans. Having taken position in a trench we wondered how we were supposed to mount the things. With ammunition I doubt we could ever have fired them without spraying half the countryside or burning our hands on the barrel as we attempted to hold them in place. Mind you, I suppose we won on points as our adversaries came through the bushes holding cricket stumps in lieu of rifles

Apart from the course of ex-seamen who had departed when we began flying there were two other courses ahead of ours. One consisted of R.N.V.R.s - the peacetime volunteers - and the other of R.N.S.R.s - the naval equivalent of the militia or National Servicemen. In a sense I suppose these chaps were the first direct-entry A.G.s though it was our group who were "the first 100 regulars." The R.N.S.R.s were the cream of the called-up 20 year olds who had volunteered to fly. Many had a public school background and in due course obtained R.N.V.R. commissions and pilot training. Not before qualifying as A.G.s however. Eventually these courses passed out and we became senior course and duly strode around in our flying boots showing off to the new juniors. About this time one of the Instructors got a draft chit to a squadron in the Orkneys. It shook him as he thought he was safely established and that only the new A.G.s would get sent to the front line squadrons. It was noticeable how he came to talk to us as equals rather than pupils. We never saw him again. I think he had a premonition.

Finally we were sent over to Aldergrove, an airfield outside Belfast for gunnery training. We went in two batches and I was with the second batch. We only got in a couple of air-to-ground firing practices when the whole school was shifted to Evanton near Inverness. Of course we were helping to shift squadron stores -what else ? - which meant a long loading and unloading effort. That journey was quite a nightmare. The Irish Sea can be nasty at any time. This time it laid it on hard and the small ferry boat bucked like a bronco. By the time we got a train into Glasgow from Stranraer we'd gone many hours without food and were quite whacked out. I shan't forget the sausage and mash laid on for us all by the Station Hotel and paid for personally by our officer-in-charge - a First World War R.N.A.S.Observer. That meal was more memorable than a banquet and was made the more delicious by the creamed potatoes -unknown to Naval cookhouses.

At Evanton the aircraft used was the Fairey Swordfish and this was our first introduction to the beloved "Stringbag". As also to their method of starting. It was a manual inertia starter which required two men to turn laboriously on a handle just behind the engine while balanced precariously on the wingroot and undercarriage. The effort required was considerable and it had to be taken up to a fair speed. When the pilot judged from the whine that it was sufficient he called "contact" , flicked on the ignition switches and pumped the petrol plunger while he or one of the handle turners pulled the inertia contact. The men meanwhile had to continue turning until the engine burst into life. It was by no means unusual for the engine to only respond with a few coughs and a splutter whence the whole process had to be repeated. The dying wail of the inertia flywheel was excrutiating. This happened as we now watched for the first time and when it failed we laughed. A certain Petty Officer Pilot Nelson heard us and promptly detailed two pupils to get turning on the handle. That wiped the smile from their faces whilst the rest of us melted away to grin out of sight.

We eventually began our gunnery course firing at ground targets and air-to-air firing at drogues towed by other aircraft. This was with both the Lewis and the Vickers Gas Operated (GO) or K guns. In the classrooms we stripped and reassembled the guns till they became like old friends. Fire a machine-gun on the ground at a firing range and you nearly jump out of your skin at the noise. Fire it from an aircraft with nothing to reflect any echoes and it is quite different. With background engine noise dominating, and wearing a helmet to deaden what noise there is, the gun sounds quite docile. In fact one can count the shots and it really does sound like a pop-gun. There is none of the film screen style crescendo of noise. We used short bursts to keep the cone of fire narrow and we hoped accurate. The whole affair was something of an anti-climax and hardly awe inspiring.

After two weeks of gunnery we returned to Worthy Down and the great day when we were given the course results and sewed on our aeroplane badge officially as fully fledged Air Gunners 3rd Class. (well "acting" then - it took 6 months to become confirmed !) There were quite a few course failures, mostly on morse, and as we discovered later many of these men were chosen to take a pilots course. We would have given our eye teeth for that. Who were the lucky ones ? A few of us who came out at the top of the list were told we might be considered for commissions later.

As we waited for the next move, four of our number were detailed to wire up a new outstation style classroom. An outstation was simply a small hut fitted with a radio transmitter-receiver which the pupils manned and operated just as they would in an aircraft. We had used these when on course before commencing flying training. This new room was similar but had half-a-dozen such equipments so it could be used as a practical classroom. We carried out the work under the direction of Nutty Richmond, a C.P.O. T.A.G. of similar standing to Bobby Maskell. Our course had been theoretical about the radio and the practical side limited to operating, so wiring up the cable forms was a new sphere of experience. The room was situated quite close to the hangers of which there were three at Worthy Down.

Early one afternoon without any warning we heard the whistle of bombs falling. Though this was a previously unheard sound nobody needed telling what it was and we hit the deck. The stick was well planted right down the line of the hangars. As we rushed for the door the rear gunner sprayed around and we hit the deck again. Finally we made a dash for the nearest shelter expecting some further visitors. The shelter was already full so some people must have moved fast. Then the air raid siren went but this was actually the end of the raid and soon we were out checking the extent of the damage. It had been a lone JU88 on a hit and run mission in an overcast sky. The R.A.F. got him all right and we received a signal "Your bird was caught". There was a repercussion to this raid without warning. That same evening we were all mustered on the parade ground to see if anyone was unaccounted. Somehow we all felt this was asking for trouble - what a target for another raider ! There was the sound of aircraft engines and in no time we were scattering in all directions. The officers appeared to be as concerned as we were and apart from a moments hesitancy were finally running with us. It was of course a false alarm. In the attack all the hangars had been hit but the most noticeable feature was the scattering of soil from the chalky ground. Subsequently Worthy Down stood out like a white splodge from the surrounding green countryside.

On summery days we had lain in the sun and watched large groups of German aircraft fly overhead quite high and heading east for London and the southern airfields. This seemed a strange approach course as it must have given lots of time for interception. Maybe they came from French airfields further to the West. It was all rather remote until we had our own visitor. Now we knew the war was really with us.

The move from Aldergrove to Evanton had interrupted our full gunnery training so, whilst the first half of the course went off to Lee-on-Solent, our group went back again to Evanton for further air firing. This time it included experience in the Boulton-Paul 4-gun turret as fitted to the Blackburn Roc. This machine was very like a Skua and intended to fly with them and give rear protection. However, the turret would not depress below the horizontal and so there was a nasty dead space under the tail. It also meant that during exercise firing at ground targets the pilot had to bank over. Surrounded by 4 Browning guns and all the feed channels for the ammunition belts the gunner couldn't see out much. There was a most odd sensation if the aircraft was turning and the turret was swung at the same time. One lost all sense of direction. Coming in for one run the pilot jinked to get on course before he tipped the plane the other way so that I could fire at a sea marker in a general seaward direction. I was too sharp in swinging the turret around following his first jink and to my horror a village crossed my sights. Fortunately I saw it in time though my finger was on the button. Needless to say I didn't fire at the proper target either as I didn't get it back round the other way quickly enough.

All went fairly well on subsequent runs but it was disconcerting that for these exercises only one gun was loaded and I got a stoppage in that. In fact the guns were arranged to fire in pairs so usually any stoppage put a pair out of action. There was a blanking-off system to prevent shooting at your own tail. As the tail was quite large and the guns switched out in pairs there was quite a high probability that you only had two in action and a fair probability that you wouldn't have any at all. Not a very satisfactory defence arrangement. The turret could even dislodge from its mounting if the aircraft flew certain manoeuvres. An elaborate system of fairings gave streamlining and these worked off the aircraft air pressure system. This fact was unknown to me at the time and coming in to land I parked the guns facing forward and opened the rear hatch. Down went the fairings using much of the air in the system and on went the aircraft virtually without brakes. We did eventually stop and the pilot was quite furious with me. At the time I didn't even understand what he was ranting on about.

There was then more free gun firing at drogues. Beam on, on the quarter and under the tail at various passing speeds until finally we were considered satisfactory and made our way back to Worthy Down. There we were greeted with the news that one of our course mates, Grant Howe, from the first half of the course, had already been killed in action over Holland. We wondered if we were all to go like that, once in a squadron. As we waited for our turn to be drafted I was sent across to check out some Swordfish. It was something of a surprise to find that such a squadron existed at Worthy Down as we had only seen the T.A.G. training squadrons. This one was at the far side of the aerodrome. They received aircraft from the manufacturers, usually new, but sometimes refurbished, and cleared them for delivery to squadrons. The pilots gave them a right aerobatic thrashing and it was my first experience of being thrown all over the sky. Quite a thrill. I was there simply to give them an air-to-ground radio test. For the first time I noted a certain respect from the ground crew presumably because they watched the air display and also because no longer was I a mere pupil. However, it wasn't long before we were back under instruction, this time at Eastleigh. On what else but the Boulton-Paul turret ? As usual things had got back to front. We could have done with this course before going on the air firing exercise. Nevertheless the practice was needed. Not only did we learn all the intricacies of the turret operation but spent much time swinging the turret round the horizon outline and onto aircraft circling the airfield. The whole turret was mounted on a ground trolley and we achieved control with a joystick lever with a fire button on the top. On this course we met up again with some of our colleagues from St.Vincent who had taken their A.G.s course at Eastleigh. In fact we had seen a number of them from time to time when they had to land at Worthy Down. Whenever there were air raids in the Southampton area the balloon barrage was raised and this prevented aircraft landing at Eastleigh. It became such an embarrassment that shortly after this the A.G.s school at Eastleigh was closed.

In a Swordfish. An air gunner checks a pan of ammunition before mounting on a Lewis gun. This gun of 1914/18 vintage was still in use in 1940

The Vickers 'K' gas-operated gun which superseded the Lewis gun was the standard throughout much of the war. This is also in a Swordfish but note that this aircraft has an overload tank in the Observer's cockpit behind the gunner

Blackburn Roc

The second half of 13 Course at Evanton, July 1940 to complete gunnery training.
Back Row, L-R: Frank Sharples; George Skeen; Bill Thomson; 'Tiny' Le Croir, Bob Hogg, Jimmy Rooke
Middle/Front, L-R: 'Sprog' Stockman; Stan Melling; DA Stevenson; Ted Kennelly; AE Liddiard; Ken Sims; Ron Roberts; Harry Pickup; Norman Train; 'Jock' Harper

Eastleigh, 1940. Receiving instruction on the Boulton-Paul turret as fitted to the Blackburn Roc

17

CHAPTER 3

Learning The Ropes

Following the turret course the next stop was Lee-on-Solent known as H.M.S.Daedalus, the Air Branch Barracks and drafting centre. It had recently suffered a heavy air attack and everyone was very jittery. In fact, as I learned later, several of the first half of our course including Bill Gold were actually at Lee during this attack and were pressed into some nasty clearing up actions on the various casualties. I had barely completed joining routine when I found I was duty watch and due to spend the night at the top of Lee-on-Solent's tower on the seafront (now demolished) as an aircraft spotter. There was an air raid warning during the dog watches and I repaired to my position on the tower. The guns started up at both Portsmouth and Southampton so we knew someone was catching it. Some Spitfires came down the Solent at low level. They didn't seem to be chasing anything and were probably just enjoying themselves on the way home to Tangmere. I duly reported them as instructed. One by one as they came into view until the chap at the other end got quite shirty and said he didn't want to know about any more.

At about 1930 I received a call telling me I was on draft to the Orkneys and leaving first thing in the morning. There followed one of the most desperate nights I can recall. I was told point blank that no one could be found to relieve me of my duties - a ridiculous situation - yet I had to do leaving routine. Everywhere had black-out fitted and it was a place with which I was unfamiliar. What is more, the usual sirens had sounded and aircraft buzzed around threateningly all night. Most of the people I required were in the air raid shelters and not available to stamp my card. So I stumbled round in the dark finding who I could and then went back up the tower to do the middle watch.

I was still trying to get my card stamped during the morning watch. Finally I reported to the Drafting Office without sleep and short of several signatures. No sympathy. No understanding. There were even threats of a charge, but the draft was overriding. I was packed off having lugged my kit halfway across the barracks (they can't bring the van to you !). To this day my opinion of those Drafting Office personnel is highly derogatory and unprintable.

With my parents living in London I was able to call on them as we passed through. Over the years I have always found this a reasonable possibility. Most drafts take one through London ; coming up from Portsmouth to Waterloo and then on via Euston, King's Cross or Paddington to wherever one is going in the North, Scotland or the West Country. One didn't have a set time table. War time trains were unpredictable. So long as one turned up within a reasonable period then half a day was not noticed. You got your kit across to the departure station, earmarked a suitable train out, say about midnight, and then had several hours to spare. Not that it was particularly pleasant to hang around in London at this point in the war. Needless to say the sirens went and anyone I tried to visit had either been evacuated or were down an air raid shelter. However, at this time - September 1940 - they were still coming over in strength during daylight and the night raiders were sporadic. So I just said hello to my parents and got away without incident.

Once more I was on a train to Inverness similar to the second visit to Evanton. I was dog-tired and recall doing the whole journey asleep on the luggage rack as someone else had bagged the seat. Of course I had a crick in the back from the centre support when we got there, but that was of little consequence. At Inverness there was a change of trains for the stopper to Thurso. I humped my kit for the umpteenth time - one kit bag (large), one flying kit bag, one hammock, one suitcase, one attache case, one gas mask and tin hat -and settled in a compartment. Not for long. The guard came through to ask if it was my kit in the after carriage, except that he didn't use the seafaring term. If so, move it, as that carriage was being uncoupled. So I carted it all up the corridor to the next carriage. Next station he came round again - move it, that carriage was being uncoupled. On my questioning him it became clear that carriages were being dropped off every so often until only one remained at Thurso. He didn't come out and say so to begin with. So I humped my kit the whole length of the train up the corridors to the front carriage and it took several journeys. There wasn't time to get it along the platform at any of the stops.

We got to Thurso and boarded a ferry for Kirkwall. In due course I arrived at the Naval Air Station at Hatston. It so happened that a P.O. T.A.G. was in the regulating office when I arrived and he welcomed me with the information that I was a replacement for someone and would be joining 801 the Skua squadron. I quite expected this and enquired about Rocs. He was horror struck and said the squadron didn't want those abortions-coffins I think he called them - and assured me there wouldn't be any.

For some unaccountable reason I was placed in a hut largely used by the F.R.U.(Fleet Requirements Unit). The chaps there naturally assumed I was joining their squadron. In the canteen that evening I met Ron Astbury and Frank Grainger from my course who had been drafted up some three weeks earlier. They were with a Swordfish squadron No.823. My new hut colleagues warned me to treat Ron and Frank with respect as they were with an operational squadron. When I pointed out that I was joining 801 the change in attitude was electric - 801 was the cream of the squadrons, even if my life span was going to be short.

In fact most of 801 squadron were away aboard Furious engaged in further attacks on Norway and only a handful of replacement aircraft and crews were working up, at Hatston. I got in several flights of fighter evasion exercises and quite liked the Skua. By Fleet Air Arm standards it was fast, fairly comfortable in the back seat with a hood and intercom with the pilot through a microphone and amplifier. Furthermore, without an Observer, the pilot treated his gunner as an essential part of the crew. A new arrival with me in the squadron was Benjy Kennedy, and Bill Crone, whom I knew as an R.N.S.R. course man had come up a little earlier. Just when I was settling in nicely after three weeks there was a call to the Regulating Office. It appeared that I had really been intended for Swordfish Squadron No.821 and had been virtually stolen by the 801 P.O., though in all fairness he was expecting another relief.

So I moved to 821 and found things very different. The squadron was at full strength and as they were a three seat aircraft compared to the Skua's two, this meant a full complement of Observers as well as Pilots. This put the A.G. in a less exalted position. As there were two P.O. A.G.s and a couple of killicks not to mention several long serving Naval Airmen the new boy found himself very much the sprog and the lowest of the low. It didn't help matters that I was almost immediately called before the C.O. and asked my age. I may have looked very young but proudly answered 18. It seems a mistake had been made on my service certificate which showed the year of birth as 1923. No wonder the C.O. was concerned. 17 year olds indeed, what was the Service coming to ?

My first flight with 821 was a night flying exercise. No problem there as the A.G. had no duty to perform. Just night flying familiarisation. The two Swordfish squadrons were at Hatston to guard Scapa Flow and carried out continuous anti-submarine patrols throughout the daylight hours. No doubt this had been instigated following the loss of the Royal Oak inside Scapa early in the war. The availability of the squadrons was largely the result of the loss of Courageous in 1939 and of Glorious during the Norwegian campaign. These squadrons had belonged to those ships and as yet no further aircraft carrier replacements were ready to take them. These squadrons continued to exercise torpedo attacks in case they were called upon to do so in earnest. If necessary, they would probably have been taken aboard Furious, as and when a suitable target had appeared off the Norwegian coast.

Soon I was sent on my first A/S patrol. These usually lasted some 3 to 4 hours. As ill-luck would have it we developed engine trouble and diverted towards Sumburgh in the Shetlands. I was given a coded signal to transmit. Up to that point I had been receiving Hatston strongly but got no reply on sending the signal. I tried a couple of times and was then told by the Observer to broadcast the message. Naturally he regarded me as very green and probably incompetent. I had however been hearing a faint response to my signals and interpretation of this was only disturbed by his thumping me on the back just when it was beginning to come through. Within a day of our return I knew just what the trouble was but it was too late then. When a strong transmission, one's own for instance, is allowed to be picked up by an adjacent receiver the latter biasses itself off and there is a long recovery time before it can operate normally again. To overcome this effect a special diode is incorporated which leaks away any biassing charge which occurs. Such a diode is seldom a source of trouble and not easy to detect as faulty, if the test is carried out with a strong local station. This time, I was unlucky enough to get a fault of this kind. If one appreciates it is happening then the solution is to disconnect the receiver whilst transmitting and plug in again immediately to receive any reply. One could not then listen-through but would get the reply. Listening-through was the art of hearing another signal through the breaks in one's own dots and dashes, and so be able to stop if someone else had a more important message. Anyway, unlucky I may have been, but green to the solution I most certainly was.

Many other A/S patrols followed and it can be very very boring just watching the wave tops and imagining periscopes in every streak of foam. At that time we had no aids to submarine detection, we just looked. Fleet Air Arm and Coastal Command aircraft must have spent many thousands of hours just looking. Such patrols were the bread and butter jobs for a great many squadrons.

That autumn was quite mild even up in the Orkneys. I recall that often I didn't wear my sidcot flying suit and was quite comfortable in ordinary overalls. Looking back today at such an episode it seems quite incredible that this was possible in an open cockpit aircraft.

We didn't have special crews but ran our own roster of who was due to fly. Hence we might go with any of the pilots and observers. In the main these were R.N. officers, as few of the R.N.V.R.officers had arrived at operational squadrons at that time. Therefore we had the regular professionals and the approach in the aircraft bore a distinct similarity to shipborne discipline. One did not chat up one's observer as might have been the case in an R.A.F. crew.

The observer had quite an amount of gear to take aboard the aircraft including his parachute, chartboard and navigation bag. Often there were other incidentals such as a Nyko coding machine and the Very colours of the day. It was expected of the A.G. to assist in carrying some of these items to and from the aircraft. As he also had his own chute and log books to handle, then he was usually well laden on the journey across the tarmac. There was a routine of handing all these things up and stowing them aboard the aircraft, plus other matters like collecting the starting handle and rigging the compasses. Each observer had his own approach to these matters and it was necessary to learn which ones liked it all done for them and which preferred to do it themselves. Some glares could be very meaningful.

On one patrol we saw an oil slick with a pronounced blob at the end. There were no ships in sight and in those latitudes such slicks were unusual as the strong seas dispersed them very rapidly. The pilot and observer seemed to agree that it might mean something more than a discharge from a ship and we dropped our depth charges on the blob. It is always quite a spectacle to watch these charges blow up such a large volume of water, even when observed from the air, as such a view belittles the effect. We circled for quite a time but nothing else happened. It possibly had come from a submarine but doubtless he was miles away before we appeared. At least it helped to relieve the monotony and to know that our weapon worked.

Not that it was monotonous for Sid Craig on one of his patrols. His Swordfish was attacked by a Dornier 17 "Flying Pencil" which chased them most of the way back to base. A jinking Swordfish can be an elusive target despite its slow speed and for an aircraft not equipped with the fire power of a fighter the Dornier was really being a bit ambitious. Sid got off some useful return bursts from the rear gun to keep the Dornier at bay. All this in between sending off signals to let everyone know what was happening.. Their machine was hit a few times but they made it safely home.

Sid was one of our killicks and he usually took charge of swinging compasses. This was a never ending chore with 12 aircraft to deal with. There was always yet another one which had just had an engine change. We A.G.s were always used as the handling party and standing around for an hour or so on the most exposed part of the airfield was no fun. In these circumstances we did feel the cold. As the aircraft was moved to each heading I recall the repeated order "steady the bobs" meaning the plumb bobs hung on the wing tips. We each tried to get the job of looking after the bobs just to give us something to do.

About a month after I joined the squadron some bodies from a lost aircraft were washed up on the beach and funerals with full naval honours were arranged. I was told that the A.G. was the chap I had come to replace. As I was also detailed as one of the bearers it was not exactly comforting to know this. Fortunately my mind barely dwelt on the subject as we were more amused by the things that went wrong. First of all the hearse failed to start and as we had reached the church door on the way out we were obliged to stay there until a replacement could be found. This turned out to be a van which was really too small. We had to tie the doors together with string. The driver had not been properly briefed and he accelerated away heading directly for the cemetery. This left a guard of honour and the rest of the naval party solemnly slow marching down the hill without a coffin. A policeman at the bottom of the hill was holding up the traffic on our approach and as we rounded the corner his face showed a look of disbelief. At the grave the sexton quickly briefed three of us. I thought he said I was to pull and he would let go. We lowered the coffin. He gave a sharp pull and I finished up one foot in the grave !

The days of routine, if uneventful, flying were very useful to me in getting experience without the pressures of action even though the patrols were operational. About this time, late in 1940, we were all made up to Acting Temporary Leading Airmen. It was the first gesture on the part of the Admiralty to recognise what their rating aircrew may have to endure but did not match the R.A.F. action in making all their aircrew Sergeants. We only equated to Corporals but at least it took us away from the drudgery of falling in with the duty watch and being detailed for cookhouse chores and similar duties.

We had a fairly full routine to keep us busy. Apart from flying on patrol every other day, there was the Daily Inspection to carry out. We had no Radio Mechanics in those days and it was the Air Gunners duty to maintain and service his equipment. This responsibility was jealously guarded. To the A.G. it was "his" radio set. These were the same radios we had used on course and keeping the accumulators topped up was the prime rule. For the record, this radio was the R1082/T1083, popularly known as the "Geep" from the identity G.P. or General Purpose. We carried spare valves with us and could if necessary replace these in the air. Periodic overhauls were the responsibility of our P.O. A.G.s 2nd Class though in fact we each did it ourselves with the P.O. signing to say we had carried it out. I.F.F. (Identification,Friend or Foe) was introduced. This was a radio response gadget that was so secret we weren't allowed to touch the insides. We merely listened in the phones for characteristic whistles that were supposed to tell us it was going all right. It was fitted with a gravity trip and an explosive charge to blow it up in the event of a crash in enemy territory. I don't know how they fared in the event of a heavy deck landing. Then there was the rear gun. We cleaned these about once a week and always when fired. Our ready room was quite a little radio workshop and armoury. Any quiet periods were always filled with lectures such as ship and aircraft recognition or P.O.W. escape techniques. If nothing else, one was handed a broom and told to get sweeping. Being a killick (Leading Hand), meant nothing in the crew room when everyone else was the same.

So we patrolled throughout the latter part of 1940, but in December came an order to disband the two squadrons 821 and 823. One assumes that the lack of submarine activity around Scapa, or at least detected activity, led to the belief that the two squadrons were wasted up there. Furthermore it is probable that the many senior and experienced pilots and observers were required to form squadrons of their own ready for the new carriers that were due to appear. One flight of 6 aircraft was to remain in being and be flown out to the Mediterranean. It was a composite bunch from the two squadrons and the 6 A.G.s detailed were P.O.Maddox, Ginger Hayman, Fred Faulks, Ron Astbury, Frank Grainger and myself.

The breaking up of the squadrons led to one glorious farewell booze-up in the canteen. By this time I was learning to swill it down with the best of them. The barrack-room shanties were sung with gusto and most of the P.O.s put in an appearance to add depth to the repertoire. I recall first seeing the redoubtable Donkey Bray at this gathering. He was a well known Rating Observer. Finally the canteen trestle tables got knocked over and the place was swimming in beer. Several of us climbed onto the cross rafters of the roof trusses to be clear of the flood and continued our 'singing ?' from there.

The following morning we took off for Donibristle and after a grand shoot-up of the aerodrome we cut round the back of the island and flew between the Old Man of Hoy and the cliff face. I'm sure there was bags of room but it didn't seem like it. The rock formations appeared to be just off the wing tips. At Donibristle which is just north of the Forth bridge we were packed off on overseas draft leave and repeated the dreary train journey back to London.

By now the capital was under constant night attack and this leave was anything but enjoyable. My mother and younger brother had been evacuated and the house was deserted. It took me some time to trace my father who had moved out to lodgings at Hatfield to be near where he was currently working for the Ministry of Supply. I couldn't stay there so it was a case of returning back home to North London and sleeping at night in a cupboard under the stairs for want of a better air raid shelter. Hardly any of my old friends were around - most had joined the Services - and their parents disappeared at night so I got little response when knocking at doors. A parachuted landmine had knocked down a complete block of houses not 200 yards away from home and some heavy guns in Gladstone Park were close enough to rock the house and wake the dead when they started up. Several times when in the street I heard the fearsome whistle of shell nose-cones whirling down and found these more frightening than bombs. One could easily judge whether or not the bombs were near and lie flat if necessary, but the cone whistles seemed to chase you around. I went into the city centre a couple of nights but there were so many fires and obstructions that it was difficult to move around and mostly I had to walk back. On other nights the fires from the centre lit the sky and I deemed it prudent to stay put. Jerry always seemed to be turning over the top of us and I believe he used the Welsh Harp reservoir as a suitable landmark to denote the edge of the target area. Finally I was glad to get out of the place but spent a last few frightening hours groping around Kings Cross Station at the height of a raid.

So back to Scotland and Donibristle. At no time was it explained to us ratings exactly what this flight of 6 aircraft was destined to do or how we were to get wherever it was we had to go. It didn't seem likely that we were to augment the Illustrious squadrons who were fully fledged unless another Taranto was planned. Events doubtless changed the intentions.

Blackburn Skua

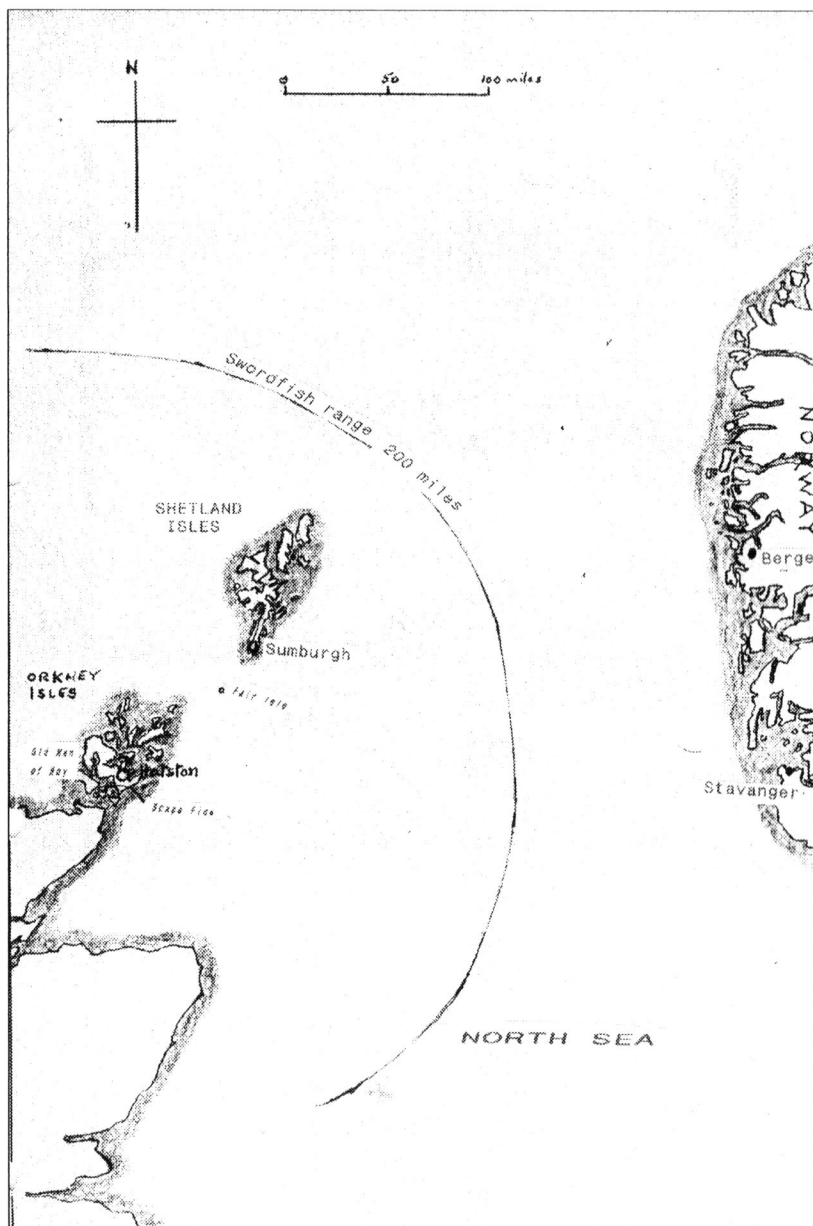

N

0   50   100 miles

Swordfish range 200 miles

NORWAY

SHETLAND
ISLES

Berge

Sumburgh

ORKNEY
ISLES

o Fair Isle

Old Man
of Hoy

Scapa Flow

Stavanger

NORTH SEA

CHAPTER 4

"...The Grand Life of The Sea"

Our first move was to fly to Prestwick. The field was literally smothered in Tiger Moths. I'd never seen so many aircraft. Clearly a massive pilots training scheme was under way. A short stop and then we were heading for HMS Argus steaming off the Clyde. This would be my first deck landing. I wondered how long it was since our pilots had done a deck landing. The first chap on dropped too heavily and spreadeagled his undercarriage. A nice inauguration for Frank Grainger in the back. Now Argus was a rather old carrier with a flush deck and very little modern equipment such as a Jumbo. This was the name given to a portable crane. So they had to rig sheer legs to shift the crashed aircraft and get it down into the hangar. Meanwhile we circled and circled for hours, with plenty of time to think about our turn. In the end the rest of us all made it safely. Once aboard we soon realised that the hangar was full of dismantled Hurricane fighters. Also two other operational Swordfish who came along to give A/S protection. One might have thought we could have done that job, but then there was of course the return trip.

Soon we were part of a large convoy heading across the Bay of Biscay and had been joined by Furious and an escort of Cruisers and Destroyers. Furious had some Skuas aboard for fighter cover. Probably she too was otherwise full of dismantled Hurricanes. Not that we saw a great deal of all this. We were experiencing our first days afloat on the High Seas and it wasn't exactly pleasant. The Bay lived up to its reputation by throwing us around and our Mess conditions were very primitive. A lot of extra people aboard as well as ourselves meant that we were crammed into a glory hole well below decks. The two A.G.s with the A/S Swordfish were experienced leading hands and they regarded us young upstarts with hooks on our arms with some disdain. We had to learn to do the mess chores like any O.D.. Argus was unusual in that she still operated the system of canteen messing. What this meant was that the meals were prepared by yourselves and merely cooked by the galley staff. It did have the advantage that you made your own choice - well collectively by messes - and could spend what you liked at the canteen. A certain minimum was subsidised plus a free issue of the staple items like bread and potatoes, but for the rest you paid. If you had enough money and wanted to eat luxuriously you could do so within the scope of the canteen goods. Most messes would skimp on breakfast - a cup of tea and a slice of bread - in order to spend more on dinner. It also saved work at a critical time of the day. However, we were approaching Christmas Day 1940 which would certainly be spent at sea. So after much discussion it was agreed that Christmas Day breakfast would be special with bacon and eggs. We couldn't run to a traditional Christmas Dinner but would do what we could with Roast Beef and so on. There was a rude interruption. As we sat down to our Christmas breakfast the alarm bells went. The convoy was being attacked by a Hipper Class cruiser and a troop-ship had been hit. Not that we knew this at the time - the information filtered through later. Our action station was in the hangar with our aircraft. We heard some distant gunfire and that was followed by a boring wait. I crept back to the mess to put my cold egg and bacon in a sandwich. The hatch to the mess had been clamped down but an inner manhole was still open. I dropped through to find that several others had the same idea. Then some duty rating threatened to close the inner manhole and shut us all in. We made a hasty exit back to the hangar. There we learned that the Hipper had disappeared into the mist and that flying conditions were not good. Nevertheless a strike was being organised. Unfortunately Argus had no torpedoes but there were some aboard Furious. The Skuas could not carry these. So the two A/S Swordfish took off from Argus and landed aboard Furious to be fitted with the tin-fish. All this was quite an exercise in itself. Meanwhile some bombs had been unearthed in Argus's magazine and these were brought up and fitted to our Swordfish. There was much deliberation as to how these old weapons should be fuzed.

Then we waited. Where was the Hipper ? Could we find her in the conditions ? Our Cruiser had come round from the other side of the convoy and engaged the enemy but she slipped away in the mist and now some hours had passed. For us it would be looking for the proverbial needle in a haystack. There was no further report of contact from any ship so we were stood down and that was virtually the end of that, from our point of view. The other aircraft did not return aboard Argus until the next day, when we had our belated Christmas lunch. We ran into better weather as we moved south. The sun came out and the sea became blue instead of grey. There is an immensely heartening feeling to watch this change in the sea colour and it is an impressive sight to come into Gibraltar for the first time. There was the Ark Royal towering majestically in the harbour. We'd looked her over in Portsmouth during our training. Now we were going aboard.

The transfer was done at the dockside. Aircraft and kit. We swung those compasses again in the difficult dockside conditions. As to the kit there were tons of it or so it seemed. Of course we A.G.s were the prime humpers. Off Argus, along the quay and aboard Ark Royal, in short stages so that it was handled as often as possible ! This was not the first time either. There had been the loading of the aircraft at Hatston, partial unloading at both Donibristle and Prestwick and again aboard Argus. We had everything with us. Kitbags, hammocks, suitcases and the officers gear. Tin boxes galore. Never have I so loathed the use of ceremonial rigs that led to the need for hat boxes, sword cases and tin trunks. We moved them piece by piece up and down countless ladders until all were aboard.

At least Ark Royal was different. Two hangar decks and the A.G.s had their own mess deck in an above water line position port side forward. Airy and pleasant with lots of our own kind as messmates. The ship had squadrons of Swordfish and Fulmars all with back seat crews and there were many of our recent classmates. It was time for a run ashore to sample the Gibraltar bars.

Then we put to sea and turned east. The bustle aboard such a carrier is quite an eye-opener and we enjoyed goofing at the deck landings. We went off ourselves for an air test and made deck landing No.2 in comfort on a wide deck with ample wind speed and lots of arrester wires. Being on passage we were left very much alone and not chased for duties though it was noticed that the ship's A.G.s also had plenty of freedom. They were really cashing in now on being leading hands. I never knew where next to find my aircraft. With two hangar decks the lifts were of double tiers but only traversed one deck. So an aircraft from the lower hangar would traverse one deck, be pushed off and the lift lowered. On again with the aircraft, up one deck with the lift and it had arrived at the flight deck. In fact they usually moved two aircraft at a time; one on each of the lift levels. The result was a continual movement around the two hangars like a double version of the tin mosaics which were popular pre-war puzzles with one square missing to allow movement. I never did learn to recognise the signs which identified the hangars and would arrive at a ladder not knowing if it went up or down.

At sea a hangar can be quite frightening. The aircraft are lashed down and one has to pick a way very carefully past all the deck bolts and guys. The aircraft themselves strain at their fixings as the ship rolls, shrieking and moaning like some prehistoric monsters trying to crush you. There was one obstacle for which I didn't bargain. Going through the Ark Royal's hangar one day looking for my aircraft to do a D.I. I was attacked on the legs by some stinging reptile which caused me to dance and kick violently. It was an A.G.s trailing aerial tied by string to another aircraft and he was transmitting ! This was of course quite against the rules apart from being unnecessary. Low power contact was all that was permitted and even that only when close to harbour. At the time I was very green about ships and was in fear of doing wrong things like treading on boats gunnels or not saluting the quarter deck. So when this A.G. swore at me for pulling down his aerial I apologised for not seeing it. I wonder who he was ? At a later date he would not have got such a soft reaction.

Sometimes an Air Gunner might wonder if his presence in the aircraft was really necessary. The pea-shooter at the back was a bit pitiful against fighters with cannon. So his key purpose was to operate the radio. In wartime, however, there is W.T. silence to avoid giving position away to the enemy. For hours on end the A.G. would merely listen to static and never touch the morse key. It was a little better when flying from shore stations. At least they transmitted and there was something to listen to. At Hatston we could send one signal per trip - an E.T.A.(estimated time of arrival). From an aircraft carrier -nothing. The ship would keep silent and not even send a DF bearing if you were lost. Unless the Fleet was being shadowed and her position was obviously known to the enemy. Our radio dials were only marked in arbitrary divisions so it became essential that all frequencies were pre-calibrated. This could only be carried out in the hangar when the lift was up, on low power such that the metal of the ship screened external transmission. We spent quite a bit of time calibrating all our likely frequencies by wavemeter.

Ark Royal had a most intriguing games room. Quite a large through deck had been set aside as recreational area presumably for dominoes and uckers (ludo !) - what, no billiard table ? In fact it was like a grand casino. All manner of betting games went on from 'Crown and Anchor' to 'Spot the Ace'. The amount of money changing hands made my eyes pop. They didn't get any of mine - I didn't have any - but men at sea built up quite a pocketful and the luckier ones would for a short while pick up even more until the money-grabber bankers copped the lot. They had their look-outs in case the Jaunty paid a sharp visit. He probably tipped them off when he was coming or else he would have carpeted half the ship's company.

Came the day when we flew off the Ark for good and headed east for Malta. Ginger Hayman's aircraft went U/S on the deck and he stayed aboard to join an Ark Royal squadron. So only 5 of us moved on, though Frank Grainger had to get a lift aboard a cruiser. That must have shattered him somewhat, as he wasn't the best of sailors. We left the ship somewhere south of Sardinia so it was a long haul along the North African coast and then past the islands of Pantellaria and Lampedusa. We had taken off just before dawn and flew singly to avoid attracting attention and being a bunch of sitting ducks if intercepted. Those islands were in Italian hands. Off Pantellaria an Italian seaplane came up and had a look at our machine. He seemed equally scared of us. It would have been an even match. I kept the gun trained on him but he was wary and didn't want to get involved. He flew parallel about a thousand yards away and eventually shoved off. Doubtless he recognised a carrier borne aircraft but by now we were so far from the ship that he couldn't tell if we had simply come out from Malta.

An E.T.A.signal was allowed and this went through OK though for some unaccountable reason we'd been given the wrong callsign for Malta. It seemed incredible that such a glaring mistake could be made, not about some obscure outpost but for a major station. They acknowledged us all right but however did we win the war?

Malta is always an attractive island and none more so than in the early light of day after a long flight over the sea. At this time she had suffered little more than a few hit and run raids by high flying Italian aircraft. How were we to know what suffering we heralded ? Though it was January the sun shone warmly and life seemed very different from the black-out and nerve shattering existence in London streets.

We were housed in an airy living quarters block at Halfar, the Naval airfield - a block shortly to be flattened. At once we sensed the difference in being a serviceman abroad. There are fewer of you and the conditions therefore vastly improve. Local help is hired to carry out certain tasks and the attitude of Chiefs and P.O.s eases. You are their kind and share the common ground of men who are "away from home". Not merely in Malta but anywhere abroad both then and since one notices this enhanced status of being English servicemen.

In our case at this time the position was further improved by our being leading hands. Other Air Gunners already at Malta had not so far received the A.F.O. which authorised their promotion. As they were senior A.G.s to us you can imagine their annoyance when they observed the treatment that left us free of duties.

To my great surprise Bill Gold turned up the day after we arrived. He had been drafted from course to join 830 squadron in Malta and after 3 months travelling via South Africa and Egypt, we were there one day ahead of him with a lot of squadron experience and a hook on our arm. The reunion of course called for a few drinks to celebrate. Going over to see him and other A.G. friends in his new squadron crew room we were surprised to find that 830 had several Corporal W.Op/A.Gs. These chaps were virtually unique in occupying a Naval A.G.s role. It had come about during the formation of 830, when both the aircraft and some of the crews had been made up by the R.A.F.,which had been using the Swordfish in a training role. We noted that they had not yet picked up the rank of Sergeant but this was remedied shortly after. We were intrigued to see that these chaps carried chartboards and navigation gear. The reason was clear when we saw the petrol tanks in the centre cockpit of their aircraft. The long range tank had reduced the crew to two.

At this point it became known to us that we would be joining H.M.S.Illustrious and had in fact been appointed to her since leaving the U.K.. It was not clear when we would be flying aboard. We carried out an air test and learned that the ship herself was in the vicinity of Malta.

Then the balloon went up. Illustrious had been attacked by a large force of Stukas and had been hit. Some of her planes came into Halfar and we helped ground crew rearm the Fulmar fighters which took off again as soon as they could be refuelled. There did not seem to be all that many armourers out at the dispersal where this was happening and our help was evidently appreciated. These few aircraft went out and back several times and then the ship came into sight over the horizon, listing heavily. The two Fulmars covered as best they may and we watched with heavy hearts. Now there were diversion strikes on Malta itself by JU88s which brought the half dozen R.A.F.Hurricanes into action. We watched one JU88 turn across Marsa Xlokk at no more than 500 feet apparently undetected or at least unopposed. At last the ship made it into Valetta harbour. We felt like raising a cheer. There were further strikes and she suffered another hit whilst alongside. Now though, she was defended by the Fleets's guns as well as the island's fighter aircraft, few though these were, and eventually Jerry had had enough. Some of the squadron personnel came out to Halfar and we were shocked by their on-the-spot stories. Then some of us were sent to the ship to help collect whatever spare aircraft stores could be salvaged from the shambles. Our view of the wrecked hangar was so shattering that for many weeks after we felt that we had been part of it ourselves.

We got airborne again the next day and left Malta to begin its siege in earnest with more devastating attacks yet to come. 830 squadron was to become a legend in its contribution to the story. The speed with which we departed makes me think that we were not due to fly aboard Illustrious at all.

Our first stop was Candia near Herakleon in Crete, at that time the only airfield in the island. It was little more than a pasture. We were well looked after and housed in a hotel with meals at a restaurant. The hospitality was generous and we appeared to be special guests. I suppose very few visitors ever called there.

We flew onwards the next day to arrive at Dekheila, the Naval Air Station near Alexandria in Egypt. Outside of the lines marked by the Nile delta Egypt is just sand. True, some of it is rock but this is still the colour of sand. The first sight of the coastline is enough to confirm the all pervading white yellowness which glares on the eyes and reflects the sun till it hurts. Dekheila is on the sand. This time we didn't stay long enough either to get used to it or to commence to hate it. Almost immediately we prepared to return to Crete. I believe this was our destination regardless of Illustrious's misfortunes. Even so, we were no longer a Flight of 821 Sqdn. but would form the nucleus of a reformed 815 squadron and gain the remnants of Illustrious's 815 and 819 squadrons. They had lost many of their aircraft in the attack on the ship though a few had made it to Malta. Yet it was said that we formed 30% of the total Middle East air strength as the R.A.F. were so short of aircraft at that time.

In terms of personnel 815 would be the Illustrious squadron and we were honoured to join such a group. In company with aircraft from Eagle these were the victors of Taranto. They were also the scourge of the Italians throughout the Eastern Med.. The ship itself had managed to slip away from Malta and was now on its way to the U.S.A. to effect repair. The ground crew came to look after us, and over the following weeks I found myself sitting in the back seat behind a succession of Taranto pilots. Our immediate task was to squeeze the Italian Dodecanese Islands which were trapped between Greece and Crete. In particular we would search for the submarines believed to be keeping them supplied. An aspect doubtless clear to our Admiral, but which only became evident to us at a later date, was that from Crete we dominated any exit south from Taranto into the rest of the Mediterranean.

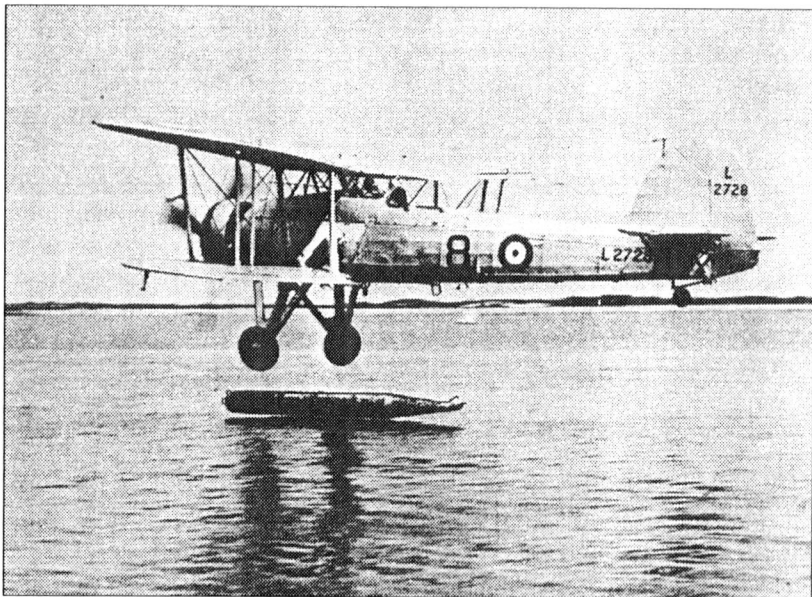

Swordfish drops a 'runner'. ie an exercise drop

HMS Argus

HMS Ark Royal

Fairey Fulmar

815 Squadron Swordfish flying in formation over England before joining
HMS Illustrious

CHAPTER 5
"A New Airfield"

I travelled to Crete aboard the cruiser HMS Ajax. Many of the squadron shipped over on a small coaster with all the squadron stores. We sailed into Suda Bay and were to set up a new airfield at Maleme some 15 miles away. At this time it was no more than a dirt strip which was being enlarged by removing small trees and bracken. Its position was on the northern coast of the island rather towards the western end. We would live in tents set amongst some trees on the side of a hill to the south and overlooking the airstrip. First though, to shift the stores from the boat to the field. It was all hands to the wheel and we split into groups each with a lorry. These were very ancient and evidently had been commandeered locally. The populace welcomed us - we'd come to defend the island from those Italians next door. They stood in the village streets to watch us go through. Those who stopped were offered wine. I think everyone sampled some of this. It befell our particular group to go back for a final load. We rather overdid it at a stop halfway back. A real party was in full swing by the time someone came out to see where we'd got to. Fortunately the C.O. was very understanding. One doesn't get welcomes like that every day. I don't think we'd done any harm except perhaps to toast the only Greek leaders whose names we knew such as Metaxas. He may well have been an anathema to the peasants entertaining us.

There were confabs between the officers and the local village headman as they tried to recruit men for various tasks. There appeared to be some success but it was a long process in broken English and even more broken Greek. We started flying A/S patrols almost at once and I have one recorded as early as 1st February 1941. There followed some bombing sorties against the Dodecanese particularly Leros but the A.G.s weren't taken on any of these. They all took place at night and there wasn't need for an air gunner. The aircraft could get off more easily with a bomb load if there was one less man in the back.

We A.G.s were kept pretty busy. On the edge of the field, in a small clump of trees, a corrugated iron shed was put up, and this became the operations room. In it was placed a field telephone exchange of ten lines. The A.G.s were the operators and we manned it in shifts. Lines went to the Bofors Guns, to the H.Q. of the Black Watch who provided airfield ground defence, one to the Naval Officer i/c Suda Bay and the most important of all to the A.M.E.S. station at the top of the hill. In today's parlance this was the radar. Then it was an Air Ministry Experimental Station. Also in the hut we rigged our pack set. This was a standard aircraft radio wired into a box for ground use. When our aircraft were on A/S patrol another A.G. also manned this set as a ground station.

We hadn't been at Maleme long before the Italians mounted an attack. About 8 SM79s came over in daylight at 8000 feet and dropped a pattern of bombs across the field. In terms of damage done it was pretty ineffective. Holes in the field could be filled in. They should have aimed round the edges where the aircraft were dispersed or even up the slope where the camp was in the trees. It certainly wasn't good for morale. Our Illustrious boys hadn't got over the ships bombing and they felt they were the prime target again. As to the A.G.s in the corrugated hut on the field edge we felt a bit exposed. The local church bell was "borrowed" and rigged on a tree outside the hut to act as the air raid warning. When we got the buzz from A.M.E.S. we would rush out and ring the bell and then rush in again to phone all other lines. We then awaited the Duty Officer and stand-by A.G. to come and assist in whatever else might be necessary. Eventually sandbags were put round the hut - not that we felt any safer. The Italians began making regular visits and several times I found myself trying to dig a hole in the concrete floor as we lay flat and attempted to lie flatter.

The heavy guns from Suda Bay were moved up one night with the intention of surprising the SM79s which had been coming over just out of reasonable range of the Bofors. The tactic didn't get a chance to prove itself. For the next raid the Italians switched back to Suda Bay. Did they perhaps get wise to the move or was it sheer luck?

Shortly after this 3 Fulmars joined us. We cheered them in. This was 805 squadron. They too brought a pack set which was also put in the Ops.Room. As they were short of A.G.s we manned it. This set operated on a different frequency to our ground station and was used to control the Fulmars and direct them towards the enemy aircraft. There was no R/T and so the route of control was a bit tortuous. From A.M.E.S. via telephone line. Then verbal to the pack set operator. He sent off in morse abbreviated code to the A.G. in the back of the Fulmar who then relayed it by voice to the pilot. How clumsy it all sounds. Yet quite effective if all the links worked. Unfortunately such was not always the case.

With the advent of the fighters we felt a lot happier. The Italians were probably having difficulty in maintaining the pressure and fewer machines were coming over. One day I was out on the airfield doing a D.I. on my aircraft. The wings were folded to break up the aircraft shape from the air. This made it very awkward for climbing in and out. There had been no bell but I happened to look up at a strange engine noise and there were the SM79s approaching. I beat all records for getting out and made a beeline for the nearest slit trench. This was next to a Bofors gun but was rather shallow. So as the bombs began to fall I crawled into the narrower walkway leading to the gun-pit. The gun was banging away but at this moment the sergeant in charge decided his gun was not making the range and ordered his crew into the slit trench. They ran all over me and afterwards found it very funny. I had to join them in that.

I had never flown in a Fulmar and was quite interested in such a "fast" aircraft. In any case it was the usual thing to look up other A.G.s where possible. 805 had camped further round the field to where we were, so when I was off duty I took a walk to see them. There were two A.G.s with them at this time, Bagsy Baker and Bomber Newman. Neither were previously known to me but welcomed another A.G..Bomber said he had flown across Africa from Lagos with these Fulmars to form a new squadron. Yes, I could have a trip. They were going up in pairs and being short of back seat men the second aircraft usually had an empty seat. I collected my Mae West and helmet and stood by for a joy-ride. It had to be on a scramble but several of these were likely to turn out to be false alarms. The bell rang soon enough and as luck would have it Bomber twisted his ankle running for the plane. They switched me to the leading aircraft and I found myself up there with two aircraft to control. Fortunately I'd done my stint on the ground pack set and knew the frequency and codes so that was no problem. It was however with a sense of relief that I got the message "return to base". Then I couldn't raise the pilot. They were using inter-com not Gosport tubes. In a Fulmar you can't reach the pilot as there is a petrol tank between you. He was even buzzing "speak" at me in morse on his alarm buzzer. All I could do was shout back "I am speaking" and consider how I could push a piece of paper at him on a long stick -if I had one. It seemed ages before he twigged that his plug had come out. Then he was all apologies and I was glad it wasn't my fault. In a strange aircraft one might press the wrong switch. I was even gladder that there were no enemy aircraft about.

One day a lone SM79 appeared and a Fulmar got airborne literally amidst the exploding bombs. The Fulmar took a bit of time catching the Iti but eventually shot him down. That seemed to shut them up altogether and we had a distinct lull. Meanwhile a Bren gun had been rigged on a central stand in a pit outside the Ops.Room. This gave the A.G.s yet another thing to man, though if it was thought the enemy were likely to attack that low I didn't really want to know.

The A/S patrols proceeded quite without success. No doubt any submarines kept well under in daylight anywhere near the island. Up to this point we had only had one flight of six aircraft at Maleme, mainly crewed by those who had come out from England. The other flight, which were the ex-Illustrious crews, had been operating up the desert in support of the Wavell push. This flight now arrived in Maleme and it was obvious that something more should be attempted than a few A/S patrols. Soon came the news that we were going to Greece with the object of making torpedo attacks up the Albanian coast to stop supplies crossing from Italy. I did not know until afterwards that this idea was something arranged almost at local level. Most of the aircraft were fitted with extra petrol tanks in the observers cockpit thus limiting the crew to two. The C.O. was carrying a full crew of three but to our surprise three of the other air-craft were to carry an A.G. in the back. This was partly determined by the need to use the Observers for navigation on the A/S patrols but also because it was likely that there might be air opposition as we moved up to the forward base in daylight.

We had to rush around a bit to get organised and I found myself without a helmet. This had been loaned to some non-aircrew who was being ferried up to Herakleon. When I let it go I didn't know what was in the wind. Finally I managed to borrow one but it didn't have gosports. "Don't worry", said my pilot, "I'll zog to you" ! Thank goodness that wasn't necessary. At the last moment someone ran up with the missing bits but the helmet itself was several sizes too large. I was stuck with that helmet for a long time before getting a chance to change it.

We took off on March 11th and flew to Elevsis, an airfield outside of Athens where an R.A.F. squadron was stationed. The ground crew, or rather a few of them, followed by sea and we didn't see them for several days. On arrival we were allowed a quick visit into Athens where I managed to win a bottle of champagne in one of the night clubs with their version of "Churchill says......". There was an odd situation in a hotel visited by our officers. The German Embassy staff were in residence as at this time only the Italians were at war with Greece. One wonders what sort of deduction the Germans made about Naval fliers (evident from the wings on their uniform) and whether the Italians were tipped off to expect something.

After some detail arrangements were sorted out it was agreed that we were to use the forward landing ground known as Paramythia which nestled up in the mountains and was supposedly unknown to the enemy. Only a few R.A.F. Gladiators were sta-tioned there, though the Mk.1.Blenheims from Elevsis also used it to refuel and rearm. So the events moved up to the attack on that first night. I pondered on these events as I waited alone for some news of the next move.

CHAPTER 6

"Strike by Moonlight"

On the second day the other four aircraft returned and I was glad to note no further losses. It was also a relief to talk it over with Laurie and Sid. It seemed that their attack had been much more successful and less perilous than on the first night. They had crept in unobserved using the same silent glide tactic as we had used. Only when opening throttles low on the water had there been some reaction and by that time they were mostly underneath the flak. A much more heartening situation. They claimed some torpedo hits on various vessels.

The ground crew had arrived with more torpedoes and all the aircraft were rearmed, with the aircrew assisting the few armourers to move the trollies around. We prepared to go up again to Paramythia that evening. Now there was a general shuffle round amongst the crews and I was detailed to fly with "Mac". I stayed with him for the next three attacks. After refuelling at Paramythia we took off for this one almost immediately. The moon was up much earlier than on the first night. Getting started was a bother. The R.A.F. weren't used to our rather laborious starting mechanism. They provided only one man per aircraft and our chap didn't have much idea of how to use his weight. The other crews had the same problem. So the A.G. had to give a hurried briefing and then himself take on the major role of turning the handle. All this with an awkward sidcot on. Not just on this trip, but every time from the forward field without our own crews. I would flop into the back whacked out and sweating heavily. As we climbed to height this situation changed until I was shivering with cold. Cold feet you may say and you'd be right. I was wearing sea boots and my feet were frozen. I cursed the days we'd spent marching round Worthy Down in flying boots. Now those boots were worn through and I was miles away from a flying clothing store.

We flew up the coast as before and came in over the neck of the headland dipping down with silent engines. Long minutes passed but all was quiet. Finally they got on to us, probably as someone blipped his engine to level out. We were still at 1000 feet but the Breda fire was sporadic and nowhere near as close as on the first night. It wasn't long before we got down underneath it. Judging the height was easy. For there in the middle of the harbour, lit up like some glittering crown, was a hospital ship. If we'd already sunk one how could they produce another so quickly ? We skirted by this ship and picked out the dark shape of a merchant ship towards the jetty area. Mac didn't go for long shots. He seemed to know just how much he needed to get the fish running and primed and that was the range at which it would be dropped. The shape was looking pretty big when he let go. We banked away and watched. I was expecting something spectacular but the flash when it came was quite subdued. It could even have been a reflection from the gun flashes which were still spraying around mostly above us, but we believed we had gained a hit. We skirted the hospital ship again and headed for the harbour entrance still at no more than 100 feet. From the hospital ship I could see a winking light amongst the rest of the lights but if it was meant to be morse it made little sense. As though the origin was partly shielded and hence breaking up the letters as we moved past. We slipped quietly out and as we headed down the coast I felt warmer and calmer. It was of course still dark when we got back, but Mac unerringly found the correct valley and we dropped down safely on the hurricane lamp flarepath. From Paramythia these visits to Valona took no longer than three hours for the round trip. So we got in a few hours sleep and in the morning hastened back to Elevsis to rearm with another tin-fish. Our ground crew had now settled in and gave us a very quick turn round. Getting the ground support organised must have been a prodigious task for the one officer and a mere handful of men. Torpedoes alone were quite a bother but they met all the demands. Whilst I was giving a hand I turned sharply and walked into the propeller. I had to go to the R.A.F. sick bay for a bit of sticking plaster on my forehead. The doctor seemed startled at my explanation, until I hastily added that the prop wasn't turning !

That afternoon we were on our way back to Paramythia. Our R.A.F. friends had been taking photos during the day which gave us some confirmation of our attacks and pinpointed positions of further shipping. As there was no Ops.Room as such and just a tent into which everyone crowded I only caught a glimpse of these photos but everyone seemed highly delighted so we must have been having some success. It was rather typical of the approach at this time that we A.G.s were never fully briefed on the intentions other than what our pilots might say to us before take-off. By now the five machines had got a bit split up. Some engine difficulties, plus the shuttle arrangements, meant that a few had been left behind and we began to operate in twos and threes. This trip I believe there were but two of us. We still formed up on take-off but if we lost each other we pressed on independently. There was little point in surprise now. I guess they knew we were coming. The moon was still holding out but it meant an earlier take-off. Straight off down the valley more or less South, then the turn West across an open plain, and then a turn North up the coast. We did not bother to gain a lot of height this time but crept in over the hills of the isthmus and down into the harbour. There was the bejewelled crown all lit up again some few miles up near the harbour entrance. Of course they were expecting us. As we weren't gliding but using engine all the way then we could be heard and pinpointed. They set off the usual barrage and seemed prepared to shoot low whilst we were still on the approach run with only hills behind us. I was scared but not so shattered as on the first night. It was fascinating to watch the flaming onions curl lazily and slowly up towards you and then suddenly gather speed and hurtle by with a swishing sound clearly heard above the sound of the engine. When we got right down on the water the barrage rose above us and eventually petered out as they realised we were no longer a good target. We turned in towards the dock area and then I was surprised to see the outline of a warship, possibly a destroyer, but we were rather on its quarter. Mac turned away and we circled to come in on the beam. They wised up to us then and the fireworks started all over again including plenty from the ship. We jinked around a bit, steadied, dropped the fish and turned away. One has to count the seconds very deliberately because it seems such an awfully long time before the fish reaches its target. Again I never saw a positive explosion but at precisely the expected moment all firing from the ship suddenly stopped. Knowing Mac I think he'd chalked up another one. We hung about a bit peering round to see if there were any further results, perhaps even from the other aircraft, but there was nothing noticeable. Personally I didn't like the hanging about. Charlie, as we called him, was flashing away aboard the hospital ship. I read a few letters which made no sense. Was he trying to tell us something ? Surely people ashore could see it, so would he dare ? Or was he just telling his friends where he thought we were ? You will note that he had been seen from other aircraft.

By this time we had got ourselves back up the harbour, so instead of aiming for the entrance we aimed to go back over the bluff where we came in. This meant we had to climb and as we climbed the Bredas started off again so that hadn't been such a good idea. Though they were too close for comfort we persevered. There were some moments of suspense and then we were clear. Back down the coast and it was rather more difficult finding our valley. The moon had gone down and the night was black. At least we were a little more used to spotting the landmarks, few though these were. Up till now Mac had been quite happy under his own steam but this time he asked if I thought he'd got it right. To be honest I wasn't at all sure, but said it looked OK to me as I had seen one or two familiar bits. Sure enough the line of lamps came into view but I didn't like the blackness of the valley walls as we circled and dropped down.

Back again the following morning to Elevsis and on the way we had a minor scare. A main bracing wire suddenly snapped and then whipped upwards to stick itself through the upper mainplane. Never at any other time had I known one do that and I think it was weakened by being hit rather than fatigued. We watched it closely but nothing further happened so we landed safely.

From the first night I had been concerned about the possibility of searchlights which would have critically disclosed us. I felt we should be prepared to shoot them out if necessary. On the other hand tracer and incendiary give away one's position and I wanted some pans of purely ball ammunition. Had we always flown in the same aircraft I would simply have done this independantly. As there was a continuous swap around between crews and aircraft I had to "sell" the idea to everyone else. They acquiesed but were not convinced. Nobody else believed there had been or would be any searchlights or that it mattered what ammunition was used. I suppose they were right but there was so little we could contribute to the activity except start the engine and be another pair of eyes that I was desperate for a job.

At some time during those first few days one pilot had done a ground loop at Paramythia and put a Swordfish in a ditch. So more aircraft and pilots had flown across from Maleme but no more A.G.s. At this point the reconnaissance photos indicated that Valona had shut up shop. What shipping hadn't been sunk had cleared away out of the port and virtually no targets were left. So we turned our attention to the port of Durazzo further up the coast. This was a very different proposition. The harbour was not land locked like Valona but was contained in a harbour wall. So there was a lot less water to allow the run of a torpedo and the approach would be a bit exposed. Photos did indicate a certain amount of shipping. There were also suggestions of a few balloons.

In the circumstances it was thought that bombs would make a better attack weapon and so most of the aircraft were switched to carry bombs. One aircraft, however, would have a tin-fish, just in case a vessel was anchored in the roadsteads or some accessible position. The Swordfish actually made quite a good bomber if it could get above a target unmolested, because it was capable of a vertical dive in the true Stuka fashion. We were all to gather again as a complete force and in the various deliberations there was much coming and going. This included some R.A.F. officers having been transported to Paramythia in the Stringbags and when it was decided to start an observer and myself were found to be at Elevsis. So we were flown up in a Blenheim. The R.A.F. pilot was assured I knew how to use the gun and I was bundled into the turret. The first thing I noticed was that there was no gunsight. Probably it was removed for safety by the gunner but where did he keep it ? I couldn't find it anywhere in the cockpit so guessed he must have taken it away entirely. By now we had taxied to the end of the runway and I didn't dare hold up the proceedings while it was found so said nothing. Sighting along the barrel would have to do. The gun was a Vickers K mounted in a manual turret. I spent the trip swinging it round and getting the feel. It was just as well I didn't have to use it.

On the second night we were complete and ready to go. Four aircraft each with 6 x 250lb bombs and several flares and one aircraft with torpedo. Mac and I got the tin-fish.

It was a long slog up to Durazzo about 100 miles past Valona. We took a line well out to sea in the hope that the latter place wouldn't notice what we were up to and give warning. After 2 hours we turned in, came over Durazzo at about 8000 feet and started dropping flares. The harbour certainly seemed quite full. So was the air - full of heavy anti-aircraft fire. The place was well defended and they had our height well pinpointed. A largish ship which looked like an oil tanker stood away from any jetty with a fair amount of water on one side of it. I guessed that was what Mac had his eye on. We did a copy book attack such as was often practised but seldom achieved. A vertical dive with a jink halfway to line up direction and check speed then down again to pull out and level off low on the water close to the target. We seemed terribly unmasked out there in the light of our own flares. The vertical dive did the trick as far as return fire was concerned. I looked back up to see the air full of gunfire above us but we got in close with little visible reaction at our level. By the time they started with the small arms and Breda we had dropped the fish and turned away. There were several moments of suspense before we crossed the harbour wall but much of the fire trailed out behind us. I saw no balloons but I did see a hit on the target, lit as it was by the flares. Nothing spectacular but nevertheless a hit. The display went on for some time behind us. I expect the boys with the bombs had not dropped them all at once and pulled back up for a second go. I wished them luck. We'd had a fairly easy passage and were on the way home. It was dawn when we got to Paramythia and the field was no trouble to find.

Talking to Sid and Laurie as we ate breakfast off tin plates at trestle tables in the open they said they'd had a hot time. They'd always been a bit contemptuous of Valona's efforts, ever since they first slipped in unnoticed, but now they had a healthy respect for Durazzo. As usual with bombs no one cold say how effective they'd been. Hits and near misses yes, but hardly guaranteed to sink a ship. They confirmed our hit however. So once again back to Elevsis.

About this time lots of things started to happen at once. Our own force was augmented by a few more Swordfish such that the numbers left at Maleme were severely reduced. Other A.G.s also came over as did more ground crew in the support ship. Not enough however to relieve the enormous pressure put upon these few stalwarts. We did get a welcome break from ops. during the no moon period and were able to explore Athens beyond our earlier visit and made a point of going to see the Parthenon. Then the Germans declared war on the Balkans and started sweeping through Yugoslavia and eventually into Greece. The Italians could be held but the Greeks and a few British troops were no match for the German Army. We knew our days in Greece were numbered. Jerry started night raids on the harbour of Piraeus and he dropped the odd bomb on supporting airfields. To approach Pireaus he crossed straight over Elevsis and we heard the distinctive unsynchronised engine notes of the JU88s, all the time wondering if it was our turn to receive. One night an R.A.F.Blenheim IV went off to intercept. He found his man alright virtually over the airfield. There was a brief exchange of fire, which we could see, and an aircraft spiralled earthwards. A parachute blossomed. We cheered. Unfortunately it was the Blenheim. His four .303s had not been enough fire-power and on coming in close Jerry proved a sharp one with his rear guns.

Again we took our torpedoes up to Paramythia but photos indicated a shortage of targets. So we brought the torpedoes back and changed them for bombs to get at the shipping by the Durazzo jetties and inside the booms. Then we found that these had done a flit back to Brindisi in Italy. So our attention switched to Brindisi - a tougher proposition. The ships were in the outer open harbour so we took the bombs back and changed to torpedoes. All this flying up and down between Elevsis and Paramythia took us through the area known as the Gulf of Corinth with the Corinth canal. Today such a flight would be a tourists dream. I'm sure we vaguely appreciated the grandeur of the scenery though at the time we were much more concerned at keeping eyes open for the possibility of enemy fighters. One Swordfish did get chased by a couple of CR42s but he managed to give them the slip. Back again once more to Paramythia where it was found that the latest reconnaissance at Brindisi showed all the ships withdrawn into the inner harbour and tin-fish were no good.

At this point the balloon went up at Matapan. This action it will be recalled consisted of an Italian Fleet including a battleship, several cruisers and destroyers, making a foray towards Crete and being engaged and routed south of Cape Matapan, a headland on the Grecian coast. Just what their objectives were are not very clear. Relief for the Dodecanese? A landing on Crete? It was rumoured that they carried German troops. I doubt it. Jerry wouldn't have trusted the Italians to get them anywhere without being in charge themselves. Perhaps they were just pressurised into making a foray to divert attention from a convoy destined to put Rommel into the desert. They probably hoped to turn and run for home when detected. They certainly had the speed. Whatever the motives they came unstuck. First they were attacked by Albacores from the Formidable. She had arrived in the Eastern Med. to replace Illustrious. These attacks slowed down some of the cruisers and destroyers. When the battleship Littorio turned away from the approaching British Fleet the Italian Admiral misjudged their nearness and allowed his cruisers to stay and help the stragglers. During the night these cruiser forces were decimated by the British Fleet. The Littorio escaped. I have only summarised the main features of the action as my story is not of Matapan but of how we missed it.

We knew something was going on but the line of communications was tedious and we couldn't get a firm picture of what was happening. There was no direct link to Maleme and I understand that such signals as reached us came via Alexandria on the R.A.F. channels which were not themselves fully informed on the Admiral's intentions. Our C.O. flew back to Maleme to find out the score and was just in time to join the Swordfish still there in a strike on the Italian fleet. This occurred about the time of the second strike by Formidable's Albacores but was not coincidental. The Swordfish were credited with a hit on a cruiser. We sat on the deck at Elevsis just not knowing what it was all about. I understand our absence was duly noted by the

These are two 815 Squadron aircraft attacking the cruiser at Matapan. No TAGs were taken as they had long-range tanks and therefore Observers in the back seats. This photograph is quite famous, as a trick of the light suggests the aircraft has lost its wing

Admiral. He wanted to know where his Cretan Swordfish were; so not only was he aware of our existence but may well have put us into Crete with this possibility in mind. The move to Greece had been a "target of opportunity" and apparently the Admiral was not advised. Even more aggravating is the knowledge that from Elevsis or Paramythia we might well have been better placed than at Maleme for cutting off the Littorio's route home. Who knows, our 9 Swordfish might have made Matapan an even more resounding victory than it was ? Unfortunately we stood by all day and no signal came to give us a sitrep and directive on where and what to attack.

Finally we returned to the problem of Brindisi and it was decided to use mines to bottle up the ships in that port. By what extreme acts of organisation our mines were produced I do not know but all aircraft except one were loaded with magnetic mines slung underneath and they were much like torpedoes in size and shape. Mac got the fish again but I had been switched to another aircraft. Our full force took off at 0145 on the 13th April and we crossed to Italy in open formation from Paramythia. It was a 2 hour haul and we made a good landfall, then adopted the usual technique of a silent glide in. It worked well and we seemed to catch them on the hop. We approached unmolested. To our utter surprise a large number of ships were in the roadstead. There was medium cloud but the moonglow diffused through it to give enough light to see without flares. They must have been forming up for a dash across to Durazzo. With torpedoes we could have had a bonanza. What to do with the mines ? There was no point in putting them at the inner harbour entrance as planned. Instead we selected a largish ship, turned over the harbour entrance and came back at her. As we did so the shore batteries woke up to our presence and opened up. These were not the light guns of the Breda variety which made such a firework display and the air bursts of the heavies did not appear anywhere near as spectacular. Our aircraft must have been spread over a wide area as each sought a suitable target and the guns seemed equally at variance as to where to fire. Our ship looked big as we flew over her at about 100 feet. She was anchored and we dropped the mine right alongside. One hoped that the mine would activate as she swung in the current. We did not know the result at the time though later I gathered it had not been effective. There was even some doubt that the mines had been suitably fuzed. A harbour entrance light was merrily flashing away and I felt this was mocking us somewhat and wanted to shoot it out. My pilot thought this was chancing our arm and not what we came for. We turned for home. As we did so I saw a large flash down on the water and it appeared likely that this was Mac scoring a hit with his tin-fish. The guns continued for several minutes more and then petered out. In the whole attack only one shell had burst near enough to us to rock the aircraft. We settled down to the two hour slog back.

All this time we had been concerned that Jerry might cut us off at Paramythia. In fact the direction of his attack was putting Elevsis under threat. It was decided we should get out of Greece as we were no longer being effective. A couple of Swordfish made one last visit to Valona and when one of these failed to return that rather settled it. We also learned later that even if our advanced field had been unknown to the Italians, then Jerry very soon discovered it and gave it a right pasting, shortly after we left. Our ground crew were set off heading for their boat at Pireaus whilst we took off and flew back to Crete.

In the short time of 5 weeks that we'd been away Maleme had expanded rapidly. Many ex-Illustrious staff had arrived and the aerodrome was approaching Air Station status even if we did still all live in tents. There were people to do the necessary ground duties previously carried out by the squadron personnel. There was even a

Chief T.A.G. - Jackie Girling, presumably to organise the ops.room.

Whilst we had been away, other squadron aircraft had continued the patrols around Crete. On one of these Fred Faulks had ditched when their engine failed them somewhere to the south of the island. With the high mountain range that runs east/west right through the middle of the island it is not surprising that their "Mayday" signal was not received. Though a search was mounted they were not found and spent four days in the dinghy before being washed ashore dehydrated, without food, and very weak. They had been unable to dissuade their pilot from attempting to swim ashore the day before and he was lost.

Before we left we used to go to the local village in the evening for a couple of bottles of krasis, the local wine, and a sing song. I recall that Bobby Beynon was one of the A.G.s in our particular bunch. On our return we found that these outings were continuing and that we had been joined by several lads from the Black Watch and from the Gunners. A favourite song was "Suvla Bay" from the Gallipoli period which we adapted to "Suda Bay". This particular one was a tear jerker and ominously prophetic but we didn't see it that way. Mostly the evening was full of laughter and the Army and Navy got on well together. I doubt if many of our army friends from that era survived the battle soon to be fought.

The Germans had now swept through Greece and were threatening Crete. Air raids were frequent and Jerry was a nastier customer than the Italians. 805 Squadron augmented its fighter strength and we were glad to see them. A very mixed bag they were too. Fulmars, Buffaloes and a single Martlet. The latter two were difficult to maintain without proper spares and their narrow wheel base wasn't very suitable for the uneven dirt airfield. The enemy radio was bombarding us with propaganda. They called us 'the island of doomed men'. We laughed, not knowing what was to come. Several old Greek biplanes came in. Chased from Greece they brought out certain political and army leaders.

Our Swordfish were now a hazard. We couldn't contribute much to the island's defence and were cluttering up the aerodrome which needed to give maximum availability to the fighters. In any case our aircraft desperately needed some major overhauls. We had flogged them mercilessly with little more than patchy repairs. So in small groups the Swordfish were flown back to Alexandria. I went in one of these just in time to miss the first parachute assault on the island. I was very glad to get out too, though mainly to escape the bombing. We hadn't rated a parachute attack very highly and thought it could be contained. When I use the term "we" this was the view of our army friends for whatever that view was worth. They were probably as ignorant of parachute attacks as we naval airmen. Everyone thought that they would eject over the top of us and be picked off on the way down. In the event their dropping zone was further up the valley and then they came down the shallow river to the airfield. Actually that first wave was well checked. We certainly didn't know or understand what other troops were on the island. In particular the New Zealanders. Then again there were others who came to Crete after evacuating from Greece. So I suppose there were rather more defenders than we thought. When the airfield was overrun during the second wave then the Germans literally flooded the field with their gliders and JU52 tugs. At this point many of our ground crew joined the troops in a bid to defend the island but as many as possible were rounded up and put aboard ships. They were too valuable to be lost carrying a rifle. However, we understand that two of 805 squadron's A.G.s,Jarvis and Jary, also joined this band of 'local defence volunteers'. Precisely what happened to them is difficult to establish but their names appear on our Roll of Honour.

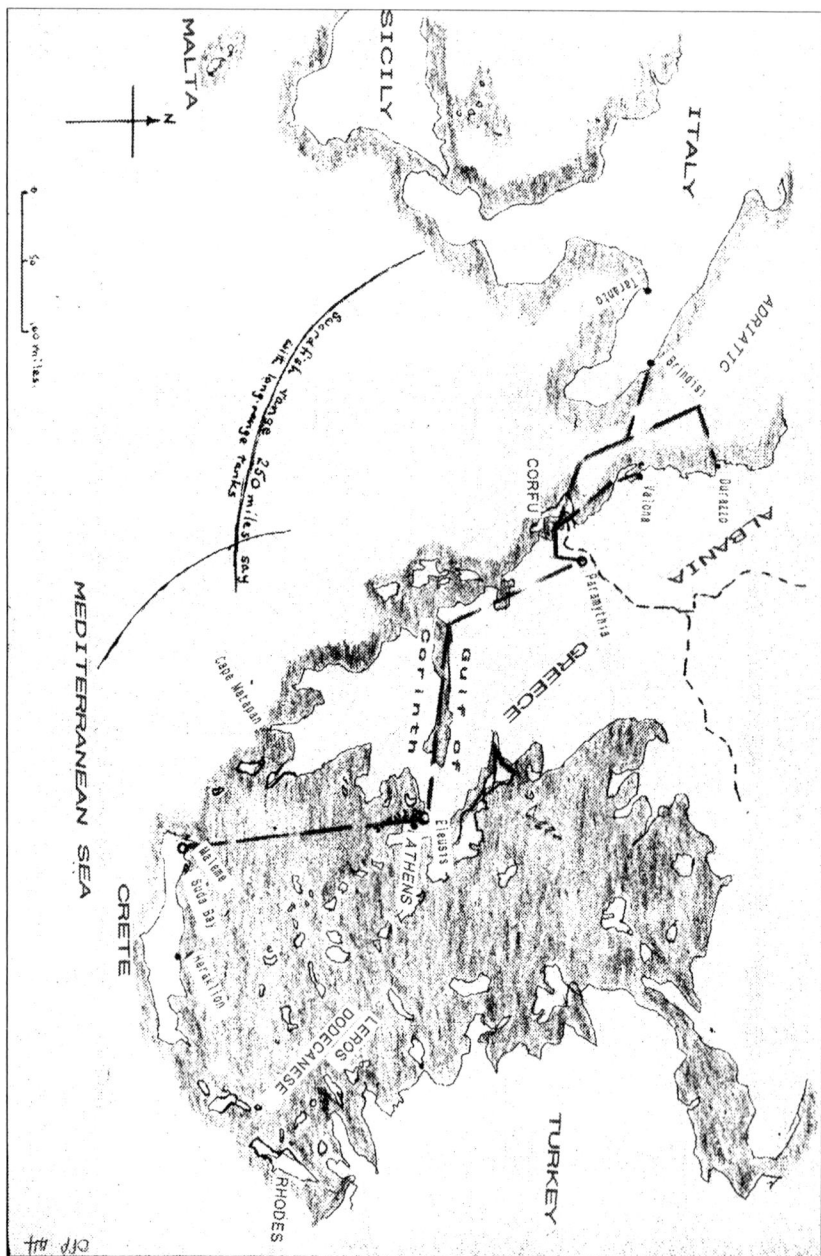

815 Squadron ashore in Athens
1941. Ashore in Athens we visited the Parthenon and are photographed
with a young guide. The photographs shows our use of battledress but with
a sailor's hat. It also shows that we still had RAF men serving with the Fleet
Air Arm. On the right of the picture are AG's Laurie Smith and Sid Boosey

BOMBING OF MALEME AERODROME

This RAF
photograph
was first
published in
the Egyptian
Daily Mail. The
northern coast
of Crete and
the east/west
road are
clearly seen.
The Fleet Air
Arm camp was
in the copse of
trees in the SW
corner – the
group to the
right of the
road. The
Operations Hut
was just north
of the point
where the road
bends

A photograph taken from the air by the R.A.F. showing Maleme aerodrome, Crete, after the Germans had
made their invasion with air-borne troops. Many of
the J.U. 52's to be seen were a crash landed, others were
wrecked in frantic efforts to get the aircraft down no
matter at what cost. The landing ground is literally
strewn with wrecked aircraft.

43

CHAPTER 7

"In The Beginning..."

It was perhaps ironic that the Fleet Air Arm should find itself carrying out operational roles from shore bases. Not only in Greece and Crete, but also in Malta, in the Desert and elsewhere.

The Royal Navy had only regained full control of its Air Branch just prior to the war, on the premise that naval operations demanded an integrated Service. Yet through loss of its Aircraft Carriers and pressures of the moment, much of the effort was diverted into fields that might otherwise have been the role of the R.A.F..

It is not my purpose to enter the arguments as to who should have controlled matters but the T.A.G. story would not be complete without some reference to the period between the wars. This in its turn leads us to a history of the early Fleet Air Arm. One must touch upon the points which led to the introduction of T.A.G.s.

It will be recalled that the Services original interest in air matters during the First World War was vested in the Royal Naval Air Service for the Navy and the Royal Flying Corps for the Army. During this period Wireless Telegraphy was in its infancy. The aircraft were fragile affairs of short range and could not readily carry the bulky early wireless sets. Yet efforts to get such devices airborne were successful in the seaplanes and flying boats, as also the airships. Where a W/T operator was needed in the earlier two-seater aircraft this was carried out by the observer. Larger seaplanes which appeared later had several men in the crew of which one at least was a W/T operator. Often such men only had the rank of Air Mechanic, but it was also possible to become a P.O. or C.P.O. Observer. There was also a specific rank of Observer Officer. Note that these operators were not Telegraphists.

Towards the end of that war the two Services were combined to form the Royal Air Force. This was a political gambit initiated by the conflict to obtain the better aircraft in which the Royal Navy appeared to have been more successful. When it was also seen that the two groups appeared to be tactically operating in parallel -carrying out strategic bombing and doing fighter patrols - then a single force looked like the answer. It might have paid the Navy better to stick to their own spheres of interest - carrier operating - which were certainly crying out for improvement. When one views the multitude and variety of ideas and methods that were undertaken one is full of admiration for those who took part. They did try. Yet it was many years before dependable and consistent methods were shown to be feasible.

With the end of the 1st World War there was the inevitable demobilisation and dispersal of all war weapons. The Fleet Air Arm element (of the RAF) collapsed to about two squadrons and a few flights. What of the W/T operators - who must be considered the forerunners of the TAGs ? If any still remained in the Service as regulars then they will have become members of the R.A.F. but probably hung up their helmets and settled for a ground occupation. At least one ex gun-layer (an airgunner) is known to have done this, though he was not a W/T operator.

Initially the R.A.F. were reasonably equipped to handle the Fleet's requirements as so many of the personnel were themselves ex-R.N.A.S.. As time progressed, however, promotions took the experienced men back into other spheres of R.A.F. work. The younger aircrew did not have a background of naval training. The Royal Navy suddenly woke up to the importance of the air and exerted considerable influence to ensure that a proportion of the pilots were Naval Officers.

The aircraft performance began to improve and with the advent of the true Aircraft Carrier it was seen that if these machines were to fly over the sea and yet be able to return to their ship then a standard of navigation was required beyond that of any existing aircrew. Who more readily available to carry out this role than the young naval officer with sea navigational experience ? It did not escape notice that this also gave the Royal Navy another finger on the control of the Air Branch.

To really become the eyes of the Fleet the aircraft needed wireless sets to pass back their information. So again why not use their ready trained Telegraphists to operate this new-fangled but temperamental apparatus ? At that time the R.A.F. had not themselves a ready source of such men, and so, with the introduction of full Naval crews the Royal Navy gained a foothold into an otherwise R.A.F. administered and manned service which they defined as the Fleet Air Arm. It is interesting to note the use of the term Observer which sprang from the early days when spotting was a prime function. Even the R.A.F. used the term well into the war years and the half brevet with a central "O" was worn. They changed the term to Navigator when they began training large numbers of such specialists. The Observer by comparison tended to be much more a jack-of-all-trades in the back seat. The early inclusion of Naval personnel in the Fleet Air Arm had far-reaching effects. At a later date when wishing to take control, many senior and experienced men were already available. As promotions took R.A.F. personnel back to their own service so the Naval pilots and observers found themselves the more senior in the Branch. Amongst the ground crew this was not so prevalent. Many R.A.F. men contrived to stay on for several years. Yet, when in due course they departed, then it was the early T.A.G.s who found themselves as the senior Chiefs on the Lower Deck of the Air Branch.

The official formation of the Fleet Air Arm (of the R.A.F.) took place in 1924, but the need for T.A.G.s was anticipated some time before this. The first T.A.G.s course was held at Gosport in 1922. It consisted of 11 Telegraphists including Leading Tels.Maskell and Richmond who later became widely known as the senior instructors in the T.A.G.Training Schools. Bobby Maskell was virtually a Father Figure as he had instructed pupils in the early 1930's, who themselves became legends early in the war. It should be noted that these Telegraphists were already considerably experienced and their course was largely concerned with training in Air Gunnery. There were certain other matters of airmanship and an interesting feature which was introduced in the 1930's was that of bomb aiming. The R.A.F. conducted the courses for many years - teaching airmanship to sailors. Further courses were held roughly at the rate of two a year right through the '20s and up to 1935. They would consist of around 10 to 12 Tels. and be conducted partly at Eastchurch and partly at Fort Grange, Gosport. Seniority was not dictated by the timing of such courses but was decided by a man's status as a Tel..At the end of the course, successful pupils proudly sewed the badge of an aeroplane underneath the Telegraphists badge which they continued to wear on their arm. They also began to receive the princely sum of 3/- per day flying pay. These were lean years for the man in the street. A sailor could be considered somewhat better off than many. With their extra shillings of flying pay the TAG felt Lord of the Earth.

Though the aircraft were slow their reliability was suspect and as techniques of flying over the sea and landing aboard carriers were still being learnt the element of risk was high. Even from the beginning fatal accidents occurred. For example Nick Carter was killed on course in 1926 and T.A.G.Burton from No.1 course was killed in a Bison crash at Halfar in 1927. There were others. Such incidents began the web of common bond which drew T.A.G.s together.

As naval ratings they found they were in the unique position of being associated with R.A.F. personnel who were themselves somewhat outside the control of the Royal Navy. This led to the time-honoured phrase "you can't touch me, I'm Fleet Air Arm", usually expressed to any busybody of a Duty Petty Officer. If, however, the R.A.F. officers and N.C.O.s interfered, the TAG would rapidly shelter behind his naval uniform. Necessarily he worked closely with his Observer and as these officers rose in rank so the TAG always had a sympathetic ear in the right quarter.

In those days the Royal Navy had plenty of ships and would show the flag around the world. Thus a lot of time was spent overseas. The Mediterranean and China Stations were the most frequent spheres. With seaplanes and amphibians attached to the large ships the TAGs got scattered around but would always make a point of getting together when in port. In the early '30s when there where no more than 200 of them all told it is probably true to say they all knew each other. Of course they liked a drink. All sailors are believed to have this in common. With the extra money in his pocket the TAG could usually afford it.

The number of aircraft carriers built up over the period and included the Argus, Eagle, Hermes, Furious, Glorious and Courageous. In the early days the aircraft units were Flights. Amalgamation of the two flights into a squadron of 12 aircraft did not occur until 1933. Various types of aircraft were used through different periods of the time scale from 1922 to 1935 both as operational units and as trainers. These included Flycatchers, Bristol Fighters, Darts, Ripons, Baffins, Blackburn Spotters, Seals, Harts, Wapitis, Fairey 111Ds and 111Fs. Each known with varying degrees of nostalgia or hate by the TAGs of the day. The TAGs prime concern was Telegraphy so his sphere was dictated by the morse code. In common with all Tels., every morning he would read a Standard Buzzer Exercise to maintain morse receiving efficiency. If I appear to be overstressing the S.B.X. and morse aspects one must realise that this did dominate a Telegraphists life. Even in later years one finds old Tels. dropping the occasional "X" code signal into letters to colleagues. One of the more presentable barrack room shanties was sung to the tune of Old King Cole. This ran the gamut of all personnel in a squadron and when it came to the TAGs it went:-

Diddy-diddy-dah-diddy-dah said the A.G.s
Merry merry men are we,
For there's none so fair than can compare,
With the boys of eight two three.

(or 813 or whatever. The words could easily be changed to match).

Another form of communication was known as zogging. In the days before voice radio, aircraft in formation had to use hand signals. The pilots had elementary gestures to indicate their intentions. Further information had to be zogged. The arm was held upright and swung from the elbow. Short swings for dots and long swings for dashes very much like sending morse by flag.

As the TAG was required to know semaphore and all the ship's flag signals he became the complete signaller. It was also necessary to learn the many abbreviated codes that were in use. Though some of this sounds antiquated in fact it was possible to communicate basic information quicker than by voice. It didn't cope with the unusual and some amusing tales can be told of misinterpreted signals.

The TAG was quick to put his skills to use in unofficial ways. At Fleet Regattas it was recognised custom to allow totes to be run aboard the larger ships with betting on the prowess of the various boats. If one knew that say the Stokers Mess crew was good - they would probably be rowing a whaler -then very likely it was heavily backed aboard their own ship with everyone in the know. So the odds would be short. Aboard other ships longer odds could be obtained. TAGs acting like Tic-Tac men would run a syndicate amongst their own kind and get the best of the betting.

In another instance, a good amateur act was built up as a Music Hall turn. A TAG (Alfie Poulter) dressed as an Eastern Potentate wearing a turban was the Mind Reader. His turban hid a small earphone and a wire ran down his leg to a metal plate on the sole of his shoe. By treading on the bare end of a wire on the floor he could make contact with a confederate at the back of the hall. The latter sat sending morse from a key in his pocket and could describe articles hidden from the stage. At a time when the public were unused to electronic tricks this was most effective and the lads were very popular at social functions. Of course they had to have time to run their wire, usually under some lino, and they pulled it out from the side of the stage before inquisitive disbelievers investigated.

Around 1935 it became clear that stirring things were afoot. The Fleet Air Arm was to be taken over by the Royal Navy and administered by them instead of by the R.A.F..The hand-over date was aimed at 1937 and although much was achieved by then, in fact the final official seal did not come until 1939. Meanwhile a whole series of events marked the beginning of a new era. Lee-on-Solent was set up as the headquarters of the branch and the TAGs school moved there from Gosport. At first everything was still under R.A.F. control and the first two TAG courses at Lee were still all Telegraphists. At about this time, it was made possible for ratings to become pilots and observers. Volunteers from the Fleet were selected for training as pilots and a few TAGs were included. Only the TAGs could enter for the Observers courses. When qualified, they were known as Observer's Mates, though this was something of a misnomer. After being trained in navigation they carried out the airborne duties unassisted. More popularly, they became known as Rating Observers. All the rating aircrew of this era soon got to know each other.

Many new aircraft were introduced. First came the Nimrods and Ospreys. The former were single seater fighters and the squadrons which were formed by combining the earlier flights, usually included some Ospreys. These were two-seaters and offered some rear gun protection plus an Observer for navigation. Yet other aircraft had been specifically designed to carry out the innumerable requirements of general duties. These were known as T.S.R.s - Torpedo Spotter Reconnaissance aircraft. To demand all this from one aircraft plus deck-landing facilities and wing folding was a designers nightmare. At a later date, when engine power had been considerably boosted, then it was met with all metal monoplanes. In the 1930's, however, the available engines were limited and wind-tunnels were unknown, and so it is not surprising that the result was hardly an aeroplane of high performance. Yet the Swordfish displayed a capability which was held in high respect. Oddly enough it wasn't first choice. The Blackburn Shark was to the same specification and having a metal skin was the first to be put into squadron service. Certain disadvantages caused it to be rejected in favour of the Swordfish.

The Fairey Swordfish became popularly known as the "Stringbag". There are various explanations of this. I'm inclined to support the most obvious. Consider a filled string bag - it protrudes in all directions with many articles poking through the holes. A Swordfish would suffer a wide variety of extras being added, most of it on the outside. Bomb racks, radar aerials and on more than one occasion when squadrons moved, bicycles. Either strapped underneath or between the wings. The resulting appearance may well be likened to a string bag.

The TAG found that his old TF/T21c or TB4F wireless set was being replaced by the TR1082/83 which was promptly dubbed the Geep. This was long before the American buggy was so named for similar reasons. The Geep receiver had reaction tuning and correct operation was determined by tapping a small pin. This was helped by a wet finger and led to the expression "lickers and tappers" which was sometimes later used in unrelated circumstances. Such was the radio on which we received our training and was used operationally through the early years of the war. Its various frequency bands were covered by separate coils kept in boxes, for both the transmitter and receiver. Much of the training activity consisted of wave changing, when we would need to get out these coils and change them all around. Nothing simple like flicking a switch.

This period also saw the laying down of a new aircraft carrier which was to become the Ark Royal. Whereas all previous carriers were adapted from existing ships this one was designed from scratch. With two hangar decks and many other features it represented an enormous advance in the state of the art.

Another new device for the TAG to operate was the R1110 beacon receiver. This gave crude bearing directions to assist in finding the ship. Theoretically up to 80 miles but in practice was usually rather less. With radio silence it could often not be used during the war, as the transmission came from the ship. Sometimes it was allowed depending on the circumstances.

At this point I shall have to break my rule about not mentioning the officers by name. It concerns Earl Mountbatten and I really cannot recount the story without naming him. Lord Louis, as he was popularly known throughout the Lower Deck, was at this period the Fleet Signals Officer in the Mediterranean theatre. As such he was very well aware of the Telegraphists who were also Air Gunners. At a period after the war, and during a social gathering, he was reminded of the TAGs, and showed that he certainly hadn't forgotten, by referring to them as "that undisciplined lot" ! A few were a little upset by this remark, but if the choice of word was harsh, it was perhaps not meant quite in that way, but rather to indicate their tendency to be unconventional. In a similar manner, another admiral was later to describe the R.N.V.R. pilots and observers as "the Dead End Kids". I suppose it went with the job.

In fact, at another post-war social gathering, a certain ex-TAG, by then an Observer, had the temerity to confess to Lord Louis, a pre-war prank that took place in the Med. and perhaps had been forgotten. Actually the man concerned was a Boy Seaman at the time, but was probably thought of as a TAG by the great man. It seems that when an officers party went ashore at one of the islands near Corfu, they took several bottles of beer which were then kept cool by dunking them in the sea in a cache. They then all went off for a swim. Now a small group of Seamen were also out for a swim and happened across the beer. To them, this was most fortuitous, and one doesn't have to explain what happened to it. It is not clear if they knew who's it was at the time, but they certainly heard not long later. No one owned up then. Now, however, these many years later, one of the culprits had confessed. Of course, Lord Louis was actually tickled pink. It gave him a nice story he could tell to various Wardrooms, and Commissioned Observer Germon found he had become instantly infamous.

With war looming and the Air Branch expanding, more TAGs were required. The Fleet were unhappy at losing so many trained Telegraphists into this slot, which was perhaps not so demanding in its knowledge of Telegraphy though requiring other skills. The first step was to open the doors for transfer from other branches of the Service. These included Signallers, Seamen, Stokers and Marines. Certain educational standards were set and the courses had to be extended to include morse and wireless instruction. There had been 32 courses of the original TAGs since 1922 and at about 12 pupils each a total of some 380 TAGs had been trained. Only about half of these were still active at this time. The new courses began at RNB Portsmouth in 1935 and continued at Lee-on-Solent in 1936. A new number series was initiated for such courses and the size jumped to about 20 pupils and gradually increased. In 1937 when Lee prepared to become the H.Q. the courses switched to Ford, the School of Naval Air Cooperation and thence in 1939 to Worthy Down and Eastleigh. Finally came the direct entry Air Gunner of whom I have given earlier account.

Each year there had been various fly-pasts as the Air Branch was getting stronger, but the Fleet Review in 1937 had a special flavour. It was the Coronation Review. It was marred by the loss of TAG Di Baxter who unaccountably had failed to fix his G-string and during a manoeuvre was thrown from the aircraft.

At this time R.A.F.personnel were invited to change uniforms and join the Royal Navy. Several did, but others were not tempted and had to be retained, still in R.A.F. uniform, to maintain the strength until replaced by new naval trained personnel. This mixed bag continued until well into the '40s with Flight Sergeants and Sergeants providing the technical expertise and authority.

TAGs had always been classified as executive branch. In those days it was broadly distinguished, though not entirely, as those who wore square rig. This is the sailor suit or more precisely men dressed as seamen. Artificers, Writers, Cooks, Stewards etc. wore the reefer jacket known as fore and aft rig. The principle was that non-executive grades could achieve higher rank on grounds of their technical ability but at that point were not qualified to take command of men on general duties. The executive branch, which was in the main Seamen and Stokers, had to pass examination boards which tested their power of command to qualify for promotion. Such were the conditions for the Air Gunner to achieve higher rank.

At least this approach ensured he remained in the Air Branch. At an earlier stage this need not have been so. When the accent had been on Telegraphist rather than Air Gunner then those with ambition who passed for Petty Officer would find themselves returned to Fleet duties in their higher rank. They might subsequently return to the Air Branch as Instructors, as did Bobby Maskell, or even be appointed back as a Warrant Officer, as was Charlie Messenger. In general, those who wished to stay with the Fleet Air Arm did not aim beyond Leading Hand. The new system now allowed them to become Petty Officer Airmen. There was some confusion with regard to the badges. As Air Gunners the main badge was now the aeroplane worn on the arm. Those who wanted to indicate their origins as Telegraphists would put the Tels. badge on their cuff.

By 1939 another 9 courses had gone through, adding some 200 to the numbers, such that about 400 active TAGs existed at the outbreak of war. They could not all claim to know each other, but the clan system still held good. Most of the older TAGs were retained as instructors. Their flying days were over but they were invaluable in the schools. Every one was a character and they exercised their influence in moulding the new pupils. Those of us who came in at this point would marvel at the dexterous and impeccable morse sent during S.B.X.. In 1938 when it was clear that war was not far off there was a considerable recruitment of transfers from the Fleet. Thus at the outbreak, when Worthy Down had but recently been opened, there were some 4 courses in training, each of 40 pupils, whilst another two courses of the same size were also going through Eastleigh. This big influx was vital to the demands for expansion and replacement of losses that came about as 1940 unfolded. These men were not available at the outbreak and so it was the active regulars who were manning the carriers at sea and who would take the brunt of the wars first casualties.

The first shock was not long in coming. On the 17th September 1939 HMS Courageous was torpedoed by a U-boat and sunk. The last TAG to land aboard was Doug Hemingway. It was fortunate that the sea conditions were reasonable and the destroyers were able to pick up a large number of survivors. Doug was a survivor but four TAGs were lost.

It should perhaps be mentioned that many of the pre-war regulars did not relish the war. They were professional sailors and aviators, yes. Such risks they were prepared to meet, but with families at home they were as anguished as the average Mr.Civilian. However, like Mr.Civilian when called upon later, they did not shrink from having a go. At the end of a stint of operations, most were happy to fall back into second line squadrons. TAGs who came in later as volunteers knew what they were in for, but usually they too were glad of a rest after getting some of the stuffing knocked out of them. All reliefs were very popular. By and large TAGs didn't ask for trouble. A few were known to go to some lengths to avoid it !

TAGs maintained a considerable grapevine. They were communicators in more than one sense. The comings and goings of those in the communication squadrons did much to assist this and the very chumminess of all the crew rooms ensured that much gossip would be passed on. The tales would include not only details of prangs, casualties and movements but also of more nefarious deeds. Certain TAGs names became household words to people who never met them.

In the early war years the individual aircraft on the larger ships played a considerable part. This was the period of the Sea Raider and there was much searching for them by both ships and aircraft. On one such search the Swordfish from H.M.S. Malaya sighted and shadowed the Scharnhorst and Gneisenau. On return they could not find the Malaya in bad visibility and came down on the sea. The TAG was Russell George. Next day other ships were amazed to hear signals from the lost aircraft. She was in fact a seaplane and still afloat. The crew were rescued by a Spanish ship, the Cabo de Buena Esperanza. The aircraft that was perhaps used most often on this type of work was the Walrus. An amphibian able to land on the sea or ashore or on an aircraft carrier. It did have an Achilles heel. When landing in the sea they had to check that the sea plug was in and the camera hatch closed or the plane would fill and sink ignominiously. I fear one of these machines was promptly shot down quite early in the war when they ran into three Messerschmits.

Fairey Swordfish floatplane

This early TAG aviator shows the Rig of the Day, circa 1924. The TAG is Reg Powis

Fairey Seal

A TAG hooking on a Walrus early in the War

Fairey IIIF

The end of HMS Courageous, 17th September 1939

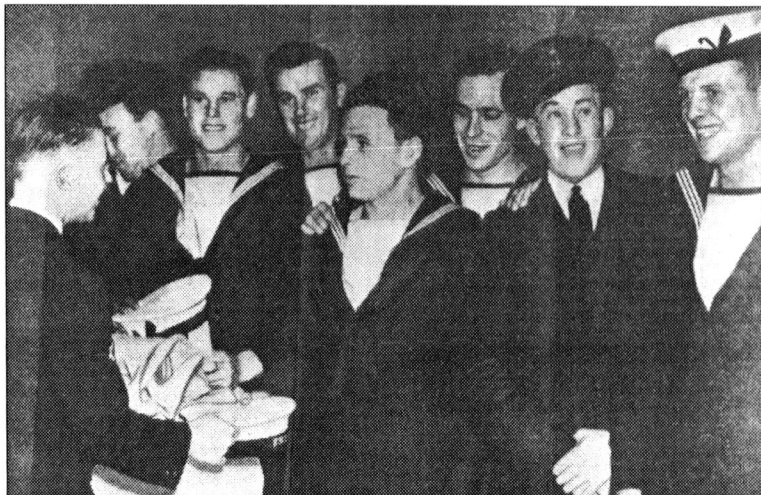
Courageous survivors. The group includes sveral AGs

Tel Bracebridge; L Tel Chandler; Tel Budgen; Tel Thompson; L Tel Brown
LS Howatt; L Tel Stimson; L Sig Mardlin; Tel Hill; Tel White; Tel Fitzpatrick; L Tel Barnard
PO Holdsworth; PO Kingson; Yeo Brown; CPO Richmond; CPO Maskell; PO King; PO Barrett

This group includes the famous Bobby Maskell and Nutty Richmond. At the back
are many other well-known, perhaps 'infamous' characters. Notice that even at
this date (1939), they were still using their substantive ranks and had not yet
transferred to the rankings of 'Airmen'. CPO Tel Maskell never did transfer

HMS Ark Royal, North Sea 1940. Ranged aboard Ark Royal about midnight, Jun
12/13th 1940, Skuas of 800 and 803 Squadrons en route to Trondheim to attack
German warships
[Photo: Courtesy Dickie Rolph]

CHAPTER 8

Norwegian Campaign.

As part of the improvement in the fighter power of the newly constituted Fleet Air Arm, the Nimrods and Ospreys had been replaced by Sea Gladiators. This was actually quite an improvement and a few of these Glads made their mark for a short while. Perhaps the most famous were those taken out of their packing cases and used by the R.A.F.in Malta as "Faith,Hope and Charity". Yet the Navy did not pursue this aircraft but placed their hopes in the Skua. So the Glads were replaced by the Skuas. One might say that the Skua was never much of an aeroplane because it did not have the speed or fire-power to be a good fighter and couldn't carry enough weight in bombs. It is however a bit unfair criticising in retrospect because the Skua was a big step forward in its day. It made quite a reasonable dive bomber as the Konigsberg found to its cost. It bore the brunt of the Fleet Air Arm effort in Norway, and, if it paid the price of being obsolescent, it was because it was called upon to do too much by too few. There were three squadrons, Nos.800, 801 and 803. They were two seaters and manned in the back seats by Rating Observers and TAGs in some numbers.

Almost in the first week of the war two Skuas got into action against a U-boat. These aircraft were from 800 Squadron and each had a Rating Observer in the back seat. These were P.O.s George McKay and 'Willie' Simpson. Now it must be supposed that the pilots were not fully aware of the effect of their weapons - up till then they had probably dropped practice bombs - but in their exuberance to attack they came too low and blew off their own tails. The sad part, is that whilst the pilots were picked up to become POWs, the chaps in the back were both killed. This attack occurred on 14-9-39 off Rockall Bank.

At a period when the country was desperately short of the means to wage war the Norwegian campaign was very much a 'do-it-yourself' affair. One TAG who was left at a supposed air base that was little more than a field, recruited local help and made prodigious steps towards turning it into a useful operational airfield. For this work he was commissioned in the field. Another TAG, George Russell, when shot down in German held territory, trekked 60 miles across the mountains with his pilot until they reached Namsos and rejoined with British forces. Another TAG, Ken King, also trekked out after being shot down. In his case he gained the sanctuary of Sweden, from where he was eventually repatriated.

The Norwegian support was flown from the Ark Royal and Furious and backed up from Hatston. Not only the Skuas, but Swordfish squadrons 816,818 and 820 had also been active in attacks supporting the campaign. A heavy blow fell on the 9th June 1940 when HMS Glorious was sunk by gunfire after being intercepted by German ships. The circumstances meant a large part of the ship's company was lost and this included a number of TAGs. In retaliation for this loss Swordfish and Skuas attacked the German ships at Trondheim with unhappy results.

We are indebted to TAG Dickie Rolph for a first hand account of this action :-

"Having covered the withdrawal of British, French and Polish troops, (who had shortly before captured the town of Narvik from the Germans), from the area of Narvik south to a little north of Trondheim, the ships carrying them back to England and France were being escorted by units of the Home Fleet. The Ark Royal closed on Glorious and we were treated to the sight of five Hurricane fighters being landed on Glorious by RAF pilots who had not seen a carriers deck before and did not have the benefit of arrester gear. All made a good landing and we thought that perhaps this would be the starter for a better fleet fighter.

We, Ark Royal and attendant destroyers, parted company to go about our own business of providing wide cover for transports whilst the Glorious and her two destroyers set off for Scapa Flow. The German heavy ships, Scharnhorst and Blucher among them, caught up with Glorious early next morning and sank the lot before any clearly read alarm signal was transmitted. Later that evening, on receipt of information, Ark Royal changed course towards the Norwegian coast. It appeared that the German heavy ships had come to rest in Trondheim and secured close to the town jetty.

An attack on these ships was planned using 15 Skuas armed with 250lb bombs. We were to have the protection of 6 long range Blenheim 4Fs as fighter cover and 6 Beauforts of Coastal Command which would bomb Varnes airfield near Trondheim to keep the numerous German fighters on the deck.

The scheme of the attack was that the Beauforts were to attack at 0158 and our attack was to begin at 0200, using our usual kind of approach, gliding from about 13000 feet to 9000 feet before going into the final dive for dropping bombs.

We had a bit better briefing than before on such occasions, but much was still left unanswered, particularly so when we were handed ú40 in Norwegian money - its import was not lost upon us. We were also given better maps and a departure point for return.

All a/c were ranged and loaded by about midnight and in those latitudes at that time of year it was dusk, but by 1 am it would be clear daylight again. The photograph shows the group just before take-off and it was my fortune to be on the starboard side right aft so we would be the last to go but had a long walk with all the bits and pieces one felt it was necessary to carry. My pilot, Petty Officer Monk, and I shared the same mess and had had some discussions about our antics in the air against German fighters and came to the conclusion that since we were much slower it would serve us best if we flew slower still under provocation. You see, even though we were fighter dive bombers no effort had been made to drill us in any form of air evasion tactics : air fighting was hardly discussed by anybody. It was assumed you would automatically know all about it.

The sky was clear of cloud and we could have been seen for miles as we came in from the sea. At the beginning of our glide I could see the hangars on an airfield some miles from Trondheim well alight and on looking up I saw 6 twin-engined aircraft some three thousand feet above us and reported to my pilot that we did have the 6 long range Blenheims above us. Shortly afterwards these 6 a/c put their noses down and their twin tails came into view. I changed my report to 6 ME110s and by this time there were more than 6. At this time also all the AA guns in the world seemed to open up on us, heavy stuff from the ships, batteries along the jetties and main streets of the town, and short range stuff so thick that there wasn't a gap to get through at all. It looked as if a circle of people were standing around throwing up handfuls of lighted stones.

The ME110s were almost shoving each other out of the way to have a go. As I started firing at the first one I was sure I was about to accomplish the air gunner's dream by shooting down an attacking fighter because there were flames coming out of the front of the 110. I soon realised that the flames were from his cannon and machine guns fitted in the central nacelle and his shells and bullets were going above, below and either side of our aircraft. I thought his harmonisation was pretty poor and then realised he was inside his normal harmonisation range. He had to violently alter course as my pilot really did his stuff in literally bringing the Skua to almost a stop.

The 110 pulled up very sharply followed by others. Each time P.O. Monk carried out the same stunt - back throttle, up nose, turn towards. There was one occasion when there was a group of 110s tearing round in a circle just below us, about 8 of them, all their rear gunners having a go at just us ! I thought it was a bit unfair. I hoped that I was faring better than they were. Finally they gave us the benefit of their departure for which we were thankful. By this time we were miles away from the target area without bombs, having got rid of them during the first attack. Heading north up the fjord away from Trondheim we had a discussion and decided to make for the island given us as a departure point. From there we would set course for the carrier.

On nearing the coast, with our departure island a long way ahead we met a group of German twin-engined aircraft which we took for JU88s returning from bombing the Fleet. It was a case of closing one's eyes and hoping you would not be seen. We believe that the Jerries must have done the same for no violence was forthcoming and we simply passed slightly below them and well to one side. On leaving our departure point (the Island of Hitra lighthouse) we climbed so that I could quickly get a good signal from the beam of the homing beacon from which we calculated our course to steer back to the 'Ark'. This was successfully obtained and P.O.Monk showed great faith in accepting my new course to steer - a difference of some 60 degrees. After what seemed a long time we sighted the Ark dead ahead.

It appeared that much had been going on since our departure some 3 hours or so before. Fog was responsible for a collision, I believe. There were also some attacks by the Luftwaffe. We were not kept waiting long before being allowed to land on. We were the first back and were hustled up to the 'office' to report to the Vice-Admiral. It went something like this. "Well, Monk, what happened ?" "Well, Sir, the bloody fool who laid this trip on ought to have his head tested". "Now, now, tell me all about it". P.O.Monk did do that. I was hardly spoken to. I offered a drawing I had made of the ships' positions in Trondheim and the torpedo nets, but no one seemed to want that kind of thing. No one seemed interested in the air fighting part of the trip. We were ushered down to the Wardroom and I was offered a pot of very flat beer. Now I ask you -flat beer, empty stomach, 'shaky-do' just completed and all I wanted to do was to tell someone how successful our tactics had been in getting the better of a huge gaggle of German fighters. Not a soul seemed interested. It was this attack and the indifference shown that made me specialise in air gunnery when the opportunity came. I was able, when I was the Chief Air Gunnery Instructor at the TAGs school in Canada, after a struggle, to arrange for fighter evasion exercises to be part of the air gunnery course, using a Canadian built Hurricane for the purpose.

Five Skuas returned from this attack. The C.O. became a P.O.W.. Rating Observer 'Cuts' Cunningham was shot down by two ME110s carrying out a scissors attack. He had the experience of using a smouldering parachute when he had to bail out. He was rescued from the fjord and taken before the German Naval Captain for interrogation. On being pressed to admit that he came from the Ark Royal he had the pleasure of telling the Captain that was impossible since the Germans had already sunk it twice. I understand that the Captain was far from amused.

Who can say that such an attack was worthwhile ? It was an awfully long time ago."

Another action in these Norwegian attacks concerned the fate of one of the Swordfish crews. TAG Jack Skeats' aircraft was hit by flak and with the bottom of his cockpit torn away and on fire, and with both legs injured, he beat out the flames with his hands to save the aircraft and his companions. Jack was awarded a DSM. His injuries kept him grounded subsequently.

A little later when the Warspite led a British Force into the second Battle of Narvik the battleship's Swordfish floatplane had a grandstand view of the whole affair. This was perhaps the most enthralling incident ever to befall these aircraft individualists. They didn't just watch though. They warned of enemy ships that lay ahead and tucked up the minor ravines and fjords. They even did some bombing of their own and sunk an enemy submarine. This action caused them to collect a spot of gunfire in opposition. Almost every German ship was sunk. Rating Pilot Ben Rice flew the Swordfish and Maurice Pacey was the T.A.G. in the back.

An interesting sideline to this episode concerns TAG Frank Smith. His aircraft had been damaged in an earlier attack and they ditched alongside a destroyer, HMS Hero,and were picked up. This destroyer was one of those in the forefront of the Narvik action and Frank was still aboard. Are you manning the aircraft wavelength he asked ? Not so. Destroyers haven't that many operators and the aircraft wave is not usually of interest to them. So Frank hopped on a spare receiver and was able to give the destroyer Captain all of the Swordfish signals which he otherwise would not have had.

Viewed from this point in time the activities of the first year of war appear pitifully weak when compared with the sterner efforts yet to come. For the Fleet Air Arm participants these were grim times. It was a young Service. There were few of them and they were pitched into every breach. None felt this more severely than the TAGs. All the 1939 fleet transfers had been drafted rapidly to squadrons as soon as they came off course. The courses of all the men trained since 1935 had been decimated. Not all were fatalities but who then knew how many were Prisoners of War ? The TAG grapevine could not give this information. Those who were left counted the faces and noted that over 50% weren't with them any more.

Now the new groups of Air Gunners -the direct entries (including RNVRs and RNSRs) - were beginning to come off course. The new boys had a lot to learn in a very short time. They had had a long course, yet when they joined a squadron they were green. Inexperienced and lost. One must appreciate that two years in Service time is an enormous gap. During such a length of time all the Fleet transfers had soaked up a wealth of naval experience and were quite at home aboard ship. Such was not the case with the new intake. They had to be put through the hoop -and quick. However it wasn't long before they were holding their own in best TAG tradition.

Perhaps they couldn't send morse very well. Their training stood them well for receiving but with W/T silence there weren't many opportunities to transmit. When the call came some pretty rough morse was likely to be heard.

The influx of these men corresponded with an all round increase in Fleet Air Arm strength. The work of 1938/39 was coming to fruition. R.N.V.R. pilots and observers appeared, as also the first naval trained ground crews. Five new Fleet Carriers had been laid down. HMS Illustrious was already in operation and the second, HMS Formidable was working up. These ships were somewhat different from Ark Royal in having only one hangar deck but a thick metal top deck. This later proved invaluable in the Pacific.

Following Dunkirk there had been the threat of invasion with the enemy within a stone's throw. Naval aircraft squadrons destined for the new carriers diverted from their work-up preparations to help break up German attempts to gather an invasion fleet. Flying from R.A.F. airfields in Kent, squadrons such as 825 and 826 carried out bombing and minelaying operations and found this useful experience, but inevitably lost some of their number. TAG Chas Homer was awarded a DSM for an encounter with enemy aircraft.

Then came the new Fleet fighter - the Fairey Fulmar. It had 8 guns like the Hurricane but performance was lost by putting in a back seat. It was probably thought necessary to provide navigational and radio facilities for carrier operation. TAGs, particularly the new direct entries, occupied these seats in some numbers in squadrons such as 805, 806, 807, 808 and 809. Within their limits the aircraft gave a good account of themselves. The movie world has always used a lot of licence in presenting this period. For the sake of a gripping story it has always been implied that voice communication with the pilot from the ground was simple. This was just not so. VHF sets did not come out in numbers until 1943/44 and the HF voice radios had poor performance, apart from being somewhat scarce. The R.A.F. got what there were. Our fighters circled the Fleet and chased what they could see, aided by such direction as was allowed by W/T.

The greatest fillip to the Air Branch and indeed the country as a whole came in November 1940 when Swordfish attacked the Italian Fleet at Taranto. 815 , 819, 813 and 824 squadrons flew from Illustrious, the latter two on detachment from Eagle. No TAGs took part in this action. The long range tanks left only room for the observers.

Previously the two carriers, Illustrious and Eagle had been the scourge of the Italians throughout the Eastern Med.. They had attacked the Dodecanese, Tripoli and other Libyan ports. Many TAGs had taken part in these operations. Some had been lost at Rhodes. This was a badly planned attack which was met by Italian fighters. One TAG was killed and three others made POW. Yet other aircraft had to ditch on the way home. A nasty set-back all round. The Eagle squadrons had battered Italian destroyers at Massawa in Somaliland. Again there were TAG prisoners-of-war. Later the Formidable's squadrons also attacked Massawa on the way to the Med.. AGs Brown and Shiel were shot down and taken prisoner.

Reverting once more to comment on the Norwegian theatre of war I shall jump the gun a bit and move on to the middle of 1941. This is a little out of time sequence but as subsequent episodes occur mainly in the Mediterranean the following is mentioned here. By this time the third of the new Fleet carriers, the Victorious was in operation. Four squadrons of Albacores and one of Fulmars from Victorious and Furious made a daylight torpedo attack on the ports of Kirkenes and Petsamo in northern Norway right up on the Russian border. In the event it turned into a sacrificial raid and was perhaps the greatest shock to the TAG world at that time. The story is best described by one TAG who flew on the attack.

"A brilliant Arctic sun shines on two aircraft carriers steaming east, about 80 miles north of the northern tip of Norway in July 1941. They are accompanied by a Cruiser and a Destroyer escort. Every member of the flying crews aboard has been keyed up for the last twenty-four hours wondering what is to come.

At dawn the look-outs spotted German aircraft shadowing the force. It looks dodgy - we know every move is being reported. Why didn't we fly off a couple of Fulmars to shoot the shadower down? My guess is that a Fulmar would never have caught up with it......

At 1300 we go for briefing and we are told that we take-off at 1400 (in the brilliant Arctic sunshine !) for a torpedo attack on massed shipping in Kirkenes harbour while the other carrier does the same at Petsamo. We are told that we should meet practically no opposition from enemy aircraft as Jerry has only a couple of worn-out ME109s in the vicinity and that the area is only lightly defended by guns. They tell us that we will go in low, with the Fulmar squadron as top cover, and that there is a German hospital ship between us and the coast - and that we must not attack it.

We get airborne, with some misgivings on my part, as I do not consider 2 p.m. on a summer's day the ideal time for an attack. Why not dawn ? The Germans must sleep sometime.........We climb to 2000 feet and force on. After half-an-hour we sight the hospital ship about two miles to starboard (probably telling the shore base all about us) ; there was no reason for a hospital ship to be in that position.

Approaching the narrow entrance to a fjord at cliff top height, what seemed like thousands of guns opened up, the guns trained horizontally on us as we went by. I felt like throwing my Vickers K at them. We climbed to get over the hill at the end of the fjord and down the other side was the harbour with about four small ships in it (massed shipping ?). The ground gunners are still firing and as we turn to starboard to line up for a torpedo run on the largest ship I see a nice formation of ME110s half-a-mile away at about 500 feet (of course they didn't know we were coming - they just happened to be there !). It's every man for himself. Torpedoes careering through the water and Albacores going all ways hotly pursued by 110s. My aircraft did a smart about turn and retired at full speed (100mph) the way we had come followed by the rest of the sub-flight, hopping over the hill and down the fjord. My No.3 hit the sea in flames ; we cleared the mouth of the fjord and my No.2 turned away towards the Russian coast chased by two 110s which eventually shot him down. By this time we were about eight miles out to sea and the last of the attacking 110s returned to base.

Back over the carrier and one aircraft is in a big heap on the deck ; we landed after it had been cleared and then waited for the rest of the seventeen aircraft that had taken off. We waited in vain. The score turned out to be eleven aircraft lost and one TAG dead on arrival back on board.

Our fighter escort ? We heard afterwards that it consisted of three Fulmars - and they got tangled up with a dozen ME109s. (No fighter opposition !)

So much for daylight torpedo attacks on a defended harbour with Albacores........."

Another report explained a feature of the German fighter tactics. With his cannon harmonised at maybe 800 to 1000 yards range he could sit off and hosepipe into the target without the AGs return fire from a Vickers K being in any way effective.

Many of those lost came from the group of direct entries. Chill were the hearts of those who heard the news as the names filtered through the grapevine. Percy Fabian, Frank Sharples, Harold Wade, Harry Pickup, Norman Train, Spike Lancaster, Harry Griffin and Jimmy James plus others. It was a long time before we heard that some had managed to survive and were P.O.W.s.

Fairey Albacore

CHAPTER 9

"The 'Eagle'"

HMS Eagle

From the foregoing accounts of operations off Norway it might be assumed that life was cheap in the Fleet Air Arm in the early war years. This was true enough in that theatre but there was another side to the coin. Around the world aviators from numerous ships were clocking up countless flying hours patrolling and searching with only infrequent glimpses of the enemy. Whilst the threat of action was always round the corner, and not encouraged by the many, there was much boredom with the routines. In these circumstances memories of the times mainly reflect the funny odd little happenings.

I have been fortunate in obtaining some reminiscences from TAG Gordon "Blondie" Lambert of this period. As a pre-war regular his story goes back to cover his introduction to aviation and in this chapter takes us through to the loss of HMS Eagle and a shade afterwards.

by Blondie Lambert:-

"Shortly before the war, when it was obvious that more and more naval air crews would be required, volunteers from General Service seamen were called for, to be trained as full time aircrew and not on a part-time basis.

I started my naval career at the boys training establishment at Shotley near Ipswich - HMS Ganges - and after a very tough and strictly disciplined 15 months was drafted first to the Iron Duke and then to the flagship of the Home Fleet HMS Nelson. It was whilst I was on the Nelson as a young ordinary seaman that a notice appeared on the notice board calling for volunteers for flying duties with the F.A.A.. A three badge A.B. who happened to be in my mess, had been a parachute packer and he said to me "get yourself in if you get the chance".

He sang the praises of the F.A.A., the promotion prospects, the healthy outdoor life and the "thrill of the air combined with the romance of the sea ". To a youngster whose experience of naval life was scrubbing decks in bare feet at Scapa Flow, cleaning brasswork, painting ship and a host of other equally unpleasant tasks, the idea of being an aviator had a great deal to commend it.

I submitted my name, could read morse at 10 w.p.m., had the necessary academic qualifications and passed a very severe medical check, which as far as I remember were the main requirements. I was accepted for training and along with several others - all of whom were of similar background to my own - a new and totally different career began.

A couple of months in H.M.Signal School at Portsmouth before going on to the Naval Air Station at Eastleigh for flying training. During the course of our flying training a couple of weeks were spent at RAF Aldergrove in Northern Ireland to undertake air gunnery practice over Lough Neagh. The RAF couldn't quite get used to sailors flying and we were something of a novelty to them, especially when we would turn out for early morning parades with trousers and overcoats over our pyjamas.

A mile or so outside the camp was a kind of civilian run NAAFI. It was a bit more classy than the camp canteen and of course being in Northern Ireland, food, eggs, ham and such like was more plentiful than in England. The only snag being that it cost money and that was a commodity which was always in short supply.

We were discussing our gastronomic needs one day and the shortage of cash to buy when our conversation was overheard by one of the "Crabfats".

"Don't worry", says he, "just go along, order your meal and ask 'Auntie' to put it on the slate. She's a delightful old lady and adores servicemen ". After all, we'd be getting paid before we left, and we were good honest sailors - weren't we ?

Smartening ourselves up, a dozen or so of us set off for the meal of a lifetime ; ham, eggs, chips, sausage, tomatoes, beans, anything they sold we'd have.

The first one in the queue gave his order which was duly plated up and passed over, the second gave his order, by which time No.1 man had reached the cash desk. "That will be 3/11d", said the charming old dear with an angelic smile.

"Put it on the slate ", says our hero, "the name is....."

He never did get his name out, no lovely old lady could abuse anyone the way she carried on.

We were a crowd of thieving jackals robbing old ladies and taking advantage of their generosity. What was the world coming to ? Put it on the slate indeed !!

Needless to say we went back to camp sadder and wiser but with vengeance in our hearts. We never clapped eyes on our Air Force friend again, which for him was fortunate.

On our return to Eastleigh we took our examinations and those of us who qualified spread our newly found wings and were away.

After a brief spell with 806 squadron at Hatston in the Orkneys flying Skuas and another short stay with the communication flight at Donibristle I returned to Lee-on-Solent to await whatever fate had in store. I did not have to wait long before getting a draft chit to join HMS Eagle which at that time, late 1940, was in the Eastern Mediterranean.

Along with two or three other TAGs I took passage in the submarine depot ship "Woolwich", around the Cape and through the Suez canal to Alexandria.

We made quite an impressive entrance into Alexandria harbour by colliding with a Hospital Ship. Fortunately no real damage to either ship and before long those of us taking passage disembarked.

After the usual organised chaos which is commonplace on such occasions we eventually found ourselves at the Naval Air Station at Dekheila just outside Alexandria where Eagles' squadrons were disembarked. We were living in tents, if living is the right word. Sand was everywhere and mosquitos were in super abundance. On waking each morning it was not unusual to find several bloated mosquitos inside the mosquito net and face and arms covered in bites. In spite of the conditions all the F.A.A. personnel made light of these irritations, drank warm beer, ate indifferent food and longed for the day when we would re-embark in Eagle.

Life was not without its lighter moments such as the time one of the TAGs "sold", to a rather well-heeled businessman, a Walrus, belonging to one of the cruisers, and which had been flown ashore. The TAG, knowing he was to return aboard next day, had, along with other members of his flight gone ashore for a "quiet run".

When going around the better class night spots - after all we were getting about 6/- a day - he had managed to get into conversation with a rather well-to-do Arab. Talk apparently got round to flying and aeroplanes and our very generous TAG said "come round tomorrow and I'll sell you mine -I don't like the damn thing anyway ".

Early the next morning a bleary-eyed, still somewhat unsteady on his feet TAG, took off to return to his ship. Later that same day a very irate Arab was storming around the camp threatening all kinds of unpleasant acts which would be performed on our con-man TAG if ever he should return again to Dekheila.

Like good times, even bad times come to an end and it was without regret that we eventually rejoined Eagle. In fact I was joining her for the first time not knowing quite what to expect.

Eagle had two Swordfish squadrons 813 and 824 and the TAGs for these two squadrons were all messing together. They were a great crowd and no one could have joined a better group of people. It should be remembered that a number of them had not been in the U.K. for over two years, having been on the China Station since before the outbreak of war, and in fact did not return home until Christmas 1941.

In addition to the Swordfish squadrons, Eagle at that time had three Gloster Gladiators. It was the responsibility of the TAGs in H.Q. to ensure that their radios were kept in perfect working order. Air-to-Air communication being of paramount importance especially when engaging enemy aircraft attacking the fleet.

Living conditions in the Eagle were by modern standards primitive. Storage capacity precluded unlimited supplies of fresh vegetables and fresh water was at a premium.

Fresh water to a naval man is almost as important as the air he breathes. To anyone who was trained in any of the boys training establishments "Ganges", "St.Vincent" or "Impregnable" it was every bit as important. We were accustomed to bathing at least twice a day and clean clothes after each bath or shower - it was just our way of life.

When at sea the usual routine was for water to be rationed. It would be turned on for say half-an-hour in the morning and again for half-an-hour in the evening. Whilst this was not too bad for those actually on board at "opening time", for those who had the misfortune to be flying on our almost continuous anti-submarine patrols it was annoying not to be able to wash or to do dhobying, and living in such cramped conditions - your best friend would tell you! However, such was the spirit in the mess that buckets of water were always put aside for those flying. The routine was almost a religious ritual. The bucket of water which the TAGs got for their oppos who were flying was always set aside for their exclusive use after landing on. Because it was never certain if the tanks of drinking water situated on the various messdecks would continue to meet the demand, the first call made on each bucket of water was for drinking. When thirst was satisfied the water was then used for personal hygiene. After that the water could then be used for dhobying. Rinsing was relatively easy. All that was required was to tie the washed articles to a piece of rope and tow them in the sea for a few minutes, or fasten a rope to a bucket handle and draw unlimited water from the sea. The bucket that was set aside was sacrosanct but on one occasion I was surprised to find that a bucket I had set aside for my oppo had been used. Standing close by was a TAG who had just completed his dhobying. Rather hastily I accused him of using the fresh water for rinsing. He denied doing so but nonetheless the resulting fracas was most unbecoming. I had reason to regret my hasty outburst when shortly afterwards my oppo landed on and on being told of the incident calmly announced that he had washed and shaved in the water before taking off.

On one occasion when patrolling in the Eastern Med. we had to take on board survivors from one of the City Class cruisers. They had been picked up by a destroyer and were being transferred to us for passage back to Alex.. Naturally there were plenty of spectators, myself included. I could hardly believe my eyes when I caught sight of an old chum of mine, "Nutty" Pulsford. We had been together in the Comms.Flight at Donibristle. It is usual I suppose, when survivors are mentioned, to conjure up pictures of unshaven, bedraggled men in torn clothes and looking the picture of abject misery. Nothing could be further from the truth in Nutty's case. He was dressed in almost clinically clean overalls which had been washed so frequently they were almost sky blue instead of the familiar navy blue.

He had on a pair of white gym shoes, his face was shining and his jet black hair was immaculate. He was carrying a small "Pusser's" suitcase. I couldn't help but comment on his appearance when he came aboard but when I heard his story it didn't surprise me.

The cruiser carried a Walrus amphibian, Nutty being the TAG. He had completed an anti-submarine patrol and returned to the ship and been hoisted aboard. When all was secured he'd gone for a bath and tidied himself up for the evening - he too was an ex-boy seaman.

No sooner had he settled himself down when the ship was attacked, set on fire and damaged to such an extent that it was necessary to abandon ship. A destroyer was called alongside to take off the first batch of survivors and the F.A.A. personnel not being required for damage control or guns crews were the first to leave. With foresight typical of the man he had packed his No.1 suit, set of underclothes, shoes, socks and perhaps most important of all his Post Office Savings Book - after all you can't have a good run ashore without money. He was a man who always got his priorities right.

There was one incident however, when we were together at Donibristle, when things didn't go quite right for him. We were flying in civil aircraft with ex-civil pilots and civilian ground crews. One of the aero-engine fitters had been working on a Proctor engine and "Nutty" had been checking the radio. The fitter climbed into the cockpit to do a cockpit check and to run up the engine. "Nutty", having completed his radio check was playing cowboys with a verys pistol showing the fitter how quick on the draw he was. I don't think the fitter was too impressed. Anyway he returned to his job and leaned forward to press the starter button, at exactly the same moment our Naval Tom Mix made a quick draw and squeezed the trigger. The pistol was still loaded ! Because events happened simultaneous the fitter thought the engine had blown up. He leaped out leaving our hero inside. "Nutty" eventually clambered out coughing and spluttering. The fire engine and ambulance were called and as no one would climb back in to stop the engine the tail was raised until the propeller struck the ground and the engine was eventually stopped that way. The fitter and the TAG were made to lie down and await the ambulance and no one would listen to Nutty's explanation - everyone chose to believe the fitter who said the engine blew up when he started it. Truth will out and Nutty eventually appeared before the Captain. The fact that he had a fair amount of operational experience over Norway stood him in good stead and he was treated leniently with merely 14 days stoppage of leave.

We did not stay long in the Mediterranean, though the time we were there consisted of an almost continuous round of A/S patrols morning, noon and night.

Early 1941 saw us go through the Suez Canal to Mombasa, Durban, Capetown and then into the South Atlantic. Our routine was in the main anti-submarine patrols and long range searches for German raiders, armed merchant ships and submarine supply ships.

On one such sortie a Swordfish sighted a supply ship almost at the farthest point of his patrol. The TAG having made a sighting report was told to shadow until a relief aircraft could take over. Eventually he returned to the ship long after his fuel supply should have been exhausted. On catching the arrester wire his engine cut out.

The crew of the relieving Swordfish was told to ensure that the crew of the supply ship did not attempt to scuttle her and abandon ship. At one stage the crew started to climb into the lifeboats so the aircraft went in close in order that the TAG could use his Lewis gun to deter them. The pilot obviously went in a little too close and had one of his wings almost completely shot away by the supply ship. Such was the wonder of the Swordfish that it made the return to the ship quite easily.

HMS Dunedin which was in company with us on this occasion was dispatched to intercept. It was alleged to be a very prized cargo of ammunition and supplies for the submarines operating in the area at the time.

It was a very trying time for all concerned. The long hours spent looking over the side of an open cockpit searching for subs. and enemy shipping, the heat and the cramped conditions.

Rats were ever present even in the most unexpected places. We were at dusk action stations and it was usual to have mugs of "kye". The air crews' action stations were in the hangar - no modern crew rooms in those days. "Kye" for those unfamiliar with naval language is a beverage not unlike cocoa. Its consistency is much thicker than traditional cocoa and tinned milk and brown sugar were added to the individual's taste. It was usually so thick that a spoon would almost stand upright in it.

At the particular time in question one of the TAGs went along to the galley to collect the "kye". As it was being ladled into the mess kettle there was a splash as though a piece of the slab cocoa had not been thoroughly melted. A ladle was used to fill your cup from the mess kettle and after two or three had filled their mugs one unfortunate TAG ladled out a dead rat. The splash had not been caused by unmelted chocolate but by the rat being transferred from galley boiler to mess kettle. No kye was drunk that night. The incident, however, resulted in a rat extermination campaign thought up and put into operation by one of the TAGs George Wells, who was later to lose his life in Korea.

The rats often ran quite unmolested along the various pipes which festooned the ship. George's idea was to make loops of thin wire hanging in the path of the rodents. As they came running along they would get their heads through a loop which would pull tight, jerk them off the pipe and so hang themselves. It was a simple and very effective means of execution and George earned all our gratitude for considerably reducing the numbers.

By and large TAGs had a fairly good time in terms of routine. If there was no flying and the radio and Lewis gun were clean and in working order we were left largely to amuse ourselves playing crib, uckers, reading or writing. Mah Jong was a very popular game, many excellent sets having been bought when the ship was on the China Station.

It was probably because of our easy going routine which led one of the ships regulating staff to have a grudge against the F.A.A. in general and TAGs in particular. He never lost an opportunity to find fault. The TAGs' mess was next to a passageway which led out onto the weather deck. At each end of the passageway was a canvas screen used at night time to contain the light from the mess deck and hence ensure a dark ship.

After one rather unpleasant incident it was decided to take some action of our own. It was the custom of this particular crusher (R.P.O.) to walk through our mess deck each evening, along the passageway to the weather deck and then through the hangar to the regulating office.

One rather foul night, blowing half a gale and no moon, a group of us gathered on the weather deck to await his coming. Word was passed along and when he emerged through the canvas screen he stood to allow his eyes to become accustomed to the darkness. Before he knew what was happening we had put a sack over his head, fastened his arms and legs and lifted him bodily over our heads, to shouts of "over the side with him" and other cruder expressions. He was absolutely petrified as would anybody if threatened with being thrown overboard miles from anywhere. After jostling him about for a few minutes we put him back on the deck, someone threw a bucket of water over him and we left rather hurriedly. Our action seemed to have the desired effect, we were never again subjected to his spiteful outbursts and he never again walked through our messdeck. I don't think it was ever reported, at least we heard nothing further.

It was usual practice to carry aluminium dust bombs whenever carrying out patrols and these when dropped left patches on the water to mark a given spot. For example, finding wind speed and direction or marking where subs. had submerged. On landing, the safety pins had to be replaced, the bombs removed from the racks and replaced in the ready use lockers. They were only very small, some 18" long and weighing two or three pounds.

One of the Swordfish having returned from an A/S patrol was struck down into the hangar and the armourer started to remove the dust bombs. It would appear that in removing one of the bombs it was allowed to fall to the deck where it exploded. As is to be expected in a ship's hangar oil and petrol is everywhere. In a matter of seconds the hangar was an inferno. Fire curtains were lowered, sprays operated but nothing could be done to save the aircraft.

Only two or three aircraft survived and that was because they were in the air at the time. The fire caused untold damage and regretfully the armourer died during the night from burns he received when the bomb burst.

It's an ill wind as they say and we all had visions of going to Cape Town for a refit. Our base up to this time having been Freetown. The Captain cleared lower deck to tell us what was going to happen to us. After all, a carrier with no aircraft was virtually useless. He started by telling us that he had requested permission from Admiralty to go to Cape Town for a refitting. This he said had been turned down. Imagine the disappointment. He then went on to say that we were to return to the U.K. and would refit at Liverpool.

We arrived just before Christmas 1941.

Early in 1942 we were on our way again. There were some new faces in the mess as we sailed again for the Med.,only this time it was the Western end and Malta convoys. The journey to Gibraltar I recall was not without incident. All was well until we entered the Bay of Biscay. I am sure many people have passed through the Bay when the sea has been as calm as a mill pond and have reason to doubt the veracity of tales of gale force winds and hundred foot waves.

On this occasion the weather deteriorated very rapidly indeed and one of our Swordfish with Herbie Goddard as TAG was doing the usual A/S patrol. Eventually it was time for him to return aboard. The ship was rolling and pitching and the wind so strong that the dear old Stringbag was having a job to catch us up. On touching down the ship lurched and in no time the kite complete with crew had disappeared over the side. Our attendant destroyer which could only be seen when it was riding atop of a wave with its propellers thrashing the air before plunging into the trough was warned of the incident. With a degree of seamanship bordering on the miraculous she was able to pick up all three of the crew. It gave all of us aircrew great confidence to know that we had such excellent support. We were being tossed about like a cork, but Herbie Goddard on returning on board after our arrival in Gib. told us of the appalling conditions aboard the destroyer. As he so aptly remarked, "the bloody thing did everything but turn over and you just held on to anything you could, your feet left the deck and you were fluttering out like a bleeding answering pennant ". He had been a bunting tosser !!

If anything, this period of the war was, for the Swordfish squadrons, the most frustrating of all. Malta was besieged and supplies of food and materials had to be got through. Aircraft too were needed for the defence of the island. We took on board RAF personnel and crates of "do it yourself" Hurricanes.

A convoy would sail from Gibraltar and the limited number of Swordfish we carried did one continuous anti-submarine patrol. We were to learn to our cost that subs. abounded in the Med. at that time.

On leaving Gibraltar, the RAF lads would break open the crates and start building from scratch the Hurricanes so desperately needed in Malta. A couple of days out from Gib. and the fun would start. Submarine attacks, high, low and dive bombing attacks and airborne torpedo attacks. Ships which were alongside one minute were no more the next and still we plodded on.

Our own fighter cover was virtually nil. We required all hangar and deck space for the Hurricanes as they were built up. Naturally our own speed was governed by that of the convoy and so these attacks would go on for three or four days at a time.

Eventually we would be close enough to Malta for the Hurricanes to fly off and be able to reach there. Once they were airborne they had to go, it was their point of no return. They had no arrester hook and so could not land on again - at least such were the instructions ; it would seem no one remembered the original success aboard Glorious. Once we had despatched our cargo we would return to Gib. to load and stand by for another run. The convoy and protective screen of destroyers had to go all the way and very many didn't make it.

The TAGs at this time could only sit back and take it. If you weren't flying you just kept your head down and hoped for the best. If you were flying when an attack started you kept out of the way as the fleet opened up and let whatever fighter cover we had do their best.

I eventually got lucky. My relief joined the ship and I was to return to the U.K..In fact several of us were relieved and we took passage home in a well worn merchant ship. Chas Thompson and myself soon weighed up the situation and felt that in an old tub like that the safest place would be on the bridge. The biggest danger we reasoned, en route from Gib to the Clyde, would be from subs.. So we volunteered to act as signalmen for the journey home. It was an uneventful trip but we managed to get special accommodation as "crew members" as opposed to the cramped unpleasant conditions suffered by the others.

At that time there were two signalling codes in operation -The Royal Navy Code and the International Code. It was rather unfortunate that in some cases each code had identically coloured flags but different meanings. It was essential therefore that the correct code was used. I have no doubt that our R.N. escorts had some rather harsh things to say about Merchant Navy signalmen !

The day after arriving back in the U.K. we heard that the Eagle had been sunk whilst on another Malta convoy.

After a very short stay at Worthy Down, Taff Beynon and I were drafted to St.Vincent as instructors. St.Vincent had of course been a boys training establishment before the outbreak of war and was now being used for the initial training of aircrews.

The daily routine was fairly strict although discipline was by no means as rigorous as before. We managed to get in a few "quiet runs" ashore and generally make a nuisance of ourselves in the mess. In the main the instructors were reservists called up for the duration and taught basic seamanship and squad drill. For our part we were required to teach Morse Code, aircraft recognition and Fleet Air Arm procedures both ashore and afloat.

There were about half a dozen of us. My old pal Nutty Pulsford, Taff Beynon, Jack Cornwall, "Honest" John Bignall and Taff Stenner. One really great character was Vince Labross. He was a well built Charles Atlas type whose cap size was something of the order of 7½. He was always immaculately dressed and wore leather gloves. Taff Beynon on the other hand was small and stocky. It was his favourite party piece to put on Labross's cap and scream out "about turn". This he would do and leave the cap pointing in the original direction when he himself had turned about. Vince was never really amused !

Nor was he amused when after one rather hectic run ashore he returned and, having undressed, climbed into bed. However, before getting his head down he decided to have his final cigarette for the day. Half way through he felt that was enough and he put the dog-end under his pillow for "in the morning". It was not long before the dormitory was in an uproar, smoke billowing round his head, buckets of water thrown over the bedding and Labross complaining bitterly. He said afterwards that he had a faint recollection of putting his fag under the pillow without putting it out.

It was not long before their Lordships at the Admiralty decided I'd been having it easy for too long and soon I found myself bound for Northern Ireland and the Mac Ship squadron No.836. I am sure that many tales of hardship and heroism can be told by many who served in that squadron but for me the stay was short because I promptly qualified for the award of the "Most Highly Derogatory Order of the Irremovable Finger".

A newly qualified TAG was sent to the squadron and as was usual in such cases he was allowed a few days to settle down and get to know the drill. One day the Senior Observer told me to take him up and do some Homing exercises. A young Sub.Lt. pilot climbed into his cockpit and our newly qualified friend and myself got into ours. We got clearance from the ground station and off we went. After making the usual exchanges of signal strength we then got down to the meat of the job.

Briefly the routine was to call the ground station and ask for a bearing. We would then keep on a steady course and after a given period ask for another bearing. This would confirm which side of the ground station we were and ensure we flew towards and not away from it. The early D/F sets were often unreliable in ensuring that you were given a true bearing and not the reciprocal, hence the need for two bearings. We continued to ask for bearings and gave the pilot a course to steer and so it went on. After about an hour or so we decided that was enough for one day and I told the pilot "Home James".

"Course to steer please ?"

"Say again"

"Course to steer please ?"

Now any bloody fool knew we were only playing and the pilot had only been going round in circles. After all the ground station didn't have a D/F set anyway. Even I knew that !

It seems that the pilot was new to the squadron and he didn't know the drill either. Anyway, there we were somewhere over the Irish Sea or was it the Atlantic ? Now came the moment of truth. I told the TAG to make a plain language message to the ground station to say we were lost and required a true bearing. We were instructed to change frequency to an emergency wavelength and to make our callsign. The ground station then alerted other stations with D/F equipment. We were relieved when first one station and then another came up and passed bearings to us. That was fine but I had no chart board and did not know the location of either of the two stations, so we were still lost. Eventually they got together and took simultaneous bearings which produced a fix and so they could pin-point our position and give us a course to steer back home.

I will omit the dialogue which took place when we got back -but we didn't even get congratulated for the successful completion of the exercise.

Whether it was because of that incident or in spite of it I don't know, but what is a fact is that very soon I was back at Lee and appointed to "X" squadron and of course X is the unknown.

Blondie Lambert's story continues in Chapter 18.

There is, however, another aspect of Eagle's activities which Blondie has glossed over and I feel should be duly noted.

This situation was when they were actually on the way from the Med. to Cape Town. This time they had quite a party in the sinking of Italian destroyers at Massawa towards the end of March 1941. TAG Ginger Tyler has been loquacious about the affair and indeed it was one of those rare Fleet Air Arm successes not clouded by substantial losses. It was, however, the follow-up to an attack by Formidable's aircraft against the same target of Massawa on 20th March, when they were moving up to the Mediterranean, and in which they were not exactly successful. Formidable had lost at least two aircraft in which the TAGs became POWs. They were Buster Brown and Paddy Shiel. Both were eventually released when we finally overcame resistance in that part of Africa. Paddy then went home to take an Air Gunnery Instructors course and so became the scourge of all new TAGs going through course in Canada. This was because all such AGIs had taken a course at Whale Island and this put them in line to emulate the dreaded G.I.s of the Fleet.

CHAPTER 10

"Island Defenders..."

The Naval Air Station at Dekheila was some 20 miles from Alexandria, and, in a sense, marked the beginning of the Western Desert. The Nile Delta paints a strip of vivid green through the yellow of the surrounding area. This is no attempt at being poetic. It literally looks just like that from the air with the demarcation lines drawn precisely by the outer edges of the delta itself. Alexandria sits on one of the major river mouths. Round the bay to the west is Dekheila with hard rock and sand. Beyond that it stretches away exactly the same except that there is little or no sign of human occupation other than the coastal road and for part of the route a single track railway which follows the road.

We weren't going that way yet. First we were going to look at Alexandria and enjoy the attractions of a cosmopolitan city virtually unaffected by the war and still bright with lights and cinemas. This was an anomalous situation brought about by Egypt not being a country at war even though its defenders, the British, were. Even the enemy when they came to attack were careful to keep strictly to military targets. After all, they hoped to take Egypt and didn't want antagonised locals.

To get to Alexandria we had to traverse the 20 miles aboard a naval bus and we travelled through some of the more squalid areas of the city, not to mention the stink of a tannery about half way there whose smell was still lingering around even when we were dismounting. Jolly Jack usually began his rounds at the Fleet Club because there he could obtain most services such as beer, eats, haircuts, shoeshines and such like at reasonable prices without being rooked. Even though he may well get his shoes squirted with yellow goo as soon as he walked out through the gates. In the Fleet Club the winning kitties at Tombola were really worth having when the Fleet was in. Those who won were advised to return to their ship immediately with an escort. Once the Tombola was over, inevitably most men made their way out into the town. Despite various disadvantages Alexandria had a definite appeal. It was a cosmopolitan town and had life. The place was full of bars and cabarets and Jack enjoyed a run ashore there. However, at this dark period of the Mediterranean war not many ships were coming in. They were going to the bottom under heavy air attacks as they endeavoured to evacuate Greece and Crete. The survivors appeared in their hundreds and Dekheila became thronged with men wearing pyjamas. This was the only rig the stores could issue to men in such large numbers. Oddly enough they weren't incongruous in a country in which the standard local attire is a nightshirt. We felt rather small rubbing shoulders with men who accepted the loss of their ship and all their belongings as just one of those things. They were in no way demoralised and looked forward to the day when another ship could be found for them.

Whilst in Crete we had been issued with khaki battledress -much more appropriate than blue for field use ashore. Soon we were also to get the summer issue of khaki shirt and shorts. We had been given a forage cap but Jack persisted in wearing his white sailor hat. Later this was officially approved. It was perhaps desirable that he still looked a sailor rather than a soldier, even if it appeared a bit odd. The officers and P.O.s matched in well enough as they could put on a khaki cap cover on their peaked caps. Jack was oblivious to camouflage requirements and kept his cap in all sorts of conditions. Admittedly the white often rapidly turned khaki in the desert.

69

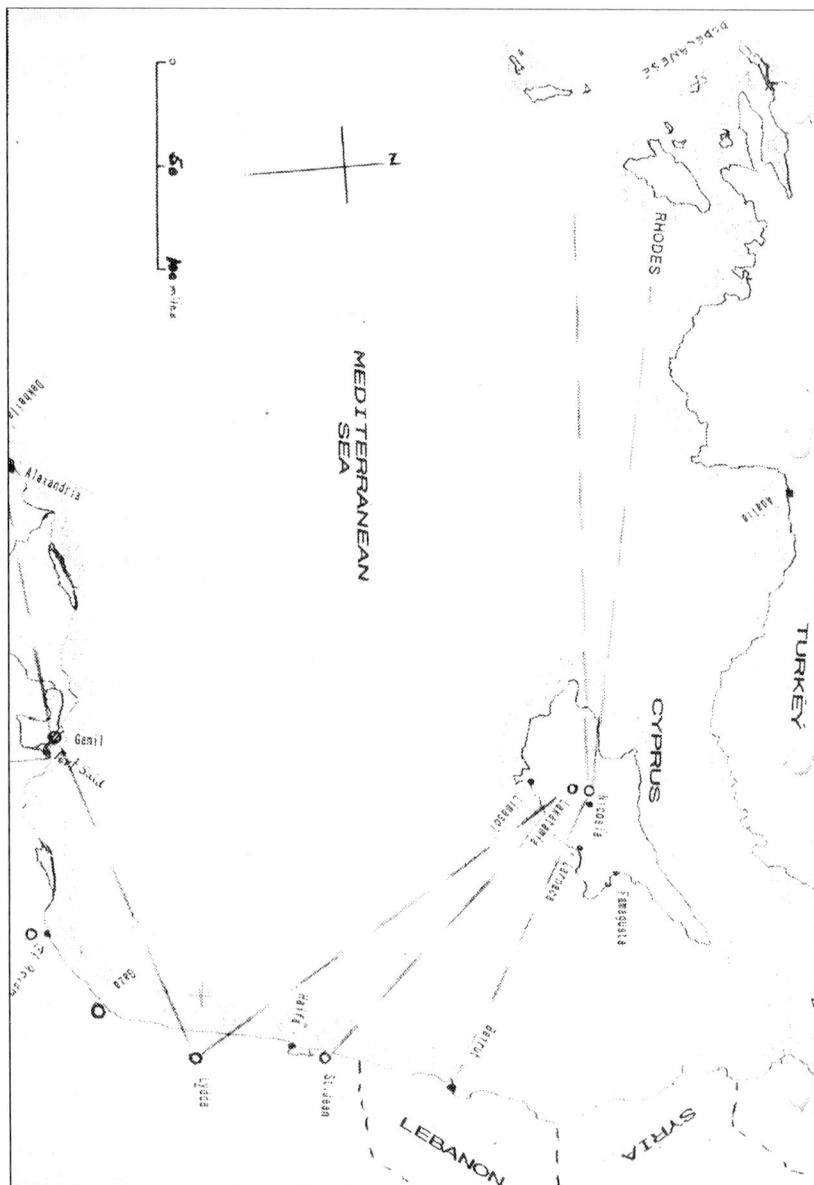

At this point it was leaked to us that Laurie, Sid and myself had been recommended for D.S.M.s. It was quite a surprise as I couldn't see what we'd done to deserve it. Later it was realised that this was more a reflection on the gallantry of our pilots. In any case it wasn't certain until gazetted. We heard no more of this for so long that I forgot about it. When it did appear no one told me officially - in the desert one sees nothing of documents like Admiralty Fleet Orders - and it must have been months afterwards before Laurie got confirmation and showed me the ribbon he had.

815 Squadron spent most of May 1941 reforming, getting new aircraft, and servicing those that were left. In particular gathering the ground crew who continued to trickle in from various ships bringing them back from Crete and replacing those who had been lost. What next ? We expected the desert but as it so happened we were destined for Cyprus. An advance flight went over but this only included two A.G.s. What was our purpose ? After the fall of Crete it appeared that the position of Cyprus looked somewhat precarious. It was well within range of aircraft from Crete and the Dodecanese, though rather far for a seaborne invasion. Flanked to the North by neutral Turkey and to the east by Vichy French Syria and Lebanon it was as far from British support as from enemy territory. After the losses in Crete and the demands of the desert forces there was no military strength to spare for Cyprus. Not that all this strategic information was known to us. It was a problem for generals and admirals. What we very soon did discover, however, was that there were few troops on the island, no R.A.F., and that we were mounting daily patrols to the westward up to Crete and the Dodecanese with the clear object of keeping an eye open for any activity that spelt invasion. The island could easily go under to a determined parachute attack but would need back up with heavier support from the sea to hold such a place. Even so, I'm not sure what we could have done to hold out if Jerry had not taken a breather to digest what he had gained. We weren't to know that his airborne brigades had received such a mauling that never again would they try such an attack on that scale.

I flew over early in June in the Walrus from HMAS Perth. We landed at the airfield for Nicosia, the islands capital city. Somewhat to my surprise I found that the two A.G.s already there were not flying but manning a pack set ground station with only the pilots and observers doing the flying. It appeared that as there were no RAF aircraft there was no ground station on an aircraft wavelength. The one WT station that existed was manned by the RAF but was on continuous base-to-base working with Alexandria. So our pack set was pressed into use to provide a ground station to listen for any signals from our aircraft.

In many ways Cyprus didn't know there was a war on and therefore presented a welcome interlude. It was a green island with attractive vineyards and under British rule had achieved standards of roads and buildings and a level of prosperity way above the pitifully poor status of Greece and Crete. We also appreciated the absence of the irritations and smells of the fellareen of Egypt. The island garrison of the Sherwood Foresters had a peacetime spit and polish to their appearance on guard duty that was a delight to behold. We were messed with the Sherwoods in their barracks though our radio was situated in the main Nicosia police station not far away. It wasn't long however, before a small group of our ground crew arrived and then we were all housed in one of the town's hotels. This was because the airfield was little more than a refuelling station for the old Imperial Airways and had no living quarter facilities. We had not brought camping equipment and enjoyed living in that hotel with all the advantages of the town right there in our midst. We were quite popular with many of the mainly Greek inhabitants when they learnt we had played a part in the defence of Greece and Crete. We were also made aware of the smaller but still considerable Turkish element in the town.

We had our problems with the radio station. The proximity of the R.A.F. transmitter also in the building would swamp out our reception and in due course it was agreed that we manned their station and carried out the point-to-point duties whilst also listening out for our aircraft. In that way we could ensure we didn't transmit to swamp our aircraft signals when they came through. It also gave us more to do than just sit and listen, though it meant round-the-clock working. This was trying until more A.G.s arrived to share the duties. The three of us kept it up for a while and did we need the practise. We hadn't touched a morse key for a month or two. Eventually more of our kind arrived and whilst we continued to do the watch keeping there were now enough of us to do flying duties as well. This also was a relief as we had some doubts about the standard of signals we might receive from the observers. They were probably more rusty than we were.

In mid-June other factors changed the tone of our activities. It was found that Vichy French ships were passing through the channel north of Cyprus and thence to France, which from our point of view was enemy territory. Lebanon itself was a threat to Cyprus and a campaign was mounted to blockade it. Our aircraft were to search for and intercept these ships. I started flying again on one such torpedo search. The object was to signal them to turn in to a Cyprus port. If they refused to do so they would be torpedoed. As it happened on this particular flight we had engine trouble. A single-engined aircraft over the sea has no safety factor and we limped back to the coast with our fingers crossed. We dropped the fish on the way to give us a chance to get back and then force landed in a field outside Limasol. With only half a field and half an engine the pilot did well to get it down with no more damage than a broken tail wheel. The locals came up to look but at least we were near civilisation and a phone call brought a lorry to take us home. They towed the aircraft back along the country lanes with its wings folded.

Two nights later we were off again with a torpedo, this time looking for a French destroyer. These vessels were of a class much bigger than the usual destroyer size and almost large enough to be called a light cruiser. She was the "Chevalier Paul" and would doubtless have given us a hot reception. In fact we were unsuccessful but she was later found by another of our aircraft and duly torpedoed. Sid Boosey in the back agreed that they had put up quite a lot of opposition and he was relieved when his aircraft turned away. There were yet other destroyers still in Beirut.

On the morning of the 21st June I was due to go on the recce patrol to the Dodecanese. The Nicosia runway ended in a sort of escarpment with the adjacent field some 20 feet below. As we took off the engine cut. We lost all power and dropped like a stone off the edge of the escarpment and into the field. The pilot did well to hold it straight on such rough ground and we stayed all in one piece. The ground crew rushed up in a lorry and peered over the edge expecting the worse. They merely saw me hanging on to a wing tip as we tried to turn the plane round and taxy it back to the aerodrome. We switched to another aircraft and did the patrol in that. I was a bit apprehensive at take-off. Recent experience suggested our serviceability had taken a plunge. This should not have been so. We had done quite well in Greece with little support, since when all aircraft had been overhauled at Dekheila.

That same day, after return from patrol, a submarine was reported off Larnaca. We hurried off to look and though we searched and patrolled the area nothing was seen. This was followed by another flap. Someone reckoned the destroyers were about to do a midnight flit from Beirut and attempt to dodge us on the way back to France. If we were prompt we ought to catch them just outside the harbour and so avoid the need to search for them.

For some reason we were short of an observer and I was chosen to make up the final crew. All the aircraft for this sortie had long range tanks. These tanks had now been changed to the self-sealing type which gave one a modicum of confidence. For the first time I was present at a briefing and felt quite important. I was actually going to contribute something. Having been armed with a chartboard and C.S.C.(course and speed calculator) - did I think I could cope alright - could I find my way back ? This from the Senior Observer. Full of youthful confidence I answered yes. Actually I believe this was quite true for the pilot could easily have got back by himself. The weather was good and there was little wind. The situation of crossing the sea was rather different than our jaunts up the coast of Albania but Cyprus was too big to miss and we had become very familiar with its landmarks. In the event some further information caused the strike to be cancelled and I missed my first chance to be a navigator. Around this time there were a great many on/off affairs which kept us busy swopping bombs for torpedoes, for depth charges and so on. It was all hands to the wheel and the A.G.s always helped out in this. In fact, as ever, the A.G.s did a lot of humping. All our petrol at this time came in thin 4 gallon cans and we hoisted them around and filled up by hand for long spells. The ground crew were trumps the way they stuck to all this manual filling and changes of weapons. We still only had a token number of the proper crews and just one Sergeant.

It was finally decided that we should attack the two destroyers sitting in Beirut harbour with bombs. Keeping constant patrol for them was getting tedious and they might still slip the net. So we were either going to flush them out or put them out of action. Being alongside a jetty and safeguarded with nets we could not use torpedoes in the harbour. So a bomb load of 6 x 250lb bombs was put up together with racks of flares. This time there were no overload tanks. I was back again with Mac but now we also had an observer.

There were 6 aircraft and we made our way independently. This took about 1 1/2 hours and we could see the target area from way off. Evidently the R.A.F. were also busy and had warmed things up. We came in at around 8000 feet and so got an immediate response from some heavy guns. We dropped a couple of flares and the target was clearly illuminated. A quick turn back and a peel off brought us diving nearly vertically down and I watched the target over the top of the upper mainplane. They started with medium stuff then, the usual flaming onions curling lazily up and rushing past. It was less frightening looking forward and seeing them miss than looking back and wondering if they were going to get more accurate. We pulled out of the dive and banked as we moved away. Bomb bursts hit the jetty between the ships, but where were the other bombs which would have scored hits from either end of the stick ? A quick lean over the side of the cockpit confirmed we still had them. The tail fins were just visible. Our flares had gone out but others were still dropping. The gunfire had swung away from us. A consultation between pilot and observer and then the latter relayed it to me. We were going back to try and shake the bombs off. This I didn't like. It told me that Mac had certainly intended to drop them all at once. We clawed back a bit of height but nowhere near as much as before, maybe 6000 feet. As we turned back in all the other flares went out. That meant we had the target area to ourselves. They soon got nasty about that. We dropped a flare but it wasn't going to do us any good. It was not so much an aimed dive bombing attack as a "here you can have these we don't want them" shudder as we went into a shallow dive and shook the wings. Suddenly the nose of the plane whipped up and we flipped nearly on to our back. Much of the observer's loose gear fell out as did one of the compasses. The air seemed full of flaming onions. We turned round on one wing tip and dived rapidly away seawards. The guns stopped as though turned off by a switch and all went black.

The observer sorted out what he had left and we headed home. Not much to show for that bit of excitement. Just two near misses. We still had one bomb hung up. I never saw the going of the others. We landed gingerly but I didn't really expect any trouble. That bomb just wasn't going to come off. After we got out I asked if they thought we'd had a shell explode underneath to throw us on our back. Oh no, said Mac, he'd simply taken violent evasive action when he saw a lot of medium stuff coming up straight ahead. Next morning the ground crew said they counted 56 separate holes in the machine. Some of the other crews thought they had been more successful with bomb hits on the target and interest switched away from these ships.

It was about this time that I got into a spot of bother. We'd been on the island some four weeks and hadn't had any pay. To some extent this was expected as the Fleet Air Arm were real cinderellas. Away from R.N. support they had to go cap in hand to the R.A.F. or the Army for administrative help. In Crete nobody bothered at all -there was nothing to buy - the wine was almost given away. Here in Cyprus though, it was rather different. There we were in the hotel in the middle of town with a couple of night clubs round the corner and the money flowed quite freely. Being a little more restrained than some and with a higher rate of pay as an aircrew I'd had a few pounds to spare in my pocket. I didn't make a habit of lending money, having previously been caught by scroungers, but I knew this bunch of lads very well and was happy enough to subsidise a few of them. In the end though, even I ran out of cash. We had been told to muster for pay but the rumour got around that for the second week running some slip-up had occurred and there wasn't any. Now Jack can be very bolshie when he thinks he is being sat on and the boys were hurt. They'd done miracles at all hours and now they snapped. No pay, no work they said and that included the A.G.s. We were under the command of an R.A.F.Sergeant (a Fleet Air Arm man) and he was aware of trouble. He wouldn't normally order A.G.s to do anything but knew they would always give a hand. Coming out of the squadron office, the only hut at the dispersal, he saw we were all sat on the sandbagged wall. "Get that aircraft filled up". No one moved. So he began at the end of the line individually. "Get down and get over to that aircraft". It was me. I didn't move. "Right, you'll see the Senior Pilot". Thence to the next man. He moved and so did all the rest. I was left carrying the can. I think the Senior Pilot was a bit put out when he saw who it was. I got the lecture all right. Near mutiny -gross disobedience of orders - lucky not to be court-martialled. I crawled away in disgrace. However, the officers were sympathetic and even had a whip round to advance the lads 10/-each. I don't think they had much money left either and were suffering from the same nasty move that baulked our cash supply. We did not find out until later, but the officers were well aware at the time, that one person in the chain by which our money was to reach us had used it make a convenient personal car purchase. In due course the boys bought me the beer for that one but it was a narrow squeak.

We continued the Dodecanese patrols though these only came round every second or third day as more and more of the squadron arrived from Dekheila and we were nearly at full strength. Other 815 A.G.s not previously mentioned and now in Cyprus were Beezel Butterworth, George Dodwell, Fred Hazeldine, Charlie Taafe and Bob "Spud" Murphy. Most of these had been in Illustrious and all had been around at various phases of the Cretan effort. It is impossible to remember who was where at any particular time as there was so much coming and going. I shall only refer to any of these when they were specifically involved in an episode that I can recall. By and large, 815 A.G.s led a charmed life and we didn't lose many. They'd all been in the drink at some time or other and everyone had stories of forced landings all over the place. An endearment of the Swordfish was that you could walk away from a prang. We also had the advantage that quite frequently there would be long range tanks and then the A.G.s weren't carried. The squadron had its losses to the enemy and otherwise. It was surprising how often that fatalities occurred to ground crew who were being ferried in the back seats or were up for a joy ride. We were always being required to tell such personnel all about safety equipment (parachutes,G-strings etc.)in about 2 minutes before a flight knowing full well that it wasn't sinking in.

Sid Boosey had experienced one of the more unusual kinds of forced landing incidents whilst in the desert and prior to the Crete period. Flying up behind the advanced patrols which had swept behind the Italians with the Wavell push, his pilot had put down miles inland and somewhere south of Derna when the engine had coughed and spluttered. Believing they were not far from one of the east/west roads which in this area were some way inland from the coast, the pilot decided to walk north for help. Sid was instructed to stay with the machine. He did, for two days but then,being without water, thought he ought to make his own way out. He left a brief note to indicate his direction and off he went. In due course he fell in with a party of desert nomads. Or strictly speaking with one of the young boys who took little notice of Sid but eventually led him to the elders when it was clear he wasn't being antagonistic. It must be remembered that this was effectively enemy territory as the army had by no means conquered it but merely infiltrated. On the other hand these desert bands probably no more recognised the Italians as masters than anyone else. At least it would appear that Sid had no need for a gooley chit - he probably didn't have one at this stage. In due course they put him up on the back of a camel - his feet being by now a bit of a mess. His description of the ride is that it wasn't exactly smooth comfort. More like a combination of the big dipper and dodgems. The most obnoxious part however was the smell that constantly arose from the rear end of the vehicle. When they finally hit an occupied area and met up with an army patrol, the officers of the party told him that his pilot had been scouring the area in a search for him. It appeared that this pilot had returned to the plane after failing to find anyone. Then he had somehow succeeded in restarting the machine on his own. No mean feat. Presumably it was still coughing and spluttering but had managed to get him to the nearest forward air base which he came across by good fortune. Evidently the engine problem was easily solved, after which he flew round and round looking for his Air Gunner. Once we had learned the elements of the story it was a source of some amusement for everyone to hold their nose and walk to the opposite end of the hut or tent when Sid appeared. This was only in fun and we didn't persist once the joke ran thin.

Returning from a patrol in Cyprus one aircraft was forced to land and crashed in the mountains. This aircraft had Laurie Smith in the back and he walked away with only a twisted ankle. We recognised a near miss but his injury was enough to make him take to his bed for a few days. It was quite amusing to see the V.I.P. treatment he received from the hotel staff and the number of friends from the local population who came in to wish him well. It made us realise that we were regarded as the defenders of the island. As we had the only aircraft that were around, ours was the responsibility.

During the final stages of the withdrawal from Crete, Formidable had been hit by bombs and so she too had to retire for repairs. So once again the ship's squadrons were put ashore to augment the Eastern Med. air strength. This time at least the major portion of aircraft and crews were still operative. 829 Sqdn. were in Palestine supporting an advance into the Lebanon. 826 Sqdn. with their Albacores were reforming at Dekheila prior to supporting the Western Desert Forces soon to be known as the 8th Army. The fighter strength was similarly deployed.

At this point one of our aircraft sighted a Vichy French ship the "St.Didier" trying to slip along the Turkish coast from Beirut. Circling and threatening with a torpedo he succeeded in getting her to turn towards a Cyprus port. When his patrol ended and he had to return to base she promptly turned away to her original course. A follow-up aircraft found her and this time she refused to alter course. So the tin-fish was dropped and it passed right under the ship without exploding. It was daylight and the observer brought back a perfect picture confirming the torpedo track. I was able to see this picture but regretably could not get a copy. We were now using magnetic heads and evidently this one had some defect. So the ship got away. It must have had some important political aspect -possibly top German or Vichy French officials aboard, because the order went out that this ship must be sunk wherever she might be. 826 Squadron arrived post-haste in Cyprus and were sent off to find her. In fact we had already got three Swordfish airborne and I was in the back of one of them. Though the Albacores were only 10 knots faster than we were they soon caught us up, outstripped us and disappeared. We didn't know how far we might have to chase -perhaps even to the Dodecanese. In fact we caught up with it in the Turkish port of Adalia. By the time we arrived all that was visible was the bows protruding from the water. The Albacores had done the job. Turkey was of course a neutral country and protested. This was not our concern. The orders were to sink wherever she was. Someone at the top must have had good reason to suffer the diplomatic row that ensued.

A full scale advance into Syria and Lebanon soon put an end to the nuisance of the Vichy French territory and this action was about the last of our contribution to the affair. Henceforth we were only patrolling to the Dodecanese. The squadron began a period of refurbishing. Replacement aircraft were coming through and those we had needed overhaul. The replacements were often Blackfish - a Swordfish aircraft made by Blackburns. Externally indistinguishable from the original, but we knew the difference. The back seat had fractionally less space and there were other minor features which varied. We also got a different radio. This was the T1154/R1155 known as the Wurlitzer. Not really much advance. A superhet receiver not needing plug-in coils and the transmitter had more compact and fewer coils. They would keep sending them without the vernier needed to tune the receiver and this was a pain. Or again, when we fitted the vernier it stuck out where everybody kicked it off, getting in and out. We had to stow the vernier in a box and let the A.G. fit it as required after take-off. Though we got used to the Wurlitzer most A.G.s continued to prefer the Geep.

I was flown back to Dekheila in a Walrus from HMS Leander for a rest and then to help check-out the radios in the new aircraft. Already doing the job back at Dekheila were two of our A.G.s, Keith Allum and Bob Boddy.

Whilst at Dekheila the opportunity arose to take a Leading Airmans Board. This was an examination in power of command in which one was required to take a class through a P.T.lesson and then march a squad of men around the parade ground through all the usual manoeuvres and any special ones that the examining officer thought up. Being already Leading Hands, if only Temporary, we hadn't thought much about qualifying for this on a regular basis. It seemed the thing to do if we were to be confirmed in the rank and perhaps advance further. Before the Board we got in some practise on each other until we were foot and voice sore. Mind you, it is quite difficult to exercise power of command over your own kind, who were quite likely to answer back and even drop out if they felt like it. Our voluntary practises were always a bit of a fiasco. The lads would "misinterpret" any command if possible. "Change arms" during rifle drill always led to the rifles being exchanged between each other. We had to have the fun to make a boring chore acceptable. Also included in the examination was an element of seamanship. Nothing very advanced. Only some elementary questions. Many of the other A.G.s from Cyprus had come over for this board including Ron Astbury and Frank Grainger. Also one of our number who was an ex-seaman. It happened that he went in first. When the examining officer looked at this man's record he said he wouldn't waste time asking him the elementary questions but would range a bit wider. So when this man came out of the room we taxed him "what did he ask you ?" Amongst other things apparently was the query "what do you call the stay coming down from the bowspit ?". We wouldn't have known that but the answer was "the dolphin striker". Soon the next man went in. The examining officer was a shrewd gentleman and in due course innocently enough asked the same question. The answer he got was "the porpoise pusher" which I gather was enough to pass that man for at least providing a laugh. In fact most of us got through. Not I believe because we deserved to, but because we were all equally bad and after all we weren't really going to train a squad of men to march around a parade ground.

We began ferrying action to get the new aircraft to Cyprus. We went via Port Said and Lydda in Palestine. It took longer going this way but there was no point in chancing the long sea flight unnecessarily. Four hours or so of petrol and a 400 mile range doesn't offer much safety margin. By the end of August we were all back in Cyprus at full strength. After taking one aircraft across I had returned with another for overhaul. As all the replacements had now gone across I had to travel via an Australian frigate HMAS Paramatta. This ship was sunk shortly afterwards.

The squadron had moved to Lakatamia, an airstrip a few miles from the airport at Nicosia. No longer were we in a hotel. This time we were in tents. The R.A.F. had established themselves at Nicosia with such few Hurricanes as could be spared from elsewhere. This just about terminated enemy daylight air activity such as it was. I've mentioned nothing of this so far because it was almost negligible in Cyprus as compared to earlier experiences. We were hardly bothered at all in the town. There had been sporadic raids on the airfield by high flying Italian aircraft and they did succeed in setting the fuel dump alight. On one occasion we heard the bombs coming down in Nicosia and their target turned out to be the hospital just outside the town. I suspect it was a mistake - they probably believed it to be the barracks. I actually got some photos of the bombs exploding taken from the hotel roof. I felt quite heroic going up there to snap the action but my ear told me they weren't falling on us. We were much more circumspect out on the airfield. Mostly the chaps wore tin hats and anything but a Swordfish engine sent us into the nearest slit trench. It was indicative of the state many of the lads were in. They'd suffered Illustrious and then Crete. The relative calm of Cyprus was beginning to work but it took time. At Lakatamia we still had intruders coming over at night and they flew round and round presumably looking for our airfield. They must have known where Nicosia airfield was - we could pick it out quite easily at night. Our dirt strip wasn't so easy to see. We developed a quite efficient if Heath Robinson method of dealing with the flare path whenever our aircraft were night flying. Though there was an A.M.E.S. at Nicosia the warning didn't get to us and the first we knew was enemy engine noise. The flare path was simply a line of hurricane lamps and we fashioned empty petrol tins to act as covers. The crafty bit was the handle of stiff wire. By riding crouched on the running board of a 3 ton truck and with a man to feed out the cans from the cab, we could douse the flare path in the time it took to drive down it with the merest pause at each lamp. When our own aircraft arrived it was even quicker to pick up the cans by spearing the handle with a stick. Those railway guard pick-ups had taught us a thing or two. As duty A.G. I often did the stint on the running board.

About the middle of September a new C.O. was appointed to the squadron and he was lost bringing a Swordfish from Dekheila. The squadron mounted a full scale search for the missing plane but it was unsuccessful. Several of the original Illustrious pilots and observers had been replaced and we now had quite a sprinkling of R.N.V.R. officers. About this time I started to get seriously aquainted with navigation. Ever since flying as a two man crew I had taken an active interest in this, but my efforts had been limited to map-reading and plotting tracks using predicted winds. Now I read up the books, equipped myself with a chart board and C.S.C. and started duplicating the observer's activities. Once they saw how keen I was I got plenty of airborne instruction and was shown how to take a wind and running fixes. Even more important I learned how to note a change in the wind and estimate this from the state of the sea. Some observers even let me change seats with them so I could actually do the navigation while they tried their hand on the radio. The patrols to the Dodecanese were an ideal training ground with landfalls to be made both ways and little chance of going astray. To keep this up I started volunteering for all such trips and most of the other A.G.s were happy to let me go. I flew nearly every day for a month and as we were still working mixed crew rosters the pilots and observers didn't find it strange that it was always me. The Senior Observer and C.O. did when they saw my log book and soon put a stop to my hogging all the hours.

In October we started getting the new and highly secret radar. It wasn't called that at the time but R.D.F.(radio direction finding). Even this term wasn't allowed to be used. Instead it was referred to as the R3039, the number of one of the units. One special technician came to look after it -Jock Cameron. Being a strong Scot it soon became identified as the "thirrty thirrrtynine". Though it was only a metre-band device of mediocre performance and suspect reliability, to us it represented an enormous step forward. We could now "see" in the dark - well sort of - even if we didn't fully understand how it worked. Night searches commenced, though this was largely a matter of training and gaining experience with the equipment. As the Indicator with the picture screen was placed in the observer's cockpit he became the operator, though we could see it by looking over his shoulder. This was much to my disappointment as I'd listened carefully to all that Jock Cameron told us and often I felt that the gain level wasn't being set correctly.

It was clear that our usefulness in Cyprus was at an end. By mid-November other things were afoot. The Eighth Army was making a push up the desert under General Auchinleck. We were withdrawn to Dekheila and many of us travelled back to Alexandria aboard the sloop HMS Erica. Our actual sea time might be minimal but what there was of it included a wide variety of craft.

After Crete, 815 Squadron personnel were highly sensitive to possible air attack. At Nicosia airfield they mostly wore tin hats and anything but a Swordfish engine sent us into the nearest slit trench

Bringing up the torpedoes over rough ground was no easy task. As the various flaps caused much changing from bombs to torpedoes and back again to bombs, all hands were constantly under pressure

Humping petrol by hand in 4 gallon cans was the order of the day for all hands. Here, Fred Hazeldine, Laurie Smith and Bob Murphy are assisting this group. Ken Sims excused himself to take the picture!

Ken Sims, Cyprus 1941

The advent of a few Hurricanes scared off most of the daylight raiders except for the high-flying reconnaisance aircraft. With little else to chase the fighters would practice their pursuits on any convenient Swordfish. Our evasive manoeuvres during this game were not taken too seriously

The Cyprus countryside was picturesque. None more so than the quaint port of Kyrenia on the northern coast

CHAPTER 11

"The Illuminators"

In October, before leaving Cyprus, we had started getting Albacore aircraft as replacements. These did not have R3039. I wasn't sure if this was because Swordfish were in short supply - they had to be taken out of service to have the radar fitted - or as a security measure relating to the radar. If we were called upon to make a torpedo attack it would be unsatisfactory to use the machines with the secret apparatus. These innovations arrived in ones and twos until we had a mixed bag of aircraft. It made an interesting diversion to familiarise with a new aircraft. Though the Albacore was to a degree not unlike a Sword-fish, and the layman might even mistake them when seen in the air, they were really quite different. The Albacore had a completely enclosed cockpit which gave somewhat greater comfort. One climbed in through a side door instead of over the top. The back seat men that is -the pilots cockpit towered up almost out of our realm. It had a metal skin and the whole aircraft was so much heavier that in spite of a far more powerful engine in the Taurus as compared to the Pegasus, the cruising speed of 100 knots was still only 10 knots faster than a Swordfish. Perhaps it would do 120 knots if unladen and in a dive. It carried out all the same functions as the Swordfish and was nearly as manoeuvreable. Being a biplane it is hardly surprising that to some it appeared to be the same machine. We knew different. Gone was the painful inertia starter with its handle. Now a cartridge was fired to start the engine and it became the A.G.s job to keep a spare box of these in the back and to know how to fill the breech when at some remote airfield.

On our arrival back at Dekheila our mixed aircraft squadron was promptly split into two flights. The Swordfish flight with the radar would carry out anti-submarine patrols along the North African coast whilst the Albacores would carry out night attacks on the enemy land forces. 826 Squadron were already fully active in this role and our flight from 815 would augment their strength. I was to join the Albacore flight and travelled up by road to the airstrip at Maarten Bagush satellite. It was my first experience of the Western Desert proper.

The 8th Army advance was moving fast so we didn't waste any time getting aclimatised but prepared at once to join in. We were to fly largely at night and act as target finders. The slow machines with good downward visibility (the observer had a bubble side window) made an excellent spotting platform. Furthermore it was navigated across the desert as though over the sea and could often arrive with fair accuracy at map reference points that had no ground landmarks. Extra flare racks were fitted and the usual load was 16 flares with 4 x 250lb bombs. If thought desirable we could take an entire flare load of 32. The bombs were fitted with a protruding metal rod on the nose some two feet long. The idea was to make them explode at surface level to give maximum effect, rather than bury themselves in the sand. Unfortunately to fit this rod meant excluding the nose safety pin and this could make the bomb live on the plane, so it was desirable not to bump the sticks with any force.

When Rommel pulled his surprise move of turning east instead of retreating west when outflanked, he provided us with the first target at Sidi Rezegh. Both squadrons were briefed to maintain a continuous illumination of the target area throughout the night. The aircraft took off at twenty minute intervals. We were quite early in the queue and had no difficulty finding them. The spot was a short flying run in from the easily identifiable port of Bardia. The target - tank divisions with their supporting

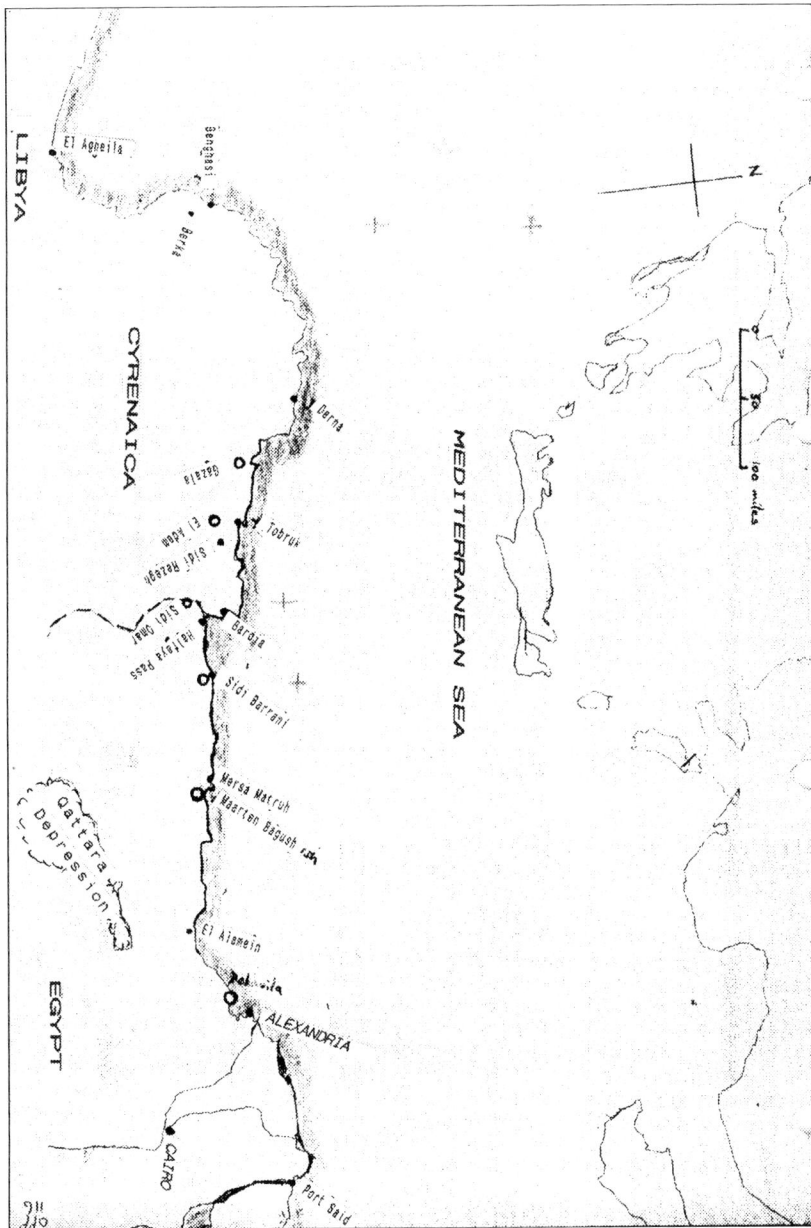

In the winter months the desert lost some of its traditional appearance. Heavy rain would transform it into a typical muddy quagmire in which the vehicles would get struck. These were Italian trucks captured during the first major push

After Tobruk was relieved during the second push, the enemy left behind much equipment when they hurriedly retreated. This had been the area from which Tobruk was under siege. Our troops had moved on and we enjoyed exploring these areas and acting the victors

M.T. were camped over an extended area. Our first parachute flare showed them up all right though I was doubtful that it was so. In the bright light of a parachute flare every ground object throws a deep black shadow and one gets an effect similar to pictures of the moon. This part of the desert is in fact rock to a large extent and certainly had wide areas of rocky outcrop and loose boulders. So I peered down looking for tell-tale tank tracks and regularities in the shadows which would identify trucks rather than rocks. We were at about 5000 feet to give the flares the best survival times and from that height the terrain was difficult to assess. We scouted around and dropped two more flares singly looking for the extent and maximum concentration of vehicles. While I was still in doubt as to what I was seeing, my pilot and observer had decided that this was it and proceeded to drop 3 or 4 flares in a group. Almost immediately the ground beneath erupted in clouds of dust as Wellingtons released strings of bombs across the site. We picked up a cluster of shapes on the edge of the spot, dropped another flare over them and dived to add our bombs on this particular target. As we pulled out at about 2000 feet I could see more clearly that these were indeed vehicles, though many had netting draped across breaking up the outlines.

Our bombs fell well across the group but as they were scattered and there was subsequently much dust cloud it was impossible to say how effective they had been. It had not occurred to me to have the rear gun ready for strafing and we pulled away before I swung it up. There was no ground fire though this may have been misleading. One cannot always see small arms fire if it has no tracer. Certainly there were no heavy guns, though we had been warned that they might have some medium stuff. Later we learned that they tended not to use anything which would disclose position until it was obvious they had been seen. So the danger was that one might come too low not sensing trouble and suddenly run into a deluge of small arms fire. This night seemed very quiet though I did spot one stream of tracer lick up towards what was presumably a Wellington. We regained height and dropped our remaining flares singly whilst holding position to give the follow-on Albacore something to aim at. Then we turned for home and looking back watched a continuation of the illuminating process. Jerry must have had a very disturbed night. The round trip lasted nearly 5 hours. On the one hand this indicated the somewhat better endurance capability of the Albacore even without long range tanks. It also highlighted the fact that we were a long way from the front line. Our target at Sidi Rezegh had even been behind the point reached by our forward land forces. It was difficult to define any front line in the normal sense. This push had outflanked many enemy strongholds and they still held places like Bardia and Halfaya pass which were east of Sidi Rezegh.

Though still maintaining our base at Maarten Bagush we began the principle of using forward bases for refuelling. The first of these was to be at Sidi Barrani, further west than Bagush and near Halfaya. So we flew there the next morning to establish that it was suitable, that they had the right grade of petrol, and would be able to deal with us that night. Then back to Bagush to rearm and return to Barrani. All this up and down stuff meant we were landing with the bomb load but that was how it had to be.

That night we took off again at 0200 somewhere in the middle of the stream of Albacores continuing to run at twenty minute intervals. Rommel was still in the same general area but much of his stuff was now strung along the Bardia to Tobruk road. It was even easier to find with the road to help and there wasn't any difficulty in identifying the trucks and tanks now we had become familiar with what to look for. Only a few vehicles were actually on the road. Most were camped in groups just off the road. We flew up and down dropping one flare at a time until we found a sizable bunch and dropped a triangle of flares round them. Before we'd even finished this, bombs from Wimpies were exploding in the centre. I even saw one plane way down below the flares at little more than a thousand feet. I reckoned he was in some danger from his own kind dropping bombs on him. They seemed to swarm in like moths to the light. We kept out of the way as it had brought some response from the ground in the shape of light flak. We had to go and find another smaller group of trucks for our own bombs. These suitably burst across them and I let fly with the rear gun. Our last flare hit the ground and fizzled out as we completed the attack so I really couldn't pick out any target to fire at. We slogged back to Bagush and landed at dawn after over 4 hours in the air.

Now the Navy wanted to get into the act. Considerable enemy forces were cut off near the coast, north of the Bardia to Tobruk road, and a gunboat wanted to shell them. We were asked to flare drop and spot. At last there was a good use for the radio, though the observer would do the spotting with the A.G. maintaining contact. That afternoon we flew up to Barrani fully armed. It was a shorter journey from there and gave us more time over the target. There was a longer time interval between take-offs and only a few aircraft were required. I think the other aircraft went back to Rezegh. We were second in our list and took off just after 2000. Approaching the target area we could see the previous planes flares and heard them on the radio. It was still all morse transmission. I don't know what the ship thought of our variable standard. After I got through and handed over to the observer it became a bit painful. The target was somewhat scattered but obvious enough. Various tents and slit trenches with transport dotted about. Not much to aim at with precision but a large general area to drop shells into. We picked up the plot and it became immediately obvious that this wasn't going to be over successful. Not more than two shells were fired at a time, mostly only one. They were way off target usually short and took about 3 or 4 minutes between each firing. What I didn't know until later, was that these gunboats were of light construction but with a couple of quite large guns. Apparently they had to be in an outward turn or the recoil would send them heeling over. So with each run the laying must have been like starting afresh and each time we were waiting for them to get into a turn. Anyway the whole affair was very long-winded and ineffective. The target was probably really out of their range. After an hour it was time to hand over to a relief aircraft. To carry more flares we only had two bombs. We now went in and dropped these on the group of transport and this seemed to us more effective than all the shelling. We landed back at Sidi Barrani, refuelled and went on to Bagush that same night.

With Bardia still in enemy hands it was considered likely that fuel and support for Rommel's tanks could very well come from there. The positions of fuel dumps were well known and in fact most of the small towns along the N.African coast such as Bardia and Tobruk had by this time become nothing more than military strongholds. So Bardia needed a visit. That same afternoon we again flew up to Barrani. From there it was but a short trip across the bay to Bardia.

As was to be expected we had a hot reception. This wasn't a night stop for transport but an established port and it had some regular defences. We came in high above the worst of it and, having dropped some flares and identified the target, we carried out a dive attack. They didn't seem to be aiming at anything in particular just spraying around to create a barrage. So we dived through it and all the bombs went together. As far as I could see they were in the right place and we didn't stop to observe but shot away at low level. If you can consider an Albacore doing anything fast. Then straight back across the bay and on to Bagush without stopping at Barrani.

When the tank battle had concluded at Sidi Rezegh and Rommel's forces retreated westward, suitable targets had moved out of our range. There was a brief period of rest as new arrangements were organised. We picked up the names of various places along the coast as though we'd been up and down there as often as the Army. In fact a great many of these places were little more than references on the map and the arab names referred to almost indistinguishable features such as wadis and rock outcrops. On the other hand some had grown into sizeable military camps, and could be identified as petrol dumps or even a canteen such as at Fuka. Put back there today, I doubt if we'd know where we were. Our spelling of the names was almost anything we liked so long as it sounded right. A lot of places were referred to only as numbers and this was particularly the case with strip landing grounds such as LG121 and LG75. Why did we want all this ? To put in our flying log books of course. This was the winter period and there was a great deal of rain. We wondered what had happened to the traditional desert. In these conditions it was more like a European mud bath. We paddled around in the mud at Bagush satellite and often got the lorries bogged down. We began to see why the Italians were using machines with a double gear box and umpteen gears. This captured transport was what had been issued to the Fleet Air Arm for desert use because inevitably they had nothing of their own.

On the 13th December 1941 the situation clarified. A forward landing ground had been established at El Adem south of Tobruk. From there we could reach well forward into enemy territory. The full strength of 826 and 815's flight flew up to El Adem that afternoon. We carried the normal full load of bombs with sticks. The target area was to be Derna. Take-off interval was cut to 10 minutes. We wouldn't hang about illuminating over the port. This was more of a bombing attack. The C.O. of 826 went first. Then we heard No.2 open his throttle. Something was wrong. The sound told us this at once and we looked at each other. He was taking off from the wrong end of the flare path ! On a strange field with no runway control such a mistake was unfortunately too likely. With such a bomb load he needed the wind against not following him. We waited for the chop of the throttle. It never came. He hit a fully bombed up Blenheim at the edge of the field and the lot blew up, with us lying flat on our faces not far away. He might as easily have hit another of the Albacores. They were all parked quite close. The A.G. in the machine was Carmichael from my own course. We gathered in a silent group. Course mates Ted Kennelly, Jock Harper and myself were perhaps the most shocked. We had lost friends before - it was a sign of our calling. To lose one in these circumstances right under one's nose was shattering. The attack was called off on the premise that other aircraft might be damaged. This was very likely only too true, but if the officers felt like we did then it was the only safe thing. Someone else would surely have made mistakes. A tot of rum all round put some heart back into us. I think it was R.A.F. emergency issue. All the other aircraft returned the following morning but we burst a tail wheel as we were taxying and got stuck. A spare had to be flown up for us. The field was in use as a forward fighter base and there was plenty of activity. We wandered around during the day watching all that was going on. A point of interest was a captured German Warrant officer pilot who had been shot down in a Messerschmitt by Hurricanes the day before. He had a personal armed guard but messed with the visiting officers whilst arrangements were made to get him back to a P.O.W. camp. In such casual surroundings with the front line within a stone's throw his escape might not have been too difficult and I suspect he was looking for the opportunity. Doubtless he cursed our presence because it meant he was under continual casual surveillance.

We got away the following morning and trundled easily back at 1000 feet. Quite by accident we found ourselves crossing Sidi Omar and suddenly guns opened up all round. Small arms fire but with plenty of tracer and there was no doubt who it was aimed at. The pilot stood the aircraft on its tail flicked over and down to the deck. We cleared the edge of the field at zero feet. How they didn't bring us down I don't know. Neither do I know if this was a pocket of enemy resistance which hadn't fallen or some of our own chaps a bit trigger happy. After all the Italians did use biplanes.

Back at Bagush that afternoon we prepared for another bombing attack and took off to fly up again to El Adem. As it happened we ran into a major sandstorm and had to turn back. To be flying in a sandstorm is about the most hair-raising experience I know. It combines the sightlessness of fog with the continuously drumming racket of the sand on the wings and fuselage. We did a smart about turn and fortunately were able to outstrip the storm and come out into the clear. Was I glad to get out of that. It was two days later before the weather improved enough to get airborne again. This time we went to Sidi Bu Amud. It was quite near El Adem but ensured that the latter place was clear for fighter operation and not cluttered up with bombers. The Senior Pilot's aircraft developed a minor fault and he promptly took our machine on the attack. Our sole contribution was to take his aircraft back the following morning. The Army's drive was still on and Jerry was breaking from the Gazala line and falling back to Benghasi. Next day found us again loaded up and on our way to Sidi Bu Amud. Our target this time was to be up at Benghasi itself - a long haul. To cut this a little shorter we took the step of flying forward another half-hour to Gazala South which had just been cleared for use by fighters. We refuelled there and took off at 2150. We were still going independently at twenty minute intervals. Our objective was a crossroads just outside Benghasi. Here the direct road across country from El Adem crossed the coastal road from Derna running south to El Agheila. There should have been quite a bottleneck of traffic at this junction as the German columns fell back. In fact when we got there all was quiet. A couple of flares only disclosed a few trucks. Nevertheless we bombed and hit the junction with good accuracy. We waited for the dust to clear and observed the holes neatly positioned at the crossing and on each of the approach roads. Doubtless they would fill in the holes and even run diversion tracks round the junction but we had done enough to make it awkward for an hour or two and perhaps some follow-up aircraft would come across a nice little bottleneck which they could exploit. We had flown there in a direct route across the desert. Now we headed home along the route of the cross-country road, AND THERE WAS THE GERMAN ARMY ! Hundreds of trucks and tanks nose to tail retreating with headlamps blazing. With their own engine noise they couldn't hear us coming. We'd dropped all our bombs and now the rear gun was our only weapon. For at least half-an-hour I was firing down at them from 800 feet and got through 10 pans of ammunition. Mostly I just gave short bursts along the line of the road and watched the ensuing chaos as they ran off the road and doused lights. None behind seemed to realise what was going on ahead and kept coming full bore with lights on. We didn't orbit or hang about to invite any retaliation. Here and there I tried to pick a specific target in the hope of something spectacular. However, between mainplane and tail nothing remained in view for more than a few seconds which was only time for two quick bursts and you can't expect much from that. So the disturbance factor had to be the most effective. Sometimes the road took a turn and I had to swing the gun over to the other side. The aircraft designers had not thought we might want to fire downwards and there was no high step. I was standing on the seat but even this was not high enough to get an eye behind the sight. I put a foot on the radio and succeeded in breaking the phone plug. It was all highly exciting even if a bit ineffective. A few fighters with 8 guns or cannon were wanted. They could have decimated those columns. Nearing Gazala we gave it best in case there were British elements following the German tail. We landed back at Bu Amud and the following morning returned to Bagush, with me spending the flight back mending my broken phone jack.

Clearly we were now too far from the front line at Bagush. So arrangements were made for a shift of base up to Sidi Bu Amud and we struck camp and set off with all the ground crew. Though we were tending more often to fly as regular crews there was still no hard and fast rule about this and we did continue to switch around. Furthermore we had more crews than aircraft and so it fell my lot on this move to go with the ground party. Halfaya Pass was still held by the enemy so it was necessary to make a detour across the desert to go round it. The track was marked by occasional oil barrels but as luck would have it a sandstorm blew up and visibility dropped to a few yards. So we groped around driving on compass bearings. On Christmas Day 1941 we were due south of Halfaya and feasted on corned beef, ships hard tack biscuits and sand. Recalling the previous Christmas Day in the Atlantic I began to think I was destined not to enjoy a real Christmas again. Next day we came down over the escarpment near Sidi Rezegh and viewed the burnt out tanks in the area. Once established at Sidi Bu Amud we awaited further attack orders. The situation had moved too quickly for us and the enemy had retreated beyond El Agheila. It appeared that our own forces had also run out of steam and were spread too thinly to immediately follow up. There was a period of consolidation.

While we awaited developments we explored our surroundings. We found that this was an area in which large enemy forces had camped as part of the besieging forces surrounding Tobruk. Several wadis ran down to the sea and in caves in these wadis Italian troops had been garrisoned. German troops had camped in tents at the head of each wadi. Obviously they had departed in a hurry and large amounts of equipment were left scattered around. None of our own troops had had time to gather this up. We explored delightedly if dangerously because there were many booby traps. Mostly these were rigged hand grenades. They hadn't had time to be subtle and we became expert in spotting the traps. The wadis rang with rifle fire as various guns were tried out and almost everyone had a B.M.W. or Italian motorcycle to tinker with. The faults on them were negligible. We were intrigued to find one cave full of womens clothes and cosmetics. It looked as though there had been official prostitutes. I discovered one hole which led to an underground cavern. Descending the ladder the interior was black. I waited until my eyes became accustomed to the gloom and peered around. It was an ammunition dump and appeared quite full. Anticipating a trap I had stayed on the ladder. Now, looking down I could just make out something tied on the lowest rung. Amongst some rubbish underneath was a bottle of liquid hiding a hand grenade. I gingerly climbed out and warned our other lads. Then I hunted round until I found a bit of red rag which I tied to a stick and stuck it at the top of the hole. I hoped the Army would understand, but there was no one around to tell. Anyway the area was probably full of such places.

Soon came an order to withdraw to Bagush. We hadn't even flown an operation from Bu Amud whilst stationed there. So it was back across the desert and round Halfaya again. The weather was a little better this time. No sandstorm. just a lot of haze and dust limiting visibility. There was an odd little interlude. One of our R.A.F. corporals was driving a B.M.W. motorcycle as an outrider to our convoy. Like many of us he was wearing one or two items of German kit such as knee boots which were very suitable for the conditions. He got a bit far ahead and an armoured car intercepted him. They were highly suspicious, as well they might be, for Halfaya was still in enemy hands. The Fleet Air Arm ? Who the hell were they and what were they doing in the desert ? They brought him in to the convoy for authentication. They then became extremely dubious about the lot of us. Somehow we managed to convince them - I think it was the sailor hats that did the trick, now a dirty brown instead of brilliant white.

As a matter of fact it was really quite difficult to know who was who in the desert. Everyone seemed to be in on the act. Australians, Free French, South Africans, Sikhs, Greeks, and Scots and English regiments of all kinds. Each wearing unusual rigs with quite a few personal variants. Special parties like the Long Range Desert Group abounded and both sides were using each others trucks and equipment.

We finally arrived at Bagush to be told that this time we would be using the main airstrip rather than the satellite. We set-to to pitch camp. Towards the end of this activity there were various heaps of equipment scattered around where they had been unloaded. Our Sergeant told me to get a couple of lads and collect these heaps together. Now I couldn't drive but had always hankered to have a try. I'd listened to a lot of verbal instructions and now for the first time I saw a chance to try it out. After all I only needed to take the lorry slowly between piles of gear. This I did, but the Sergeant spotted me. "I didn't know you were a driver". I'd have to brazen it out now. "Oh yes". "Good. You are due for a rest. Drive this truck back to Dekheila tomorrow". Oh,heck - what do I do now ? Tell him I was lying ? I said nothing. Well, they might have made it easier. On to a 3 ton truck went two German B.M.W. motorcycles - downright plunder this was -promptly covered over by all manner of other unwanted stuff such as spare tents and broken aircraft parts. Then with two passengers in the cab making me sit well over to the right, I set off in a right hand drive vehicle on a right hand drive road. 150 miles to go and no driving experience. Furthermore two Australians cadged a lift and sat on top of our load taking pot shots with rifles at tin cans by the roadside. With every shot I jumped a mile thinking I had burst a tyre. Overtaking slow convoys was a difficult manoeuvre. I had to get the passenger in the outside seat to tell me when the road was clear and then take all manner of chances to get out and round. Finally I hit a pothole when doing about 45 m.p.h. and the overweighted lorry took charge and started to swing. Being inexperienced I didn't accelerate out of it, but braked and fought it side to side to a standstill. At this point our Australians abandoned ship - I wonder why ? We got going again and otherwise did all right - we arrived at Dekheila in one piece -though my passengers did say they hadn't previously ridden with such an unusual driver ! I now became an acknowledged driver with the squadron, though it was some time before anywhere near competent. The Fleet Air Arm wasn't geared for desert operation and drivers and all support personnel were in short supply.

We now discovered what was behind the move back to Bagush. 815 Squadron was to revert fully to its submarine hunting role using the new radar in Swordfish. The one flight which was doing this was insufficient and further Swordfish had been delivered. Our Albacores were to be used as replacements by 826 Squadron which would continue in the target finding role. The Italians came to call them "the helicopters" and they were feared. Orbiting around a wingtip at no more than 100 kts overhead at night they must have seemed almost stationary. Those underneath would know that as soon as more than one flare was dropped a barrage of bombs would hurtle down from the

Wellingtons. On the other hand a slow orbiting aircraft can be very vulnerable. Flying night after night at no more than 5000 feet is bound to create enemy reaction and the response when it comes can be drastic. 826 Squadron lost many aircraft on these activities. Ted Kennelly was killed only a few days after Carmichael. Even moving up to forward bases in daylight brought its toll. On March 9th 1942 Vic Coulter was in an Albacore jumped by a couple of ME109s. At that time he was usually known as Sammy. He describes the encounter as follows :-

"On our way to advanced base for some night bombing of enemy supply bases between Tripoli & Benghasi, we were met by 2 ME109F's. They had just shot down a Wellington in very short order before attacking us. They attacked singly at first. Then they decided to come in together attacking from our rear on either side. The pilot, ably guided by the observer, did a splendid job of side-slipping. This action, together with our slow speed, seemed to confuse our enemies. but it also made it difficult to hold my gun on target.

I had my left hand wounded almost at once, so was reduced to operating with only my right hand and steadying the gun and mounting with my chin. In changing amo pans, I lost an empty one over the side. In the second run I received my chest wound.

When the ME's came in on either side I had to make up my mind to concentrate on one of them. I got a burst into it as it passed on my right -it shuddered violently and pulled away. The other put us down with a shell in our tank and a shoulder wound to the pilot.

I had an enthusiastic recommend after this encounter. My buddies visiting me in hospital told me that a decoration was coming my way. It is still coming after 47 years.

My observer who had escaped injury in the air was very seriously wounded when we were attacked again on the ground, as we crawled out of the plane. That pilot was, perhaps, giving us extra punishment on behalf of his friend. The observer lay flat on the ground, as we braced ourselves for the attack, while the pilot and I knelt down on one knee. I don't think we were being clever about making a smaller target. At any rate the pilot escaped further injury and I received only an additional wound in my left leg. There were two ground attacks.

My observer and I communicated for years until I left for Canada - he with just a thumb and forefinger of his right hand. He lost his left hand, had wounds to his face, lost an eye and had a huge wound in his back. Ironically he was given a job as recruiting officer when the doctors finally patched him up. He became quite famous while in 64th General Hospital for being a model patient in spite of his awful injuries. The staff regularly sang his praises.

Sandy Saunders, our T.A.G.A. Secretary was in 64th General Hospital, Alexandria, when I was there. He was recovering from serious burns and was most helpful to me in many ways. Since he was mobile by that time , he visited Ward 9 daily to assist in various ways, including trips to the hospital canteen for several of us. I recall his genial presence very readily."

In his account Vic readily names both his pilot and observer and it is perhaps unfair of me to suppress this to conform with the rest of my narrative. It is, however, noticeable that Vic dismisses his own injuries in relating the problems of others.

I put some questions to Vic to clear up a few points from his narrative. He says, yes, they certainly did see the Wellington go down so they knew what they were in for. It happened too close for them to make themselves scarce. After the ground attacks they crawled to better shelter and Vic himself went to higher ground to look around. They feared they were in the middle of nowhere, but an army jeep appeared from a unit which had watched the encounter. They were taken to a field hospital and then by train back to Alex..No, there were no survivors from the Wellington, and they could glean no information about an ME109 which had been forced down anywhere.

Just a few days prior to this event, on 5th March 1942, yet another Albacore had been shot down, this time by a JU88. The aircraft was from 821 Squadron which had been formed to augment the 826 effort. Two A.G.s were killed in the aircraft shot down, Ernie Stuttle and Norman Leslie. It happened that the latter was an 826 man who had been awarded a D.S.M. and was taking passage in the 821 aircraft back to Dekheila.

These events indicate how German aircraft roamed the coastal area in daylight. Though we had air supremacy the enemy aircraft continued hit and run forays throughout the desert campaign particularly at night. There was no air raid warning system - it couldn't be worked and wasn't worth the bother - everyone carried on without worry. Yet our ears were well tuned and we were quite prepared to dive for a slit trench if necessary and sometimes it was. Mind you I once found myself sharing it with a scorpion and nipped out smarter than I nipped in.

So, in January 1942 we left 826 to pursue their special tasks and returned to our beloved Swordfish.

Albacore BF677 of 826 Squadron which crashed in at Dekheila from 200ft on return from illuminating and bombing the 21st Panzers at El Alamein
[Credit: Air SMO Howe (TAG)]

CHAPTER 12

"Elsewhere at Sea..."

As mentioned earlier, several of the Fleet Air Arm's key actions have received ample publicity including TAGs eye views. Yet if this book is to be a coverage of the TAGs involvement then we must again range through these incidents and endeavour to highlight any aspects which have so far escaped notice. Necessarily they include some of the most moving moments in our brief history.

Though the early loss of Courageous and Glorious followed by the crippling of Illustrious and Formidable had done much to clip the Fleet Air Arm's wings there were fortunately other carriers still able to operate. This even included the old Albatross which could act as mother ship to several amphibians. Mention has already been made of the sterling use to which the Walrus was put in the search of the Atlantic for seaborne raiders. Albatross operated out of Freetown, from where she could cover a fair expanse of the Atlantic. In fact her squadron, No.710, spent much time flying from the air station Hastings on the West African coast. Living conditions for the TAGs there were hot and sticky in an area earlier known as "the white man's grave". On one search mission TAG Mick Dale was instrumental in rescuing survivors from the SS Eumaeus for which he received the B.E.M.

As I rather glossed over the battle of Cape Matapan when describing 815 Squadron's minor part in the action, I must now say a little more about the major effort. There were two main attacks on the Italian Fleet, by Albacore aircraft of 826 and 829 Squadrons flying from the Formidable, augmented by some Swordfish. Both were in daylight on the 27th.March 1941, though the second attack was nearly at dusk. It

Supermarine Walrus

was thought that at least one hit was obtained on the Littorio causing her to slow down, but certainly some of the cruisers were hit. That is why our Fleet was able to catch up with them, though the Littorio herself escaped. Getting TAGs eye views of this action has proved difficult, beyond the usual description of considerable flak and the inability to be sure of any hits. Apart from this, TAG George Blenkhorn, who was recommended for a DSM after the first attack, failed to return from the second. However, both John Montague and Bob Hogg (from 13 course), were awarded DSMs for the action. We also lost Frank Coston who was in a Fulmar of 803 squadron. In general the Italian Fleet was not defended from the air - they were too far from their fighter bases, but aircraft were sent to attack the British Fleet and it was one of these with which the Fulmar tangled.

Besides the effort from the Formidable, the Swordfish floatplane from Warspite also took to the air to shadow and report on the Italians. Yes, it was the same two as from Narvik, Ben Rice and Maurice Pacey, plus a famous Observer. In the morning they had to hook on again whilst the ship was chasing hard and returning from their second flight they landed at night in Suda Bay on their own line of flame floats. It was gratifying to note that at last Maurice Pacey's successful transmission of all the reports was acknowledged with a Mention-in-Despatches. He got nothing at Narvik.

93

They had been relieved by an Albacore from Formidable in which was TAG Alex Japp. This aircraft continued the night shadowing of the Italian Fleet with appropriate signals on their position and disposition. This aircraft also had return to Suda Bay as Formidable had moved out of range. In their case, not being fitted with floats, they had to ditch in the Bay.

Formidable continued to make her presence felt after this action , but was kept very much a part of the fleet, rather than being allowed to roam afield to harass the enemy. As a result it was her fighter aircraft which largely featured in enemy interceptions during the next few weeks. These were still mostly Fulmars with TAGs occupying the back seats. Then Formidable also suffered hits from enemy air attacks and needed to retire for repair.

Other Aircraft Carriers still afloat were able to operate with sufficient strength to cause havoc wherever they appeared. A carrier's mobility is its greatest asset. The German and Italian enemy, who had no carriers, must have wondered where next their tormentors would appear.

Ark Royal, which we have already met in this narrative, was part of Force H operating out of Gibraltar. This meant that she could move as desired either into the Mediterranean or out into the Atlantic. Even perhaps back to home waters if necessary. It is true that when she was used to support convoys to Malta then the enemy was on to it in a flash and the element of surprise vanished. No doubt there were many observers in neutral Spain noting which way the Fleet moved and advising accordingly. Yet she was able to make several other forays to catch the enemy on the hop, notably to Sardinia and to Genoa. TAGs were in the back of all the Swordfish on these excursions but fortunately not often called upon to get dramatically involved.

Yet shortly after the fall of France, the British Fleet made a foray to Oran in July 1940 in an attempt to persuade the French Fleet to come across actively onto our side. Forcibly if necessary. It fell to the aircraft from our carriers, notably the Ark Royal, to make these sabre rattling gestures. Unfortunately the French weren't having any of it and promptly shot down a few of our planes with their own shore based fighters. TAG 'Chats' Chatterley with Rating Pilot Tom Riddler in a Skua were a couple of those killed in this action. A similar situation was then repeated at Dakar two months later on 24-9-40. This time it was rather more ill-timed. TAG Frank Moore was killed as was C.K.Bunnett from the R.A.N..The latter was flying in a Walrus from HMAS Australia. Two TAGs were made POWs, Norman Jarvis and Fred Dawson, the latter after baling out of his aircraft. Doubtless those involved did not have any heart for what they were doing, but still had to act against the enemy. Here Percy Clitheroe was awarded a DSM. He was later lost looking for the Bismarck.

Apart from these excursions the Swordfish activity was mostly to carry out endless A/S patrols. The TAGs in the Fulmars on the other hand found life more hectic. The Ark Royal was constantly harassed by Italian and German bombers and as her Fulmars were the main fighter defence then almost every flight was likely to see action. What did the chap in the back do ? Mostly he just sat there feeling superfluous. There was no rear gun. His presence was considered desirable to pick up any signals on the W/T directing the aircraft - there was no R/T. The ship just might transmit if it was evident her position was known to the enemy. Or yet again they might offer a D/F bearing to a lost aircraft. However, most air defence occurred within sighting distance of the ship.

So the chap in the back thought up his own defence measures. The first ideas were to fire brown smoke puffs from the Very pistol at any approaching enemy aircraft. It was thought this might put them off momentarily - enough perhaps for the pilot to jink clear. The next was a typical TAG inspiration. Toilet rolls. These were dropped down the flare chute at a crucial moment and unrolled in the slipstream to produce a devastating secret weapon calculated to unnerve any attacking pilot. If they actually recognised what it was, which they probably did, then perhaps they thought it was our crews way of suggesting that this is what they needed.

Finally the lads talked the powers that be into letting them take up a Tommy-gun. At first this seemed more practical, though a TAG with familiarity of the Vickers 'K', which itself was little more than a pop-gun, might have anticipated the result. The muzzle velocity of these hand-held guns was so low that, when fired, it was possible from a position behind the gun, to see the bullets lose their forward speed and watch the trajectory trail downwards. They really weren't much use at all unless the enemy came up real close. Still they kept taking them. It was something to do, and perhaps the enemy fighters might not be expecting response from the rear of such machines. If they saw the muzzle flashes it could be enough to deter them slightly. It should be realised that in order to fire the gun anywhere astern it was necessary to lean out of the cockpit.

On one occasion Dickie Woodhouse's aircraft got tangled up with 7 CR42s off Pantellaria. They made it back all right but with a few holes here and there in their aircraft.

At an early period in Force H's activities of running convoys through to Malta they had actually come across the Italian fleet to the south of Sardinia. A daylight torpedo attack by Ark's Swordfish did not meet with much success but the point of my comment relates to the TAGs eye view as the attacking aircraft turned away. The Italian warships also turned, but towards the approaching torpedoes as is the normal defence to such an attack. Some of the TAGs swore that the enemy ships were overtaking them! As was usual, the Italian fleet did not fancy an engagement, and effectively retired.

In May 1941 Bismarck was known to have left the Baltic and to be in a fjord at Bergen, with the cruiser Prinz Eugen also in a near-by fjord. RAF reconnaissance had kept track of it up to that point using high-flying camera equipped Spitfires, but then the weather closed in, causing cancellation of an RAF strike and putting a stop to further air spotting. The Admiralty was most concerned when this information ceased. A senior and experienced Observer at Hatston considered he could navigate under the cloudbase. With the assistance of an experienced pilot from the F.R.U. at Hatston they took a Maryland with TAGs Armstrong and Milne, and flying at wave top height groped their way under the murk into Bergen fjords. Bismarck had sailed. This was a remarkable flight and one of some surprise for TAGs in an F.R.U..Armstrong sent the W/T message that set up a big chain reaction.

In fact Bismarck and Prinz Eugen were spotted by our cruisers Norfolk and Suffolk as they came they came through the Denmark Strait between Iceland and Greenland. TAGs Jan Coles aboard Norfolk and Bob Aggas aboard Suffolk, each expected to get airborne in their ship's Walrus to continue the shadowing, but with Bismarck doing 30 knots the aircraft could not have been recovered without the ship losing touch, and so they were not catapulted. Suffolk was able to shadow at extreme range with her newly-fitted advanced radar. Not so Norfolk with her older radar, and so she had to join Suffolk and follow her movements.

HMS Hood and HMS Prince of Wales had already put to sea, and now with the receipt of the Maryland's message, the Home Fleet also sailed from Scapa and with them went the Victorious. This must have created an enormous flap because Victorious was a new ship which had not worked up. The squadron of 9 Swordfish

(825) which they took aboard, together with a flight of 6 Fulmars, were both newly formed squadrons which had had no time to get fully organised. Normally the ship would have had at least twice as many aircraft.

As has been described in detail elsewhere, Bismarck was engaged by the Hood and the Prince of Wales with the former being disastrously blown up. At this point, Bismarck's whereabouts was only too well known. It was found by the Swordfish aircraft from Victorious and duly attacked. During this attack the leader of one sub-flight was not satisfied with his approach and turned away. In the back of this aircraft, TAG Les Sayer says he knew the fish had not been dropped. Not only is it usually possible to feel a slight lift as this occurs, but Les had noted a slot in the cockpit floor through which he could see part of the tin-fish. So they went back in a second time on their own. Contemplating this action many years later, when he was making a model of Bismarck for a grandson, he found himself sticking on the guns, turret after turret of the anti-aircraft variety. How could they possibly have missed us, he mused ? Miss them they did, perhaps because on their second approach they came in from the West on Bismarck's starboard side and therefore were not seen against the setting sun, which was still visible, though late at night, in those latitudes. This sole aircraft dropped its fish and turned away before the party began again. It was believed one hit had been made and this was probably the aircraft that did it, a view later confirmed by the senior German survivor, though he also mentions a prior hit which harmlessly exploded on the blisters.

Subsequent to this strike Prinz Eugen was detached to operate independently because it was clear that Bismarck would have to return for repair. Actually the cruiser also decided to make for France and reached Brest without further interception. Bismarck had tried to shake off her shadowers a couple of times without success, yet when they made a slow and large turn to starboard during the night they unwittingly chose a fortuitous moment when the Suffolk was on an outward leg of her anti-sub zig-zag. Thus Bismarck completed a full circle to take it behind the pursuers, who now lost their target and thought it had escaped to the West, whereas it was actually steering South-East.

Its position was in fact known to a Fulmar aircraft which shadowed it during the night. The exploits of this aircraft have only become generally known of more recent date, because it would seem that those who sent it off were not very interested in what it saw. Whilst this is not directly TAG related, the actions of the Observer in the rear cockpit are just those which a TAG would regard as his province. No doubt it was a TAG who set up the radio on the required frequency for the Observer before take-off. Yet I doubt if a TAG would have had any better success in communication in the circumstances. This Observer must have worked hard on this flight - my later experience of navigating and operating W/T in a similar machine tells me just how hard, and he was doing it at night against an enemy battleship.

They had little difficulty in finding and following the ship. It was hit all right and was leaving a trail of oil. From a subsequent German account it would appear that the original damage was inflicted by hits from the Prince of Wales. These had been shored up and overcome by the damage control parties but the air attack had caused Bismarck to take violent evasive action. This and the shock of the final torpedo hit had opened up all the seams and once again oil spewed out into the ocean. This was what the Fulmar followed. At any point when they thought they had lost it, they just found the slick and flew up it. The faster speed of the Fulmar made this reasonable. A Swordfish might have had difficulty catching up ! So the observer sent out his sighting reports. He wasn't surprised that the Carrier didn't answer. They wouldn't wish to give away position, though when one thinks about it, they were the pursuers and in an area where they were not likely to be pursued. As no other aircraft was airborne he could not use the 'intercept' method and just had to broadcast.i.e. send his messages twice. That must have kept him busy, for a man not in morse transmission practice.

So finally they turned for home. Where was his ship ? It was quite dark and their courses round Bismarck were dubious. So he asked for a bearing on his radio. By W/T naturally. Now it so happened that an Air Direction Officer aboard the Victorious, who was short of a job with so few aircraft to direct, thought he ought to enquire on the progress of the shadowing Fulmar. Finding his way into the W/T Office he identified the operator on the aircraft wave. This man was reading a book. Now this ADR officer had evidently been trained by a TAG at one point - perhaps he had even been one? - anyway, he said to the Tel. on watch "Aren't you going to swing round the dial ? Aircraft radios can't be put spot on the frequency." This made the operator jump. Whether he agreed, or not, you don't argue with an officer. So he swung the dial, and there was the aircraft asking him for a bearing and it seems he did have the facility of taking such a bearing. "Aren't you going to answer him ?" Once more the operator thought he ought to more or less do what he was being told. He actually got as far as transmitting the bearing before being stopped in his tracks by the Duty Communications Officer. We will draw a veil over what was probably said between the two officers. The point is the Observer got his bearing and arrived safely back over the ship, where the pilot did his bit in getting them back aboard. A carrier landing at night in an unworked ship. Hair-raising.

Of course, nobody had received any of the aircraft's other signals, so subsequently there was nothing on paper to say what was what, and where and why. This crew duly appeared in the operations room, but there for some reason, the S.Lt.(O) RNVR didn't seem to count much amongst the top brass discussing where Bismarck might be. Didn't they know he was the man who had followed it for the previous two hours ? He was able to point a finger at the place where last he had seen it and to say it seemed to be making a beeline for Brest. So he went off to his bunk. Was his information ignored or not recorded or just not believed because of his lowly rank ? This we don't know. Certainly in the morning he and his pilot discovered that a search was being organised to go off in a totally different direction. At the time they didn't question this as it was assumed that further information received during the night had changed the scene.

I imagine that there was quite a bit of heart searching amongst the operational staff aboard the ship and possibly some argument. Yet it would appear that the order came from Admiralty in London to search to the West, and who were they to argue against that, purely on the strength of a S.Lt.s say-so ? Admiralty's view was understandable. They had several forces coming up from the east, it just required Victorious to scotch any possibility that Bismarck had gone westwards.

So the searches for Bismarck went off in the wrong direction and it escaped detection for many hours. Our concern here is for the TAGs who went off on these searches. One was Percy Clitheroe who had already been on the attack the prior day. His aircraft landed in the sea and the crew were lost. Another was Fred Sparkes, again from the attack on the prior day. In this case the crew boarded an empty ship's lifeboat which they had miraculously ditched alongside and they survived several days at sea before being picked up, but Sparkes lost his toes through frost bite. His pilot believes this would not have happened if only he had removed his boots and applied massage but he would not. Another crew that also ditched was from a Fulmar but no TAG was involved. This was the end of May 1941 and the Atlantic sea condition was pretty rough. To survive in a dinghy one had to have a lot of luck. That three aircraft should all have ditched suggests that the ship altered course without advising them. Very likely under the stress of the chase with more important considerations prevailing. Yet, with so few aircraft and some of these apparently abandoned, this just about denied Victorious any further part in the affair.

Bismarck remained undetected until an RAF reconnaisance aircraft picked it up and reported the sighting at 1030. It was now Ark Royal's turn to get into the act. She had come up from Gibraltar with Force H and already had aircraft airborne on a search pattern. One of these made contact and got off a sighting report at 1115. Another Swordfish aircraft joined in a few minutes later. It is clear from the timings that they were successful independent of the Catalina's report. Much has been said of Ark Royal's attacks but little about her shadowing activity. Before the strikes could get under way the position of the RAF sighting had to be checked. This shadowing effort was kept up throughout the day by continued relief aircraft. Two shadowers enabled the 'intercept' signalling method to be fully exploited and ensured no loss of the quarry should one aircraft have to return. In one shadower we find that the TAG involved was Bagsy Baker, one of the old school of Tels. but also notorious for his addiction to rum. This time, in a sober period, his evident skill with a morse key kept the information flowing from an equally proficient observer. This was not the only crew involved in the shadowing process and another TAG, Harold Huxley, who was later killed in a flying accident, was decorated for the effort. No doubt Baker had blotted his copy book in some off-duty exploit. Their activities would have concentrated on the whereabouts of Bismarck. They were not there to give warning of the proximity of Sheffield, whose presence should have been known to the strike aircraft. Such was not apparently the case and so she was attacked, though it seems several crews recognised what she was and held off. Also it was discovered that the Duplex proximity fuzes were firing prematurely.

Thus they had to mount a second attack, in sea conditions which made the take-offs and landings somewhat hazardous. Fortunately Ark Royal carried three squadrons of Swordfish (810,818 and 820), and though in each the numbers were reduced by earlier losses, and by the aircraft on shadowing and A/S patrols, nevertheless they managed to put up a total of 15 aircraft this time using direct contact fuzes and succeeded in making two hits, one in the vital area aft which damaged Bismarck's rudders. She commenced turning in circles and the rest is history. There were TAGs in the back of all but one of the attacking aircraft and incredibly none were lost, though Dickie Seager was wounded by the anti-aircraft fire.

In the previous paragraphs you may have noticed that I have persisted in referring to Bismarck as "it" rather than "she" as we would for a British ship. This is because the Germans refer to their ships as masculine,but I could not bring myself to referring to it as "he" !

After this, Ark Royal returned to her actions in escorting Malta convoys or a very similar action of taking RAF fighter aircraft to within flying distance of Malta. The latter was slightly the less hazardous, but they were usually picked up by enemy reconnaissance anywhere south of the Balearics and then the party would begin. The Tiger convoy took place in April/May 1941, Style in July 1941 and Substance (the return of ships from Malta) in August 1941. These were followed in September 1941 by Halberd. Fulmars were active all the time and on one of these Bill 'Gerry' Germon's aircraft was badly hit by return fire and had to ditch alongside a destroyer. It so happened that this ship was due to escort the convoy all the way, much to Bill's dismay as he couldn't get back to his carrier and this turned back somewhere short of Pantellaria. However, one of the other escorting ships hit a mine and lost some of its bows. The ship Bill was aboard got the job of escorting back the lame duck, and as she finally caught up with the rest of the fleet they were cheered through by every ship present. Bill felt mighty proud to be part (if only a passenger) of such an episode.

Ark Royal's charmed life finally ended in November that year, hit by a submarine lurking off Gibraltar. However she stayed afloat long enough for almost the entire crew to get off without getting their feet wet. They almost saved the ship. It so happened that two of the TAGs who were rescued were subsequently put aboard the Audacity for the journey to England. That ship was sunk on the way, 21-12-41. Yet again both survived, not this time with dry feet however. Even so, two ship survivals in a month for a couple of aircrew was something to write home about (if they had been allowed to). These two Tags were Mac McCulloch and Cyril Coventry. Most likely there were many seagoing men who had more than two ships sunk under them. One of our own former TAGs, who was commissioned via the rank of Warrant Tel., Fred Fieldgate, was aboard three separate destroyers which were lost. Yet for an aircrew, such was more the exception. One of our rating obervers, T.E.Andrews was torpedoed twice on the way to Trinidad.

Now it so happened that the Swordfish squadron which was active against Bismarck, when flying from Victorious, had been transferred to Ark Royal. This was 825 squadron. Aboard Ark there had been a few transfers of crews, but now, along with the other ex-Ark squadrons, or what was left of them, they were now without a ship. Yet the crews existed and were regarded as those with the most experience of torpedo attack ability. It is hardly surprising that they were earmarked to play a key role in the event of any break-out of the German battleships from Brest, though six aircraft is a pitifully small number. Of course, it was never envisaged that theirs would be a near solo effort, and at that period we could hardly afford to have lots of aircraft just standing-by.

This episode has been recorded many times from different sources and it is not my intention to repeat all this. Yet when covering TAG activities, one cannot ignore this sad yet heroic epic. Not that the TAGs had any option about taking part. One wonders just what their feelings were. Sick yet hopeful I suppose. At least they had cause to fire their gun. Better than just sitting watching. For some, this was by no means the first time they faced a German battleship. Johnson, Wheeler, Clinton and Bunce had all been involved in the attack on Bismarck. Only Smith was a new boy, whilst Tapping had been Mentioned in Despatches when flying over Norway in 1940. I think I can shed a light on one description that came through. It was said that one TAG was sitting astride the fuselage beating out the flames with his gloves. It sounds a bit far-fetched. Actually one was quite sheltered from the slipstream in the back of a Swordfish, and if one's G-string was opened up to its limit - and this was quite normal - then one could stand on the seat or even climb up onto the gun mounting without feeling one was likely to fall over the side. I can believe this was what he was doing.

There is one TAG who feels utter dismay at what took place. This is Les Sayer, who knows full well what it was like to face Bismarck. He was now the P.O.TAG and during what was supposed to be a stand-down he agreed to go up to Scotland to check out the radar on some replacement aircraft. On his return there was just no squadron.

The one TAG who survived this debacle was Don Bunce. Like all but one of the other survivors he was wounded and his aircraft ditched. I recall that in one description he said he found there was no floor to his cockpit. He had probably been standing on the gun steps, which were small cubby-holes in which we kept spare valves for the radio. Despite this shattering experience, which was doubtless quite traumatic, he has given calm interviews on the operation of a Swordfish, which have been echoed in praiseworthy terms by other TAGs of his era. All feel his C.G.M. was more than genuinely earned.

Very shortly after this Channel Dash, another balloon went up when it was believed that a strong German force was at sea east of the Shetlands. This was within two weeks of the action in the Channel and perhaps had been intended as a diversion or maybe an attempt to take advantage of that action. The major German ship was believed to be the Tirpitz. As it happened the weather was quite appalling. Aircraft were sent up from the two squadrons aboard Victorious on a night search for the enemy. These were 817 and 832 squadrons, which were now equipped with Albacores. From the reports of those taking part it was a bad decision to send them off. The conditions were so bad that they could see nothing, not even their flame floats, so navigation became impossible. In any case they were being thrown around so much that the pilots could not hold course. The radar was just a mass of jumbled sea returns and the radios a constant hammering of static. All of the aircraft required D/F homings and those TAGs who were successful in getting through worked hard to bring their aircraft back. Not all were so fortunate. Two aircraft from 817 and one from 832 were lost. It is believed some may have tried to fly to the Shetlands. The lost TAGs were Hibbs, Dryden and Clive Clark (a colleague from my Course).The date the 23rd February 1942.

Just two weeks later aircraft from these squadrons found the Tirpitz. There followed a copybook episode between two of the aircraft on the search with the sighting reports being transmitted and repeated between them. As Harry Robertson, who was also airborne and listening, relates, it was as though they were carrying out an exercise at Worthy Down. This was a rare example of the use of all our training in the "Intercept" method. The second aircraft also turned toward Tirpitz such that a sighting was possible. Then following this information a strike was initiated by the two squadrons. This was a daylight strike and Tirpitz made the usual fast turns toward the torpedo tracks. She had all the luck. Later reports told us that in fact there were two hits and neither torpedo exploded. Two of the attacking aircraft were shot down. These carried TAGs Sivewright and Hollowood. The German Command decreed that the Tirpitz should not again put to sea if an Aircraft Carrier was in the vicinity.

Back in the Mediterranean the convoys to Malta continued. No longer with Ark Royal, but Eagle, Furious and Argus kept the pot boiling. Convoy Harpoon took place in June 1942, and then a very big effort was made with 5 Carriers. This was Pedestal in which Indomitable and Victorious joined the other three, in August 1942. Sadly it was in this effort that Eagle was sunk, and Indom was damaged. It will be appreciated that by now some single seater fighters such as Sea Hurricanes were in operation, yet the Fulmars were still doing much of the fighter work. As always the Swordfish were lumbering round on A/S patrol. It was during this operation that one TAG excelled himself and attracted some attention. During an air battle with enemy fighters this Fulmar took some punishment and both the pilot and the TAG were wounded. It so happened that the pilots wounds included a bullet which had gone across his forehead causing the flesh to drop down over his eyes. Therefore, although he could still fly the plane he could not see, at least not well enough to watch the batsman. He pushed the skin up from time to time, but when it came to a hand on the throttle and one on the stick he was in a fix. So the man in the back opened his hood, stood on the seat and watched the batsman out of the top of the open cockpit and over the pilot's head. You will understand that from the back of a Fulmar normal forward visibility is nil.

In this manner he told the pilot of the batsman's signals and effectively guided him to a deck landing. For this he was awarded a C.G.M. The TAG was Len Barrick. When asked subsequently during various sessions round the bar to expound on his effort he invariably replied:"I'm here talking to you, aren't I ?" His attitude to the whole affair was that he was merely saving his own skin, and that whatever he had to do to achieve that was well worth the effort.

Bismarck fires a salvo

CHAPTER 13

"George Cross Island"

I have already made mention of Malta's 830 Squadron. After leaving the island we followed their activities with considerable interest. This was heightened in my case by the knowledge that Bill Gold was with them. We felt that here was a sister squadron -another bunch of Swordfish operating ashore in the same theatre of war. We didn't get hold of all the details, but the news items were frequent enough to let us know they were right in the thick of it. Furthermore our squadron was sometimes called upon to fly them replacement aircraft and we knew that some of our pilots had been sent across by other means to bolster the effort. With their operational losses and constant bombing they were desperate for more aircraft. Some could be flown in from the west the way we came but only if an aircraft carrier was close enough. To get them across from North Africa was only possible when the airfields in the Tobruk area were in our hands. From that point the distance was some 650 miles which was just about the extreme range of a Swordfish with a long range tank. There was nothing to spare. Any greater distance was out of the question. We ourselves were short of aircraft so when the call came there were probably none in the pipeline and as like as not an 815 machine was selected to make the run. If an experienced 815 crew went then they had a reasonable chance of making it. With a replacement crew there was some doubt. Malta was not particularly large and some crews were known to have finished up in Sicily. They always took an all officer crew as it was considered that the key feature was accurate navigation. On the other hand we listened in to Malta radio every night and heard them giving D/F bearings to RAF aircraft. We knew that a German station in Sicily often pretended to be Malta and gave false bearings. With our experience we were quite able to tell the difference. In my view the run might have been tried with a TAG. D/F bearings would have simplified the final run in. I am confident I could have got there if the aircraft and engine were willing. You will see that the continued existence of 830 Squadron was very much in our minds.

830 Squadrons presence in Malta was something of a circumstantial happening. At the time of the fall of France a Swordfish squadron No.767 was stationed at Hyeres in the south of that country. Though basically second-line they soon switched to an operational role when the Italians entered the war and promptly bombed Genoa which was a bit cheeky in daylight in a Swordfish. The Italians then retaliated by bombing the Naval Air Station at Hyeres. The Vichy French authorities took a poor view of this. 767 Squadron had to leave in a hurry on the 18th June 1940 with the French naval ratings training machine guns on them as they left. The ground crew shanghaied a ship and acting as stokers sailed for Gibraltar. The Swordfish flew to Bone in N.Africa. Here they split with one half returning via Gib. to the U.K. with the other half going to Malta. Already operating at Malta was a R.A.F. Communications Swordfish squadron. There was nothing odd about this. All aircraft and aircraft spares were routed to the R.A.F. and continued to be identified under R.A.F. part numbers for years after the take over. The two groups now amalgamated and were renumbered 830 Squadron. To make up the aircrew numbers most of the R.A.F. crews stayed on and thus six W.Op./A.G.s flew with 830 for eight months in the traditional TAG role. Three of these men were awarded D.S.M.s and through this information I was able to follow up their history. Two were subsequently commissioned, though none are alive today. They are Sgt.G.R.I.Parker.DSM.Ment.W.Op/AG.550085.later_Flt.Lt.died

1963   Sgt.M.Parke.DSM.W.Op/AG.543666.later_Warrant   Officer.killed   1946
Cpl.L.S.Carter.DSM.W.Op/AG.550974. later__Flying Off.died 1966 The other three,
L.A.C.s Stripp, Clark and Hendry I have been unable to trace.

When Bill Gold was finally sent home he came out the way he went in -eastwards
via Dekheila. At the time I was up the desert and so Bill sent me a letter - by hand.
Because of the manner in which it reached me he could express himself freely. The
bottled up strain and emotions of the previous 12 months were let loose and in reading it I lived through those 12 months as he had done with fear gripping the stomach.
On every operation two or three faces would disappear. Whose turn was it next ?
When they landed after an operation Jerry would be over the top of them and, following the letter in gripping lower-deck prose, I ran with him, wildly and stumbling,
in flying kit, trying to find the edge of the airfield and some sort of sanctuary but
instead tumbling into a recent bombhole, and lying there choking for breath until the
raid eased. It was a long letter and included many such incidents written when they
were vividly in his mind. I was a pal of many years and could appreciate every word
and he knew it. Unfortunately I no longer have the letter. It was left with my kit in the
baggage room at Dekheila and, as I didn't go back that way when heading home, it
had to be sent for. Some interfering busybody must have confiscated it along with several other items when checking out my bag before its despatch.

We can turn to a more recent article written for me, by Bill, for a description of his
stay with 830 Squadron. Not so expressive as the original letter but equally
enthralling. He begins with a description of the formation of the squadron and continues :-

" The operations which followed were predominantly torpedo attacks, mine laying,
dive bombing and, strange as it may seem, 830 were also front line defence of the
Island. Our aircraft, built in 1936, had no night flying instruments or sights.

The record of 830 was never equalled by any other squadron. From May to
November 1941 they sank 110,000 tons of enemy shipping and damaged a further
130,000 tons in the same period. By the end of 1942 in collaboration with 828 they
accounted for something like 400,000 tons of enemy shipping.

Life on the island was not pleasant. At times we were short of food, torpedoes and
shells, the latter having to be rationed. There was continuous bombing with scream-
ing bombs, and raids of over 100 aircraft at a time on one target (during April 1942
750 tons of bombs fell on Hal Far alone) -and then all hands were spread across the
drome to pick up shrapnel or fill bomb craters. The sharp shrapnel could tear our own
aircraft tyres apart. Our living quarters were so badly damaged that we were evacuated to a house in the village of Zurrieq which we shared with rats, mice and fleas.

We normally flew during the period when the moon was up, taking off at midnight
and returning around 0600 to 0700 the following morning. After this we were
debriefed, invited to have breakfast in the Officers Mess, then turn-to to service our
aircraft. This was a difficult job, the aircraft being dispersed and Jerry keeping up continuous alerts. At noon we were granted a make-and-mend and it was advisable to
sleep in the air raid shelter during the afternoon. At the end of approximately a fortnight the squadron stood down and the A.G.s went to a rest camp for a few days at
Ghain-Tuffieha where they ate, swam and got gloriously drunk.

On the 9th September 1941 the people of Malta presented 830 Sqdn. and the R.A.F.
with shields for the work each had carried out in the defence of the island. They also
treated the squadron to a free booze-up spread over a period of two days which was
appreciated by all.

I might briefly describe some of the operations carried out by 830, which reflect the courage of F.A.A.pilots. As A.G.s we sat in the back and went along for the ride. Pilots had to have the guts to push home the attacks. Petty Officer Charlie Wines was one of our best dive bombing pilots.

On the night of 19th March 1941 the squadron was briefed to lay mines in Tripoli harbour. These mines were magnetic and fuzed with delays from one to eleven 'ships'. (The number of ships passing over it before the mine is triggered.) A normal operation of this kind would be 4 to 5 aircraft carrying mines and perhaps 2 to 3 aircraft dive-bombing ack-ack positions to attract gunfire, each aircraft carrying six 250lb bombs with blast rods on the nose and at least two screamers on each tail. We usually lost one or two aircraft on this type of operation. This night I was flying with P.O.Wines and we were carrying bombs. It normally took two hours twenty minutes to fly from Malta to Tripoli - plenty of time to reflect. Why we had to dive-bomb I could not understand, because R.A.F.Wellingtons which took off after us arrived over the target first and carried out high level bombing. Tripoli always put up a box barrage with plenty of searchlights. After the Wellingtons completed their mission they flew around the target to watch 830 go in. This kept the radar and barrage going, consequently when we arrived it was nicely hotted up. We complained about this but nothing was done. Whilst we observed strict W/T silence, the R.A.F with their more powerful sets hogged the air waves. Therefore when any of our aircraft were in trouble it was the devil's own job to make oneself heard. Thanks to some very good operators at Bombay, Ismailia and sometimes Chatham, who kept listening watches, they unknowingly saved many lives by signalling Malta to advise that he was being called.

The mine-laying aircraft would approach the target at approximately 4,500 feet, break formation, cut engines and glide down to 100 feet. They had to get in as close as possible to the entrance of the harbour, drop their mine, turn and glide out to sea before switching on. When on this task it was a wonderful sound hearing that old engine cough into life again, but very disturbing having the searchlights sweeping across the water.

On arriving at the target, Charlie yelled through the gosports - "Look at that beautiful ship in the middle of the harbour - I'm going after it !" As a passenger what could one do? To me it seemed no different to flying down the barrel of an anti-aircraft gun...

We went in at 4000 feet, and straight into a vertical dive. I clung on for dear life and then something big hit me in the stomach. It really hurt -I thought "I've been hit" - and then realised that a spare pan of ammunition resting on the gunring had slipped off and hit me. I hooked my arm over the side of the aircraft to heave myself up - the sight before my eyes frightened the life out of me ! It was like daylight, tracer coming up from all directions, swishing and cracking ; the ship looked enormous. I clung on to my position as we straddled the ship with our bombs. I heard all six explode - Charlie had timed it beautifully. As the bombs exploded we were pulling out at 800 feet and turning away and the ack-ack fire eased. Charlie threw that kite all over the sky and we were free. We lost one aircraft on this operation (the A.G. was Bill Thomson who fortunately ended up in Tunisia).

A Midshipman (I cannot remember his name) turned out to be another excellent pilot. Very cool, the type of pilot one felt safe with. Our brief, a torpedo attack on a convoy comprising five destroyers and two merchant ships. We took off from Hal Far in total darkness and formed up in the usual tight 'V' formation. The Middy, being the lowest of the low, flew on the end of the 'V'. The dim formation lights of the aircraft in front could just be seen. The last aircraft in, we were to commence our attack so many minutes after the second flare had dropped. Over the target we received the signal to break formation, and then suddenly it was like daylight -the first flare illuminated our aircraft - panic stations to get clear.

I suggested to the Middy that it might be a good idea to drop a flame float in front of the leading destroyer to attract gunfire. (It had been done before to generally upset a convoy). This we did with good results. The second flare dropped and the Middy manoeuvred into position. The destroyers were putting up a smoke screen and as we flew over one of them the flare went out. It was now as black as the ace of spades. We turned to fly in the general direction of a ship. Up to then the guns had stopped firing, but then some clot on the destroyer we had just flown over opened up with tracer and sprayed it about. Another gun opened up ahead of us and this tracer went through the main plane. Then a large dark stern of a ship loomed up. The Middy dropped our torpedo. We did not hit the ship. We were much too close -the torpedo must have gone underneath.

Charlie Wines was also on this operation attempting his first torpedo attack. Unfortunately he was shot up and crashed in Tunisia. Charlie and Toddy, his A.G., were interned. (Toddy was not happy about going as it was a year ago to that same day that he was shot down off Norway dive bombing a Cruiser - the Konigsberg).

On arriving back at Malta, Jerry was waiting over Hal Far dropping the odd anti-personnel bomb. We landed in pitch darkness. That night we also lost another aircraft with A.G.Bungy Edwards. It was believed one ship had been sunk.

One pilot tried but failed. He 'chickened-out' on each operation he attempted. On his last flight, on the 11th Nov.1941, he took me, as I had gained some experience. (Experience allowed you to fly with the C.O. on one operation and the most 'goon' pilot on the next, to give him confidence). I was not at all happy ; one of the escorts of the convoy was a Cruiser and knowing the prospects of this pilot I felt our chances would be very slim. However, after one and a half hours he turned back. We were the only aircraft to return. The rest of the squadron, six Swordfish, together with the shadowing aircraft, an R.A.F. Wellington, never returned. What remained of the squadron received sympathy from Churchill and all the other big-wigs. This pilot left the island on the next available aircraft. I felt extremely sorry for him, yet grateful for probably saving my life. The whole operation should never have happened.

On the 14th July 1941, the squadron went out to attack a convoy but failed to locate it. On the return journey, through the mist, could be seen two Merchant ships and a destroyer. This was not the convoy we had been looking for, but the C.O. decided they were worth having a go at and gave the signal to break formation and attack. This was my first experience of a daylight operation. The ships did not appear to be moving very fast, their bow wave hardly disturbed the water. We were to attack last, and as each aircraft went in, every torpedo missed. Not a shot was fired as we went down and made our attack on the leading ship. As we pulled away my pilot cursed -our torpedo had hung up. So round we went once more and made a second attack. Again our torpedo remained with us. My pilot would not chance his luck a third time so we carried on to catch up with the rest of the squadron.

It was ascertained during debriefing that all three ships were already sunk by our own Destroyers and were resting on a sandbank! We were complimented for bringing our torpedo back...

Whilst on the island I only went on one A/S patrol. A duty of this nature for Swordfish from Malta was far too dangerous during daylight hours. On this particular occasion the Convoy was extremely valuable. There were six merchant ships, a

Cruiser and six Destroyers. At least one ship had been damaged. Two Swordfish took off during the night but failed to make contact. I flew in one of the next two aircraft. Dawn was about to break and this could mean attacks by ME109s.

We found part of the convoy, a large Merchant ship, torpedoed through the bows and well down in the water, being escorted by the Cruiser and a Destroyer. The sun was now up and the next thing I knew we were amongst ten Stukas which had flown out of the sun. I grabbed my Lewis - cocking handle back - "what did they say on 13 Course at Aldergrove about deflection and speed ?" I never answered that one, things happened too quickly. I found myself grovelling on the cockpit floor forced down by 'G'. I finally staggered to my feet, the gun had swung round on its mounting and was pointing at me ! We were now at wave-top height and Jerry was dive-bombing the ships, fortunately without any direct hits.

So much for my gallant action.

Our duty done we landed at Hal Far after approximately seven hours in the air and no breakfast - it was now almost midday.

Later that day the pilot and myself received a message of thanks from the skippers of the merchant ships and endorsed by the Captain of the Cruiser. It was gratifying to know that we had been of some comfort to hundreds of men - little did they realise that at times we had probably been more scared than they were. "

Bill Gold was Mentioned in Despatches for his participation in this special episode.There followed a list of all the TAGs who had served with 830 during Bill's stay. Many were killed, missing, P.O.W.s or interned. It had been stipulated that an aircrew tour in Malta should last no longer than 9 months and this figure was later reduced to 6 months. In fact Bill and another A.G. S.S.Clark stayed for 12 months as there had been no reliefs.

Of those who came through their tour, whatever the duration, three were killed subsequently. There were little comments about each. Evidently he had talked at a later date to some of those interned in Tunisia. They had been treated worse than P.O.W.s. There was an intriguing little piece about Taff Evans. His stock phrase was "Mr.Brink will get you tonight - he will tap you on the shoulder". When sitting down in a Swordfish with an overload fuel tank in the observer's cockpit, the slipstream would catch the spare length of parachute harness on the shoulder and one would feel a sensation of someone tapping you on the shoulder.

Bill concludes his story :-

"Although 830 Squadron reformed several times in subsequent years, somehow I feel 830 was part of Malta, was conceived and died there on an island approximately the size of the Isle of Wight, which shook from the impact of over 14,000 tons of bombs during the siege. When I think back, I try to remember not only the dead, but the living, the pilots who brought me safely back, the wonderful comradeship - and appreciating how sweet life really is before going into action. Let us pray it never happens again."

Though getting only passing mention in the foregoing narrative, 828 Squadron with Albacores joined 830 Squadron in Malta and were active with them during 1942. On their arrival they even had to lend 830 some aircrew so heavy had been the attrition.

I did not see Bill at Dekheila. By the time I got back there on one of our rest periods he had been shipped home round the Cape. We only met up again on my return to the U.K. when by good fortune we were both at Lee-on-Solent. I felt that we were somewhat lucky to have both come through without mishap. At that point we were in the P.O.'s Mess and Bill had chummed up with Donald Bunce who I vaguely remembered from 15 Course at Worthy Down. Bill and Don had both opted to become Air Gunnery Instructors and were awaiting transportation out to Trinidad and the Observer's School. Not surprisingly Don Bunce also knew Len Barrick as both held a C.G.M.. It so happened that Len was also in the Mess, and so, after drawing our tots the four of us gathered for a typical chin-wag. At the time I did not regard it as any more than a bunch of TAGs having a chat. On reflection I suppose it was a shade historic but I was very small fry in such august company.

Nat Gold

Swordfish ex-Illustrious, Cyprus 1941.
Leica photo by Carton Speight, 7 Div. Cav. Regt. A.I.F.

CHAPTER 14

"Finding The Needle..."

We didn't particularly like Dekheila and I don't think they were too keen on us. To them we were the pirates who wanted to dress as they liked and do as they pleased, without concern for normal discipline. This was only too true. We would work all hours - night flying programmes demanded such an approach, but once off duty we objected strongly to any other pettifogging routines. We only looked forward to the run ashore in Alexandria. Otherwise the sooner we got back up the desert the better.

So I was happy to fly back up to Bagush on January 19th 1942. It was back again to A/S patrols. This time with a difference. We now had our secret weapon - radar - and hoped we could find them at night. The North African coast was always busy with our shipping. First there had been the support of Tobruk under siege, now it had been relieved and they could run supplies in there for the Army. There were also the runs across to relieve Malta. Though it meant diverting goods brought all round the Cape for use in the desert, they could reach Malta more readily from the East than from the West. They could hug the coast under our own air cover as far as possible and then run the gauntlet across as best they may. The shipping was a right mixed bag with a lot of small vessels, but enough to attract a row of enemy submarines. We also still had some warships that made prime targets.

The squadron immediately embarked on continuous nightly searches. With radar these were not patrols any more but searches. We were the hunters now. With a squadron effort of about 8 aircraft we were able to keep at least one and usually two aircraft searching the coastal area out to 50 miles from the beach and from Alexandria right along to Tobruk. With overlapping airborne times we might have as many as four aircraft in the air at once. From dusk to dawn all 8 aircraft probably got airborne in a night. The squadron strength was 12 aircraft but the other 4 would be at various stages of maintenance back at Dekheila.

On the sixth night - the 25th January - we struck lucky about 30 miles off Mersa Matruh and hardly an hour after take-off. We had the first stint that night with a start at 1800. Being winter this was a dusk patrol with still a hint of daylight though very hazy and dull. The observer got an echo at about 8 miles. He tapped my shoulder and I could see the echo by looking over his shoulder. We homed on to it and the pilot got a sighting during the final mile. The half light was fortunate and very helpful. Without needing to illuminate, it meant we did not disclose our presence, though if we could see them probably they could see us, if keeping a sharp watch. It all happened very quickly and I didn't see much of the final approach as I was hastily reeling in the trailing aerial. When I got up and looked forward we were right down on the water and coming over the top of the sub.. She was lying stationary and seemed caught completely unawares. Our two depth charges dropped in a perfect straddle diagonally along the subs line and therefore each was close in. I was watching so closely for these that I didn't even notice whether anyone was in the conning tower, though I think I would have seen if there was a face looking upwards. As we pulled up and turned the sea erupted with the sub lifted up on top of a volcano of water. When it subsided she was still visible but now it was on end with its bows sticking out of the water like a buoy. We circled around watching but it was getting darker and it was difficult to pick out detail. There seemed no point in using the rear gun, the bullets would just bounce off. There was no sign of oil but I was convinced it would sink. After some minutes the bows slowly disappeared below the surface. Surely nothing could survive those huge explosions. It was only later that I began to have doubts that it was anything other than sunk. The observer gave me a position and I signalled back on our attack. Follow-up aircraft would search the area. They did so without finding any further sign of our target. We landed feeling very elated. After so many hours of A/S patrols it was something to even see a submarine. It is now known that this was U453 and it was certainly badly damaged. They limped home to Pola in the Adriatic.

Though this metre-band R.D.F. could do no better than about 8 miles on a surfaced submarine it was a great stride forward. We could now find them at night as they charged their batteries. After this initial success we were sent chasing all over the place wherever submarines were reported. There were a few further searches from Bagush and then during February we were detached to search up the Palestinian coast and even back to Cyprus. Then over to Beirut. It was quite an experience to see again from the air a place we had attacked and got such a hot reception, but now in quiet circumstances. We also landed and saw it from the ground. I kept quiet about our previous visit. Then we moved south again to Palestine. On a patrol from St.Jean (Haifa) we ran into the worst electrical storm I've ever experienced. The lightning flashed all round the aircraft as it jumped between clouds and to the ground clearly hitting us on the way. The aircraft was thrown all over the place and our compasses became useless. This was worrying to say the least as the night was black, apart from the lightning flashes, and we were some miles out to sea. We turned round and the pilot had to fly by instinct back towards the coast. Needless to say the radar was useless and, though I wasn't consulted, I could tell from much use of the Gosport speaking tubes that the pilot and observer were in some doubt about which way to go. Before we hit the storm I had my trailing aerial out. I thought it prudent to reel in when the lightning started. When I tried to put the earth plug in to bond the aerial to the aircraft huge sparks jumped across the gap and my arm became rigid. I only got it into position by moving my whole body and my leg and boot to get the plug finally in place. Reeling in was quite an effort with the static discharging through me. It was fascinating to watch sparks jump the gap from my fingers whenever I reached out to touch something. I could feel it, though it was evidently of low current. It seemed my flying clothing was insulating me from the aircraft. Finally we found the coast and there we had got clear of the storm so there was little difficulty in recognising exactly where we were. I had the last laugh after we landed. With some foresight I jumped down from the plane. The observer, not thinking, climbed down, and got a discharge to ground through himself. It was one of the best impromptu dances I'd seen for a long time. The pilot, still standing on the wing root, and myself, found it most amusing. Our rubber wheels ought to have been impregnated with enough metal to discharge the aircraft but it would seem that in this case the charge was excessive.

All our searches round these coasts were fruitless and we returned, first to Dekheila, and then to Bagush, but doing a further search on each leg. Other aircraft had meanwhile maintained the Bagush patrols and a couple had been fortunate enough to get contacts and put in useful attacks. Did the enemy really have a string of submarines along this coast ? Or were we finding the same two or three boats again and again ? If the latter was the case we were certainly giving them a headache. On our first resumed search from Bagush we again had electrical storm problems and returned. All aircraft under maintenance at Dekheila had been completed and the squadron was now up to full strength of 12 aircraft. This eased the demands on the crews and patrols only came round every other night. We were now nearly working on a regular crew basis. There were changes from time to time due to sickness or other reasons, but it made quite a useful contribution to team slickness to stay together.

This period saw the squadron really settling down to become a compact unit. There had always been a distinct comradery stemming from that "we are ex-Illustrious" spirit and fostered by the Cretan episode and other periods of stress. On the other hand we had had detachments here there and everywhere, such that there were times when one forgot just who was in the squadron. Now we were nearly one. The aircraft tail-fins sprouted an emblem consisting of a large eagle carrying a depth charge in each talon and scanning the sea with a telescope. Such may have been frowned upon by their Lordships but it did a lot for squadron spirit. Even the C.O. appeared in a distinctive navy blue forage cap which was at variance with the usual cap with khaki cover as seen in the desert.

We Air Gunners were enjoying the opportunity of using our radio. Except when escorting convoys, strict W/T silence was not enforced as we could give little away by position. We ranged up and down the coast and the enemy knew we were doing so - his subs had been attacked often enough. We only exchanged a brief contact every half-hour but it was very comforting to make that contact and know that we were "in touch". We still had our own ground station -somewhat of a pirate perhaps on Coastal Commands wavelength. It was still an aircraft style radio but now it came complete with a WT van. Two Naval Telegraphists had joined us earlier when we had our flight of Albacores and these chaps now manned our ground station and eased the demand on A.G.s to do a ground watch. As it happened, when I went back to Bagush the spare bed space was in the Tels tent and so I moved in there and happily took watches to help them out. The desert in winter can be very cold at night so we moved the radio into the tent because it was warmer. It also meant we could more readily shake each other for relief or to take special messages without deserting the receiver. The sand made it very difficult to get a good earth and so we rigged a counterpoise consisting of a row of petrol tins on a rope under the aerial wire. These were filled with water and linked with wire. During the day the water evaporated and we had the strange sight of a Tel tuning the output from the transmitter by pouring in water until a peak reading was obtained. Our frequency was overburdened with signals from R.A.F. search aircraft reporting all manner of things - often enemy convoys off Malta. From our particular position we could act as a link to pass some messages on to Alexandria whenever it appeared that the latter hadn't heard signals that we had. Even Jerry latched on to our ground station callsign. He was fond of coming up and, using Malta's callsign, would pretend to be Malta. Then he would accept signals meant for others or transmit false DF bearings and so on. We think his transmitter was in Sicily but we could recognise its note and somehow there was a distinction to his morse. It was a subtle and indefinable difference which gave it away, but those of us constantly listening on the air knew it at once. To make a change he sometimes used our callsign to "accept" R.A.F. aircraft transmissions as he must have heard us so do. I wonder if he knew who we were. I doubt if the R.A.F.crews were told our callsign or whether to expect a German station.

We suffered quite a bit from static. There was usually a bit of sand blowing about outside and this drummed on the aerial to increase the normal background noise. On occasion one of us in bed and supposedly asleep, would wake and tell the operator he was being called. The signal was reaching the man in bed even if faintly whereas the operator with the phones on couldn't read it through the static. In such circumstances one often found it better to put the phones on the bench. Our Telegraphists should have been T.A.G.s. They fitted our outlook on life and were accepted into our circle. They would sometimes rib us over bad morse. We pointed out that it wasn't easy from a shuddering aircraft. One day we got each of them up on a test flight and briefed the pilot to give them the "works". They kept in touch perfectly through all this and we didn't dare admit that the manoeuvres were exceptional.

As the camp was a little more permanent than previous spots, we built up the tent walls with sandbags. This had the dual role of an air raid shelter and forming a dry island. When it rained the ground got very muddy and the sandbags kept all this out of the tent once a couple of bags were added across the entrance. Some of the original A.G.s had left the squadron at this time. Allum and Hazeldine had gone to join 826 and Boosey to the Leander. Thus we got some new A.G.s joining, Freddie Taylor and Taffy Way. It made a change not to be junior bod any more though I suppose I shared this position with Astbury and Grainger. We began to get regular issues of Victory V cigarettes - all right for those who could stand them - and some beer. We were never really short of this. Not everyone fancied the Canadian and Australian bottled beer which had a sharp chemical taste, lots of burp and a fierce hangover kick. So there was always an extra bottle going begging for those who could stomach it. The one small detachment we still had in being was situated at LG121 - our alternative landing ground at Sidi Barrani. It was manned by only half a dozen chaps as a refuelling party but had a Royal Marine in charge of the bar. He made a point of a regular run round the various issue depots. At each he would draw "the Fleet Air Arm's" issue. As we didn't belong to anyone in particular each depot happily issued it out to him. He reckoned he ran the best pub in the desert and was never short of beer. We always looked forward to landing there and would manage to bring back a few extra bottles.

We had several Marines with the squadron all ex-Illustrious. They acted as Wardroom Attendants. All were characters. Mostly they were reservists, who perhaps were no longer suited for the Royal Marines more strenuous roles, but did sterling service for the squadron with their experience in "knowing the ropes". We also gained some R.A.F.Regiment chaps at Bagush. They manned machine guns to give us ground protection. I recall being asked to lecture them on aircraft recognition - I was assumed to be expert mainly because I carried several books of silhouettes. One of their number turned out to be better than I was and named every silhouette I had and knew many more aircraft that were quite new to me.

At this time we started brushing up our power of command preparatory to taking a Petty Officers Board. We could see more sense in this. The Leading Airmans Board with a hook already on our arm was a bit of a non-event. At least it had given us the feel for the more important one yet to come. I was gaining confidence though it was obvious we weren't going to pass this time out of sympathy. It was hard work being part of a voluntary squad in the heat of the desert and marching round the dusty uneven ground. Our camp was right alongside the road and passing soldiers in trucks were probably amazed at this sight of the Royal Navy's extreme discipline. As it happened I was sent off on another detached series of searches and missed that particular Board. I took another some three months later and was then the only P.O.candidate amongst several Leading Airmen. This probably aided my pass as I could do better than the others and there was no competition at my level.

If our reversion to an anti-submarine role was less spectacular than attack missions it was none the less active and interesting. We had been lucky to find our first target in twilight. Other squadron contacts were made in darker conditions and the problem was to illuminate the target so that the pilot could drop the depth charges visually. We started using illuminating cartridges fired from a Very pistol. These were quite effective in giving light for a few hundred yards ahead but did not last long and a continuous string of them was necessary. The cartridge itself was twice as long as a normal Very and they gave a much bigger kick. There was a sharp corner on the back of the breech and this would recoil on to the back of one's thumb. Firing a string of these could be a bloody business. There was also the question of misfires. We kept a spare pistol loaded in readiness for such an event but what did one do with the misfire which might still go off ? As each crew met these problems they tried to solve them in their own way. The misfire could be handed to the observer to hold over the side but he, as like as not, was still watching the radar screen conning the pilot on. On one flight an A.G. put a misfired pistol in the gun mounting. There it vibrated round towards him and then went off. It hit his forehead -luckily not his eyes - but then bounced down into his box of cartridges. Where else ? This set the whole rear cockpit alight and the ammunition started exploding in the pans. The A.G. started throwing just about everything over the side. This included much of his flying clothing which itself had also started smouldering and had to be discarded. As the A.G. described the situation subsequently, the pilot decided that he didn't want to be party to the display in the back and tried to distance himself from the activity. Thus he made a very hasty landing. They got back on the ground all right and the fire was contained but there wasn't much left in the back. Even the radio was well scorched. It taught us a lesson about keeping lids on cartridge boxes and not putting misfires in gun-rings.

To keep a string going the problem was to empty the old cases and reload. There was little time to get one's fingers round the rim of the spent cartridge and that itself meant the fingers had to be free. I liked to wear gloves to guard against the recoil of that sharp corner and then you couldn't shift the cartridge. So I evolved the simple process of holding the gun over the side in the slipstream and letting that whip the case out. It was just necessary to tie a piece of codline from gun to the aircraft so you didn't lose it if dropped - we had been doing this anyway - and then to open the breech. The arrangement worked beautifully and it was just the same for a misfire so it solved that problem as well. I became happy that I could keep a string going no matter what. I'm told that much later someone had the idea of making up a board with a battery of Very pistols which they fired at intervals. I never saw such a board in use and can't say I savour the idea. It appears somewhat limiting and must have been the devil to mount. We were interested to read about the R.A.F.'s Leigh light. We might have been able to mount something like it but had no facilities for doing so and certainly didn't have a powerful enough lamp. Someone though, I believe it was the C.O., did have a bright idea. Carry a flare on an external rack but detach the normal parachute and replace it with a length of codline. This was then tied to a practice bomb on an adjacent rack. It worked well. Drop the flare and lo ! A bright light towed behind which shone a long way ahead. To release it just select and drop the practice bomb. We started to be fitted like this.

The next problem was striking power. At this time we were carrying two ship's type depth charges of about 450 lbs. apiece. sometimes fitted with crude fairings front and rear to give some streamlining and to make them drop without toppling. Later we got smaller charges filled with amatol which gave about the same explosive power for less charge. These were easier to handle and not so much drag on the aircraft. Yet our aircraft continued to find surfaced submarines which stayed on top without diving. We soon realised that a charge bursting underneath even at minimum depth was only sufficient to shake them up and did not prove lethal. Another idea, again I think from the C.O., was to link the two charges together with a wire line. A good straddle across a submarine would swing the two charges together and double the bang in one spot - right underneath. The C.O. tried it out on an exercise and guess what ? One charge hung up. So there he was flying round with a charge dangling on a length of wire. These things will go off on impact if the bump is heavy enough. He tried various manoeuvres hoping to break the wire but without success. In the end he had no choice but to take it down to sea level and let the drag break the wire. Luckily it made a 'soft' impact and, though nearly pulling the aircraft down, the wire did give way and they were able to pull clear. A good idea spoilt by unreliability and so this idea had to be abandoned. Quite a number of ideas were explored around this time. There was encouragement to improvise and some useful ideas were developed. We would certainly have welcomed rockets had they been around at that point. As it was we had to continue with the depth charges and aim to make the attacks as accurate as possible.

We started getting several uncomfirmed contacts. With doubtful serviceability of the R3039 and odd small craft in the area plus flocks of sea birds floating on the surface we could not be sure what these contacts were. Perhaps the submarines were getting wise to the fact that we had metre-band radar. We didn't know it at the time but learned later that in the Atlantic they even got round to monitoring the frequency and would dive at the approach of a searching aircraft with this device. Here though we believe it was simply a case of greater vigilance and a dive at the sound of aircraft engines. I don't think they were monitoring our frequency in the Mediterranean, as our biggest successes were yet to come. We did have one abortive experience. Crew communication was still the crude voicepipe or Gosport tube. Its great advantage was basic reliability and the fact that the pilot and observer did not need to be irritated by breakthrough from background morse. Microphones and masks in the open noisy cockpit would have been an embarrassment. So everyone accepted that electronic inter-com was not necessary. On the other hand the A.G. wasn't in on the Gosport system which simply linked pilot and observer. The A.G. depended on the observer keeping him informed by direct voice sometimes helped by the short length of Gosport tubes on the A.G.s helmet. On this occasion we got a contact and the observer tapped me on the shoulder and pointed to his screen. For some reason we weren't carrying a trailing flare and I stood by with the illuminating Verys as it was a black night. As the target reached the bottom of the screen the observer turned and nodded. We would now be half-a-mile from the target as the radar did not cope with very short range. I started firing a string of the Verys and had reached about the fourth when a voice shouted "....stop firing". I did so but wondered why. I had seen nothing but perhaps the pilot had seen whatever produced the radar blip. I thought I might be told to continue or get an explanation of why I was told to stop but no order came. We searched the area for some time but the echo did not reappear. On landing I was asked to my surprise why I had stopped. "You told me to". "Oh! no, I said don't stop firing". So that was that. The pilot gave the observer a very scathing look and nothing more was said to me. The wind and poor means of communication had defeated us. I would have continued that string by every means possible. As I saw it, any order could only be read as a countermand. This was not my regular crew though we had flown together before, without I might add, the experience of a contact. It was an example of the need to exercise procedures and the desirability of regular crews.

Searches continued throughout March and April using LG121 and LG05 quite regularly as well as Dekheila and Bagush to cover the whole stretch of coastline. The military front line had now fallen back to Gazala. Tobruk was still in our hands and convoys still went up that way. On one rather lengthy patrol for a convoy off Tobruk we watched that port under air attack and saw a J88 pass quite close to us in the moonlight. It was a reminder to keep our eyes peeled. I don't know if this chap saw us but he evidently had other things on his mind and he made no pass to attack us.

Though all our patrols were at night we were often up in daylight moving from airstrip to airstrip or doing air tests. The C.O. kept us busy. On some air tests we would drop sea markers and practise gun firing. I was gratified to note that I seemed to be able to hit the marker all right even from 1500 feet. Doing the same thing at night against a real target one is usually unable to tell how effective and accurate it is. Towards the end of the month of April we had to return from a patrol with engine trouble. Not an unknown situation and with only one engine a prudent move. As luck would have it we had to do exactly the same thing the following night. I heard the missed beat alright but the ground crew could not fault the engine and there were knowing mutters. So we tried again two nights later to redeem our faces. After half-an-hour we ran into some appalling weather. The radar screen was cluttered with heavy sea returns and static bright spots. So we turned back. It may have been coincidence but next day we were flying back to Dekheila. Well, we did need the rest.

It was a fortnight later before we went back to Bagush to continue the routine as before. A large convoy was going up and we covered it for two days in a series of patrols. On the first night enemy aircraft dropped flares over the convoy throughout most of our stay. These were I think from shadowing aircraft as attacks on the convoy did not come until later. We kept well off round the outer ring of escorts in case they didn't know who we were. Again we watched for enemy aircraft but we must have been well below their height. The second night was quieter but a ship that had been hit was trailing behind and we had a double job to look after him and also to circle the others. This night we left before the enemy made further air attacks.

The following night found us escorting yet another convoy. This time one that was returning back along the coast. We had been on patrol about an hour when we got a contact ahead of the convoy. It was always a bit tricky with this type of radar, distinguishing targets from ships of the convoy. The presentation was not a map or P.P.I.(plan position indicator) as more modern devices show it. We had what was known as Left/Right or 'A' scope, which only gave a distance and a direction straight ahead and a very rough idea of whether an echo was to left or right of that line. This time however there was no doubt. The contact was well clear of any other group of signals. We turned towards. Just in case an escort vessel had got ahead of station we maintained height and manoeuvred to get the contact up moon. There it was - a submarine. Even as we tipped the nose down it crash-dived and we were still some 4 miles away. We dropped our depth charges just ahead of the last sighting point more in hope than expectation. I got off a radio sighting signal as we were diving and followed this later with a position. These were sent to the shore station. We never knew whether the convoy escorts were keeping watch on the Coastal Command frequency and were able to intercept such messages. Somehow I doubt it. We then dropped some flame floats at the last known position. The convoy altered course away though this action could well have been part of their normal zig-zag. No escorts came to have a look at our marked position and in due course we returned to LG121 without seeing anything further. The following morning we did a sweep across the area and around the convoy which appeared to be intact some miles beyond the overnight position. So we made our way back to Bagush.

There were further patrols every other night for the rest of the month. On one of these we had to return with the R3039 U/S. On the whole its serviceability was very good and this was much to the credit of Jock our one radar technician who had his problems. The boxes came out often enough during D.I.s.

On the night of 2nd June 1942, we took off from LG121, to which we had flown the evening before. We combed the bay from Sidi Barrani across to Bardia and up to the point where the coast turns for Tobruk. We had been searching for more than two hours when we got a contact at 7 miles some 20 miles off the coast nearly in the middle of the bay, which I believe is called the Gulf of Sollum. It was a good positive signal and again we were lucky with the light. Though about 0300 there was some moon above low patchy cloud which produced a diffused glow allowing visibility of about half-a-mile. Thus as we approached at no more than 100 feet a submarine was clearly recognisable. Again we apparently achieved complete surprise and there was no response from the target. This time the light was far too dim to sight anyone on the bridge. Furthermore, as we crossed we were heading down moon and so would lose sight of the submarine. So as we went over the top I fired two illuminating cartridges. It was a good straddle and the two charges seemed to explode simultaneously lifting the sub on the peak of the explosions. This time, as the water subsided the submarine retained an even keel and just sat there. By now we had come to expect such results from the attack reports of other crews. It seemed that though we could give them a good shaking, charges under a surfaced submarine were not powerful enough to be devastating. Yet this time they made no effort to submerge. Perhaps they were aware that we had no further weapons. On the other hand they must also have known that we would call up more support so I guess we really had done them some damage. A sighting signal had gone off even as we ran in. This was now followed by a position and a situation report. Once this was acknowledged by our ground station we waited for the follow-up aircraft. As we orbited at 800 feet the observer indicated that I should use the gun. It couldn't do any damage but might make them keep their heads down. Actually I found it quite difficult to see the target. It was only a darker patch against the sea when viewed from above, which was worse than the silhouette we got on the run in. When looking through the gun sight, which was a faintly illuminated red ring, the target tended to disappear altogether. However, I spent half-an-hour triggering off sporadic bursts as we orbited without getting a shot back in return. I found my tracer disconcerting. There was only about one tracer round in each burst and it didn't go anywhere near where my experience told me the rest of the burst should be going. Orbiting a stationary target there isn't much deflection so I ignored the tracer and stuck to basics. In due course I heard the relief Swordfish contacting base. I could tell he was close so gave him a call and repeated the position. Then we sheared off so he wouldn't be misled by any radar contact on us. We could still see the sub and considered he would too. He didn't want illumination that would light him as well. We were running short of fuel and had to leave at that point. So we were too far off to actually see his attack. However we saw the sub spring to life when a stream of tracer went skywards. He had a hot run in. So my half-an-hour of target practice must have been effective after all. Perhaps we ought to have stayed and kept it up as the other aircraft came in. We landed after four and a half hours which was just about our limit without a long range tank. As my pilot said, we couldn't have stayed any longer. The second aircraft did not report any progress from his attack. The sub was still on top and not submerging. There was some feverish phoning from LG121 to Bagush to get a machine armed with bombs. However, the situation was resolved by the R.A.F..

As we operated under Coastal Command it was logical that they would act on our sitreps.(situation reports) They sent out aircraft at dawn - Blenheims of 203 Squadron I believe. Sure enough the sub was still there in the morning and they bombed and claimed a sinking. It was as well a Swordfish didn't have to make a daylight attack. We were credited with a third of the sinking, subsequently confirmed as U652.

However, this isn't quite the end of the story, though our further knowledge has only recently come to light. From a German source we learn that U652 was actually sunk by a torpedo from U81. U81, incidentally is the boat which sank the Ark Royal, so was quite a thorn in our side. It appears that the RAF did not sink U652 as claimed. It was however, badly damaged and U81 took off the crew before sending it to the bottom. I suppose we can still claim that our attack, and those of the others, were responsible for the end result.I think a veil should be drawn over one other piece of news. It seems that yet another aircraft from 203 Squadron actually came across the two U-boats during their crew transfer and took no action. They say that the boats fired some sort of red recognition verys and so they were left alone.

When we had returned to Swordfish and A/S patrols I had again taken up the interest in navigation. On all these trips I was duplicating the plot -it made the time flash by. The chartboard fitted all right under the gun-ring for stowage without interfering with its working. Then it came out onto my lap for me to use. The observers were always helpful - and arrived at the aircraft with their own gear so that I could stagger aboard with mine. When escorting convoys I was allowed to occupy the observers seat and navigate courses round and across the convoys path followed by a course home. The convoy position itself ensured one wouldn't get lost and I usually came up with a good course home which was necessary because the coast all looked much the same around this area.

We had often experienced some difficulty with a radio "dead space" about 50 miles off the coast. This is a natural radio phenomenon where a weak ground signal fades and before the so-called "air-wave" reflected from the upper layers has come in with any strength. The effect varied with weather and day/night conditions but at the frequency we were using it could range from 40 to 60 miles. The Petty Officer A.G. asked if he could plot the likely area of difficulty to exonerate those A.G.s who had had communication problems. So a trip was arranged to criss-cross the area with the P.O. plotting signal strengths. I was allowed to go as navigator and the whole thing was laughingly referred to in the operations log as "Search for a lost wave". It all went off quite successfully and afterwards the C.O. sent for me and asked if I was keen to become an observer. Certainly I was, but understood that Rating Observer courses had ceased. Why not a commission asked the C.O. ? He would start the necessary papers and recommend me. Now I had never considered this possibility. I came from the wrong background with only an elementary education and an accent and attitude that had lower-deck stamped all over it. I still didn't believe it possible but from that day my sights were raised somewhat higher.

The technically minded may be surprised to note that I've often referred to using my trailing aerial, yet from the foregoing description it would be clear that we were using HF and not MF. In fact I found it was possible to tune the trailing aerial on HF with the Geep and this gave me a multi-standing wave pattern which was highly directive. This might be unsuitable for some situations in which case one would then simply switch over to the fixed aerial. On the other hand, when flying directly towards or away from the ground station then the directivity gave a very distinct advantage. One could detect this quite readily whenever it was at first difficult to get through. I recall that once when flying over Palestine, Malta came up to say I was loud and clear (in morse language strength 5). It was as though he was expecting me to say I was about to land there. This wasn't bad for our relatively low power sets and I credited the trailing aerial. I switched to fixed aerial and Malta ignored me.

As we moved into the summer months the desert developed its more expected standard of being hot, dusty and irritable. Fortunately, apart from air tests, our work was at night which gave us much of the day to rest in the cool. Being on the coast we also could slip down to the beach for a swim within a few hundred yards. This particular bit of beach was a real humdinger that would have graced any seaside resort and put many to shame. Most of the nearby units used it, Army, R.A.F.,Navy - in fact all and sundry.

June was a very busy month. We took to doing regular air tests in the evening before each night flight to ensure satisfactory operation of engine and radar. We flew so many sorties that I filled two pages of my log book -even more than when I hogged all the trips in Cyprus. The squadron had recorded 30 anti-submarine attacks to date, over a period of some 6 months. Clearly several had been unsuccessful - the enemy couldn't maintain all that many submarines in the area. It was a pity our form of weapon lacked punch against a surfaced submarine.

As June wore on we knew the Army were being pushed back and eventually we found ourselves watching the entire 8th Army trundling back along the coastal road. Bagush main airfield actually straddled this road with the airfield on the south side and our dispersal to the north of it. Our aircraft would taxy across the road for a take-off. So we literally sat there on the roadside and watched the trucks, guns and tanks go by. Why weren't we moving ? No one in our chain of command told us to go. One senior army officer stopped and said we should get out. The C.O. was still trying to get someone on the phone in our own field of authority to say move. As he waited for word he called for volunteers to defend the White Ensign and they actually dug a defence ditch in front of the flag pole. No one seemed very keen to volunteer. By the morning of the 27th June we were all packed, though no tents were struck. We still had not received any direct orders to shift. A Feiseler-Storch came in to land at the airfield. I expect it was being used by our own forces as a very convenient observation machine. One of our touchy ground crew let off some rifle shots at it before he was stopped. Then a Major called in to say he was officer-in-charge of the rearguard company and that they were just pulling out of Mersa Matruh which was but a short distance up the road. Therefore there was little or nothing between us and the enemy. Again the C.O. struggled on the phone. The news that came out of that call was that an enemy tank force had by-passed Mersa Matruh and was 8 miles south of us. That led to an order to evacuate and no one needed telling twice. The ground crew were set off first - most lorries were already loaded and there was no attempt to take down any tents. An amusing sight was that of our Italian P.O.W. cookhouse messmen running after the lorries clamouring to get aboard. They didn't want to be rescued. All were bundled in. Then someone pointed south. A line of tanks was coming down the escarpment on the far side of the airfield about 4 miles away. I never did find out if these were ours or theirs but from what the Major had said, I had no doubt about it. From the phone report and lack of any heavy forces in our rearguard there was only one conclusion. We ran to our aircraft and swung on that inertia starting handle like never before. This was no time for a false start. The ground crew were miles down the road. I think the observer was helping me but he needn't have bothered. The worst part was taxying across the field and towards the tanks with clouds of dust from our airscrews shouting our presence. I don't know why we didn't come under fire. Perhaps they were too busy negotiating the escarpment and unable to take up a firing position. We took off and keeping low made our way back to Dekheila. We had been told not to risk any aircraft carrying the vital radar. One machine which was not so fitted was allowed a retaliatory sortie against the advancing enemy forces with bombs. This had been planned the previous night and he was ready loaded. I think everyone wanted to do this. It was galling retreating without a blow and there is seldom so obvious an opportunity as when the enemy position is known and moving in the open, yet in advance of his own air support. We might have felt vulnerable on the ground but once in our own element the urge to strike back was strong. It was a little strange that enemy aircraft had not put in an appearance, but I suppose they found it as difficult as we did to organise a suitable advanced base when the ground forces moved forward rapidly.

We had no idea about the military situation but it was evident that our own army was still very much in existence. There had been no rout and the withdrawal that we had seen was sedate and organised. It was to be expected that they would stop before Alexandria though perhaps it surprised us that it was so close. El Alamein meant nothing to us. It was just a mark on the map with nothing to distinguish it beyond a whistle stop train platform. There was a single track rail line that stretched down to Mersa but I never saw any trains or even an engine. We were more familiar with places such as Fuka and Burg-el-arab perhaps because these were the refuelling stations with canteens. Once we seriously looked at a map with the military situation in mind then Alamein was obvious. It lay at the narrow point between the Qattara Depression and the sea. Now all was clear.

With the enemy approaching Alexandria the Eastern Med. Fleet began to pull back to Port Said. To cover these movements one flight of 815 squadron was moved to the airfield of Gamil at Port Said. The rest of the squadron stayed at Dekheila. The Naval Air Station was now only a stone's throw from Alamein and it became a front line airfield from which 826 and 821 squadron Albacores made nightly forays to harass the enemy. Though some of Dekheila's personnel continued to provide on-the-spot back up services other elements were moved back and southward to Fayid on the canal in case further withdrawals were necessary. German aircraft were seldom in evidence during daylight, a tribute to our air supremacy but they did send over night intruders. We had one visit from Jerry whilst we were at Bagush when he dropped some bombs and machine-gunned around. He also made a few attacks on Dekheila and I recall biting the dust there one night as a string of bombs whistled down without warning.

I was soon on my way as one of the flight sent to Port Said. Here we found that our enemy was disease. The airfield at Gamil was situated on a strip of coastal sand. The area to the south was part of the Nile Delta and was a large expanse of dormant water thick with mosquitos. These pests as well as flies always presented some trouble throughout Egypt. At Gamil it was critical. We paid a lot of attention to our mosquito nets. The insects weren't the only trouble. With a change in water supply, many men, even hardened desert types, went down with dissentry. What with pleurisy and malaria, in no time 50% of our strength was in hospital or sick-bay.

The aircrew had changed radically. All our ex-Illustrious pilots and observers had long been replaced. With a shortening of operational tour duty time even some of the replacements were now going home. The A.G.s found that initially they were not being considered on a tour basis, as were the officers, and were treated like the ground crews, in terms of foreign commission time which could amount to two and a half years. Eventually though, it was becoming recognised that operational flying should limit the time and so at last the ex-Illustrious A.G.s were being released to return home. Most had completed two years since leaving the U.K..These were followed shortly after by the A.G.s from my group ex-821 squadron. I might have gone with them but had asked to remain. This is perhaps difficult to explain but basically I was happy with what we were doing and couldn't imagine a better squadron than 815. I suppose I loved the piratical mode of living and didn't wish to conform to the more normal disciplines. One other A.G.aquaintance from the days in Crete had now joined us - Newman. It seems that he had remained with 805 even when that squadron changed to single seater fighters. Someone had to service the radios. That meant he had done little flying and so didn't qualify for an early return home. He soon made up for it with 815 squadron.

This motif of an Eagle sprouted on the tail fins of our Swordfish at Marsa Matruh. I hope my drawing is a reasonable recollection of how it looked. Needless to say it was promptly ordered to be painted out once we returned to Dekheila.

CHAPTER 15

U-Boats Galore

Even as we were settling in at Gamil, the Fleet was dealt a nasty blow. A U-boat sank the depot ship 'Medway' just outside Port Said. She was the mother ship for all our Eastern Med. submarines and was being moved from Alexandria to Port Said. I don't know why we weren't actually covering her – not that we could ensure immunity. Perhaps someone else was doing the job. As soon as the news came through we got airborne and scoured the area.

The ship was necessarily stacked with torpedoes. As dawn broke we could see that the sea was covered with these, many in crates but still floating. Destroyers and escort vessels were hastening to the spot. We dived and dropped markers on the larger groups of tinfish. There was no sign of survivors and those that there were must have already been picked up by the many ships. Various vessels started to recover the torpedoes and we could do little more the help. There were so many they couldn't miss them. After one final sweep we returned to base.

We immediately mounted a series of night searches to find the culprit. In fact I note that on the 7th July I actually did two, three-and-a-half hour patrols, on the same day. Taking off from Gamil at 0200 we covered the stretch back to Alexandria and landed at Dekheila at dawn. After a snatch of sleep during the day – difficult in the heat – we took off again at 2100 and covered the same stretch up to 50 miles out, back again to Port Said. All without the ghost of a contact. The following night we tried the area further eastwards and landed at Aquir in Palestine. Again, patrolling back to Port Said. Nothing. Nor from the other aircraft of our flight overlapping us in time and area.

At this point the Admiral took a hand. (Did he think we were doing nothing?) He was doubtless incensed at the loss of his depot ship, not to mention a few other ships that had gone to the bottom. He was very anxious to retain sea supremacy in the Eastern Med. in spite of the threat to the base at Alexandria. He sent for our Senior Officer (the CO was elsewhere), and this Lieutenant was told we would fly and fly and fly, but we would find that submarine. Destroyers would mount a continuous sweep of the area with us patrolling ahead of them. For a 5 aircraft flight (one A/C had been seriously damaged), and with only 50% of fit air and ground crews this was a tall order.

So began a hectic three days. One aircraft was always with the destroyers during the dark hours and it was a case of keep the pot boiling.One up on patrol, one on his way back home and one preparing to be next relief. An aircraft went seriously unserviceable on the second day and then there were four. The crews were in similar straits. I believe that at one point an observer climbed out of one aircraft and straight into another. We were that short of fit men. I don't know how long we could have kept it up, but on the third night we found the submarine.

Our aircraft took off at 2240 to do the second patrol. It was pitch black. Not the sort of period we liked for a hunt – much better with some moon to aid final sightings. We found the destroyers by radar and took up patrol position flying across a line 10 miles ahead of them. At this distance it was just possible to get them on radar as we turned and so keep a check on our station. After a couple of hours we were beginning to think our relief should be preparing to take off when we got a contact. Down we came to the usual 100ft as the observer conned the pilot onto the echo. It was usual to bring the target up slightly to port as this was the comfortable side over which to peer. To

A big submarine, and we were coming up on it fast. Unfortunately this was on the wrong side to the one we were expecting

815 Squadron, Gamil, Port Said 1942

U-Boat. This is more or less as we saw them. Perhaps more in silhouette as it would be darker and we were usually somewhat lower

121

Another
U-Boat

A composite group at Mersa Matruh, Christmas 1942. This Heinkel
was found wrecked on the airstrip.
Left-Right: Jock Cameron; Flight Sergeant Burlington-Green;
Pete Bromley; Ron Gobbett; PO A/M Curtis; Jan Holden; Ken Sims

starboard one got the full force of the slipstream. Over the observer's shoulder I could see the port response slightly larger on the left/right presentation. At just over half-a-mile range we dropped our trailing flare – the first time we had used this home-grown gadget in anger. It worked well, trailing behind us on about 100ft of codline and brilliantly lighting the sea ahead. Where was the target?The sea was empty. Pilot, observer and myself were all leaning over the port side. I glanced back at the radar. A big echo reaching the bottom of the screen. Half-a-mile. It must be there. Then I looked over the starboard side. A big submarine and we were coming up on it fast. I thumped the observer on the back and pointed. He shouted in the Gosports. It seemed we would hit it with our wingtip as we passed by but this was probably my fancy. Figures moved on its bridge and we seemed laid bare with that flare lighting us better than a searchlight. They opened fire and a stream of tracer licked up. I too had the gun up and was pouring a burst back at them. Nearly a pan-full – no time for finesse here – the target was enormous. The observer thumped me on the back and signalled stop. I didn't want to, but he was right. They were firing more at the flare than at us, possibly somewhat blinded by it. My gun flashes would only give the game away. So instead I hastily sent a sighting signal. What was the pilot up to – why hadn't he turned to attack?Well, he had his problems. Our aircraft was full of things that didn't work. Hardly surprising with only skeleton ground crews and the planes constantly in the air. Not only was one of the radar aerials out of alignment but everything was choked with sand. The tail shackle was jammed upwards and prevented violent rudder movement. This had not been noticeable during normal flying turns when turns were effected by the ailerons, but down at a hundred feet when attempting a sudden manoeuvre it was apparently vital. Then the practice bomb hung up and we couldn't drop the flare. To crown it all we lost our depth charges. These had been selected on the run in and in the effort to get rid of the flare these had gone instead. So we could only do a gentle turn back. The flare had now burnt out. There was no contact. Clearly the sub had crashed dived. Only the destroyers could cope now. With a position given me by the observer, I sent out a full report and got acknowledgement from our ground station – still the same tireless Tels in the WTvan. Whether or not the destroyers ever intercepted this I never knew. We flew back to these boats and repeated the information by aldis lamp. They evidently knew something was on – I guess they'd seen the gunfire – as they were headed full speed for the spot. We hung around for a while over the contact point but there our contribution came to an inglorious end, and we slunk home feeling a bit deflated. We understood later that they did get an asdic contact and after many depth charge patterns, sat over it for a long time and finally claimed a kill. All we could say was that we found it. At least the pressure came off.

Not for long. Three days later the same destroyers went up to bombard Mersa Matruh and we went up with them to give A/S cover. First we landed at Dekheila to refuel. A new long range tank had been introduced for the Swordfish. An external type that fitted on the torpedo rack. Clearly we could only then carry bombs or depth charges. With the latter and the long range tank we quite literally staggered off the ground and our airborne speed was down to 70 knots.However we could still have a crew of three and the endurance time was over 7 hours. This is a long time in a Swordfish. I don't know how the pilots stuck it. No co-pilot, no 'George'. I believe they asked the observer to call them every so often to ensure they hadn't dropped off. It was bad enough for us in the back. At least we weren't flying the thing if we did happen to nod off. In fact we took benzedrine to keep us awake. We went out like a light afterwards and woke up with a hangover.

We tried the change to anti-submarine bombs. This not only meant a tactical change in the method of attacking surfaced submarines but could also relieve the monotony by dropping these on enemy targets on the way home. Such was only really suitable when going up the coast held by the enemy. It appeared that the other half of the squadron who were operating from Dekheila, went up this coast regularly and found our old camp at Bagush popular. If Jerry was using this he must have got fed up with the intruders giving it special attention. Accurately, too, after all we knew exactly where it was and could find it at night in the dark. On this trip, however, we ruled out Bagush. First we watched appreciatively as Mersa was bombarded. The destroyers could put up more firepower than the gunboats. Then on the way home we found a coastal searchlight post. Presumably there were also some guns there, aimed to pick off any of our shipping which tried to creep up the coast. The searchlight was sweeping without success.Our bombs soon put it out and as we pulled away they got a good strafing from the rear gun as well. This trip only lasted 6 hours but we certainly needed the benzedrine. So back again to Gamil.

Two nights later one of our aircraft at Dekheila was lost. The AG was Taffy Way. We flew over from Port Said and joined in a daylight search of the area without success.It was vital to our morale to know that the whole squadron would always mount a search for anyone missing, even though these were seldom successful. Then back again to Gamil to continue the never ending patrols. We didn't use the long range tanks or bombs unless going up the enemy coast. Yet we were pushing endurance to the limit of 4 hours. We still had the scent of the fox in our nostrils and the hunt was on. This made the long flights endurable.

On the night of August 3rd, flying from Gamil, we got a contact. There was a brilliant moon and this gave us the best approach sighting we'd had to that date. As we conned on there was the submarine, a long low, starkly black shape, silhouetted in the middle of the silver path of the moonlight. As we saw it from some 5 miles distance, the approach seemed far too slow. We crept in at 50ft fearing to use too much throttle. Surely they would hear us and disappear beneath the surface. No! We got right over the top and dropped an excellent straddle. These moves of an attack had attained almost carbon copy situations. Up goes the sub on the top of the eruptions and then it wallows stricken as the water settles. Have we hurt it this time?It doesn't go down, intentionally or otherwise. Presumably, again just damaged. Once more I send out an attack report and a position and get an acknowledgement.

We orbit and I begin strafing to make them keep their heads down as we wait for a follow-up strike. It was a bit different in this moonlight. Up moon the sub was clear and black. Down moon we kept losing sight of it. Presumably he could then see us. So we took to flying back and forth down moon of him. I then had to use quite a bit of aim-off and swing the gun either side as necessary. I could see my shots landing and that was helpful. Not a thing moved on its upper deck for the half hour or so that we hung about.In the end we had to leave it, still surfaced, and hope that the next aircraft would find it alright. In fact he did so and the sub was still surfaced, but it was then dawn.There had been an unserviceable aircraft and the crew had to make a switch, hence they were very late. So they found a damaged sub apparently prepared to battle it out on top in daylight. The Swordfish with AG Newman in the back got a right royal reception and had to break away. They tried again by coming in high and diving. Once more they had to break away. Those last hundred yards when it is necessary to go right over the top to drop the charges left them too exposed in daylight at 90 knots. In the end they came in quite high in cloud cover and dive bombed with the charges which went off on impact. By this time RAF aircraft were over the top and they joined in to give the coup-de-gras. The last Newman saw, it was wallowing in a sea of oil and looked to be sinking. We think we had another share in a certain success. In fact I believe this to have been U372 but we seem to have been squeezed out of recognition. The destroyers we had signalled eventually came upon the scene and put paid to this particular boat. Inevitably they claimed the credit for the sinking, but to aggravate us, the aircraft named as involved was one from 203 Squadron RAF. This does seem somewhat unfair as they were hardly primarily responsible. The ships were HMS Sikh, Zulu, Croome and Tetcott.

Shortly after this it was leaked to me that some crews had been recommended for decorations and my name was featured. "We know you have one," said my informant, "you will get another."

It was not to be.

The submarine HMS Thrasher was due to come into Port Said and surfaced at the edge of the submarine sanctuary. This was an area plotted as an arc for a few miles outside the port. I cannot recall the exact distance but it was probably about 7 or 8 miles. The information that the Thrasher was there did not reach our squadron until too late. One of our aircraft was already on patrol. It intercepted and attacked. They had to tow the Thrasher in and our name was mud. The Naval authorities appeared unable to accept that we could not be expected to recognize submarine types at night with but a few seconds to make a decision. There was much argument as to whether the position was inside or outside the sanctuary. Evidently it was a borderline situation in which an experienced crew might have been more cautious, or yet again Thrasher might have come in a little closer before surfacing. After all, German U-boats were waiting just outside the port; the position was just about where the Medway went down. That we hadn't been advised was clearly not the squadron's fault. Such information came to us via Coastal Command and somewhere along the way they had delayed. I recall sitting in the W/T van waiting to take off when the duty officer arrived in some consternation. Could we raise the patrolling aircraft and send a signal? He had just received the Thrasher notification and recognised the danger. At that moment the aircraft came up with its attack report. Amid much criticism and recriminations the squadron list of recommendations for decorations went into the waste paper basket.

We kept up the pressure throughout August with four hour searches nearly every night. It came round this often because we were so under strength that the fit just had to fly. On the 9th we had a scare on our homeward leg. The engine spluttered ominously and we jettisoned the charges and struggled back with two pots missing. The Pegasus engine was good for a struggle.We were mostly sweeping between Port Said and Alexandria and would sometimes land at Dekheila to refuel. That was where we kept in touch with the rest of the squadron and also to know that 826 and 821 squadrons were still hammering away at German positions behind the Alamein line. If we were at Dekheila we would do a daylight sweep along the coast on our way back to Gamil, either at dusk or dawn. We didn't expect them to be on the surface at midday.

About this time Newman succumbed. He'd had malaria before and it was a wonder he kept going. Eventually there was a relapse and he went into hospital. What was even more surprising was that his mosquitos didn't give it to me. Though we were fairly particular about our mosquito nets there was always the odd night when we weren't flying and toddled across to the RAF canteen. On such occasions we might not be so careful!

A relief A.G. named Frank Brown arrived from Dekheila. This was a young lad not long off course and though he'd had a few months travelling out and acclimatising. This was his first squadron. I welcomed him in and explained that we would give him a day or two to settle down and be shown around. We still had three A.G.s flyable who would cope that night. I went off on the evening of the 16th on the first patrol. Arriving back after midnight I was sitting as usual in the W/T van having a cup of cocoa and chatting to our hard working Tel. He had just been in contact with the aircraft on the second patrol At that moment the door opened and our third A.G. Bob Gregory fell in. This was quite disturbing as we couldn't imagine what was wrong with him. Malaria didn't usually get them like that. Later his problem was diagnosed as pleurisy. He had got up off his camp bed when shaken but in the W/T van passed out with nausea. We managed to get him picked up by ambulance from the RAF sickbay. Now who was going to fly on the third patrol? I thought at first that I would have to do it but I was nearly out on my feet. Having flown the previous night and been up all day repairing the radio fault that was giving us trouble, I could hardly keep my eyes open. It had to be the new A.G.. I shook him and asked if he felt capable of operating at short notice. Yes, he was keen. So I briefed him on frequency and call signs, made sure he had all the kit and established him in the back of the aircraft with instructions to get through to the ground station as soon as possible. Then I had to explain to the pilot and observer that their own A.G. had gone sick. Off they went about 0300 and I crawled to my own camp bed, dead beat. Within the hour, so it seemed, I was being shaken. Actually it was 0600 and dawn. The third patrol was missing and there had been no radio signal. We were to go off and look for them. Their intended track was known and the weather was fine with excellent visibility. They had been heading east about 10 miles off the coast. In an hour we had spotted the dinghy. Seldom is a rescue search with one aircraft so lucky. There was no one in it! A line was pulling down the side of the dinghy to something under the water! The Swordfish was fitted with a large circular dinghy in the upper wing which automatically inflated on the aircraft's impact with the water. It was tied with a line to the aircraft to prevent it drifting away. One had to cut this line to float free. Clearly the dinghy was still attached to the aircraft which must be lying on a sandbank not far under the surface. I got off a signal with the position which was acknowledged. We circled the area in wider and wider sweeps but could see nothing else. If not in the dinghy then surely they must be in the water, but where? In the end we had to return. Later we were told that a Walrus had gone to the spot. He found the dinghy all right and landed alongside. One of the crew dived down. The Swordfish was there alright. THERE WAS NO ONE IN THE COCKPITS. I was unaware of this and simply flopped into bed to catch up on sleep. Rising about midday for lunch I was chatting to our Tel and debating the possibilities. I also asked about our A.G. in the sick-bay. Then it hit me. No one else knew of our switch of crew. I rushed to see the Duty Officer who was aghast. They had sent off a missing signal naming the original crew. He rushed to correct this, yet I understand a telegram did get to the wrong address before being rescinded. Sod's law had worked again. Any other time and the signal would have been held up for days.

We had no time to dwell on the situation. That same evening a search was laid on with the destroyers again. Off we went at 2300 for the usual side to side sweep ahead of the ships. I'm not sure if they were astern of intended station or whether we were too far ahead but the distance was more like 20 miles instead of the usual 10 miles. On my own chartboard I had the relative positions plotted but it was not for me to question the observer. We were to the north east of Port Said, roughly in the area where our plane had gone down and we got a contact. It was a brilliant moon and so, with previous experience we manoeuvred without turning directly in. Sure enough there she was. The unmistakeable slender black shape squatting low on the water some five miles up moon. Just as on the previous occasion we came down to 50 feet and we closed her without a sign that they knew of our presence. Another good straddle and up she went on the top of the upheaval of water. There it sat again making no attempt to go under but surely leaking and battered. The destroyers must get this one. As we attacked I'd pushed out a brief sighting report. Now a fuller message followed giving the position. Our shore station acknowledged. Had the destroyers got it? To give them a double chance we also dropped a flare so they could get a bearing and home on to it. Pity they were so far away.

We weren't expecting another aircraft. Our resources had sunk too low. In fact they pulled all the stops, refuelling the one we had relieved and sent them off with a scratch crew just before we returned. They never found the submarine. As far as I am aware neither did the destroyers. We had to turn back out of fuel before they got to the spot. The submarine was still surfaced when we left. I hadn't strafed. First I'd been too busy on the radio sending off the position signal. Then when I got up I found that we had tracked back looking for the destroyers though still keeping the submarine in sight up moon. I don't know how the pilot/observer conversation went but we didn't get back to flash the ships a signal by aldis. So it was another inconclusive story. I expect they managed to recover from our attack and submerged when they heard the destroyers asdics. On the other hand, we wondered, supposing it had sunk as a result of our attack. What if our missing crew were aboard?

Just what had happened to them? Engine trouble? Flying too low? Shot down attacking a sub.? They surely wouldn't misjudge height in that moon. No one would bale out of a Swordfish flying at under 1000 feet. No matter what happened we would trust the aircraft to give us the best chance of ditching. So for whatever reason they ditched they would be with the aircraft. Then why weren't they in it, in the dinghy or floating in their Mae Wests in the vicinity? There are all sorts of possibilities. The chance that they were in that submarine is high and this was the official version that was generally accepted. At the time I was convinced it was so. Today, I'm not so sure. I don't suppose for a minute that the submarine sank as a result of our attack. It might, however, have been found by the destroyers who could have claimed a success of which I was unaware. Why didn't the crew use the dinghy? Perhaps it didn't operate initially and only came out after the aircraft went under. Then they may have swum to the submarine. On the other hand would any submarine dare to sit charging its batteries on top of a sandbank? Maybe it wasn't a sandbank at all and that the aircraft was being kept up by its own buoyancy (air in the petrol tanks) aided by the dinghy on the surface. I wish I knew the answer to the puzzle.

At this point my pilot and observer took an independent line that was long overdue. They flew down to Fayid, the Fleet Air Arm maintenance depot and scrounged a torpedo. Our last two attacks had cried out for such a weapon. A stationary target, well illuminated and well worth a tinfish. Why it wasn't used before I'll never know. Not perhaps the thing to bring back to a carrier but no real problem on an airfield. It is perhaps surprising that we were still catching them on the surface. In the Atlantic every move was matched by a counter move. Why were they not listening for our radar? They must know by now that we are using it and presumably know its frequency. Then again where were the extra guns that would have made our low level attacks more hazardous? I believe that some of these submarines could have been Italian, in which case Jerry wouldn't be too quick at passing on his expertise. Most, however, certainly were U-boats. Our metre-band radar was beginning to be old hat.

Well it certainly seemed that they had heard about our new secret weapon – the torpedo. After that we couldn't get a contact for love nor money. Maybe we had really cleared them away with so many attacks. Anyway our luck suddenly ran out and there was nothing to be found. We carried that torpedo on search after search through the rest of August, and much of September and October, every other night. Mind you, if we had found anything, we never knew if it would work. That torpedo was something of a rogue which was why it was back at the maintenance depot. All the time we had it the compressed air leaked and it had to be refilled frequently. The hiss it made was amusing and yet embarrassing whenever we landed at any airfield other than Gamil. The local ground crews would listen, look and vanish. It was as though we had the plague. We always had to find our own parking spot at strange airfields and if this was anywhere near other aircraft there was bound to be a figure keeping well in the distance but dancing up and down waving his arms about. We moved around quite frequently to various airfields in Palestine as we refuelled to cover the area.

One choice of refuelling stop was St Jean at Haifa. Our real motive was to have a look at the Yanks who had now got into the war and were flying Liberators from Haifa. It was quite an eye-opener. Used as we were to running everything on a shoestring the wealth of their equipment made us quite jealous. Then I thought they spoke English but I worked my way through the words breakfast, eats, dining hall and so on before discovering that what I wanted was the chow line. Today it sounds feeble because in recent visits to the States I have had no difficulty in being understood. Doubtless in recent years we have adopted more and more to American expressions and they in turn have attuned to an English accent. Yet on that first confrontation I found it hard going. Once we got across our needs, their generosity was unbounded. I chatted to a corporal thinking here's an NCO of my rank who's been about a bit. To my amazement I found his job was to hold the nozzle of the gas pipe in refuelling. He was part of a team running a bowser which included two Sergeants and a Top-Sergeant and none of them had been in the service more than a few months. Our aircraft got a lot of interest. Like something in a museum. The questions they asked! Figures about everything – as though they mattered. I found myself quoting not only horsepower, weight, speed, range and bomb load but impossible data such as tyre pressures, arrester hook breaking strain, catapult thrust, torpedo ranges and goodness knows what else. Of course I didn't know half of these but the figures rolled out just the same and mostly it didn't seem to matter what I actually said. If they looked startled I just said ENGLISH gallons or pounds or whatever and that settled it.

Later we called at Gaza airfield. Clearly this was quite a pleasant place compared to the desert. In no time it was arranged for us to operate from there and so get away from the disease ridden Port Said area which was playing havoc with our crews and serviceability. In fact it turned out to be Gaza satellite that we used but any bit of grass was better than none. The soil, though dusty, was not in fact sand. The airfield was shared with some Greeks but we didn't seem to hit it off with them as we had with their countrymen at home.

We had a narrow squeak on one patrol when flying up and down the Palestinian coast about 10 miles out. A Beaufighter got on our tail. I never saw him, which wasn't surprising as he was down moon. We were up moon of him and he recognised what we were. It seems our IFF was not transmitting and they did a radar interception. We were fortunate he spotted us. I never did like a radio box you just switched on with nothing more than an audible whistle to suggest it was OK.

Returning from a patrol on the morning of the 1st October, dawn was just breaking and we found the field covered in a blanket of mist. Such conditions are not at all unusual at home but we did not experience them in the desert. Presumably the dry surface did not harbour sufficient water vapour. Here in Palestine was the phenomenon that is a nightmare to flying. Above, clear skies, but how without instruments do you get down through ground fog? We hung around a bit for it to clear and finally with fuel getting short we could just see bits of ground when looking vertically down. Horizontally it was still thick but we could roughly line up on the runway and then just groped our way through, felt for the ground and bounced to a standstill. Anything faster than a Swordfish wouldn't have made it and the pilot did a grand job.

On the 9th, one of the other aircraft got a contact and lost it. We followed up and searched the area to no avail. I believe they really had cottoned on to us now and were diving if metre band transmissions were intercepted.

Two nights later on the 11th, we were again on patrol in the same area and had been up nearly 3 hours when the engine checked and faltered quite without warning. It picked up but shook and clattered in the most alarming manner. We headed due south for the nearest land some 30 miles distant and I was already transmitting an SOS. One doesn't have to be told when things are bad. We dropped our charges - we didn't take the fish on a moonless night. There seemed an interminable time before the observer gave me a position. I got that out and when the ground station acknowledged I felt better. Thirty miles is a long way at 90 knots and we listened, hearts in our mouths, to that clattering engine. At last the coast appeared and we dropped a flare. A flat beach so we slipped down. Good. I didn't trust that engine another minute. By the time we touched down the flare was out and in the dark we bucked and flapped from side to side over dune after dune. Flat beach indeed! A further signal was sent to base to say roughly where we were - about 5 miles from El Arish, though the accumulator was failing without the engine to charge it. Up came a Nubian patrol and we hastily shone a light on our roundels. Actually at first we only saw the sergeant; his patrol had surrounded us and stayed in the shadows. The pilot and observer made tracks along the beach to get help and left me with the plane. I listened for a while on the radio but reception was very weak on our ground station, though Malta was coming through loud and clear. It was that wretched 50 miles dead spot again and the surrounding sand dunes didn't help. They tried to contact me to say a lorry was on the way but my transmitter petered out and I couldn't reply.

The pilot and observer soon returned with an RAF officer. It seemed El Arish boasted an airfield of which we were unaware and it wasn't far away. They put us up there for the night. Next morning we returned to the plane and the pilot decided to fly it to the airfield; it was only five or six miles. I wound it up for him and the engine started. He invited me aboard but I noted the observer wasn't having any and I also declined. That engine just wasn't healthy so he bounced off alone. We got in the truck. On the road out of El Arish we were stopped by a crowd. As we got out the crowd parted. There was the aircraft in a gully. No wings, no undercarriage. Just a fuselage. The rest was scattered far and wide. The pilot had climbed out shaken but otherwise OK. Poor old aircraft L (V4707) had ended her days. We went back and collected all the bits he had shed as he plonked down. There were two big heaps. One of rubbish and one of all the moveable gear from inside; radio, radar, guns and ammunition.

Particularly the radar. I was told to dismantle and remove all the radar aerials. Couldn't let anybody know our frequency. The locals clustered round and watched every move, just waiting to pounce on any unrecovered treasure. Naturally I was the prime humper. We got it all into a lorry and thwarted them. When the work was done, our lorry from Gaza turned up. It was some time before I could explain that our "landed on beach" signal was not made from its current position. In clambering over the wreck I had torn my shorts very badly and was in rather a dishevelled state. This was embarrassing as we had been made at home in the Officers' Mess though this was but a marquee. To add insult to injury their AOC was visiting and everyone was specially turned out. I felt a right Charlie sitting there in my rags amongst the pomp and splendour. Another Swordfish then appeared to ferry us back to Gaza. Yes, you can get five men in the back of a Swordfish - just. Oddly enough this episode about signalled the end of the saga in this theatre and within a couple of days the whole squadron was pulling back to Dekheila to reform.

The event that led to this move was the battle of Alamein. Victory here changed the sphere of our activities. We would be required to go back up the desert in support of the ships once more moving along the coast. Whenever we had called in at Dekheila we had been very much aware that the front line was but a few miles up the road. In Gaza however, we were well clear. We had listened enthraled to the news of the siege at Stalingrad and noted that we sat in the middle of the pincers from north and south. The lads had no radio and I would take down a precis of the news or perhaps read Reuter in morse to pin on the notice board in the mess tent. The result of both battles meant as much to us as to everyone else. A real turning point at last.

Back at Dekheila we had a new C.O. An observer this time and he came to put us on a regular footing. Months of living rough, flying at all hours with makeshift equipment had turned us into a right bunch of scarecrows. The Royal Navy wasn't impressed so we had a few weeks of tight discipline. The aircraft lost their distinctive markings and so did we. There were numerous air tests and exercises to bring us up to top serviceability. On one of these we simulated submarine attacks on some motor launches. The C.O. was participating and no one wanted to go in the back with him. I got detailed. I was on tenterhooks to make sure I got everything right and was anxious not to miss any signals. As luck would have it I broke a pencil. Fishing out a spare it turned out to be indelible. With a few drops of water spraying back from the gun mounting I   soon had a very smeared purple blotched log book and could feel this was being duly noted over my shoulder. On landing I waited in the cockpit somewhat nervously. The C.O. turned, looked me full in the face and said, "It's time you started shaving." Could anyone feel so crushed?

It was about this time that the Admiralty conceded that the Air Gunners might use a new badge in the form of wings. There had been requests for this for quite a while from the newer elements. All R.A.F. aircrews had identifying wings or half-wings as also the naval pilots and observers. Not so the naval Air Gunners whose original aeroplane worn as a non-substantive badge hardly indicated aircrew. So, without altering the latter, a pair of wings was introduced for A.G.s similar to an Observer's wings but without the crown and central 'O'. They were worn on the cuff except in tropical shirt sleeved attire when they were worn above the breast pocket.

With the Army fast moving forward it was time to send an immediate relief convoy to Malta. On the 17th November we moved up to Mersa Matruh and from there flew night A/S patrols round this sizeable convoy as far as we could cover them. This convoy was soon followed by several others and we were then sent to Mersa to set up a permanent base and continue to cover these convoys as a regular commitment. Once more we were back in the desert.

This time it was different. Now minefields abounded and all edges of road tracks were suspect. We had to be careful not to stray around exploring. A couple of soldiers triggered some mines right adjacent to our camp. They were actually trying to clear the minefield. They were alive but not a pretty sight when brought out.

Also the enemy was now really on the run and we were very much in the back areas. This took away the old expectancy of action and immediate fraternity with one's army neighbours. With a full squadron the rate of flying was much curtailed. There was little sign of the enemy, either as night intruders or in their submarines. The one set of airmen who did drop in was a crew of Americans from a Liberator. They baled out of a damaged machine after a visit to Tripoli. How they all came unscathed through the minefields was a miracle.

We suffered one violent sandstorm which lasted three days during which some of our aircraft suffered damage. They banged into each other and a few did a cross country trek to finish in ditches. To stake them down we used coiled spikes but the hard rocky ground at Mersa was much tougher than at Bagush and it was difficult to make an impression even using sledge hammers on the spikes. So these were augmented by ropes tied to sandbags. At the start of the storm it was realised that these might be inadequate and all hands were called out to add further lashings. The difficulty was to actually find the aircraft. Several chaps just got themselves lost. It was quite hair-raising to know that a free aircraft could be bearing down on you whilst you were endeavouring to hammer in a stake. With men and machines scattered all over and out of touch, organisation was near impossible. At one point I was sent back to central ops. to get more help. After some delay we rounded up men and ropes and I led an officer and half-a-dozen lads back to the spot and the aircraft was gone. We moved down wind a couple of hundred yards or so without finding it. Struggling back we came across another aircraft with three men desperately hanging on to it. That was finally pegged down but where was the camp? Or the minefields? With some luck we found the squadron office and gave the storm best. Thank goodness such storms were not frequent.

Shortly after this, Jock of the "thirty thirrrtynine" was sent back to base for two weeks overdue and well deserved leave. He was still the only radar man and had kept it all going for months. As the A.G. with the longest experience of giving him a hand I was left to stand in. I wasn't allowed to poke around inside the boxes but could do all the setting-up of screwdriver adjustments and change unserviceable boxes. There was a van with petrol-driven generator and going round to check out 12 aircraft was a full mornings work never mind the snags. I appreciated even more, Jock's tremendous efforts to keep us ticking. I was afraid he would return to a pile of dud boxes but it didn't turn out as bad as that. We had had an almost complete change in the squadron A.G.s. Several, such as Freddie Taylor, Bomber Newman and Jim Hawkins had gone home. We had a new P.O.A.G. in Jan Holden and some newcomers were "Flash" Hodgett and Dick Gobbet.

By-the-way, whatever happened to Christmas 1942 and my jinx? Well it wasn't quite as outlandish as 1940 and 1941 had been, but it was again spent in the desert at Mersa, and that sandstorm occurred during the Christmas period even though not on the actual day.

CHAPTER 16

Fall-of-Shot

After our previous active style I was finding this patrolling tame stuff with little sign of the enemy. So in February 1943, I welcomed the formation of an Albacore flight of four aircraft specifically to act as flare droppers and spotters for ship bombardments.The other A.G.s in our flight were Bob Hughes , Pete Bromley and Tom Maltby.

We began with some spotting exercises with the gunboat HMS Aphis. As the observer did the actual spotting, I arranged on/off control of the transmitter by running two parallel switches to his cockpit. Then it happened that our aircraft returned to Dekheila for a major inspection -evidently they'd been well used previously by 826 squadron. After settling myself in at the base, in our usual transit tents I returned to the aircraft, and was aghast to find my complete radio had been removed.

For some time we had known that the Service was training radio mechanics, but had assumed that these would be assigned only to the single-seat fighter squadrons. Who could imagine that after so many years of servicing their own radios, that this responsibility would be taken away from the A.G.? In any case it hadn't happened yet - merely that some inexperienced mechanics were appearing at the maintenance bases. To an A.G. who regarded his radio as something personal and tended it with great care it was near sacrilege for anyone else to remove it. I stalked in to see the Radio Officer in high dudgeon. Fortunately he too was an old TAG and well saw my point of view. On the other hand he had to satisfy the regulations and settled for a compromise. The inspection was to be carried out under my eye and to my satisfaction. I wasn't really happy about it but had to acquiesce. Yet they refused to allow the switches as they were "non-standard". As a display of sheer pig-headed behind-the-lines awkwardness this took the biscuit. I made it perfectly clear that as soon as we left I would have them back in again, and in fact had to put them in to carry out the particular function for which we were detailed.

Off we flew up the desert again. First to Gambut to refuel, then on to Benghasi - to the airfield at Berka 3. This was near to the furthest point we had previously bombed. Our small ground crew detachment had already slogged all the way up by road. We had our own radio van - a smaller one this time - but no Telegraphists. Within a day everyone had dysentery - the sudden change of water supply I suppose.

We did some air tests and rear gun firing. With twin rear guns. How I hated these things. They were still held on the same basic mounting and were therefore doubly heavy and awkward to manoeuvre. As they were some 18 inches apart, but with the sight central, one stood a strong chance of hitting one's own tailplane. A gun would be capable of doing this before the tail became visible in the sight. One had to press both triggers simultaneously or the mounting swivelled round and became difficult to hold. The same result occurred if one gun jammed - as happened to me on the first shoot. All-in-all a pretty awful design and quite useless. Two pea-shooters are no better than one if the enemy has cannon. One 0.5 might have been more useful.

The enemy were still retreating and the navy guns were short of targets. We did one A/S patrol around Benghasi and shortly afterwards were heading for Misurata. On this move I drove the W/T van, and though there was more hard work and discomfort going this way rather than by air, it was also interesting to view the recently won enemy territory and chuckle at the incongruous monuments of Italian empire built in the middle of nowhere. Where small towns did exist the walls were liberally daubed with "HD", meaning the Highland Division. To everyone else it meant the Household Decorators. There was also the more basic "Sirte is dirty with mines and booby traps". It was as well to be reminded.

Though we set up camp at Misurata, within days we had flown up to Castel Benito, the airfield at Tripoli. There we paused expecting at any moment to be called to support a bombardment, as the enemy had stopped near the Tunisian border. To arrive at Tripoli was cause for great satisfaction, as this had been the prime objective throughout the prior years. This was the port through which Rommel got his supplies and one of the prime targets for Malta's aircraft. Though this was the 8th Army's triumph, we felt we had contributed in a small way, and were grateful for the chance to follow them up and actually arrive at the goal. Whilst rooting round Castel Benito airfield, we came across an Albacore with Italian markings. Evidently they had attempted to use a captured machine. I don't know if they ever got it airborne.

We were not called upon to do any spotting and flew back to the base at Misurata. There, we did numerous A/S patrols for convoys moving up the coast to Tripoli and across to Malta. These were bread and butter tasks to justify our presence. They were anything but comfortable. The weather became exceedingly hot with a temperature inversion. This meant that as one gained height it became even hotter. The all metal Albacore was an oven to get into at the height of the day. Not like the "fully air-conditioned" Swordfish. As we had no radar these patrols were flown in daylight. Several times the aircraft had to return with over-heated engines.

By early May it was clear that the North African coast was going to be entirely in our hands and that the next likelihood of naval bombardments would come with the attack on Sicily. It was time to re-check our cooperation arrangements. We struck camp and flew back to Dekheila. Within a few days we were on our way down to Fayid near Port Suez. From there we spent some time working with HMS Orion which was carrying out gunnery practice in the Red Sea, shooting at targets ashore. Some of this was at night, when there were full-scale rehearsals of our flare dropping and spotting techniques. It was as well we had been acclimatised to hot weather flying. Fayid and the Red Sea can be a bakehouse. Then back up to Mersa Matruh for a similar exercise with destroyers firing at Ras el Kanayais. Once more down again to Fayid for yet another set of shoots, with HMS Newfoundland and HMS Mauritious this time. We were getting our techniques right, but it was always a bit tricky raising good communication with each new participant. Operating a radio with an observer on the key puts one in the middle-man position of being vital, but not quite having control of things. I often wondered what the ships thought of our variable morse standards.

So we were ready for the day when we could support the Sicilian landings. For this we would operate from Malta. On July 1st we flew up to El Adem and thence on to Magrun. On the 3rd we took off for Misurata, but we didn't make it. At least not by plane. The tired old Albacore had had enough of this hot weather flying and gave up the ghost. Near Beurat the engine faltered and oil pressure disappeared. We made a landing on a straight stretch of the coastal road which was fortunately clear at the time. At the end of the run it became impossible to hold on such a narrow runway and we veered off into the adjacent sand. I got a signal through to Misurata but they didn't seem to know what to do about us. We weren't too happy tramping round in a likely area for mines, though apparently there were none there. When my battery was too low to maintain contact we thumbed a lift into the airfield some 50 miles away. By the time we got there we all had splitting headaches from the effects of the sun. Our

Albacore was left to its fate and we got to Malta as passengers in a DC3. On that trip I came the nearest I have ever been to being airsick. I suppose it was because we were shut up in a bumpy tube with nothing to do. After that, all paratroopers have my sincere sympathy. Another of our Albacores also failed to get to Malta. They ditched in the sea part way over, and were lucky to be seen by a lookout with long sight aboard a destroyer. That man had to convince his captain of what he had seen and get him to go about. In the end we arrived at Malta with four crews but only two aircraft.

It was an intriguing return to the island I had last seen over 2 years before. In between it had suffered a long siege and constant bombardment. We did not go to Halfar which had taken such a blasting but to Takali. Even then the living quarters were not at the aerodrome but way off in the village of Dalgety. The island was now teeming with aircraft and men, bent on reaping revenge by invading its far larger neighbour and the major source of the scourge. Few of these men had been present at the start of the battle. Now I too was to be denied the chance to hit back. The landings went so well that there was no call for our spotting services. We had gleaned a replacement Albacore and put it through numerous air tests and our next chance to join in came with the proposal to attack the Italian mainland. To this end we flew across in August to land at Casserbile in Sicily itself. How beautiful to see greenery in the form of vineyards after so much sand, though this was the height of summer and the soil was rather dusty. The field was full of fighter planes and they were very active. Jerry put in one of his rare last gasp attacks with Stukas and we watched enthralled. We weren't at the receiving end as he was going for the adjacent port of Augusta and now he was taking some stick from the fighters. As usual, we were the unwanted cinderellas at an advanced fighter base. We took off on a spotting exercise with HMS Mauritious. It was nice to know the ships were around and meant business. I'd begun to think we were chasing after ghosts. In the end it was a fool's errand. The advance up the toe of Italy went so well that bombardments were called off and we returned to Malta.

It was at this point that we began to lose our independent flavour. Our parent squadron of 815 had been disbanded back at Dekheila as A/S patrols of the North African coast were no longer necessary. A new 815 was subsequently formed at Eglinton in Northern Ireland to carry the anti-submarine mantle so arduously supported by that squadron number. Furthermore all the aircraft carriers that had gathered to support the Sicilian and Italian landings were choc-a-bloc with fighters. Their T.B.R. elements had been flown ashore to create maximum room for the fighters. Now all the T.B.R.s were sitting at Takali waiting for whatever role arose. This meant that there was a very large pool of A.G.s from various squadrons and no one knew quite how to keep them busy. As our flight had no ground crew there was no way we could remain aloof, and we became simply a few more in the pool. There was a Chief TAG, CPO Howgate, and he was embarrassed with so many lads to look after. All this time I had been hopefully waiting for advancement to P.O. but if this came at all it would have gone to Dekheila and so had not caught up with me. I didn't fancy getting involved in any of the silly little activities that were thought up to keep the A.G.s occupied, nor less did I want Howgate to off-load his responsibilities on to me. So I kept quiet and made a point of attaching myself to the radar man. As ever with these chaps in the early days he was very much on his own and welcomed the help, especially from someone who had already plenty of similar experience. In no time we had a routine for checking out the numerous aircraft. They all had radar and included Barracudas which I was seeing for the first time. What a horrible looking aircraft. On the ground like a praying mantis and not much better in the air with its high wing and tail plane stuck on top of the fin. There must have been nearly 50 aircraft, with Albacores as well as Barracudas. It took almost all day to get round on a D.I. on the radar. Nobody called on them to fly.

By October our spotting services were deemed no longer required. Whether this would still have held good after Salerno I don't know. Anyway, we watched the Italian Fleet surrender off Malta and then made tracks for Gibraltar. We were to fly our Albacores there and then catch a boat home. This was going to be interesting. By hopping along the Algerian coast we would cover all the battle grounds covered by the 1st Army. There was no observer and Bob Hughes accompanied me in the back seat. First stop was El Aouina in Tunisia. Then on to Bone followed by Maison Blanche near Algiers. The countryside all seemed very pleasant. We found it almost laughable that some of the lads who had come in this way in support of the 1st Army landings had called it 'the desert'. Compared to what we'd been used to, this land was fertile and green, at least along the coastal strip.

We took off from Maison Blanche the following morning. Not for long. Within minutes we had an excessive oil overflow and turned back. It wasn't too serious but, on taxying in, the oil leaking onto the hot engine was giving off some blue smoke. A rather over eager crew of Americans doused us with foam. Well, that was that. One can't clear foam off an engine in five minutes. It now needed stripping and being given a good cleaning. So another Albacore was left to its fate. For a couple of days we stayed at the Naval Base. This was amusing because we drew tots. We'd never had this option in all our previous meanderings and I found it convenient not to mention that I'd been registered as T not G. (T=Teetotal,G=Grog). The joke came when we wanted to leave and needed a draft chit in order to cancel the tot. Naval routine over this is very ponderous, but necessary to prevent excess tot issues to the unorthodox - i.e. issues to people who have already left the ship. (It doesn't stop them getting up to such gags - just makes it awkward). So we had to authorise our own draft chit to the U.K.. Odd really, how easily we convinced everyone that this was where we were going without calling on our pilot to add authority. He had been busy and booked us as passengers aboard yet another DC3 to Gibraltar. We made this in two hops after a refuelling stop at La Senia near Oran. So in the end we did fly the length of the Mediterranean along the N.African coast. So ended nearly 3 years of operation with 815 Squadron.

We still had to get back to England and this we achieved as passengers in an L.C.I. (Landing Craft Infantry). These were coming back preparatory for D day after the Med. landings. Our particular craft was leading back a gaggle of them. We worked our passage -largely as lookouts. The crew were few in number and extra bodies were welcome to share the watches. Such craft were not exactly ideal for ocean going trips. They could not go too far into the Atlantic and more or less had to run the gauntlet of crossing the Bay of Biscay with Jerry still established along the coast. As passengers we were accomodated in the forward hold which would otherwise carry some 70 or 80 troops. It was quite eerie being there alone and the journey back to the deckhouse for a midnight or morning watch was uncomfortable. In a blacked-out ship with seas washing over the forecastle, every step along the low seaboard was treacherous. There is little doubt that I exhibited the typical reaction of an airman in unfamiliar surroundings. It was not expected that submarines would find us an attractive target but Focke-Wolfe Condors would. So when a Catalina appeared on the horizon there was initial alarm. I'd never seen one before but I knew the silhouette instantly.

Unfortunately, when the skipper shouted "man the gun" - an Oerlikon -I felt obliged to carry out the order as the only spare man around. From this position I found it difficult to assure him that this aircraft was probably friendly. As it happened we slipped across the Bay unmolested but other groups of L.C.I.s were heavily attacked.

It was a long slow journey but eventually England appeared. First the Scilly Isles, all shrouded in mist and overcast skies. Later Cornwall and then South Wales. I shall never forget the greenness. Deep and dark and even in that wet atmosphere very very attractive and appealing to a man returning after 3 years of yellow and dusty surroundings capped by a couple of weeks of freezing foam topped seas. We docked at Milford Haven and enjoyed every minute of the long train ride to London.

This Albacore with Italian markings was found at Castel Benito airfield

Fairey Albacore

CHAPTER 17

"A Change of View and The Indian Ocean"

It was November 1943 and the capital was still under attack, though less forcibly. The most remarkable thing was that no one took any notice. London was almost cheerful, with everyone hurrying round to great purpose and clearly confident in eventual victory. The difference from December 1940 was most striking. As ever I managed to slip home for an hour or so whilst crossing London. I was still in khaki though wearing the white sailor cap. I expected to be stopped by patrols in this odd rig, but there were so many other strange uniforms that it wasn't questioned. However, I suddenly became sensitive to my unsavoury appearance. Just about everyone suffered from desert sores and most of us learned to live with them. Nothing ever healed. My face and legs were liberally covered and none of the ointments had been any help. My parents, who were now back at home, were horrified. However, within a month the sores were gone.

I was back in London a couple of days later on regular leave in a blue suit. Aerial mines had hit my old school and a housing block close to home. On a subsequent leave a few months later I was to experience Hitler's secret weapons - the V1s and the V2s. During that leave I heard quite a few bangs which were probably some V2s. It was the V1s - the doddlebugs -which were more disturbing. When I was visiting relatives in South London, several came over. When the engines stopped one dived for cover. Yet for all that, they were less fearful than the all night drone of manned bombers. However, at this point the V1s had not begun.

I couldn't settle. Most of the old links were gone. There was an awful feeling of being war experienced and yet not to have grown up. For the next 12 months I had to go back and begin as an 18 year old and learn to live. I sensed this disparity almost everywhere. To me, at the time, it was quite outrageous that people who were clearly fresh in the Services and had seen little action, should be so supremely confident in themselves. I recall listening to a Lieutenant RNVR and a PO.Wren talking in a railway carriage as though the Royal Navy was their invention, yet it transpired in the conversation that both had joined in late 1941.

Thus when I returned off leave to Lee-on-Solent, still as a Leading Hand, I strongly resented that large numbers of A.G.s from far later courses than mine, were already P.O.s and in one case even a C.P.O.. This came about because it had been decreed that a confirmed P.O. who was also an A.G.2 could be made acting C.P.O.. Hardly anybody had previously bothered to become A.G.2s - the requirements were little more than a repeat of our existing knowledge - because it only brought in another 3d a day. From henceforth it meant taking a special course. It happened that the particular Chief whose good fortune it was to rise so rapidly, had the task of checking out all A.G.s returning to the pool, to see that their W/T proficiency was up to scratch. They were sent up in a Proctor to do a wave change exercise and he operated the ground station. So he had to check me out and I didn't like that. Before take-off I fiddled the morse key to ease the strength of the spring and in the air did the fastest wave change I could achieve. Hopefully before he had changed seats in the W/T room, I was back on the air with morse at 25 w.p.m. plus. He took it all right and made no comment either way when we landed but I think he got the message. We met on equal terms some time later and became good friends. I doubt if he even remembered the incident.

It was around this time that the Royal Navy decided that it would be more appropriate to allow A.G.s to be known as Telegraphist Air Gunners and so recognise at last their more active role with the radio. From henceforth the term became T.A.G..

After two weeks of scrubbing floors and such like, (Acting Leading Airman didn't count for much now), I eventually arrived at the Captain's table. Confirmed Leading Airman and rated Acting Petty Officer with nearly two years back-dating. What a relief. In the P.O.s mess I began to meet all the faces that had gone their separate ways since 1940. Well, those that were left. We'd taken quite a pasting and there were many gaps in the ranks. What a variety of incident these chaps had witnessed.

In attempting to describe some of these incidents I shall doubtless fall into a number of traps. One inevitably has to refer to the broad sphere of the operations involved and finally to the particular role of the Fleet Air Arm in those operations. Other people have written in great depth about these activities and it is certainly not my place to elaborate upon them in any way. Here, we are only concerned about the TAGs' role. So, I may either say too little about the role of others, or perhaps oversimplify the whys and wherefores. If the result should infer that only the Fleet Air Arm were involved, and that the TAGs were at the forefront of the action, then I apologise in advance. Actually, in many cases, there is little more to be said beyond the statement that we were there.

To follow some of these events it is necessary to go back to those dark days of 1941. Since the return of Eagle in 1940 there had been no Fleet Air Arm presence in the Far East. Very little RAF either, but that was the fault of the Country's unprepared policy than any tactical decision.

Thus when the Japanese came into the war with the attack on Pearl Harbour and their movement south towards Malaya and Singapore, from their aquisitions in China there was little to oppose their air armadas. Yet the Royal Navy felt obliged to seek out and attack their seaborne transports. So Prince of Wales and Repulse moved into the China Sea east of Malaya. At least these capital ships had Walrus aircraft for search and patrol activities and on the 10th. December 1941 one of these from Repulse was airborne and carrying out a search of the shore line for signs of an enemy landing.

It happened to have a completely rating crew of Petty Officer Pilot Bill Crozer, Petty Officer Observer Steve Damarell and as air gunner, L.Air Merv Rose. That the rating pilots and observers largely manned the amphibians on the capital ships was quite a regular situation, but perhaps it was a little unusual for the entire crew to be ratings.

Now, on that fateful day, these three watched in horror as the two ships were attacked by Japanese aircraft with torpedoes and bombs and both were sunk. Naturally they made themselves scarce and hopefully unnoticed. Perhaps the Japanese planes were at the extreme of their range and disinclined to chase a straggling plane who would no longer have a home to go to. Certainly there was no home after the enemy had left, so they had to take their only option of flying towards Singapore as far as their petrol would take them. Eventually they landed on the sea 15 miles from the coast and 60 miles from Singapore. All this had occurred during the morning but it was pitch dark that night before they heard ship engines and saw sweeping searchlights. Rather expecting it to be the enemy, they were overjoyed to hear British voices hailing them. Their rescuers were the destroyer HMS Stronghold. Their aircraft was taken in tow back to Singapore because it was fitted with radar, but after such a buffeting I doubt that it was much use to anyone subsequently. The crew was returned to Ceylon and we shall meet them again presently.

After the fall of Singapore, the Japanese Navy felt powerful enough to venture into the Indian Ocean looking for the British Fleet. Well they might feel powerful. With a group of aircraft carriers such as we had not then dreamed about, they could put up multiple aircraft strikes to dominate wherever they went, and were intent on dealing a crippling blow to the British Fleet. Had they been successful then all the Indian Ocean and every country around its coasts would have been theirs to take. Evidently they fully expected to find our fleet around Ceylon as that was where they headed. Fortunately for us they made a bad guess, or perhaps our admiral can be credited with more astute thinking. He operated the fleet from Addu Atoll. However, he was obliged to leave a cruiser force with the aircraft carrier Hermes, to patrol the Ceylon area.

There was some sterling work from a squadron of RAF Catalinas who did their best to shadow the Japanese. It so happened that one of these squadrons No.205 had been short of Wireless Operators. Two TAG P.O.s were found at Singapore, who for one reason and another were effectively spare. These were Jock Heath and Norman Hollis. Jock Heath was actually TAG aboard Exeter, but whilst ashore on the sick list, his ship had sailed. In fact she was sunk shortly afterwards. So these two were sent on loan to the RAF. This occurred in December, after the loss of the two big ships. So the Japanese were rampant and spreading further afield. Thus on Christmas Day, 25th.Dec.1941, a Catalina with Jock Heath aboard was shot down off Singapore. They spent some days in the dinghy but were eventually rescued.

These Catalinas continued to patrol into 1942, watching the whereabouts of the enemy fleet. Of course they themselves were stalked and pounced upon by Japanese fighters. Yet each managed to send out some messages of the Japanese position before being shot down. Even so, there were periods when it was not known exactly what the Japanese fleet was doing. Such lack of information caused some chaos in Ceylon when the enemy were not far from its coasts.

Our fleet sailing from Addu Atoll had with them the Indomitable and aboard were 827 Squadron with Albacores, veterans of the attack at Kirkenes. They were put up to search for the Japanese. In fact the first British ships to suffer the onslaught were HMS Dorsetshire and HMS Cornwall from the defending cruiser squadron. An air attack sank both these ships. On Easter Sunday 5th.April 1942, one of 827 's searching aircraft with Air Gunner Ken Porter, found the Dorsetshire survivors. He sent his signal by the Intercept method and it was received and repeated by A.G.Gordon Dixon in another searching aircraft. This was the last that was ever heard of Porter's aircraft. He had been shot down.

Here, I pick up the story as told by Gordon Dixon (13 Course).

'Suddenly my pilot exclaimed "—look at that lot". As he turned 180 degrees I saw the Jap battle fleet and quickly got off the signal '3 aircraft carriers,3 battleships,3 cruisers plus'. This was the Jap fleet that had just sunk our two heavy cruisers. Suddenly the observer shouted a warning as a Zero flashed past on our port side. The pilot took us down to wave top height and I got my Vickers ready. His first attack was from astern and as the pilot took evasive action I got in some good bursts. This was followed by a pass from the front followed by another from astern. I was now wounded in the left arm and left side but remember thinking "I musn't have a stoppage". So I took off the canvas bag that catches the empty cartridge cases and after that the empty cases came out of the gun like bullets and flew everywhere. I put on a new pan and the Jap made three more passes before breaking off the attack.'

Gordon Dixon has the highest praise for his pilot and for his observer who warned of each attack, such that between them they foiled all the Zero's efforts. Actually the name of the Japanese pilot has been traced by an enterprising author. It would seem that this pilot ought to have been severely reprimanded for failing to account for a mere Albacore in daylight. This Albacore got back to the Indomitable. Gordon still has the bullet which was taken out of his side. It is hardly surprising that he was concerned about the canvas gun bag. During his action at Kirkenes in 1941 he had indeed had a stoppage due to the bag filling with empty cartridge cases and so blocking the gun. He was Mentioned-in-Despatches for this action against the Zero.

During the attack on Kirkenes ten months earlier, this same crew had faced attacks by both a JU87 and a ME110 and survived. Now they had got away from a Zero. To my knowledge this is the only instance of an Albacore crew surviving attacks from both German and Japanese fighters. Come to that it might be the only survival of any aircraft, to have faced both types of enemy opposition.

Unbeknown to Gordon at that point in time, this Jap fleet had been very busy on that fateful day, and had also delivered an air attack on Colombo. To follow a little of the story of what was taking place ashore on the island, it is necessary to appreciate that Colombo is basically a civilian port and lies on the S.W. side of the island. The naval port of Trincomalee is on the N.E. side of the island nearly 200 miles distant. Hermes was at Trincomalee and her squadron, No.814, as usual for a carrier in port, was ashore at the local air base, known then as China Bay. Also at this base was a Fleet Requirements Unit, No.788 Squadron. When, from the Catalinas reports, it was clear that the Jap fleet was heading towards the S.W., steps were taken towards producing a strike force. It was a pretty forlorn gesture against such a fleet, but something had to be done. No doubt they intended to strike at night. Anything else was doomed to failure. So a strike squadron was formed from the Swordfish of 788 Squadron. As this was an F.R.U. it will be appreciated that these aircraft were all second line. Tired out hacks used for a variety of odd jobs. If sending a first line squadron of Swordfish to attack the Germans in the Channel was considered "the British mothball navy" as the Germans called them, whatever would they have thought of this bunch ? I believe there was some concern about finding suitable guns to fit and a few of the aircraft only had the old Lewis guns. There were two flights. 6 aircraft with torpedoes and 6 aircraft fitted with bombs. Crews were scraped up from all directions and we note that two quite senior confirmed Petty Officer TAGs were included. Such men would not normally have appeared in an operational unit at this stage of the war. Their experience was too useful as instructors. Also some crews were taken from 814 squadron. It will be noted that as a first line unit they too would have been armed and waiting. In their case, however, they were held ready to rejoin their ship. 788 squadron torpedo flight now set off to fly to Colombo, probably intending to use the racecourse there, which had been pressed into service as an airfield. The flight with bombs, one crew of which included Merv Rose with his pilot and observer, was to follow later. As ill luck would have it the flight of six Swordfish arrived just as the Japanese were delivering their attack. The air was swarming with Japanese aircraft and all six Swordfish were shot down.

It has been difficult to obtain first hand accounts of this action. Three of the TAGs were killed and two wounded. Their names may be found in the Appendix A, 5-4-42, under 788 Squadron. Here, I will simply draw attention to David Bolton who had been a survivor from Prince of Wales. Also to Jock Heath, the survivor from the Catalina. They must have felt that the Japs had a personal vendetta against them. Heath survived but not Bolton. The luck was just not with him. Evidently the flight necessarily scattered, and initially the pilots were reluctant to lose their torpedoes, apart from the possibility of dropping them on the civilians. This meant that the normal Swordfish ability to carry out drastic evasive action was limited. Not that it would have been much help against so many enemy fighters. Also it should be remembered that these were scratch crews that had not trained together. They were not the only losses on that fateful day. Some Fulmars took to the air in a vain attempt to stem the tide. Some of these were also shot down. Amongst them yet another TAG was killed.

It was some four days later before the Japanese discovered the Hermes. One supposes they were still looking for the British Fleet when they moved up to Trincomalee, and probably were more than a little peeved at only finding Hermes. She was at sea and preparing to embark her aircraft. When the enemy dive bombers came in these aircraft were told to remain ashore. Now most of our Aircraft Carriers had aboard some spare crews, and the TAGs were known as Headquarters personnel and used in an administrative capacity. In this case, knowing the probability of attack, several machine guns had been mounted on the bridge and these were manned by these TAGs.

They defended from the 'island', and when the ship was sunk all of these men were survivors, though one had been wounded.

Our Admiral could not chance the destruction of our fleet against such overwhelming odds and avoided confrontation. Fortunately the Japanese were never again able to make a foray in such strength, after being mauled by the Americans in the Pacific. Yet before it became clear that their wings were clipped the threat in the Indian Ocean persisted. Thus it became necessary to prop up our own defences and one of the weak links was Madagascar. This was yet another of the French Colonial countries which owed allegiance to the Vichy Government and could not therefore be relied upon.

So early in May 1942, a force spearheaded by the aircraft of 810 and 829 Squadrons from Illustrious and of 827 and 831 Squadrons from the Indomitable engaged in the campaign to take over Madagascar. Obviously it was the ground forces that had to carry out the actual invasion so if I place accent upon the aircraft it musn't be thought that they did it all on their own. However, our interest lies with them. The main attack was on the harbour of Diego Suarez at the northern end of the island. The Albacores of 831 and 827 attacked the airfield whilst the Swordfish of 810 and 829 attacked various French sloops, submarines and AA batteries. The anti-aircraft resistance was quite fierce and some of the aircraft were shot down. Air Gunner Bennett suffered a ditching. Air Gunner Haddrell was killed and P.O.AG. Ken Groves from 810 Squadron and Popeye Edmondson from 829 Squadron were taken prisoner. Yet another AG was wounded.

There is an amusing sideline to some of this action. Three aircraft of 810 Squadron dropped paratroops ! Swordfish have been credited with many unusual activities, but this one takes the biscuit. Actually they were all dummies. An account of this printed elsewhere suggests they were on the bomb racks. Not so, says Charlie Hawthorn. He was nearly squeezed out of his cockpit making room for them. Then, of course, he had to drop them over the side in a string at the appropriate position. Apparently, from all French accounts, the ruse worked and Vichy were advised accordingly. So when the real troops went in, it seemed like a pincer movement.

Once the Commando's landed the resistance collapsed and the whole affair was over in a few days. Groves and Edmondson were then released. So it was something of a storm in a tea-cup but nevertheless hectic for those involved. AG Gavin Rough force landed on a remote island and lived a Robinson Crusoe like existence for 27 days until rescued. As Madagascar is such a large island the southern areas remained independent for a while. It was necessary to go back there and repeat the landing process at another harbour, the port of Tamatave, before they too surrendered. Once more the aircraft did their stunt of putting on a show of force over the town. An unusual feature of this effort was that a squadron numbered 796 was embarked aboard Illustrious for these operations and carried out 89 sorties. Though later put ashore in East Africa to continue normal F.R.U. work, it was a further example of a 7** squadron carrying out operational duties. TAG Doug Cole was sufficiently enchanted with their efforts to later name his house "Tamatave".

Subsequently airfields were established ashore on the coast of East Africa ,primarily at Mombasa but with detachments at Port Reitz, Tanga and Nairobi. These provided most of the Fleet requirements that were needed along that coastline. Many TAGs fancied themselves as Big Game hunters, as they took their opportunities to explore these well known areas.

We have seen that Indomitable played an important role during this period and in ensuring no break in the sequence of events I have been unable to mention a certain sideline involving TAGs. I take this opportunity to sneak in this episode.

After one particularly harrowing flight by an 827 aircraft, the rear cockpit was liberally daubed with blood. This may even have come from Gordon Dixon. The point, however, is that the P.O.TAG, Jackie Lambert, set-to to clear up the mess. It will be noted that Jackie felt that such a task rested in the TAGs court and was not to be offloaded onto any ground crew. Now Jan Lock, who was actually the P.O.TAG in the Skua squadron and not 827 at all, peered into the cockpit to pass the time of day with Jackie who was in fact the much more senior man. "A right mess you've got there. Want a hand ?" Jackie knew very well that this wasn't really an offer, because it was a one man job in the cramped cockpit, but he immediately recognised the possibilities. "Will you do it for a tot ?". "Sure", said Jan, whose liking for the liquid was well known. So he got to work and duly cleaned up what must have been a gruesome task. Then he presented himself at the rum-tub next day when Jackie was drawing his tot.

For the benefit of the uninitiated, I have to explain that for a birthday one may be offered 'sippers', which quite literally means just that. It represents little loss for the giver, but several 'sippers' all round the mess can add up a lot to the recipient. Yet when one offers a tot for 'services rendered' this is taken to mean 'gulpers', an amount which can vary from a third to half the measure. It is ,however, considered very bad form to drink it all, particularly from a man known to enjoy his tot. Even so, some 'services rendered' may be thought extreme enough to warrant the entire tot, particularly if 'gulpers' was not specifically mentioned. Such was the case this time and Jan duly quaffed the lot, much to the utter chagrin of Jackie, who was so speechless that he didn't even protest.

Now many moons passed by, and some years later we find these two meeting up again. Jackie by this time is a Warrant Officer and Jan a C.P.O.. This meant that they were not in the same mess, and in fact the Warrant Officers did not have a rum issue. They could, however, quietly slip into the Chief's Mess, if invited. Thus Jackie accepted Jan's invite to come in for a 'wet' for old time's sake. To Jan this meant the usual 'sippers'. Imagine his horror when Jackie promptly sank the lot. "I've waited 7 years to be able to do that", was his satisfied remark. This time it was Jan who was speechless.

Our story is seen to be working its way back towards home waters and in a sense this is basically what was happening in our seaborne effort. Once it was clear that the Japanese had rather shot their bolt in the Indian Ocean, and were under pressure in the Pacific, then our Carriers could be used elsewhere. Indomitable had come back in August to carry out yet another Malta run. This time she was damaged and returned to UK for repair. Even more dramatic was the loss of Eagle on the operation. Though two TAGs were lost in fighter actions, none were lost with the ships.

The big new action that was put in hand was the invasion of North Africa from the Western end in November following on the heels of Alamein in October. Many TAGs will recall the odd situation of flying in aircraft painted with American markings that sported a prominent white star. All this despite the fact that they were very evidently Albacores to anyone of even limited aircraft recognition capability. However, the opposition was quickly overpowered, this time because of our much improved fighter strength, augmented by American aircraft. This was just as well, after the mauling that had occurred the previous year at Oran and Dakar. We did lose one TAG in a bombing attack at La Senia. This was Gordon Dixon, not the same man, but a namesake of the one who saw the Jap fleet. Also, during this action, AG Charlie 'Bungy' Williams, drove off an attacking fighter aircraft and believed he may possibly have shot it down. As so often with engagements of this kind, it could not be confirmed.

The end of 1942 also saw the beginning of the fight back in the Atlantic. Up to that point our shipping losses had steadily increased and we were on the verge of losing the battle, but now some small aircraft carriers were put into action and the Air Branch could take retaliatory action. These ships were generally known as "Woolworth Carriers". The Avenger was sunk in November and the Dasher blew up in March 1943. Yet both had previously been effective in their efforts. These ships were later augmented by more substantial ships known as 'Escort carriers', of which the Vindex was perhaps the most famous.

In fact aircraft were put aboard almost everything afloat. Some ships simply carried a fighter on a catapult. Once airborne he would have to ditch if not close to shore. No TAGs here of course. Yet other ships just had a flight deck built on top of their normal holds. They continued in their commercial role of transporting goods and were generally known as 'banana boats' or 'Mac-ships' because so many had 'Mac' in their name. In fact this term came from the name Merchant Aircraft Carrier. They carried about four Swordfish aircraft which necessarily remained on the flight deck, to the obvious disadvantage of the maintenance men.

Whatever can I say about all this sterling effort in the Battle of the Atlantic that can do justice to those involved ? Many books have been written in great detail to describe these events. One in particular I have in mind has covered this most excellently. As however, I am writing about TAGs, I cannot ignore such episodes, yet dare not pretend to match the fuller accounts. The 'Mac-ships' were crewed from one very large squadron, numbered 836, which was based at Eglinton in Northern Ireland. The crews did a round trip out and back and were then relieved. Thus next time out they were probably in a different ship. With so many in the pool, yet so few aboard, there was little chance of developing a squadron spirit. However, most TAGs quite enjoyed the relatively high standard of living conditions aboard these merchant ships as compared to the more spartan and disciplined naval vessels.

Flying conditions were a bit fraught with only a small deck and few arrester wires to catch. Atlantic weather also meant a pitching deck. In general they did not fly far from the ship but patrolled around the convoy, and few got themselves lost. Their presence usually drove the submarines under, so not many were able to get in direct attacks on submarines. I was, however, slightly surprised to find that those that did attack were often successful, which I haven't quite managed to explain, compared to my own limited experience of such events. This comment refers to depth charges. Rockets were clearly much better.

One particular change in the technical sphere concerned the increasing use of R/T (radio/telephony) or voice transmission. With the aircraft operating close to the ships such was well possible even on H/F. At first only the more limited H/F sets were used. It was some time before the more efficient VHF sets came into operation late in the war. So, early on, the TAG was often allowed to operate the radio because one had to have an 'ear' for it and be able to interpret what was said. Even so, the pilot would still get into the act if he wanted to, and tell everyone what he saw or was going to do. This was also the era in which a whole new range of code words was introduced, so the TAG had a list of these. In practice only a few got regularly used.

A particularly unfortunate incident took the life of one TAG aboard a Mac ship. This was Willie Shotton, a course colleague of Gordon Lambert and therefore one of the pre-war regulars. He had already done one tour with the Formidable and now found himself in the Atlantic on anti-sub work. By now the aircraft, though still the redoubtable Swordfish, were fitted with rockets, which were found to be the most effective weapons against surfaced submarines. Having only a makeshift flight deck everything had to be done 'up top'. So Willie was in his aircraft doing the usual D.I. whilst an electrician was checking out an adjacent aircraft. By some misfortune the circuits were made and a rocket was fired straight through poor Willie in the A/C nearby. As someone said "what a way to go !".

It was the Escort carriers who probably got more active in the role of U-boat attackers because they were used quite literally as submarine hunters, though this also meant flying in atrocious conditions, when perhaps patrolling aircraft might find it more convenient to sit out the storm. Submarines tended not to attack in the worst weather but might be caught on the top, themselves 'sitting it out'. Quite a few TAGs had cause to ditch on these operations, and as they had not then designed the immersion suit, such ditchings were not a pleasant matter. In fact when the chase stretched into Arctic convoys it brought a whole new element into the stress of such flying. A ditching in such waters almost certainly meant 'no survival'. In fact, towards the end, a point was reached where no TAG was taken, only a pilot and observer. This was partly decreed by the addition of extra petrol tanks. With VHF radio pilot operated and the radar in the observer's cockpit, the TAG had become superfluous.

Catalina flying boat

HMS Hermes

'The Great Escape' – by Nodrog. Depicting an encounter which took place on the 5th of April, 1942 from the Indomitable

MV Empire MacKendrick turning into wind to land on aircraft of 836 Squadron

836 Squadron 'M' Flight aboard Empire MacKendrick 1944. View from Swordfish aircraft on landing approach

CHAPTER 18

The Transformation and Two Visits to Kaa

In this narrative I have largely pursued my own story. It has not been possible to simultaneously relate the more inspiring events that were taking place elsewhere. Thus it was necessary to backtrack in time to catch up on other activities that occurred during 1942 and 1943. Now that I am moving into the era of 1944 and 1945 I propose to reverse the approach. My own actions during this time are of little consequence. Those of other TAGs are much more significant.

It will be noted that I have headed this chapter "The Transformation...". This it most certainly was. The Fleet Air Arm grew up fast. At the beginning of the war it was a Cinderella. At the end the Aircraft Carriers were the major war vessels. For the aircrews the significant change was the quantity of fighter planes. From 1944 onwards they could mount large strikes well supported by fighter cover. Whilst the Barracuda was not a very imposing aircraft, the Avenger most certainly was. The element of risk was still present and no one would belittle the courage still required to maintain a series of operations, yet it was greatly heartening to fly with large numbers of one's colleagues and see even more planes giving cover above. The Service had come a long way from a few pitiful Swordfish setting out alone.

There were several major attacks on the Tirpitz by Barracudas. All were similar in character. Though they did not sink the ship they were successful to a degree. It has been said that the armour piercing bombs might have done better if released higher, and that the pilots pressed home their attacks too enthusiastically. That is conjecture. In the end it took 4000lb and 8000lb bombs from the RAF to take the final toll. It might be recalled just how much Illustrious suffered and survived from lesser bomb sizes. Tirpitz was a tough nut to crack. The results do not detract from the courage of the crews taking part.

It is my privilege to now offer the final part of the story by TAG Gordon "Blondie" Lambert who takes us through two attacks on Tirpitz, and finally into the Indian Ocean and the Pacific to attack the Japanese. His personal story is exceptional but it also embraces the work of many TAGs in these theatres.

"Blondie" Lamberts story continues from Chapter 9 :-

Lee-on-Solent, as post-war visits have proved, is an extremely nice place. The glorious view across the Solent, the beautifully maintained grass spaces in front of the FAA Memorial which lists the names of all who gave their lives during the conflict. Such was not the case in the later years of the war. My main recollection being of Lee Tower where the local dances were held and the local pub just outside the camp gates. I was never quite 'at home' at Lee, even though it was the Fleet Air Arm Headquarters. To be in 'X' Squadron was like being a number in an enormous 'lucky dip' and only the Good Lord himself or the Drafting Master-at-Arms could decide your fate.

Such was the position in which I found myself at the end of 1943. Its an ill wind..........as they say and I couldn't believe my good fortune when I found that the Drafting Jaunty had been an old shipmate and had a special affinity for TAGs. Not to put too fine a point on proceedings I took a few soundings on the possibility of a quiet number, preferably somewhere near home and lots of week-ends.

A few days later the grapevine fed a message for me to see the Drafting MAA.

"How about a spell with the RAF ?"

"That suits me"

"OK. I'll fix you up to go to No.9 Wing."

Barracudas= forming-up prior to setting out for Tirpitz

At that time, to be fair to the Joss Man, I'd never known FAA Squadrons to have wing numbers before, so I thought at last my luck has changed.

I was, to say the least, a little surprised to find that No.9 Wing was stationed at R.N.A.S.Crail close by St.Andrews. Had the RAF taken over a Naval Air Station ?

No.9 Wing was of course a combination of two squadrons, 820 with Chief TAG 'Darkie' Holroyd and 826 with Chief TAG Len Barrick. Had I been conned ? I found I was to fly with the Wing leader. The aircraft were Barracudas and many horrific tales were told about wings folding when in flight and mysterious crashes on take off, and what might happen in a steep dive was best not thought about.

'Darkie' Holroyd was an old school chum of mine. We were in the same class at school in Redcar and in those days, when we would puncture a teacher's bike and then be given threepence to repair it, little did we realise that in a few short years we would be much more destructive and with the blessing of H.M. Government.

Although I had heard about Len Barrick, I had never actually been stationed with him, either ashore or afloat. He was a great character. He had already earned himself a CGM in the Med. and was later to collect a DSM in the Pacific.

I will always remember his antics in the mess. He was never without a pint pot in his hand and strangely enough it was always about threequarters full. He appeared to be always on the verge of being very merry but never drunk. I don't think I ever saw him with an empty glass or come to that a full one either.

When a squadron is forming up there is an untold amount of work to be done. The ground crews are getting to know the aircrews and vice versa. Aircrews are getting to know each other. In the early days of the war when naval aircrews were fewer in number nearly everyone knew everyone else, but as time went on more and more H.O.s were joining the air branch and consequently names and faces were not so familiar as had once been the case.

In spite of the fact that they had not been born in a 'Pussers Blanket' their undoubted ability, loyalty and comradeship was never in doubt. Names that even now spring to mind include Sam Dunn, 'Pincher' Martin, 'Bing' Crosby, 'King' Cole, Jeff

148

Robertson, Taff Rees, Taff Howells, Sam Winfindale and Taff Stone. Come to think of it, I believe Darkie, Len and myself were the only pre-war regulars.

Our working up was typical of the time, lots of flying, both day and night, compass swinging, radio and gunnery exercises and for the pilots lots of circuits and bumps.

Even those very tiring and trying times were not without their lighter moments.

By virtue of, at that time anyway, my fair hair I was inevitably called 'Blondie'. When on night flying exercises certain a/c were often called upon to drop flares so that the rest of the squadron loaded with torpedoes could make their attack on a well illuminated target.

The code word which was the signal to start dropping was 'Blondie' and by accident or design I'll never know, the code word to cease dropping was 'Darkie'.

A recent newcomer to the squadron who knew both Darkie and myself from days long gone was attending his first night flying briefing and it was thought prudent by the briefing officer that the newcomer should know the flare dropping procedure. He therefore asked him :-

"Do you know about 'Blondie' and 'Darkie' ?"

To which came the reply :-

"What have those two b_____s been up to now ?"

At one stage during our working up, all activity came to an abrupt halt. One of our diligent air mechanics found a very faint hair line crack in one of the wing locking pins, all carrier borne aircraft at that time having folding wings. Various theories as to the cause and suggestions for a cure were put forward, and I suppose someone, somewhere, did something, because we resumed flying and eventually came to the big day early in June 1944 when we were to fly aboard our big new aircraft carrier 'Indefatigable'.

I think it was at this stage that to all intents and purposes the 'Wing' idea broke up and both 820 and 826 squadrons became independent units. I became part of 820 and flew with the Senior Pilot. With his observer we were to stay together as a team until the end of the war.

'Indefat' was a far cry from the 'Eagle'. We had crew rooms with bunks, our mess was comfortable with our own hot plate, fridge and even the mess stools were padded. Our action station, if not flying, was in the Wardroom and our action mess was also the Wardroom. All in all life seemed to be on the up and up.

We continued our flying exercises, doing long range sorties in the many lochs which abound in Scotland. This frequently called for us to fly along valleys which opened out to a large loch and there would be a ship at anchor. We would make dummy low level, dive bombing and torpedo attacks before returning to 'Indefat' to refuel, rearm and start all over again.

It is said "where ignorance is bliss..." and this surely was the case whilst we were doing all this flying.

Then came a day in July 1944 when we sailed northwards towards the Arctic Circle. When we were clear of harbour the aircrews were called together to be told that our target was the German Battleship 'Tirpitz' which was lying alongside a jetty in Kaa Fjord in Northern Norway. Now we knew the reason for all our flying over Scottish lochs, they were not unlike Norwegian Fjords. In company with other carriers and escorts we sailed northwards.

Before sailing, in fact whilst doing dummy attacks in the Scottish lochs, a new formation was adopted instead of the old 'V' formation. Aircraft flew in slightly staggered pairs.

The leader would take up his position with his No.2 slightly below and on his starboard side. No.3 would be directly behind and below No.1. No.4 would be similarly positioned behind No.2. Nos 5 and 6 would then take up their positions in a similar manner. These six aircraft would form one 'flight'. Another six aircraft would form up in identical manner and become a second flight and so on. This type of formation proved to be infinitely better than the old method. It gave better all round visibility for each aircraft and gave better fire power - there was less chance of hitting your oppo! The value of this greater availability of guns was to be proved later in the Pacific.

As we approached Northern Norway we were briefed about the impending attack on Tirpitz.

She was an ever present threat to the Russian convoys, lying in wait in a remote almost inaccessible fjord. She was tied up alongside a jetty sheltering under almost sheer sides of the rock face which formed the fjords. Smoke generators had been built in the rock face and at the first sign of danger they were operated and covered the fjord in a thick blanket of smoke.

It was necessary therefore to try to catch them unawares and at least start the attack before they could operate the smoke generators.

Whilst the aircrews were being briefed (we had an excellent model of the fjord and surrounding area) the ground crews were doing their last minute checks and the armourers were busy loading up with 1600lb AP bombs.

Briefing complete we waddled out to our respective aircraft well wrapped up and carrying our 'survival kits'. After all, if we were shot down or damaged we could make our way to Sweden !

The Flight Deck Officer gave the signal to start engines and we knew then that we were under Starters Orders.

The goofers platform was extremely well manned with all the ghouls waiting to see if we could get airborne. We had quite a number of aircraft lined up on the flight deck and come to think of it we had never gone off before with a 1600 pounder slung underneath. We could feel the ship heel over as the fleet turned into wind and the thin jet of steam from a pipe set into the forward end of the flight deck was soon streaming back along the centre line of the deck. The fleet was now turned into wind.

We were the first to go off. The FDO waved his little green flag above his head and rotated it faster and faster until finally he dropped it to his side and we moved slowly forward gathering speed with every turn of the wheels until we ran out of deck. The aircraft dropped a few feet, the engine groaned and all I could see was the massive bow of the ship. The flight deck had disappeared from view. The engine was equal to the occasion as we gradually gained height and circled the fleet waiting for the remaining aircraft to fly off and form up.

Eventually all were airborne and in formation.

Other carriers in company were similarly engaged and finally the full striking force was assembled.

It was 0030 on the morning of 17th July 1944. The sky was clear and in that latitude at that time of year the sun never really sets, so in spite of the time, it was to all intents and purposes daylight.

We set course and flew at zero feet until we reached the Norwegian coast before climbing to about 10,000 feet for our dive bombing attack. We crossed the coast south of Kaa Fjord whilst a diversionary raid was being carried out to the north. A flight of fighter bombers, in addition to carrying bombs, had parcels of aluminium foil strips which they were to drop in the hope of confusing the German radar system.

Just how successful they were in their efforts I'll never know, but what is certain is that the Germans were ready for us.

As we crossed the coast, the midnight sun shining on the glaciers and air so clear that one could see for miles almost shut out all thoughts of the purpose of our being there. From the air the view was magnificent and it was unthinkable that such beautiful scenery was soon to give way to savage destruction.

We eventually sighted Kaa Fjord and caught a brief glimpse of Tirpitz as smoke began pouring from the smoke generators. It was absolutely essential that the attack be carried out with the minimum of delay if we were to have any chance of success at all. The fighter bombers which had come in from the north had gone in first with a fair amount of success. Unfortunately for us the ack ack guns were now fully manned and the gunners had very quickly rubbed the sleep out of their eyes. They soon had our range and in no time at all shells were bursting rather too close for comfort. In my opinion it is at this stage in any attack when the true value of all our training and discipline is most in evidence. It was as true in this case as it had been in the Mediterranean and was to be in the Pacific.

The cockpit drill immediately preceding the attack was carried out as though it was just another exercise. Guns were cocked, bomb switches made and fuses set. There was little point in going all that way if any single detail was forgotten and either the bomb hung up or failed to explode because a fuze hadn't been set. You haven't got time to cock the guns if a fighter suddenly appears on your tail.

My pilot, in whom I had the utmost confidence, called out "stand by, we're going down".

The nose dipped as he pushed the control column forward and as our angle of dive increased so did the speed. The effect of this manoeuvre is to subject the occupants to negative 'g' and a feeling of weightlessness. It can be quite disconcerting if you are not strapped in and suddenly find yourself floating around the cockpit.

Facing backwards, as was the case in Barracudas, I could see the rest of the squadron begin their dives and follow us down. It was rather strange that in spite of all the ack ack fire and the thought of going down into the smoke blanket, did not concern me so much as the thought "I wonder if they really did find a cure for those cracked locking pins". I remember one suggestion put forward that if a patch was put over the wing camera aperture it would reduce the pressure inside the wing structure. One of the pilots offered to test the theory if the originator of the idea would fly with him. He never did - but here we were and with more to think about.

Just before we reached the smoke which must have been about six or seven hundred feet above the Tirpitz I felt the aircraft lift slightly as the pilot released the bomb, and then started to pull out of the dive. Pulling out of a dive has exactly the opposite effect as going into one. The aircraft is subject to positive 'g' and forces the aircrew down into their seats, lower jaws are forced open and cheeks are forced down like a bloodhound jowls. If one is standing it is virtually impossible to remain upright as knees buckle.

Anyway, pull out of the dive we did, but not before we had entered into the smoke. The wings had stayed on and our bomb had gone, although truth to tell we never saw it land.

I now turned my thoughts to more immediate problems. The wings were still on but what were we likely to meet when we came out of the smoke ? Anti-aircraft fire there was in profusion but fortunately no enemy fighter aircraft. It was a relief to be out of the smoke - at least we could see where we were - but then of course so could the AA guns crews. The drill on completing the attack was to make our way independently to the coast where we would all meet together to be escorted back to the fleet by the fighter bombers.

As we arrived at the coast and circled a couple of times I was rather concerned as to the fate of some of the others. There certainly was not as many as started out. Eventually we set course for the Fleet.

We arrived back at our rendezvous to find the Fleet waiting. As we circled around waiting for the carrier to turn into the wind for landing several stragglers came in and joined up with us. It was a great relief to find that all our squadron had returned. The signal was given for the Fleet to turn into wind, a relief A/S patrol was flown off, and finally the signal for us to land on was given.

One by one we came home for an early breakfast.

Breakfast had to wait however for at least another couple of hours. There was the very detailed interrogation and debriefing procedures to go through. It never ceased to amaze me how reluctant the interrogators were to believe what was told to them. Every story and incident was checked and double checked.

Eventually they were convinced that we had told all and a very tired but relieved squadron sat down to breakfast and looked forward to some sleep. Later in the day we learned that at least one more attack on Tirpitz was necessary. The first raid had only been a partial success. For the next few days we stooged around the cold arctic wastes with inevitable A/S patrols.

When not flying we spent many hours playing cribbage, uckers (ludo), reading, writing, checking our radios (which we never seemed to use) and making sure the guns would fire when they were required. We would spend a lot of time with our ground crews who were a magnificent crowd of chaps. Each was confident that his aircraft was in absolute tip-top condition and many is the time the ground crew had worked all through the night to make sure his aircraft was ready for the next day. It was comforting to know that we had competent and reliable ground crews and had the utmost confidence in them. After all we frequently had enough to worry about without wondering if the aircraft would keep flying.

One day a group of us were in the hangar when a couple of aircraft were being loaded with depth charges. Now with Barracuda aircraft having such high wings a special portable winch was used to raise the bomb or whatever to the underside of the wing. The winch was mounted on the top surface of the wing and the wire rope led through the wing and attached to the bomb carrier which had been fixed to the bomb on the deck. The winch was operated and carrier and bomb were raised together, a special locking device in the wing then secured the carrier to the spars in the wing. Normally the operation went quite successfully and without trouble. Sometimes the gremlins got to work as they did when one of the TAGs was assisting his armourer to load his aircraft with depth charges. The TAG was operating the winch and the armourer was guiding the bomb rack into position. Unfortunately the locking device would not engage properly. The TAG looking from the top could see exactly what the trouble was but it could only be rectified from beneath the wing. After a few minutes unsuccessful endeavour by the armourer to the shouted instructions from the TAG, the TAG in desperation called out "use your bloody head man".

To the absolute horror of the TAG, the armourer did no more but lowered his head and brought it up with a sickening thud on the underside of the depth charge. The armourer collapsed on to the deck with severe concussion, but at least the bomb rack locked into place. After he had recovered and was asked why he did such a stupid thing he couldn't offer any rational explanation. Perhaps he was trying to 'work his ticket'.

Since carrying out the first Tirpitz raid we had done a few A/S patrols and searches looking for German supply ships without much success. Towards the end of August, about the 24th I think, a report came in about shipping movements in Lang Fjord. There was the usual increased activity. Aircraft were loaded once again with 1600lb AP bombs while the aircrews were being briefed.

Briefing complete, we manned our aircraft and the signal was given to start engines. After they had been ticking over for a few minutes we were told to switch off but remain in the aircraft. There had been a delay for some reason the exact details of which elude me.

Because of the large number of aircraft taking part it was found necessary to use the catapult for launching the first few aircraft. There was not enough flight deck for the front aircraft to get airborne.

The first aircraft to go off was to be a Barracuda and to save any embarrassment to the TAG concerned I shall not reveal his name. The signal was given to start up again but there was still several minutes delay. During this time the TAG in the aircraft on the catapult had dropped off to sleep, neither was he wakened by the starting up of the engine.

Being 'catapulted' needs to be experienced in order to be fully aware of the stresses both to crew and aircraft. When it is considered that from a standing start the aircraft is airborne flying at between 100 and 120 knots in a distance of about 150 feet the acceleration is of the order of 3g.

Blissfully unaware of the activity all around, the TAG slept peacefully on and to his regret not strapped into his seat.

Eventually the FDO gave his signal, the booster operator pulled his lever and the aircraft hurtled along the catapult track. In effect, the aircraft accelerated forward leaving the TAG behind. His seat left him and he and his radio met with a sickening thud. It broke clear from its mounting and together they finished up inside the tail end of the fuselage. He was so badly hurt that it was necessary for them to land on again once all the strike aircraft were airborne.

In accordance with our flight plan we took up formation and again flying at very low level we set course for the Norwegian coast. On approaching the coast we climbed steadily to about 8000 feet and then turned northwards towards Lang Fjord. Once again we had stretched out before us the magnificent scenery we had witnessed on the first Tirpitz raid, only this time it was mid-afternoon.

As we turned into Lang Fjord, steaming along with a couple of other smaller merchant ships was an oil tanker of some 8000 tons. The surface of the water was like a mirror disturbed only by the wake of the ships.

We attacked in sub flights of three. Going in first we were met by very intense cannon fire, I would say something of the order of 20mm. It was a very frightening experience to have tracers streaming by on either side and knowing that tracers were only about one in five, where were the non-tracer shells going ?

We had done a considerable amount of dive bombing training and so were accustomed to manoeuvring as the pilot lined up the aircraft to aim the bomb at the target, but I for one never got accustomed to being somebody's target

Personally I always felt more alarmed at the greater concentration of cannon fire at the shorter ranges than the heavier anti-aircraft fire which seemed to predominate around the Tirpitz. After all a single 20mm cannon shell can do just as much damage in the right place as its heavier brother.

Although one feels that you are never going to pull out of the dive, it can only be a matter of seconds before it is "bombs away", and then the gravitational tug as the aircraft pulls out.

By the time we had pulled out of our dive and banked around, No.s 2 and 3 had completed their attack.

The ship had made a violent alteration of course but it had been to no avail. Smoke and flames were pouring out from the bowels of the ship and the bow had almost completely disappeared. Our second sub flight was then sent in to complete the job whilst the third and fourth sub flights attacked the remaining supply ships.

Highly delighted with our success we set course for 'home'. We were still flying fairly low over land on our way back when I was surprised to see a man and woman run out from an isolated cottage and to our delight we saw them excitedly jump up and down waving a Union Jack.

On crossing the coast we were somewhat surprised to find ourselves being fired on by a 'Flak' ship which was lying close inshore. One of our flight escorts, seeing what was happening, did a half roll turn and went into a steep dive towards the ship. I could see him open fire and tracer shells raked across the deck. There was a burst of orange flame and debris rose into the air as the Flak ship disintegrated. There must be a moral there somewhere because I'm certain that had he not opened fire on us then no one would have given it a second look.

Once again we made our rendezvous with the Fleet and as it turned into wind we came in to land. All the Barracudas returned safely once again.

A few days later we were told that the second attack on the Tirpitz was to take place.

The drill for the second attack was to be similar to that used in the first. The only difference being that this second attack was to take place in the afternoon. Ah well, perhaps they'll have their heads down and not be expecting an afternoon attack.

We were to lead the attack again and it was our turn to go off the catapult. I made sure I kept awake and was strapped firmly to my seat.

I suppose we knew in our hearts that we would be expected. The fighter bombers carried out their diversionary sortie and dropped their aluminium foil. The Germans were not fooled, as we approached Kaa Fjord we could see the smoke already starting to spread out over Tirpitz. The anti-aircraft gunners were up to their usual high degree of accuracy and this time there were enemy fighter aircraft in the sky as well.

We maintained our course and up to now had not been attacked by fighters. The cockpit drill was carried out and once again we were in position to start the attack.

The signal was given to attack and then came the feeling of weightlessness as the aircraft nosed over and started to dive. At about 1500 feet the bomb was released and then the effect of 'g' as we pulled out of the dive. The fighter bombers had gone in first a few minutes before us and were milling around waiting for us to drop our heavier stuff and then escort us back to the ship.

I'm sure that it was the presence of our fighters which protected us from the German FW190s and ME109s. Several times the German fighters would try to get to grips with the Barracudas but our escort rose to the occasion and fought them off.

We in No.9 Wing all came safely through the raid although such was not the case with the fighters. Some had been shot down, one for certain had been blown up by his own bomb as he pressed home his attack at very low level. Many of the others were damaged.

It is a wonderful sight to see the Fleet when returning from a journey such as we had been on and the precision with which they turn into wind as though controlled as a single unit.

The signal to land on is given and some three and a half hours after take off we were back home for the inevitable interrogation.

I can't remember, if I ever knew, what casualties were suffered in the other carrier's squadron but we had the satisfaction of knowing that we had all returned safely.

We did not sink the Tirpitz but I believe we caused sufficient damage to put it out of action for a while. It was eventually moved to Tromso where it was sunk by Lancasters in November 1944.

The Fleet set course southwards and as we neared the Scottish mainland the two Barracuda squadrons flew off to land at the Naval Air Station at Machrihanish. We celebrated our return ashore in the fashion well established for such occasions.

Rumours were rife as to our future and we had not long to wait before being told that the wing was to be disbanded and that we were to return to Lee-on-Solent where a new 820 would be formed.

It was about the middle of October 1944 when we flew our Barracudas for the last time and I don't think any one of us was really sorry. We had to take them to the Naval Air Station at Dunino before travelling by train back to Lee-on-Solent.

Blondie Lambert's story continues in Chapter 20

Airspeed Oxford

CHAPTER 19

Friendly Gunfire

I have made an attempt to maintain some sequence in the time scale of this story, otherwise the reader may lose track of when and where. It is therefore with an apology that I interrupt Gordon Lambert's enthralling story, and suggest that perhaps we are leaving the best till last.

From Lee-on-Solent, and following promotion to Acting P.O., I was soon on draft to Yeovilton. This airfield together with its satellite Charlton Horethorne was a hive of activity almost totally concerned with advanced training of newly qualified pilots. The circuit was alive with aircraft on deck landing training generally known as circuits and bumps. There was also the fascinating sight of several pilots riding ice cream tricycles around the apron with covers over their heads. I was later to learn that they were practising radar interceptions ! What could they possibly want a TAG for in all this ?

There were some Oxfords, in which other pilots were getting instrument flying training. It seemed that though they used visors and special tinted windscreens to give a dark outlook, they also liked to get a little of the real thing whenever there was cloud about. Unfortunately this often meant they were lost when finally coming out of it. These training craft were only fitted with HF voice radio with a range of not much more than 30 miles and they might finish up a good deal further away than that. So what about putting a Geep radio in the back, together with a TAG to get a bearing ? Four of us had been sent to set up this idea. These included Stan Browning as a P.O. colleague. Stan was pretty good on the piano and drums and was keen to run his own band after the war. As we haven't managed to contact him I often wonder if he was successful. The squadron was No.759, 'E' Flight. The first step was to install the radios in the aircraft. We soon had a few fitted and started regular flying. We weren't needed much of the time, and being right there behind pilot and instructor I took great interest in what was going on. Apart from actually getting hold of the controls I soon knew the rules for flying on instruments. This had an odd sequel. When at a later date elsewhere, I was allowed to take an aircrafts controls I quite naturally watched the instruments rather than look out through the windscreen, and the pilot at the time found this intriguing.

It happened that there was frequent need for flights to other airfields that were engaged in similar training activities. We would then be taken for navigational back-up. Our efforts in this sphere were anything but satisfactory. It needed two DF stations to give us a fix and this would be given in Latitude and Longitude. The position would then have to be translated onto our maps. If lost in bad weather, with a pilot twisting and turning looking for something to latch on to as a landmark, one could become even more lost before identifying where one was ten minutes before. The DF stations didn't take kindly to multiple requests. Their system was only meant to aid aircraft flying steady courses above cloud. For a start we really needed our own DF station right at Yeovilton itself. Short of getting VHF the only hope was to know all the available W/T DF stations and be prepared to change frequency as necessary. With luck one might find a station at one's destination, from which a simple bearing would suffice. With war-time security preventing the general issue of a document like a RAFAC (Radio Aid Facility Aircraft Charts) such as came along post-war, it became necessary to glean and assemble the information from various sources. It was a collation task of some magnitude but before long we had produced a useful volume.

One port of call on these cross-country trips was Hinstock near Stafford. This place always had a gathering of TAGs in the crew room and there were some enjoyable reunions and the usual relay of information about others in the clan. On the return from one of these visits we met some bad weather and dropped in at Moreton Valence, an RAF station near Bristol. I was immediately struck by the excessive security. One gathered we should't be there. Then we saw it. The first jet. At that time it was quite fascinating and certainly no whisper of its existence had come our way. Yet it was flying around and so it wouldn't be long before everyone knew. A pity it took so long to develop further. British jets barely got into the war.

At Yeovilton I enquired about an Observers course and the chance of a commission that I had been promised. What C.W.papers was the reply ? Evidently none had been raised or they had gone astray. I was even taken to task for asking. Apparently one didn't ask to be considered ; one had to wait until chosen. At least they now did start them.

I noted that just about everyone else was drawing their tot and I was not exactly teetotal. That had simply been the automatic result when first qualifying to change from U/A (under/age) some two years previously. In the desert there was none to be drawn. Now I requested a change from T to G (Grog). The Jaunty (Master at Arms) suggested it was tradition for the first one to go to him. He was pulling my leg as it was quite against regulations. On the other hand there was a code of practice related to tots that was not in K.R. and A.I.s and it paid to be bound by them. The Jaunty got "gulpers" which meant nearly half of it. I was not put out as this move coincided with my birthday and I got birthday 'sippers' from several chums. I was fast appreciating the advantages of the P.O.s mess.

My stay at Yeovilton was short-lived and at the end of March I was drafted up to Arbroath to take a TAG2s course. This was the Naval Air Signal School as well as the Observers school and the place was therefore flooded with TAGs. Once again there were numerous reunions. The course itself was not onerous being largely a refresher of standard procedures. It did serve to introduce a lot of new equipment in the radio world that was just coming into operation. Perhaps the newest aspect from our point of view was the introduction of R/T (radio telephony). Hardly new to pilots who had been using it since 1940 but for those of us who had spent much time on a morse key this was different. We all developed high pitched voices, as instructed, to overcome the background noise typical in HF working. Some time later when I came to use it, I found that the high voice was ludicrous because by then we were using VHF.

The course only required a few trips in an Anson for W/T exercises but it did also include further Air Gunnery and for this we were sent down to St.Merryn in Cornwall. They were still trundling away down there in the familiar Swordfish and we repeated all the usual firing exercises with the Vickers K gun. So as a TAG2 I qualified to become a CPO as soon as I was confirmed PO, after one years acting time. From one extreme to the other, it all seemed untrue.

A little earlier there had been introduced a ranking known as A.G.I. or Air Gunnery Instructor. This was an alternative to the TAG2 course and still qualified for CPO in the same way. Those who opted for it went first to Whale Island, and later took a special Air Gunnery course. It was quite popular amongst those who did not get along too well with the radio side. It produced a number of senior TAGs who could carry out the prime function of Air Gunnery Instructors to future TAGs and Observers and were also proficient in giving parade ground drill. One other feature never quite came off. It was thought that in mass strikes using several squadrons they would hold loose formation if attacked by fighters. Then the defensive crossfire from several aircraft might be more effective. It would be an A.G.I.s job to brief and instruct on arcs of fire. As the guns were still small calibre it was a bit pathetic, though the best in the circumstances. In the event there were few big strikes of this kind. The RAF had similar ideas for use by large formations of bombers and ran an extensive advanced course for Gunnery Leaders. A few of our A.G.I.s later went on such a course in qualifying as A.G.I.1s.

Whilst we were on course at St.Merryn the D Day landings took place, and the progress was followed with great excitement. Most people had their fingers crossed and I heard no one express a wish to be there. When we had travelled south through London and then on to the West it was clear that big things were afoot. The traffic was considerable. As we now returned to Lee-on-Solent the support waves were going in and the roads to all ports were cluttered with every conceivable type of vehicle. However, apart from flying some A/S patrols at either end of the English Channel to give cover to the enormous invasion fleet, this was not the Fleet Air Arm's battle. They had other problems.

Somewhat to my surprise I didn't get a draft to an operational unit. Clearly there were now TAGs galore and I was in for a longer rest. I was sent to 776 squadron the F.R.U. at Speke near Liverpool. From there I went almost at once to their subsidiary flight at R.A.F.Woodvale, near Southport.

An F.R.U. is a Fleet Requirements Unit and behind that bare and uninspiring description lies a depth of activity largely unsung. In a coverage of a Telegraphist Air Gunners work I make no apology for dwelling on the F.R.U.s. In fact it would be criminal not to make much of the flying carried out by TAGs in the several squadrons that existed for these roles. It is perhaps a pity that my experience was limited to but the one squadron of this type, and that was in one of the easiest of locations. All TAGs

Boulton Paul Defiant

will have served in an F.R.U. at one time or another and for some it was their major squadron duty.

Clearly the Fleet's requirements can cover a wide range and they exercised this to the full. Senior Naval Officers of that era were not always air minded, and might well expect aircraft to be on call at any time. Often such aircraft carried out their tasks in the most appalling weather conditions. The tasks began primarily with target towing for ships carrying out practise shoots. This might be when leaving harbour to join convoys. To simulate speedier targets there would be no drogue and the guns would aim off. Faster aircraft such as Mosquitos would then be used. For another task the ships might wish to check radar, and an aircraft would be called upon to fly approach courses. There might be calls to search for missing boats. In fact this could extend to anything missing - ship-towed targets, buoys, mines, aircraft etc.. The F.R.U.s were not immune to operational roles. There was the famous flight by a Maryland from 771 at Hatston which went into Bergen when RAF reconnaissance had failed, and disclosed that Bismarck had in fact sailed.

These duties would be carried out using obsolete or operationally rejected aircraft. So not only might they have dubious flying qualities but their supply of spares would also be in doubt. Almost anything was pressed into service and with the special faster aircraft the squadrons built up a peculiar range of types such as Defiants, Rocs, Martinets, Chesapeakes and Whitleys apart from Swordfish, Fulmars, Albacores, Skuas and Walrus. There were odd ones barely heard of such as the Blackburn Botha. Name a British or American aircraft of the war era and one of the F.R.U.s somewhere was likely to have had one.

The F.R.U. squadrons would normally be stationed to serve a port and this could mean remote and unwelcome places such as Hatston or Twatt for Scapa Flow, or Machrihanish for the Clyde. Also most Naval Air Stations had a resident squadron or flight with F.R.U. responsibilities. Those TAGs who got a draft to one of these squadrons at the popular venues could consider themselves very lucky. Most Naval Air Stations, however, were in rather remote parts, particularly in Scotland. With the strains of their form of operation it is perhaps hardly surprising that the F.R.U.s had more than their share of flying accidents. A large number of TAGs were lost with F.R.U. squadrons.

I was lucky to get one of the more attractive venues. The flight at Woodvale towed drogues for the Royal Navy's gunnery school HMS Queen Charlotte at Ainsdale. This establishment had taken over a pre-war holiday camp and many of the gunners who were being trained were destined for the Merchant ships, all of which now mounted defensive guns. Ships joining convoy at Liverpool were looked after by the parent squadron from Speke, but occasionally such a task would come our way.

Though towing was regarded as a very humdrum affair it did have its moments. To begin with the winch operator was a very necessary and important crewman. He had to keep a clear head and attain some skill or he could black out half the local county. He was faced with a fearsome looking drum of cable which when winding on or off was just waiting to pounce on the unwary. Fingers, helmet leads or neckerchiefs could easily get trapped in the works. A false move with the brake might cause several thousand feet of wire to break off and drape itself over high tension cables. This was not unknown amongst pupil winch operators. Then there was the slipping of the target sleeve. This surprisingly enough was achieved by the very basic system of cutting the codline with a knife. To do so meant opening up a hatch in the floor of the aircraft and leaning out through the hole. We would of course be hooked to our G string and have the knife tied to our wrist. Even so it is quite an experience to hang out under the aircraft. The wire ran off the drum under the pull of the slipstream on the drogue. One controlled speed and amount by a manual brake. Sometimes the wire could foul or become cross-threaded from its guide. At worst this might mean cutting the wire out at sea. To wind in there was a four bladed propeller about 30" in diameter which turned into the slipstream (so that's what that extra propeller was for !). This then rotated and turned the drum. The last few feet had to be inched in to get the codline in view. Too fast and one had the whole gubbins jammed in the pulleys -a right mess. The gunners didn't often shoot the drogue off - for many of their exercises they weren't trying to - so for most tows it was just once out and then a couple of hours boredom till it came in again. Well, not quite. A towing machine once sent the now famous signal "I'm pulling this target not pushing it".

Such a signal might well have been sent on other occasions. Fortunately not very often. The offenders were the heavy guns. We would fly at some 8000 feet with perhaps 4000 feet of tow line out. Sometimes I thought these chaps practised a box barrage which included the towing aircraft as well as the target. For the light guns we only needed 1500 feet of tow and usually flew at 2000 feet. Radio was pilot operated HF on voice and we were linked in by intercom..No morse to bother about, though elsewhere towing aircraft did sometimes have W/T sets.

When I first got to Woodvale we were using Defiants, but later got delivery of Martinets which were a bit newer and more comfortable and dependable. Towing did become humdrum but fortunately the interest was soon enlivened by the arrival of winged targets. The first versions were simply 16 foot wing span gliders made of wood and fabric. They had a metal centre skid and negligible flight characteristics. They were tied on to the wire at the end of the runway and one took off with the target following behind on about 100 feet of tow wire. In the air their behaviour was just like any drogue. If not shot down one could land them for further use. The TAG would bend down through the hatch as usual and from there he could see the target flying some 30 feet below and trailing behind. He could talk to his pilot and guide him to let the target make a touch-down. Then a cut of the codline and the target stopped very rapidly on its skid. The aircraft flew on round to make a normal landing after a further circuit. It worked well except that at first the pilots, who couldn't see the target, just didn't believe how low they had to get and often a touch-down would not be made until nearly the end of the runway. This itself was almost helpful as it let those recovering the target get clear quickly before the plane landed.

So far so good, but these were soon followed by 32 foot winged targets. This device was a much more realistic affair and a near nightmare to tow. The target was built with a metal skin and though standing only two foot high it had a fuselage like a large torpedo and was fitted with pneumatic wheels. There were four of these. Two in tandem on the fuselage and one at each wing mid-point. This was unfortunate for landing as the target just ran on and on and not necessarily straight. First we had to get them off the ground. The wing span was nearly as

Miles Martinet

776 Squadron, Woodvale, 1944. 32ft wing span Winged Targets came to grief all over and around Woodvale airfield. This one finished up under a bridge carrying the Cheshire Lines railway across a culvert and farm track

much as the towing aircraft. These targets had flying characteristics only limited by a heavy weight in the nose. Once when one broke away in the air it lost its nose weight and the target glided for miles. We weren't aware of all this when we started and tried to take one off using existing techniques. We gave it a bit more wire than usual but it was still too close to us. Once airborne it lifted up to our level and then spiralled in our slipstream until it broke away. Before that it had pulled our tail round in the most alarming manner. At the time I wasn't quick enough to twig the solution. On reflection it became clear that we had to let out the tow as soon as the target became clear of the ground. This was tricky because it mustn't be so quick as to let it drop back on the deck nor yet to hit any airfield fences or whatever else was outside the perimeter track. This was one reason I hadn't dared to lengthen the tow on the first attempt. We found that a medium speed of slip could be achieved and the target stabilised at about 250 feet of tow. A crew arrived from the boffin's group which developed the things, after we lost the first one. This included TAG Alec Shimmin and they showed us how to handle them. Even they weren't familiar with landing techniques as the targets weren't meant to be brought back. Who would want to cut adrift such a sleek looking machine if it hadn't been damaged by gunfire ? Alec brought a special attachment device which was simple enough but avoided the need to splice the wire at each tow which was an aspect which had bothered us. When slipping one had to cut the wire and this would otherwise have led to a lot of tedious splicing.

Once safely in the air the tow was no bother but quite unlike the 16 foot target which followed the aircraft like a drogue, the 32 footer had its own ideas. It was fascinating on a high shoot with lots of wire out to do a 180 degree turn and pass the target still going in the other direction ! Of course it eventually felt the pull and followed the tug around.

So we faced up to the problem of not only taking the things off and towing, but also trying to land them. The 16 footer target technique just didn't work. We now had 250 feet of wire out and the target didn't immediately respond to whatever the aircraft did. The TAG could still see it out through the bottom hatch and give left or right directions but he was unable to judge the height with any certainty unless, perhaps, there was some sunshine and some target shadow. Slowing down was the problem. As the aircraft slowed the target overtook. Its heavy nose weight kept it down so that it

161

swung underneath the towing aircraft. When belatedly it did slow and the wire was pulled taught then once more the target was lifted. Thus on an approach the target would go into an undulating swing like a switchback as viewed from the ground. It was the luck of the draw whether it actually touched down when straight and level. Most often it hit nose first and broke up. If the slip was successful the target ran a long way before coming to rest. The R.A.F. threatened to ban us before we wrote off one of their aircraft. Our advance in technique was slow because every pilot and TAG was having a try and each step had to be learned again and again. As senior TAG I took a great interest in all this and tried out the idea of talking to the pilot from the ground. This put me under some pressure as E.T.A. times were variable and I might have to do a furious dash across to the control tower on a bicycle. The first tries were no more successful than before. I'd report "target at 100 feet descending -80 feet -50,30 20,10 cut" The last few heights were gabbled in rapid succession as it took its usual nose dive in. Judging height was easy. I just took multiples of the wing span. Now, though, I could see why they were diving in. ANY pilot action started the switchback. The slightest dive or throttle variation would set it off. The target would not follow a change. I stopped the talk-downs and asked each pilot in turn to set himself up as soon as possible on final and then to do his utmost on an approach not to vary attitude or speed. They began to bring the targets down in one piece.

We had one silly episode early on. At the time we had but the one special linking attachment. So when a target was shot down on Ainsdale beach I was keen not to lose the linkage. I got a driver to run me down to the beach in a 15cwt van. The tide was out but there were pools of water and a lot of soft sand. The driver got stuck and stalled the engine. I ran a mile or so to Queen Charlotte but it was lunch time and it took a long time to raise a working party.Eventually we arrived back in a DUKW. The tide had come in and the van was engulfed. The DUKW floated and like that it could not bring its full towing capability to bear. I thought I'd lost a van for the sake of a towing attachment. However they finally pulled it out, stripped it, and it was fully recovered.

At about this time my 12 months Acting period for P.O. was concluded and promotion to C.P.O. came through, with 18 months backdating. It seemed ridiculous. I was but 23 and recalled the phrase " the thrill of the air plus the grand life of the sea". Well I'd had the thrill of the air but could muster barely 6 months sea time. I thought of the R.A.F. pilots manning the Catapult Merchant Ships. They were getting in the sea time for at most half-an-hours flying time, if they ever took off. If we had met perhaps we should have changed uniforms.

In the New Year 1945 we began a variant of our target towing, although all the previous tasks were continued. We were to tow drogues on air-to-air firing for Fireflies operating from both Burscough near Southport and Inskip near Blackpool. This kept up the interest because we would carry a stack of drogues and stream, reel in and drop, one for each Firefly firing. In one flight we might stream 7 or 8 drogues and the time passed very rapidly. Our TAG complement up to this point had included Fred Rigby, Tim Barrow, Bungy Williams, A.G.'Nobby'Clark, Jeff North and Naval Airmen Inwood and Roffey. The last two were winch operators but not TAGs. This group had recently been augmented by Geoff Hearn, "Ali" Barber, George Beardsall , Herb Bearshaw and Martin Tansey. Even as a Chief I made a point of going on the flying roster. Quietly I wished I could do more as I enjoyed the flying.

It was quite usual to go over to Inskip for the day. Then there would be a trip both morning and afternoon with a landing for lunch. Having streamed a drogue - white ones for this job with large identity letters in red - a Firefly would join us and we then flew out over the Irish Sea at right angles to the coast. The Firefly would start his passes coming in beam on to the drogue. They never stopped at deflection shots. There would be a curve of pursuit until you could see the Firefly approaching behind the drogue. This meant that the Firefly should be able to see us in his sight in front of the drogue, but they didn't seem to notice. I used to sit there horrified, watching the row of flickering flashes in the leading edge of the wings. At first I fired red very lights but this simply held things up. After a green very, it would be just the same next time. I couldn't quite understand at first why they had to have full ammunition, though on reflection I supposed it was easier to let all standard functions work, rather than chance one gun stoppages such as dogged and ruined our turret exercises. The pilots had to learn how all guns would give a kick back in their speed. In the end after carefully watching what they were up to, I could see that their shots must be falling away behind us, though as we were not in a turn there wasn't much in it. They had to aim somewhat further ahead before we were in danger although there was always a chance of a stray from their cone of fire coming our way. The Firefly pilots appeared to get carried away with their enthusiasm, and would often close the drogue until it was in ribbons. On 1200 feet of tow it was really too close for comfort but good experience for us as rear gunners.

Came VE day and much celebration. As something of a joke I declared that I would have to drink lemonade in order to make it special and different from any other day. Oddly enough with the sheer enthusiasm of the occasion I found myself getting quite heady and enjoying the fun whilst still on lemonade. Then the non-regulars started flopping out - it was still only lunch time - and my services with others of the hardened brigade were in great demand carting people off to their bunks to sleep it off. We went out to Southport in the evening to join throngs of people giving expression to their relief at the end of it all. I'd rather committed myself by now and the rest of the lads were watching to see if I could keep it up on lemonade. It was the best thing I could have done, and I was able to enjoy every minute through to the end of the day. The antics of some people were remarkable. I had my own celebration the following day, but it was not so memorable !

The war wasn't over yet. The Royal Navy turned it's attention full bore on the Japs. For one thing they took over Woodvale as a Naval Air Station. White posts , gaiters and quarter-deck. The R.A.F. function was at an end but the Fleet Air Arm still had a war to fight in the Pacific. All the usual barrack stanchions arrived and the full squadron moved in from Speke. My pool of TAGs was swollen to 30, so many in fact that now I cannot remember all the names. There was no question of loafing quietly in the crew room. They were out in the hangar unloading and assembling winged targets till they stood in rows on the tarmac. It was time to go, and go I did. The Drafting Office had obviously not forgotten that a newly made up Chief was due for another operational squadron.

Grumman Avenger

CHAPTER 20
"With The Forgotten Fleet"

Continuing Blondie Lambert's story :-
On the 1st November 1944, No.820 Squadron was reformed with the American built Grumman Avengers. The squadron strength was somewhat smaller than the previously combined 820 and 826 squadrons, so there was some speculation as to who was to stay and who was to leave. Soon it was decided that my lifelong mate 'Darkie' Holroyd was the one to leave.

It was not long before we were once again starting our working up drills. The Avenger was a much more modern aircraft than anything we had been accustomed to and we were delighted with the sophisticated radio, 0.5 Browning turret, and the .303 Browning in the belly of the aircraft. In addition to which, we entered by means of a door in the side - no more climbing in over the top.

The war in Europe, as far as we knew, was going reasonably well and it left us no illusions as to our future destination. Indefatigable had arrived in Portsmouth and was having a quick overhaul, so it did not require much imagination to forecast the inevitable course of events.

After a visit to the ship by King George VI, we eventually left Lee to join the ship once again.

As we sailed southwards we continued with our working up. Dive bombing runs, air-to-air and air-to-ground firing using the front guns, the turret and the belly gun. Boosted take-offs and deck landings in addition to our routine A/S patrols were the order of the day, every day.

We passed through the Straits of Gibraltar and spent one night in Tangiers, before continuing our journey eastwards. There was more and yet more flying as we went through the Med.. I suppose it was only natural that we should compare that trip eastwards with those we had done a couple of years previously. It was a much more peaceful journey this time, although I'm sure there were many of us with thoughts

Avenger with British Pacific Fleet markings flying over Indomitable. Infatigable was of the same class as Indomitable

of Malta convoys, Ark Royal, Eagle and Illustrious. I suppose also, there were thoughts of Alexandria and Dekheila, as we went into the Suez Canal and then on through the Red Sea, Indian Ocean and finally Colombo. Before entering harbour at Colombo we flew ashore to the Naval Air Station at Katukurunda and it was while we were at Kat, that we were to learn all about jungle warfare and jungle survival.

We were issued with green linen flying overalls, foreign legion type hats, boots, gaiters, extra thick stockings and over stockings. The reason for the gaiters and extra thick stockings we were told was a protection against snake bites.

Incidental items included a machete, an extremely sharp, heavy bladed, two handed weapon for hacking through dense jungle undergrowth, a stiletto whose purpose was obvious, and, of course, a service 0.38 revolver. A very comprehensive first aid kit with all manner of medical paraphernalia thought necessary for jungle survival.

We had many medical lectures on how to use hypodermics, and the occasions when one tablet would be preferable to another, when to sleep and when to travel, in fact anything to make life bearable, should we have the misfortune to be forced down in the jungle.

Perhaps the most important event in our short stay at Kat was practical jungle survival. It was felt by someone in authority that the only real way to learn about the jungle was to go and live in it for a while, so in groups of 3 or 4 we did just that.

An instructor of indeterminate nationality, although I do believe he was a South African, possibly a Boer, was to be our guide. He took us into the jungles of Ceylon and taught us the hard way.

He showed us how to make camp, the vegetation we could eat, how to trap, skin and cook. He showed us what to avoid and what to do if we were bitten by snakes. We spent a very interesting and intriguing few days, and returned to camp determined to avoid being shot down if at all possible, but knowing that if we were, we at least had got some chance of survival.

Early in the New Year of 1945 we suffered our first set back. We had carried out a dummy dive bombing attack on a prominent building in Colombo having flown from the carrier as she was sailing towards Trincomalee. On the way back from the exercise I saw someone, or something, fall from one of the aircraft. Within a few seconds a parachute opened and then a second. The aircraft crashed into the jungle below. The third member of the crew, the TAG, was unfortunately killed and I don't know whether it was because his chute failed to open of whether he was unable to abandon the aircraft, but his body was found close by the crashed aircraft.

After a few days in Trinco, we sailed eastwards in company with Victorious and Indomitable. The Admiral flew his flag in Victorious. Shortly after leaving harbour the aircrews were called together to be told that our next operation was to be an attack on the Japanese held oil refineries at Palembang in Sumatra.

The evening before the attack was to take place we had our main briefing session. As the briefing progressed it became more and more obvious why we had undergone jungle survival training, and our recent cross country dive bombing exercise.

The refinery was, we learnt, very heavily fortified. In addition to the considerable number of anti-aircraft guns, the area was surrounded by a balloon barrage, and the whole lot backed up by a considerable number of fighter aircraft.

We were to be escorted by long range fighter aircraft carrying rockets. The main target area was to be the oil cracking furnaces and plant control rooms. The crude oil storage tanks and the refined petroleum products were of secondary importance. It was the process by which the crude oil was refined that was important.

The attack was to be a combined effort, the total strike force being provided from all three carriers. The general intention I recall, was that half of the total effort available would carry out the first raid, and the other half would carry out a second attack, should it prove necessary.

One significant part of the briefing was the arrangements made for the collection of survivors. It was expected that there would obviously be some losses but hopefully there was a chance that some may bale out or survive a forced landing. There was a lot of jungle between the point where we crossed the coast and the target, and anyone unfortunate enough to be forced down on this Japanese held island would have little or no chance of making his way to a friendly or neutral country.

A submarine was therefore detailed to be lying off shore at a given position on a certain date, and would surface for a short period, when any survivors would hopefully make contact and be picked up. The submarine was to adopt these tactics for two or three nights. It did nothing to raise our hopes when we were told that it would be some five or six weeks hence before the sub was in position. This was not because the sub had a long distance to travel, but rather that it was expected to take that length of time for us to get from the target area to the coast. Considering that the distance was something of the order of 150 miles, left us in no doubt that if we were unlucky, there was some difficult walking ahead.

Early in the morning of 24th January 1945, we were called to breakfast before our final briefing. It was at this final briefing that I was surprised to see the Paymaster. He handed to each and every one of us, first of all a "Blood Chit". This was an authorisation for us to guarantee the payment of a sum of money by HM Government, to any friendly native who gave us shelter or returned us unharmed to the nearest British or American base. It was printed in several languages and dialects of that part of South East Asia.

Then rather surprisingly we were given about 50 gold sovereigns each stuck on a length of elastoplast and folded into a compact little parcel. It wasn't that we were being given a bonus or even danger money - it was purely and simply for bribery. In the event of the "Blood Chit" being unacceptable, we could use the more desirable gold coins, although it would not do to let the natives know we had them, unless as a last resort and then only singly !

It was obvious that a lot of thought had gone in to the preparation, but frankly it gave us all food for thought.

Briefing complete we gathered our belongings together and made our way to our aircraft.

The ground crews had been hard at work since long before we'd gone to breakfast. Some of them had worked through the night making sure everything would be all right. Each aircraft was to carry 4 x 500lb bombs.

There was a rather strange subdued atmosphere on the flight deck that morning. We had heard many unpleasant stories of Japanese atrocities, especially to aircrews, so it was with apprehension that we manned our aircraft. The ground crews were especially helpful and one could sense their concern for us. Their unspoken thoughts, "sooner you than me" came over quite strongly.

The signal to start engines was given and in a very short time the FDO waved us off. It was comforting to know that we carried the good wishes of all the goofers who ranged along the Goofers platform on the island superstructure.

As we cleared the front of the flight deck the aircraft dropped several feet and I'm sure most people watching must have held their breath, until we reappeared as we gained height. I must confess to being alarmed myself, especially as I could see turbulence of the water caused by our own slipstream.

The rest of the aircraft from Indefatigable were flown off and a similar activity was taking place in the other two carriers. Once all aircraft were airborne we took up our pre-arranged formation and set course for Sumatra.

After flying for some 2 hours, mostly across what appeared to be impenetrable jungle, we started our preparations for the attack. A few minutes later we were within sight of the target, and our rocket firing fighter escorts were detached to carry out their rocket attack on the previously agreed targets, whilst we circled round to take up our position to come in out of the sun.

By this time of course the enemy fighters were in the air and anti-aircraft fire was most intense. The AA fire was initially directed at the aircraft carrying out the rocket attack, and the enemy fighters, the infamous Zeros, concentrated on us poor 'slow' dive bombers. It was at this stage that I really believe the new type formation we had adopted prior to the Tirpitz raids proved to be successful. We had been warned at our briefing to stay close together as the Japs looked for stragglers and concentrated their attention on anyone who strayed from the fold. We did stay close together so the fighters had to have a go at us collectively. Because of our formation we were able to concentrate a considerable amount of 0.5 calibre fire on our attackers and with little danger of shooting each other out of the sky. Our training stood us in good stead, and we were still a complete squadron as we went into the attack.

The turret had to be locked into the fore and aft position when carrying out a bombing run, so as not to influence the flying characteristics of the aircraft. Another, and to me important reason, it was only possible to get out of the turret when it was in that position. If we were hit I would want to be out - if I had time.

In less time than it takes to tell we had carried out our dive, released the four bombs we were carrying and pulled out of the dive. It was when we pulled out of the dive that our trouble really started. Our normal procedure on completing the attack was to fly low away from the area and reform on the way back. This time we had the balloon barrage to contend with. No sooner had the pilot pulled out of the dive, when he called out that he was too low to climb over the balloons and we'd have to take a chance and hope we didn't slice our wings off on the balloon wires. One or two of our fighter escort had shot some of them down but there was an awful lot still to negotiate.

We managed to clear the area safely and it was then that the pilot lowered his wheels as a signal to all the other aircraft to take up formation for the trip back to the ship. The lowering of the wheels naturally has the effect of reducing speed and therefore manoeuverability. Before any of the others could form up on us we were attacked by about six Japanese fighters. We had been so concerned about the balloons that none of us had seen the fighters.

We did not have to be told that we were in trouble. The pilot raised the wheels and we prepared ourselves to fight it out alone. The Japs ranged themselves on either side of us, just too far away to be in any danger from our single 0.5 Browning.

We were now in the position of having to run the gauntlet and it was rather frightening to say the least. I suppose we should have been blasted out of the sky in a matter of seconds, but their method of attack allowed us hope of being able to out manoeuvre them.

One aircraft would peel off from our starboard side, make his attack and then join up with his oppos on the port side. At this stage one from the port side would then carry out an attack and join up with those on the starboard side. The process was then repeated again and again. Provided they kept up this method and didn't make an attack from both sides simultaneously we had at least a fighting chance. Our defence against these tactics was simple. As soon as an attack started, either myself or the observer, according to whichever side the attack was coming from would call out to the pilot "stand by to corkscrew port (or starboard as the case may be)".

As soon as we judged the fighter to be just within firing range we would sing out "go".

At this point the pilot made a violent alteration of course towards the approaching fighter throwing him off aim. As soon as it was obvious that we were safe from that attack the pilot would straighten up and wait for the next one. I can't be sure how long this went on for, but it seemed an awful long time before they gave up, either from sheer frustration or lack of fuel I'll never know.

One of our adversaries, in a final attempt to bring us down made an attack from ahead and below, flying towards us. The pilot called out what was happening ahead and told me that one of the fighters was coming in from below and that I should see him appear beneath the starboard wing. I rotated the turret in the general direction and sure enough there he was. It was then that the Jap pilot did a very silly thing. He pulled the aircraft into a climbing turn to make, I assume, another run at us. In carrying out this manoeuvre he was an absolute zero deflection target and plumb in the centre of the gun sight. I managed to get in a couple of long bursts and I could see the tracers finding the target. Smoke appeared and he fell rapidly away.

I was unable to see what happened to him subsequently, but we were not attacked again on that trip.

As we made our way back to the Fleet other aircraft joined up with us, and some 2 hours after carrying out our attack we were once more circling the Fleet, waiting for it to turn into wind for landing on.

We had not got time to get out of the cockpits before we were being surrounded by ground crews and those air crews who had not been on the raid, asking all manner of questions. My first request was to the RAF Sergeant armourer, who was part of the squadron strength, to get the camera gun film and have it developed - I was anxious for an action replay. Regretfully he came back to me later in the day to say that the camera gun was not aligned correctly with the gun, consequently there was no record of my endeavour. Anyway we were back in one piece although we did lose one aircraft. It was piloted by a Canadian CPO called Mitchell although I can't remember who the TAG was who was flying with him. (This was in fact, Clifford Lewis Harris.- KS)

I seem to remember that Mitch had a premonition about that particular raid and didn't fancy his chances of coming back.

After landing on there was of course the usual debriefing and the checking and double checking of what each and every one of us said and saw.

At the debriefing we were told that, after the questioning was completed, we were to report to the Paymaster with our gold sovereigns. I don't think he really trusted us at all. In his office he had a little marble slab some 6" square. As we each went in with our little parcel of gold he unfolded the elastoplast strip and removed the coins. He then very solemnly dropped each one on to the marble slab, to make sure the "ring" was right and that we hadn't substituted foreign coins, or perpetrated some other lowly counterfeit trickery.

It would probably have been the next day when the squadron was called together in the hangar, and my pilot, who had led the squadron on the raid, gave all the ground crews a talk about the raid, and what we had achieved, and what was left to be done. It was obvious then that another raid would need to be carried out.

At the conclusion of the chat my observer came over to me and said that the C.O. was incapacitated, and that my pilot was going to lead our squadron on the second attack. The observer was going with him and it was put to me that perhaps I would like to consider going with them and so keep the same crew together. It seemed logical to me, and in any case our experiences of the day before had given us a lot of confidence in each other. I can't say that I was looking forward to it, any more than I can say I was never frightened.

The second attack was very much a repeat of the first. We had to fight our way in again, but on completion of the attack we very quickly reformed for our journey back to the Fleet. We had a considerable amount of anti-aircraft fire to contend with and, of course, the barrage balloons. The enemy fighters did not appear to be as numerous as on the previous occasion, although perhaps it was that we were more fortunate on this trip. One incident which was rather heart stopping was when one of the Zeros dived down on to the squadron. Whether he was trying to ram any of us I can't be sure, but what is certain is that he hurtled down in an almost vertical dive just missing our tail and the nose of our next astern.

For many miles on the way back we could see vast columns of smoke and flame, and I'm convinced we'd given the place a good hammering.

This seemed to be confirmed a few hours later when we were told there would be no more attacks necessary, and that we were bound for Australia. There was some rejoicing in the mess that night and the rum bottle was emptied.

On the way to Australia there was a rather unpleasant episode when certain of the Ship's Company had a minor mutiny. It was of course, to do with food. I seem to remember that the Admiral flew across from Victorious, and shortly afterwards a better and more varied diet was available.

We arrived in Fremantle and after a very short stay we moved on to Sydney, where we were given fourteen days leave. The Aussies were most friendly and offers of holidays on farms, up country, by the sea or in the bush, were in abundance.

The time passed all too quickly and it was not long before we were sailing northwards towards the Japanese held islands.

We were now called the British Pacific Fleet, Task Force 57.

During March 1945 we carried out a variety of strikes against shipping and airfields on the Japanese islands of Ishigaki and Miyako, which were part of the group known as the Sakishima Gunto. Other than the usual anti-aircraft fire and occasional fighter opposition there was nothing of great significance.

April 1st however was a day of some importance.

It would be sometime before 0800, that I had washed and shaved and was preparing to go to breakfast in the Wardroom which was our action mess. The rest of the ship's company was at early morning action stations. There was some gun firing, although I believed it to be that some spotter plane had come too close. Anyway our cover air patrol was in the air and we were some distance from the nearest land so all was well - or was it ? Suddenly the anti-aircraft fire seemed to get more insistant and as our mess was down near the water line, I thought it prudent to get up to our crew room in the island superstructure.

It was whilst I was on my way up to the crew room that there was an almighty explosion, and I could feel the blast wave come down the ladder I was ascending. My immediate thought was that we had been hit by a bomb, and if it had penetrated the flight deck to burst in the hangar, we were going to be in real trouble. I raced up the remaining ladders to the crew room to find a few others assembled and all speculating on what had happened. A voice on the tannoy system called for all doctors and sick berth attendants to report to the flight deck, and for the damage control parties. The quartermaster rang eight bells - it was 8 o'clock on the morning of April Fools Day 1945.

We went out on to the flight deck to see what had happened, and lodged between the side of the island and the flight deck was the remains of a Japanese suicide plane - a Kamikaze ! The medical staff moved about the dead, the dying and the injured giving injections and generally making people comfortable, until they could be got down below to the Sick Bay.

The damage control party set about removing the debris from the flight deck in an attempt to get the ship fully operational again. By 0830 we were almost back to normal. Seafires which had been up on early morning CAP came in to land and only one crash barrier remained inoperable. In all other respects we were back to normal. Later that day even that was repaired. So much then for the feared suicide bomber.

As soon as the initial excitement died down I decided to go to breakfast. As I was descending one of the ladders, just ahead of me was a stretcher party carrying down to the sick bay a badly injured seaman. His leg had been very badly injured, the temporary dressing had fallen off as he was being carried down the ladder in a strait jacket type stretcher, and I could see the torn and mutilated flesh and bone.

When I sat down to breakfast and was offered bacon and tomatoes (train smash) I had to refuse.

I think it was as a result of the suicide attack that our C.O. became FDO. I believe the original holder of the job was injured. So my pilot got his other half stripe and took over as C.O. of the squadron.

We spent almost the whole of April carrying out raids on Japanese airfields and shipping around the islands. One of these raids was an attack on the port of Kiirun in Northern Formosa. The attack itself had been successful although one crew at least would not agree. As we left the target area one aircraft, although not from our squadron, came down in the sea. We saw the crew manage to get out of the aircraft, but there was a motor boat on its way to collect them. Knowing of the atrocities performed by the Japs they would probably have been better off had they been killed outright.

Other than the ever present thought of what might happen to us should we be taken prisoner, the raids we did were in the main uneventful. There was always AA fire to contend with and of course the enemy fighters but at least those of us in 820 squadron kept coming back.

One or two incidents did cause the blood to flow a little quicker, like the occasion when we were approaching a target and I saw a flash of gun fire. I reported it to the pilot who said, "It's too far away to bother us". In a matter of seconds there was a resounding crack right underneath us and the aircraft was peppered with shrapnel. It never ceased to amaze me that, when flying through anti-aircraft fire one could see the shells burst but not hear any noise above the roar of the engine. Unless of course it was very close and this time it was. We did a little bobbing and weaving but we could not shake off the extremely accurate fire. We turned away and went round the island and attacked from the opposite side with considerable success and more important - no losses.

On another occasion we had to attack our target from the opposite side of the island from our direction of approach. Attack out of the sun and all that ! We had got round to the far side and were flying at about 10,000 feet when suddenly the engine cut out. We dropped several hundred feet and I for one thought it was curtains for us. Just as suddenly it cut in again and as we regained height and our position, the pilot calmly informed us that he'd forgotten to switch tanks.

On yet another occasion as we started to climb to our dive bombing height we had to go through a very thick layer of cloud. As we entered the cloud we were in very close formation but when we came out into the glorious sunshine above we were alone. We circled round for several minutes but none of the others appeared. It was agreed that we went on alone. Now I can't say that I relished the thought of being one against many, so was very relieved to see another two of our number coming up astern of us. We slowed to allow them to catch up, but instead of a full striking force only three of us completed the attack.

One evening I was strolling up and down the flight deck with my pilot having a yarn and I expressed my concern about the way we dropped off the front of the flight deck, and how I could see the turbulence created by the slip stream. "Don't worry about that", he said, "it gives the aircraft a bit of extra speed and assists in getting some lift" !!. As we were talking, one of the other carriers was flying off some strike aircraft and we were watching them adopt more or less the same drill. Unfortunately one pilot tried to pull his aircraft up into the air before reaching the front of the flight deck. He didn't have enough flying speed, stalled and crashed into the sea.

At the end of April we had a few days in Leyte in the Phillipines and we all enjoyed the short rest.

On May 1st we sailed once again for a further period of operations. The next day a signal was received with the names of people decorated for the attacks on the oil refineries at Palembang (Operation Meridian as it was called). All of our crew were decorated. The pilot got a bar to the DSC he got for the Tirpitz raids, the observer a DSC and myself the DSM. One other member of the squadron TAGs , Taff Rees, also got the DSM.

Once again the rum bottle came out and I'm afraid Taff hit the bottle rather hard. It was obvious he'd had more than enough when he collapsed, out to the world.

Someone rigged his hammock and after lots of heaving and humping he was lifted into his 'mick to sleep it off.

The next morning it was impossible to wake him. He was still breathing which was something but still dead drunk. We got him under a shower and threw buckets of cold water over him, and although we managed to raise him from his stupor he was in no fit state to be allowed to fly.

We managed to keep him out of harms way, at least until the Captain sent for us to congratulate us on our recent awards. Once again it was all hands "to the pumps" to help get him cleaned and presentable to go up to the bridge. It was at this stage that Taff noticed he couldn't raise his right arm. He had slept all night with his arm hanging over the side of his hammock and in doing so had partially stopped the flow of blood to his arm. I suppose it was fortunate that it was not more serious, otherwise he may have lost the use permanently. When we got him presentable, together, he and I, went up to the bridge. It was one hell of a job to assist him up the ladders and when we finally made it I had to jamb him up against the door frame to prevent him falling.

Fortunately the Captain came over to us rather than call us to him, and for that I was extremely grateful. If we'd had to walk freely I'm sure Taff would have fallen flat on his face. I had to do all the talking and when the Captain went to shake hands with Taff I was delighted to see Taff raise his hand to about the level of his waist. The Skipper had a rather puzzled look on his face, but to his eternal credit he turned a Nelson's eye.

May of course saw the end of the war in Europe and that was the signal for another celebration which might have had more disastrous consequences. On VE day itself we were in the operational zone and obviously could not take part in any celebrations. As a matter of fact I remember carrying out two raids that day. The first early in the morning and the second late in the afternoon. So much for VE day in the Far East.

The Captain who was a very considerate individual broadcast to the Ship's Company and explained that we would 'splice the main brace' at the first opportunity, probably when we returned from the operational zone to a relatively safer area to refuel and restore at sea.

A couple of days later we did just that. It was the custom in Indefatigable when in tropical waters to issue rum with the evening meal and not at lunch time as was usually the case.

"Up spirits" was piped and we looked forward to a very pleasant evening. Two tots each plus what we'd got saved in the bottle.

One of our number, a certain Bill Daniels who was a CPO pilot with one of the Seafire squadrons, eventually decided he'd had enough rum for one night but before turning in thought he'd go for a breath of fresh air and took a stroll along the flight deck. I don't think anybody missed him until he was returned aboard next day. The story, as I remember it, was that Bill had taken his walk along the flight deck but unfortunately had walked too far forward and straight off into the sea. Considering that it was pitch dark and all the Fleet was blacked out and that he'd fallen 50 feet or more, the fact that he was able to recount the incident was all the more remarkable.

As he hit the water he was sober in an instant. He surfaced just as he was about level with the quarter deck. His cry for help was fortunately heard by the Royal Marine sentry on the quarter deck who immediately let go a life raft. He then rang the bridge to report 'man overboard'.

The bridge made an immediate signal to our attendant destroyer, who broke all the rules by switching on a searchlight. By a stroke of good fortune the searchlight picked him up instantly and a boat was lowered to pick him out of the water. Not unnaturally the destroyer skipper started to ball out Bill, endangering the Fleet and all that. Of course he was right, but when he calmed down he asked Bill how he came to fall overboard. Events of the previous few minutes had sobered Bill and he was as alert as ever. "Well Sir", he said, "I've been flying for hours on end doing cover on air patrols and I'm so keyed up I can't sleep, so thought a walk along the flight deck to relax would help me overcome my insomnia. I must have been day dreaming and just walked off". The skipper was duly impressed, after all here was someone who risked his life every time he took off ! "Have a tot of rum",said the skipper,"it might help you to sleep". "No thanks", said Bill, "I never touch the stuff". When he came back aboard he said he would never drink rum again, and I for one believed him.

There were many incidents both humorous and tragic. The duty TAG who forgot to read the weather report which was transmitted daily at a certain time. On being reprimanded by Schoolie who was our Met. expert, he claimed he was seasick and had to leave the radio room. Knowing that Schoolie was subject to seasickness he was excused and comforted by a fellow sufferer.

I suppose I could tell the next little story anonymously but considering the passage of time and now being able to laugh at the situation as I saw it, I must confess to being the party concerned.

We had carried out a raid on one of the airfields and were carrying bombs not of British manufacture - they were probably American. Anyway, unlike the British bomb, once they were armed they had to be dropped, they could not be made safe again. If we had a hang-up we were told that under no circumstances were we to attempt to land on. The drill was that we were to set the aircraft on a course away from the Fleet and bale out, and a destroyer would pick us up. It was necessary therefore to make sure all bombs had gone after completing the attack. On this occasion as we were making our way back to the fleet the pilot asked me to check that all bombs had gone. There was a very small window through which it was possible to see into the bomb bay, or should I say it should have been possible to see into the bomb bay. The window was so dirty and cracked that it was impossible to see through. By removing a few screws I was able to remove the glass and this I did. Inside the bomb bay was so dark I couldn't see a thing so I asked the pilot to open the bomb bay doors to let in a bit of light. As he did this, the wind blowing through the now removed window was so strong I only managed a quick look. I could see nothing so assumed all was well. (We weren't wearing goggles in those days - modern aircraft and all that !).

We continued happily back to the ship and landed on. As we taxied forward the pilot opened the bomb bay doors as was the usual procedure to clear any fumes which may have built up. I was rather surprised to see the flight deck party running hell for leather for cover until we had moved a few yards further on and I could see a lovely 500 pounder lying on the deck. No wonder there was a scattering match.

Fortunately the fuze was faulty and the bomb was harmless although no chances were taken and the bomb was carefully lowered over the side and dropped into the sea.

It can only be assumed that after closing the bomb bay doors the bomb had unhooked itself and had lain on the door until it was next opened. After that episode, whenever we carried that type of bomb again, we had to fly low past the ship with bomb doors open so that the inside of the bomb bay could be seen from the flight deck and an inspection made.

Then of course there were the Seafire pilots who were bursting lots of tyres when landing on and supplies became critical. The skipper threatened them that they would fly with rope grommets but fly they would. The number of bursts reduced dramatically.

On one occasion as a strike was returning to the fleet, someone sighted a life raft, although he could not be sure if anyone was in it. A destroyer was detached to go and investigate and we were told later that it was an American airman who had been forced down and had been adrift for several days. He was very badly sunburnt and it was alleged that he had said that had he not been picked up that day he had intended to throw himself over the side and end it all. The unfortunate part about it was that for several days he had seen aircraft passing overhead but no one had seen him.

I always felt that the war in the Far East brought all the air and ground crews close together. It was not unusual for either the pilot or observer to ring down to the mess and invite the TAG to the wardroom for a drink. Considering that at that time they were limited to one short and one can of beer a day it was some sacrifice.

The Fleet returned to Sydney in June and 820 squadron disembarked for another spot of leave. I was to be denied that luxury although I suppose in one respect I was more fortunate. I had a draft chit back to the UK, where I landed about the same time as the first atom bomb fell on Hiroshima.

From the time of joining 820 Squadron until I left, we had flown many thousands of miles and spent hundreds of hours in the air from the Arctic Circle to the edge of the Antartic. We had sailed round the world crossing both the equator and the international date line, on so many occasions we lost count and yet our losses were negligible.

I can only put our good fortune down to the skill of the pilots, the navigational accuracy of the observers and the skill and coolness of the TAGs when under attack.

Finally, and perhaps most important, one must pay tribute to the excellence of the ground crews, in whom we had the utmost confidence. Those war years brought lots of sorrow and yet lots of joy. I was privileged to have known both the sorrow and the joy and had the honour of being part of the "Navy that Flew".

By way of an epilogue I must say that I have never flown since those days believing the old adage "only birds and fools fly by day - bats and lunatics at night !"

From the author (Ken Sims).

Sadly Blondie Lambert is no longer with us. He died in August 1993. He had written his reminiscences at my specific request some years ago and I still have all his original manuscript. He was somewhat embarrassed that I had singled him out as a TAG with an exceptional story to tell. When it seemed doubtful that my yarn would ever get into print, I arranged with our editor of the day for Gordon's story to appear in the TAGs' magazine. More recently, just before he died, he rang me in response to a letter, to assure me that I still had his full permission to put all of it into a book if such were a possibility.

Fairey Barracuda

CHAPTER 21

Och Aye

To pick up the thread of the story after Gordon Lambert's captivating account rather brings us down to earth. Metaphorically speaking that is, because for me it was more a matter of getting up into the air. Och aye you say ? Oh yes, it was once more back to Scotland where the Fleet Air Arm established so many Naval Air Stations, and I realised why my name was Ken.

In early June 1945 I was on my way to join 818 Squadron of Barracudas at Crimond near Aberdeen. They had already formed and were in a working up phase. Though Gordon has already given you his thoughts on the Barracuda, it will come across from what I say, that they were still regarded with many doubts. Also it will be noted, that though the Avenger had established itself as the prime and dependable strike force aircraft in use on all the major Fleet Aircraft Carriers, and quite able to stand up to Jap fighters, there were several squadrons of Barracudas forming up, which were intended to join some of the smaller carriers. At that stage it was expected that defeat of the Japanese would only be achieved after a considerable war of attrition.

By now we had dismissed all thoughts of doing radio maintenance and happily left this to the new branch of Radio Mechanics. There was a new radio, the ARI5206 - not that I liked it - it was all boxed up with only the controls to twiddle. No longer could one get at every valve or have the whole thing open in one's lap in the aircraft whilst reconnecting some wire or other. No batteries to bother about. That was a good point. In fact we were totally aircrew, and that meant a lot of time was spent on occupational training, such as lectures, dinghy drill, skeet shooting, training films and so on. By now they were working the crew system fully, and each squadron crew had gone through an NOTU (Naval Operational Training Unit) as a team. I crewed with the C.O. and Senior Observer (SOBS) though we had not gone on such a course together. I liked that NOTU system. It meant that I had a batch of experienced and dependable TAGs instead of the usual bunch of goons joining their first squadron. A couple were actually P.O.s of my era. A few others were also A/P.O.s who had been on squadrons before. There was now an Admiralty Fleet Order which promoted TAGs to Acting P.O. when they passed a Leading Airmans Board. This was possible shortly after completing course. The sight of a P.O. without a 3 year Good Conduct Badge was strange indeed.

Barracudas had gone through their bad days. The pilots now knew they couldn't be dived at more than 60 degrees or the rivets popped. So by-and-large I was fairly happy in them. Mind you they were really as obsolescent and outdated in 1945 as the Swordfish was in 1940. I was concerned over one feature. With the rear hood open, part of it stuck up above the cockpit canopy in the slipstream and gave good turbulence protection. However, in a protracted dive the pressure build up was excessive. There was a fair chance that it would crumple or at best slam shut. There was certainly difficulty opening it at speed. Some people actually tied it open with rope but I didn't fancy the possible consequences. The idea that enemy fighters might follow you down in a dive was a possibility but after giving it some thought I reckoned to leave it shut in a dive. In fact I think the pilots had opinions about this - it must surely have interfered with the airspeed and trim - but I wasn't given directions one way or the other.

About all I can remember doing at Crimond was going on a skeet shoot. I'd never actually done this before and was a little apprehensive that all the TAGs were watching their new Chief to see how he performed. I'm glad to say I actually hit some of them and so lost no face in that direction.

Shortly after my arrival at Crimond the squadron moved to Fearn north of Inverness, och aye. There we began extensive dive-bombing and navigational exercises. I was anxious to get the boys on their toes with the radio and would always man the ground station if not flying myself. I wasn't at all impressed with the range of the 5206. Maybe it had something to do with the aerial arrangement on the aircraft. One couldn't carry out the old trailing aerial dodge. The set wouldn't tune to it. I tried variations with a shorter length of trailing wire with fractional improvement but became convinced that this equipment was a backward step from the old Geep in terms of performance, though more convenient in ability to switch frequency. It remained with us through to 1953 and probably longer.

When we practised carrier take-offs and were all in a gaggle at the end of the runway I would have the TAGs tell-off on the W/T. This consisted of a rapid response from each in sequence. They got very good at it. All basically old hat and quite useless in itself but it did get them on the ball listening-out and keeping their transmissions short. Half the W/T failures to get through are because some other selfish operator is hogging the air. Do you recall the passenger aircraft that went off course and landed in the Sahara ? When they were lost the aircraft operator couldn't get through because the ground stations were too busy transmitting to each other — about him !

Fearn was hardly a suitable airfield. It was ringed with hills and the mist was likely to come up quite quickly. For local flying this was bad enough with a circuit full of aircraft - there were at least three squadrons working-up there. On the 14th July many of our squadron were away on a navex when the mist closed in. I was in the air myself and listened as several aircraft were diverted to Lossiemouth. Those of us nearer home were allowed to continue back to Fearn and we landed before the mist closed right in. Unfortunately one aircraft had not made a landfall and being a little behind the others ran into a dense wall of mist. We could only surmise this - he was missing but had been heard on the radio not long before his ETA. As ever the squadron was prepared to mount a search for a missing colleague but the weather made it impossible. We waited impatiently. At last, late in the evening, the mist lifted a shade. Enough for one Swordfish to get off. The Senior Pilot took it and an observer and I went with him. My first Swordfish flight for months, and as it transpired my last in such an aircraft. We went up and down the gullies to the north of the airfield. At first the mist was still treacherous and only a Swordfish could have negotiated the twisty ravines. As time wore on the air cleared but we had almost given up when suddenly we spotted it halfway up one of the hills. There was no sign of life and it looked as though they had seen the ground at the last second and pulled back on the stick. There was a complete plan view imprint on the side of the hill with the wreckage strewn below. It appeared as though they had hit belly on and then fallen off backwards.

The observer and I spent some time deciding where exactly it was - one hill looks very like another in that terrain. I learnt that a Swordfish engine noise is too much for a microphone without a face mask - I'd never used R/T before in a Swordfish. We returned to a subdued squadron, and another bitter pill. The lost TAG was a substitute in that crew for a colleague who was in the sick bay. Who should the latter be but Bob Gregory, the same man who keeled over with pleurisy that day at Port Said some two years previous. Again he'd lost a crew and a colleague who stood in for him. I'd had no part in the present substitution but the coincidence of my presence in the squadron and the similar circumstances were a little strange. This TAG swore he'd climb out of a sick bed rather than let anyone else ever fly in his place.

I fear a few of us older TAGs treated it quite casually. We'd experienced too many such incidents. In your hearts the feeling is there, but you just had to harden to it and shrug it off or your morale would crack.

The working up continued when suddenly, out of the blue, Keith Allum appeared to relieve me. Rather reluctantly I might add. Someone had at last woken up to the fact that I had CW papers and I was sent off to Lee-on-Solent to face a Selection Board.

No one knew at this time how swiftly the war would end following the atom bomb, and we had all expected a long tedious battle. In the event the Japanese surrendered shortly afterwards and 818 squadron never did leave the country for the Far East.

The war was over and as I waited at Lee-on-Solent for an Upperyardmen's Course the returning men passed through in their hundreds. Lee was the Air Branch Barracks and from there the majority of Fleet Air Arm men were demobilised. The messes rang with laughter at the sheer relief of it all. Whilst there, some were meeting up again with others of their kind whom they hadn't seen for many months and they recounted to each other all their wanderings, trials and tribulations of the days between. TAGs in particular were vociferous in describing all the imaginable and unimaginable happenings as they counted the heads of those who were left. It will be appreciated that I was in the Chiefs Mess, so the TAGs passing through were all from the groups trained prior to about 1941.

The remarkable thing is that squadron numbers were bandied about as though the speakers expected all listeners to be fully aware of the exploits of their own particular squadron. Early in the war such might have been possible because certain squadron numbers became a by-word for always being in the thick of it. 830 at Malta for instance or 825 for the Bismarck and Scharnhorst attacks. Later, however, the sheer multiplicity of squadrons made it impossible to recall who was who. It says a lot for the pride that Commanding Officers managed to instill into squadron spirit that many men felt that the eyes of the rest of the Service were focussed on their squadron alone.

I imagine that it was only well after the war, when some books were written on the subject, that the majority of personnel found out what their colleagues had been up to. Sister squadrons on the same ships would have been known but not many others.

Once the demobilisation dates approached these men began to wonder what awaited them as civilians. Some had it all mapped out. Others went without a thought of what they were going to do. They were just glad to be free of the routine.

Quite a few had to apply for special release. These were the men who, like myself, had joined at the outbreak of war and had no option but to sign on as regulars. A special AFO had recognised this situation and noted that such enthusiasts had really only wished to join for the duration. Now they were allowed to revoke -but not those who had indicated their intention of being regulars such as my application as an Upperyardman.

A few other regulars were also able to call it a day. For several pre-war men the completion of their time at either 12 or 22 years had taken place at some time during the war and so these were able to go. It didn't all happen overnight and some were still awaiting the day well into 1946.

CHAPTER 22

Further Enemy Encounters

Of recent years I have been busy piecing together as much information as possible of TAG history. My regret is that this work was not begun at a much earlier date when many of the participants were still alive. Somehow, at that time, we did not regard ourselves as historical figures. I suppose it was clear enough that those who had taken part in something special had some claim to fame, but for the rest it was simply the every day job. The special events had been placed on record, and it wasn't until later that we realised that even the official lists of the aircrew often had corrupted versions of the TAGs names. This was particularly noticeable in the lists for the Tirpitz attacks. Such errors arose from manual copying and perhaps because they were taken from the briefing lists. It was not unknown for crews and individuals to be switched at the last moment.

In compiling the casualty lists I have leaned heavily on the work of Ron Pankhurst , himself an ex-TAG, who has made a special study of all Fleet Air Arm losses. I have also attempted to portray who was in a squadron at any particular time and to show those who received awards for their efforts. It is hoped that all these lists will appear as appendices to this book.

In studying such lists I have more and more come to admire the men who were the crews during those early war years 1939 to 1941. Few survived. Not for them the prospect of being relieved after some set period. As far as they were aware at that time, it was a case of keep going until it was their turn not to come back. Remember too, that in 1939/40, most TAGs flew as Naval Airmen. Then we were putting our obsolete biplanes into action in daylight. No wonder they got mauled over Norway, and along the Channel coast around Dunkirk. No better, either, if they were in Skuas.

I suppose the officers may have felt that there was some prospect of reward for daring efforts against the odds. The chap in the back did not enjoy such possibilities. Often he was not briefed on the intentions. Just jump in and go. And the next day and the day after. The general news was that of losses in every theatre and overall there was an air of despair. For those at the sharp end, losing their comrades each day, it could well have been devastating. At least when I came on the scene there was a glimmer of light.

When I look at some of the pre-war TAG courses I find they were just about decimated. A few of these chaps became Prisoners-of-War, at dates in mid-1940. When they came back in 1946 they contacted the TAG Association hoping to find their erstwhile colleagues. I was unable to help. Almost to a man they had been lost. Of course, this wasn't always due to enemy action. The very essence of naval flying meant that there was the threat of destruction at every take-off.

I apologise for painting such a black picture, but I feel it is necessary to get across the feeling of utter hopelessness that prevailed during much of 1940, so that the reader can appreciate how these chaps set off to fly during those years. Gradually this attitude receded as the war progressed. Now and again it reappeared when called upon to carry out extreme actions such as Bismarck, the Channel epic and the Ceylon affair. Actually, Fleet Air Arm losses remained at an almost constant level through the war, but as our numbers increased dramatically, then in proportion they did not hurt so much at a later date. So the spirit became quite buoyant once victory was in sight.

Whilst Gordon Lambert has given us excellent accounts of his two visits to Tirpitz in Kaa fjord, perhaps a little more should be said about other people involved in these attacks. Gordon's first visit was in the attack known as Mascot, but by then the smoke screen system had been well established. The more successful attack was probably the first one, known as Tungsten on 3-4-44, when they were more able to see their target. This involved 830 and 831 Squadrons from Furious and 827 and 829 Squadrons from Victorious. During this attack TAG Ernie Carroll of 829 baled out when they were hit. He joined TAG Vic Smyth of 831, who was also brought down, and they both became POWs. Paddy Burns of 830 was less fortunate and was killed. Quite a few TAGs were awarded DSMs for this attack, and these included Jan Lock, Andrew Carr, Tom Cridland, Ginger Topliss and Oscar Halhead. Awards were not so prolific for the subsequent attacks and whilst there were fewer losses, at least amongst the TAGs, yet Doug Sansom of 826 was injured and eventually lost his leg. Allan Thomson can claim he went there three times, twice with 830 and once with 827. Other TAGs can also say they went there more than once. Frank Grainger,Sam Dunn and Ted Jones are amongst those who made three visits.

I must include some comment on the activities that took place in the Channel. Indirectly, I have already made mention of 825 and 826 Squadrons, who were pressed into action along the Dutch and French coasts, in endeavours to prevent enemy build-ups of shipping, with possible invasion in mind. 812 Squadron were similarly employed, and their action extended until March 1941. When it was clear that Swordfish wouldn't last long in daylight, they switched to minelaying at night. The redoubtable Donkey Bray was awarded a DSM here, and other squadron men included Ernie Kerridge and Stan Makin. For all of this Channel work the squadrons were under the control of Coastal Command. In fact it seemed to become almost the policy for squadrons working up for Carriers, to carry out this activity for a while. Later, yet other squadrons who had been on Arctic convoys, were sent to Coastal Command - for a rest ? Once the Germans had gained control of France, then up to the time of the Normandy landings, E boats and other German vessels were able to move up and down the Channel with some freedom. In daylight they had considerable cover from the fighter airfields in France, and it was necessary to make our attacks against them during the dark hours. This meant they had to be searched for, and it was soon evident that this was more readily achieved by slower aircraft, such as Swordfish or Albacores.

816 squadron was involved during the period January to April 1941 and after reforming the following year, they went back to the Channel. During this stint TAG J.A.Varley became a POW at Cherbourg and Dickie Dickens at Le Havre. On the same night as Dickens went down Bernard Whitehead was killed, also at Le Havre. We find 816 returning to the Channel in 1944. This would be a period when they were covering the D-Day landings.

A variety of airfields were in use for this work, including North Coates, Detling, Thorney Island, Manston, Exeter,St.Merryn and Hawkinge. One well known squadron seconded to Coastal Command for this task was 819 Squadron. They began their stint after return from HMS Avenger in 1942 and went to Bircham Newton. The TAGs included Stan Pomfret and Ollie Bridges. Ollie claims they were forgotten by the Admiralty. I don't suppose this is strictly true, but probably they didn't always receive the information available to other Fleet Air Arm squadrons, and maybe the crews were not relieved as early as was expected.

Such squadrons were able to scour the Channel at night looking for E boats and carry out minelaying. However, having found their enemy, they were at some disadvantage when trying to attack such a fast moving target, well equipped with defensive weapons.

Other squadrons did similar work. 811 in late 1942. Then in 1943 it was 823 and 833, also 842 later that year. I refer you to my lists to see the many TAGs involved in these operations. When 838 joined the party in April 1944 to operate from Harrowbear, little did they realise what a nasty job awaited them. It was one thing to attack E-boats, but a German destroyer was rather another matter. By this time such vessels had been liberally supplied with anti-aircraft armament and their techniques sharpened up against slow flying opponents. So when 838 were sent to attack an Elbing class destroyer at Cherbourg it was courting disaster. The place was more specifically Isle Vierge, and the date 1st.May 1944. As six aircraft were lost it has been difficult to get a clear picture of events. Some managed to limp home and crash land in various parts of the country. Three TAGs were killed in the attack. Albert Rockley, Brian Rowntree and Dick Grapes. I have managed to talk to Bill "Ginger" Locke, who was one survivor, about the affair, and obviously he only saw it from his viewpoint. It was evidently a right little hornets nest, with a wall of defensive weaponry from ship and shore and all stirred up by other attackers. Clearly it was not a good target for Swordfish in 1944. However, 838 recovered from this debacle and continued in the Channel until Feb.1945. Then back came 819 once again from April 1944 through to February 1945. During this period TAG George Machan was severely injured when he ditched 27-8-44. Following up the armies, once they had broken through from the landings, took 819 into Belgium from where they could continue the coastal patrols. To my mind this has remarkable similarities to the situation at the end of the first World War, when fighter squadrons of the RNAS moved into Belgium to cover the front line. In a way, it was this action which precipitated the formation of the RAF.

It was not only the Swordfish squadrons which engaged in this work. Avenger squadrons, working up before going to the Pacific, also got their hand in. However, as we learn from a detailed description from one pilot engaged in this effort, they did have some difficulty in latching on to their targets. They could pick up the E-boats well enough with their radar, but tended to overshoot when getting into position to attack. This particular pilot finally approached rather by guesswork and met a hail of retaliatory fire. He baled out to become a prisoner but not so his TAG, Stan Norman, or his Observer. This same squadron, 855, lost another aircraft with TAG Bash Selby, the following night. Also involved in the Channel were Avenger squadrons 848 and 854. Even Barracuda squadrons were not immune. We find 822 doing anti-submarine work there from Jan.to Apr.1945.

How did the TAGs like this arrangement ? I suspect they rather enjoyed it. Attached to the RAF where they could perhaps cock a snoot at authority and able to get ashore rather more easily than from Naval establishments. Very nice, even if they didn't get a tot.

Besides the dramatic, if unsuccessful, attempts to sink Tirpitz, Barracudas were also used extensively in the Indian Ocean during 1944. Sometimes this effort gets overlooked in view of the more extensive use of the Avenger at a later stage, and because Avengers also worked alongside the Barracudas in 1944. Much of the work actually consisted of sea searches plus the inevitable A/S patrols. Here and there, however, some strikes were made against Japanese outposts. It would have been unwise to expose Barracudas to the more strongly guarded positions even with extensive fighter support. In April and May 1944 Illustrious was searching for Japanese Cruisers with 810 Squadron without success. However, they also had 845 and 847 squadrons with Avengers. These together made attacks on Sabang 19-4-44 and then Sourabaya 31-5-44. There is little special to report on these from a TAG viewpoint except the good fortune of no losses. However, a few weeks later they also attacked Port Blair in the Andamans on 21-6-44. Here TAG Charlie Rogers was shot down in a Barracuda and became a POW. He was eventually taken all the way back to Japan, and whilst suffering the usual privations and humiliations that the Japanese always inflicted on their prisoners, he at least avoided the ultimate sacrifice met by other such POWs, as we shall see.

Later on that year the Victorious arrived with 831 squadron and Indomitable with 815 and 817 squadrons. All of these were Barracudas. They attacked Emmahaven/Inderoeng on 24-8-44 and on return from this Geoff Evans' A/C stalled in and he was killed. Presumably they had suffered damage from flak. After this 831 were replaced aboard Victorious by 822. Thus, a month later a further strike by this group was made by 822,815 and 817. This time they attacked Sigli in Sumatra, again without TAG loss. No doubt, by switching around they had strung out the Japanese aircraft to only a few at each target. Now the same group went up to the Nicobars, though only 815 and 817. Strikes here took place on both the 17th and 19th Oct. 1944. The first was on Nancowrie harbour and here regretably Ken Jenner's A/C was seen to dive straight in during the attack, which was otherwise reasonably successful.

Avenger squadrons were not only aboard the major carriers, but also operated from several of the smaller ones, such as Shah, Empress and Emperor. One particular episode that deserves special mention concerns 851 squadron operating from Emperor at that time. They were able to shadow the Japanese Cruiser Haguro as it made its way back to Singapore through the Malacca Straits which are 150 miles wide at that point. Maintaining a continuous stream of relieving aircraft initially taxed the squadron, whose aircraft had been previously engaged elsewhere. Yet they also managed to mount a strike which was only thwarted by our own destroyers attacking first, on the information from the shadowers. So, yet again, TAGs Ted Sherlock, Tony Traverse and others, had been able to put their communication abilities to good use. These two were awarded DSMs.

In describing for us his own view of the Palembang attack, Gordon's account, fascinating and factual as it is, has not been able to embrace all the other events that took place. Thus it is necessary to make some reference to one or two of the other squadrons. Of course, full accounts have appeared elsewhere, so I am only concerned with those aspects which involved TAGs. We know that 854 Squadron was taken down through the balloon barrage, whether unwittingly or in the belief that it would not deter is not known. What we do know is that balloons claimed the lives of TAG Barber and of CPO TAG, George Stollery. George was of the pre-war group and had been injured in the Illustrious bombing of 1941. Later he was active with 819 Squadron and so was an experienced and well known character.

Even more devastating was the action involving 849 Squadron. Being the last to attack, they first of all found that the flak defences had reached fever pitch and then on the route out they were jumped by Jap fighters which somehow had evaded the attentions of our own fighter squadrons. So 849 squadron aircraft fought a running battle on the way home with TAGs fully employed in their defensive role. Remember that the target was on the eastern side of the island and so they were flying across a large expanse of jungle country for many miles before crossing the sea to the westwards. Two of the aircraft were shot down and at least two others were obliged to ditch alongside the destroyer, HMS Whelp, which had been positioned off shore to guard against such difficulties. These two ditchings involved TAGs Dickie Richardson and Bob Taylor.

The two aircraft shot down carried TAGs Ivor Barker and Bill McRae. With their crews, both were reported as having survived and were POWs. I am not sure if this information actually reached us during the war. What is more important is that these crews, together with some fighter pilots also lost at Palembang, were all beheaded by the Japanese after the surrender, at Changi prison, probably on August 16th.1945. The story is confused because the Japanese took steps to confuse and gave contradictory accounts and dates. Certainly when the story came out, the three Jap officers who carried out the executions took their own lives, but probably others were also involved and these could not be identified. It should be understood that Allied forces took some time to get ashore after the surrender and there was much else to be done.

We now believe that the bodies were taken out to sea in small boats and dumped overboard. Another story that they were forced to dig their own graves is probably true up to a point. It was the kind of torture often carried out. In this case we do not think the bodies actually went into such graves.

Though the bald facts were known, nothing was at first done to record such horrific events. Due to the persistence of Mrs.Mavis Morton, the wife of Bill McRae, and since re-married, this has now been remedied and a plaque has been erected in Changi chapel to all these brave men. Also a stone memorial ,donated by stone-mason Tom Topham, is due to go to the chapel at Yeovilton, also marking this event. All this effort has been guided by the sterling efforts of Dickie Richardson, who has been to Changi for the unveiling and to New Zealand for a replica plaque. He has organised the collection of a considerable fund to which large numbers of individuals and Associations have contributed. At last we can say that this appalling act has gone on record.

A feature of the operations from the major carriers was that the TBR element was worked as a single squadron in each ship. The maintenance aboard was greatly improved because replacements were not baulked by squadron demarcations. Thus we find that the squadrons aboard the Pacific Fleet carriers were very much larger than had previously been the case. We have already met 820 aboard Indefatigable, and 849 aboard Victorious. The others were 848 with Formidable, 857 with Indomitable, 828 with Implacable and 854 with Illustrious.

Much effort was engaged in subduing the islands of the Sakishima Gunto. The object was to suppress any retaliation from this group whilst the Americans were attacking Okinawa. Gordon Lambert has given us some account of this effort. The other squadrons and Carriers were similarly engaged. We lost several crews along the way. Others had to ditch. From 849 Ossie Jones was rescued by Kempenfelt. Ivan Miller also ditched and Doc Dougherty was rescued by Ondine.

Such attacks continued with the final onslaught against Japan itself, before the surrender. TAG Jack Rogerson was taken as a POW when flying with 828 from Implacable. With 820 from Indefatigable, was Ron Pankhurst, whilst from the same squadron 'Jan' A.A.Simpson and Harry Evans were awarded DSMs for attacks around Tokyo in the last actions of the war.

In these few pages I cannot do justice to all the efforts of TAGs in these and other theatres. I trust you will refer to my lists of "TAGs in Squadrons" to see who else was involved and where. Also to Ray Sturtivants excellent "Squadrons of the Fleet Air Arm" and other books on Fleet Air Arm exploits.

De Havilland Dominie

CHAPTER 23

Communicators

From Lee-on-Solent, in 1946, I was sent on the Upperyardmen's Course. I will not dwell on this period, interesting though it was, as it has no TAG overtones. Suffice to say that I failed in the later stages - insufficient officer-like qualities. This was hardly surprising considering the standards demanded, though I felt that everything ran against me. I was already a C.P.O. and Air Branch to boot - hardly helpful where they wished to mould one's outlook in seafaring tradition. Finally there was no war and the Royal Navy had an abundance of officers applying for permanent commissions. More Upperyardmen were not wanted at that point in time. It was a disappointment as I had worked hard at changing my attitude and appearance.

So in mid-1946 I found myself back at Lee-on-Solent. With the end of the war there was a sudden dearth of Radio Mechanics, all of whom had been wartime recruits. So the TAG became a useful man to fill the gap. Three of us were sent up to Arbroath. Pop Lasson and Darkie Holroyd joined the Anson flight for Radio and Radar maintenance. I went to the Naval Air Signal School and found myself with half-a-dozen Wrens to supervise. If I thought I knew all about radio I soon discovered this was not so. I was faced with a cross section of every style of Service radio in use, including several new ones and many American models. The next few months were highly enlightening as I familiarised with all manner of radio matters.

The Chiefs mess at Arbroath was almost a Mecca for TAGs. This had always been the case since the days when it was an Observers school with several TAG instructors and others taking the Observers Mates courses. Now, apart from us "technicians", there were still several Instructors at the Signal School and a course for TAG 1 was going through - all Chiefs naturally. The chaps still left in the Service were the regulars and for the most part they were of pre-war vintage. When this course passed out and left, new arrivals gathered to form the next course which would be No.13. Available TAG2s were now in short supply and those of us on the Station were put in to make up the numbers. As it happened this TAG1 course was to be the last one. I chuckled at the inference of the course number. I had come across it somewhere before !

By now almost any gathering of TAGs produced a collection of characters and this course was no exception. Jan Lock, Darkie Holroyd, Pop Lasson, Frank Smith ,Ted

Churlish and Keith Allum to name but a few. The course was quite comprehensive and lasted some six months. The radar theory alone was enough to give some grey hairs - yes, at last they were telling us how it worked, and some TAGs at least didn't want to know. My earlier stint in the radio workshop stood me in great stead and eased the burden of swotting. I was able to spare time for allied subjects. One Instructor Officer was a bit nonplussed to find me wading through some calculus instead of the radio theory. He caught me out in the end. I sat near the nissen-hut stove of the classroom and had dozed off - too easy in the afternoon after a tot. Anyway I'd lost the thread of the lecture and looked very sheepish when asked a question. I hadn't the foggiest idea what it was all about. The lads laughed like hell -they'd all seen me dozing - and enjoyed seeing me taken down a peg or two. In any case it wasn't easy fitting back into the Chief's mess after an Upperyardmen's course.

During the course we did a few trips in an Anson. Radar and W/T exercises - the first flying for a year or so. Then we were hit by the winter of 1946/47. One of the bleakest winters on record. In Scotland it was just about the worst of anywhere. Villages cut off -animals stranded on hill sides. Arbroath airfield had about 4 feet of snow all over. By the time runways had been ploughed open the snow either side was heaped 10 feet high. A few of the aircraft were got off on mercy missions -dropping supplies to villages and to animals where they could be found. Some of the TAGs were employed pushing the feed stuff out of the aircraft doors. The landings were hazardous. Inevitably in the end a tyre slipped on the ice and an aircraft ploughed into the side banks of snow. We walked out one night to one of the local villages for a few beers and got greeted like heroes. It seemed we were the first ones to get through to the village for some days.

In March the course came to an end and we were sent our separate ways. My draft was merely a few miles down the road to Donibristle (still Scotland - och aye) and there I joined 782 squadron. It seemed a little odd. They must now have had TAG1s by the bucketful and hardly any TAG3s. For here we were back as W/T operators in a communication squadron. Personally I welcomed the flying job. The aircraft were D.H.Dominies - a comfortable cabin biplane which could carry 7 or 8 passengers. Apparently they had begun the war as a civilian feeder line service around Scotland. After being taken over by the Navy this service had been redirected towards the Naval Air Stations - virtually the same airfields but then doing war work. Evidently there was no immediate move to turn it back to civilian use and the 'bus service' continued for Fleet Air Arm requirements. We would fly special trips to take V.I.P.s wherever was required but otherwise we did regular runs serving all the Air Stations in Scotland and N.Ireland transporting people and aircraft spares. Airfields visited included Arbroath, Lossiemouth, Evanton, Belfast, Eglinton, Abbotsinch, Sumburgh, Machrihanish, Anthorn and perhaps less often Dyce, Leuchars and so on. As a squadron for knocking up the flying hours this was it.

It also meant one met many other TAGs. There weren't all that many of us still serving and I soon began to know the whereabouts of most of them. Landing at any of these places for lunch one could get a sip of someones tot and pass on all the grapevine news. In the air our job was to get clearance on the radio. Our bus-route Dominies were treated like airline flights and we worked the civil airline frequencies. As a stepping stone to a civil operators licence it was admirable. Many TAGs got into the business this way. Donibristle itself had an excellent MF/DF station and we could always be guided in no matter what the conditions.

On one trip across to N.Ireland we took a Wren W/T operator for the air experience. I'd briefly told her what we did on the radio and on leaving Belfast on the homeward leg let her sit in the seat and have a go. To my surprise the pilot asked me if I'd like to fly the plane. It wasn't fitted for dual - there was only one seat up front. He just climbed out and let me climb in. Then he went back and had a doze. I know these things fly themselves but I got a real kick out of taking it to Donibristle, flying for an hour or so all on my own. It was then that I learnt that I had a natural tendency to climb rather than hold a steady height. The Dominie was very docile and didn't drop its nose in a turn presumably because of the small twin engines at the C of G.

The radio was the old faithful Geep and apart from that we had no other navigation aids. That didn't stop us operating in poor conditions. We could usually get below cloud which would stop other aircraft. With a low speed and good forward visibility, hedge hopping was no problem.

Very few TAGs had a flying job at this time. Eglinton still had Barracudas on A/S work but elsewhere the switch had been to Fireflies which were two-seaters using Observers. Lots of TAGs were doing radio repair work and yet others were on Air Traffic Control or acting as Regulating Chiefs. Many of them were very happy with this arrangement. We did not receive flying pay but a rate for the ranking and if not flying who cared ? The Royal Navy was not unmindful of this and at the end of August 1947 they introduced a new concept. For those who wished to continue flying a course would be initiated which would train them as observers. Others could opt to take a Radio Conversion course, whence they would become Radio Mechanics (keeping whatever rank they held). Or they could choose to join a newly instituted branch of Aircraft Handlers. The latter covered a wide range of responsibilities such as fire-fighting, carrier hangar work and squadron administration. In fact these were just the type of jobs many TAGs were doing. Though retaining their ranks they would drop quite a bit on non-substantive pay as these were non-flying activities. Several opted for radio maintenance and only a relative handful were left to continue flying.

It was the beginning of the end for the branch of Telegraphist Air Gunner.

Fairey Firefly 1

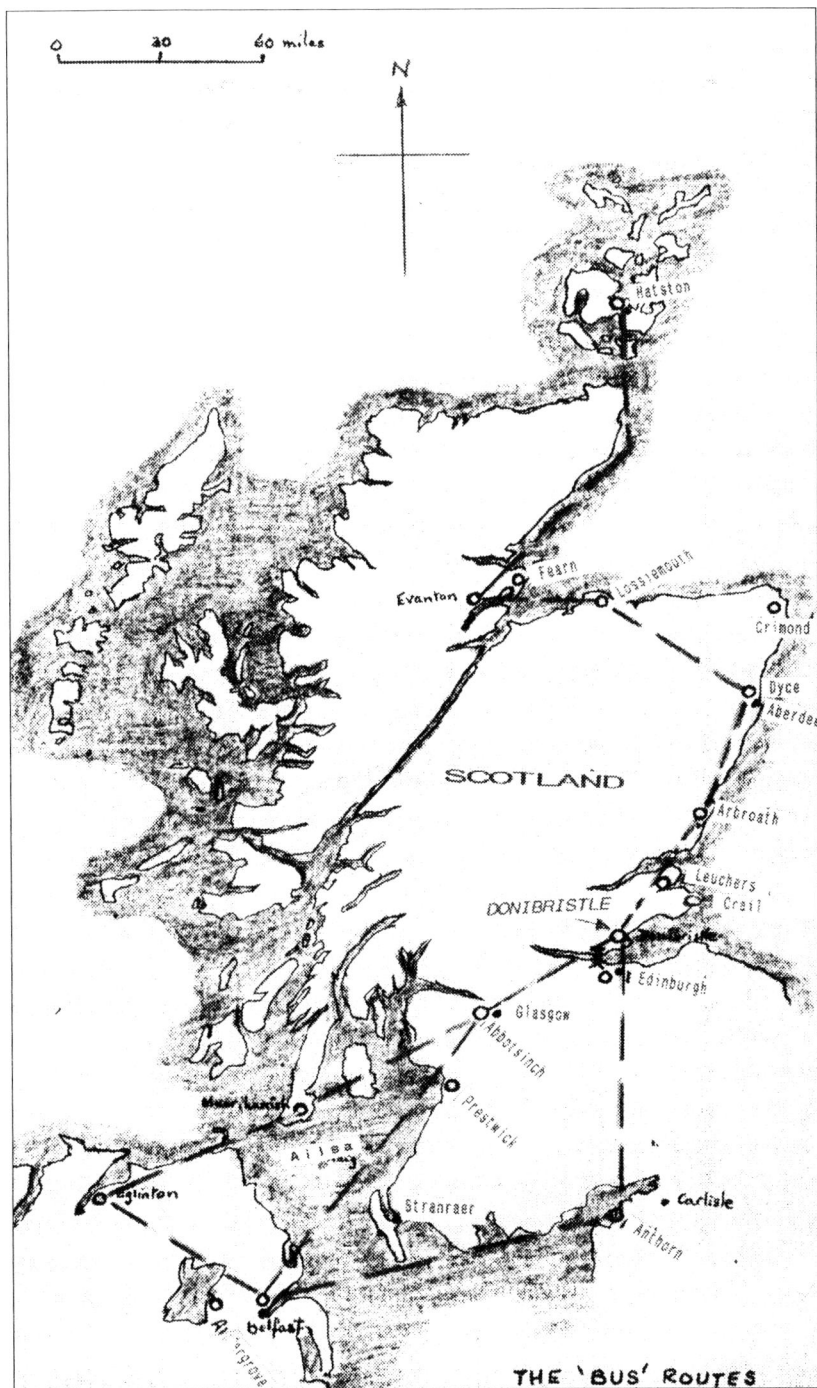

THE 'BUS' ROUTES

187

CHAPTER 24

Aircrewmen

Unquestionably my choice was to continue flying. At last the chance was offered to become a navigator. Just over a hundred of us made this decision and we went through in ten courses. The early ones were 15 or 16 strong and this dwindled later to groups of 9 or 10. It happened that I, with several of the recent TAG1s bunch, were put on the first course. I expect we were all readily available. If we thought that TAG1 group had character it had nothing on the first Conversion Course. This consisted of Nutty George,Tom Ford, Arthur G.Robinson, Bunker Ellis, Bob Sharman, Pop Lasson, Darkie Holroyd, Tommy Thompson, Tug Wilson, Blood Read, Jackie Cornwell, Scotty, Jackie Spratley, D.D.Smith, Ted Churlish and myself. Amongst this lot of regulars I was the baby of the group.

The Naval Air Signal School had moved from Arbroath to Seafield Park, just outside Lee-on-Solent. It was here that we began the course - with a refresher on W/T and Radar. Not everyone had the advantage of a recent brush-up on the subjects. This time moreover there was far greater accent on airborne radar operating and we did numerous trips in Ansons out over the Channel, homing onto any ship that was around and these were plentiful enough. The twist to the whole affair was that our instructors were TAGs like ourselves, albeit with some experience in their particular subject. Eventually they too had to go through the same course, when some of our No.1 course had come back to Seafield Park to become their instructors ! The one new subject we tackled at Seafield was Meteorology.

In November we moved down to St.Merryn and began the real part of our navigational training. There was plenty of classroom work and the airborne exercises were in Fireflies. As it was winter we were fitted out with the latest idea - immersion suits - not far removed from a space man's rigout. To see some of our more venerable members , especially the short ones, making their way to an aircraft complete with parachute and in these suits was laughable in the extreme. The rear seat in a Firefly was of the bucket type so the chute was the pilot's style that one sat on. Manoeuvres with chartboard and protractor must, to the less familiar, have been quite an effort in the cockpit. Now my previous navigational experience began to tell. Nothing was really new and I could use the course to polish up my technique till it became second nature. Scotty was another who knew his way round a chartboard, and with a click-click of the C.S.C. we could be on our way home while the others were thinking about it. We did the navex's up and down the coast, not more than 20 miles out at sea at any time. The chart paper was blank as though we were in mid-ocean. So apart from "take departure over Trevose Head" we would not refer to a map. The pilot though, had to note where we finished up. This was a shade misleading because whenever we crossed the coast on the way home we could expect a wind change and this was not taken into account for the purpose of the exercise and mostly we would find ourselves further south than the aimed at terminal point. It was like locking on to an aerial monorail that inevitably took us down towards Plymouth.

The course made its mark at St.Merryn all right. We fielded a hockey team which decimated the Wrens. Not so much skill as brute force. Our soccer team was not so successful but the remarkable part was that we could field one at all from 16 relatively old men by Service standards. There was no doubt that the course won hands down at the Sod's Opera when ably led by Nutty George as M.C..

In early 1948 we qualified and found we were to be called not Rating Observers but Aircrewmen. A term which smacked more of an airborne flunkey than anything else. Though we remained Chiefs we were not called such, but Aircrewmen 1st class. Well, we might not have liked the name but the money was better.

So to a squadron to exercise our newly won spurs. Where else but to the Mediterranean ? Clearly some of us were due for more foreign service. Six of us embarked in a troopship and at Malta we split three each to HMS Ocean and HMS Triumph. I went to 827 Squadron aboard Triumph with Darkie Holroyd and "Robbie" Robinson. The other three, D.D.Smith, Scotty and Bob Sharman went to Ocean. Our squadron had Firefly 1s and were part of the 13th C.A.G. (what 13 again !) which included a sister squadron of Seafire XVIIs.

Good old Malta with the sun burning on the white rock and hurting the eyes. The aircrew style dark glasses were very welcome. These were issued to guard against the sun's glare at heights. For now we might find ourselves above 20,000 feet using oxygen and looking up at a near black sky. We hadn't been up that far before. It all sounds a bit dated against todays jet performances and was even commonplace for fighter aircraft in the war. To ex-Swordfish types this was all brand new experience and a little breathtaking. It was also quite frightening when we went to sea and standing in goofers gallery watched an aircraft break its back on the round-down and finish up in the barrier. The sound of crunching metal like so much silver paper happening right there at the end of your nose and close enough to reach out and touch is upsetting to say the least. Yet, we were going to fly in those things !

Not a few Aircrewmen retired from battle when finally faced with the new era of flying which was so different from their previous experience. With a nasty time gap in between, too. However, this was not so with our stalwarts. We got stuck into the squadron routine of flying and began to build up an impressive list of deck landings, though not without incident. The squadron already had 4 TAGs flying with them. It surprised us somewhat to find these chaps with the squadron, but then it became clear that the new flying arrangements did not often allow aircraft to go off singly, and if observers were in short supply then the TAG was a useful stand-in. They were Windy Geale, Ron Gilbert, Ted Dingley and Jimmy Loveys. These chaps were of the younger school who opted to become regulars at the end of the war. It was almost unfair to have faced them with three Chiefs who were also Aircrewmen. They had to suffer me lecturing them about the intricacies of radar -the Senior Observer welcomed the idea of a qualified TAG1 who could fill in on non-flying days. They were dying to get away and take an Aircrewmens course themselves. When they did go, their cup must have been full to find I was their instructor again !

Without the edge of wartime strikes the story of squadron operations in peace time loses some of its bite, but for those participating it is as strenuous and exciting as ever. Any carrier working is full of incident and expectancy and as the peacetime navy simulates war, almost all aspects of the work are touched upon. My story so far has been nearly devoid of carrier background and therefore has given an unbalanced picture of a TAGs life. We have had to fill this gap by leaning on Gordon Lambert's descriptions to get the feel of carrier working. I can now expand on this by offering a picture of the post-war period. These were not unlike the problems met in the later war years except that Triumph was a much smaller carrier than Indefatigable and we did not have to face possible Kamikasi.

An aircraft carrier is a noisy sardine tin and no matter where you go there is no getting away from the noise. On the flight deck is the noise of engines all packed together in discordant harmony. Go under the fo'c'sle and you get the bang of the booster or, if not flying and entering harbour, there is the clatter of the anchor chain. Go aft to the quarter deck and there is the twanging of the arrester wires. In the hangar there is the bang-crash of the barriers being raised and lowered. If not actually landing on there is much incidental aircraft movement plus the clanging bell of the lift. Dive really down below to get away from it and there are the ship's engines. That's OK then you say, nothing excessive there. Wait, this is a small carrier and as like as not its going flat out to get up enough wind speed across the deck. So the ship shakes and shudders and the engines shriek. When there is no flying the tannoy vies with the disk jockey to make sure nobody gets bored with the quiet.

So we always welcomed a return to Valetta when we would fly off to Hal Far to enjoy a change. Not that there was a rest from flying. The object of going ashore was to keep the aircraft busy. However, too long a stay was upsetting. The pilots lost touch with deck landing technique in spite of lots of addles. A return to the ship was always the time when someone went into the barrier or over the side.

A visit to Hal Far also gave us the chance to have a drink with Nigs Hemming and Taff Beere, a couple of veteran TAGs holding fort at that establishment. We would also meet up again with the Ocean crews when their squadrons were ashore. On one of these visits we were able to quiz Bob Sharman on a ditching he'd made off Ocean. I was always sensitive to escape and rescue techniques and what to do when faced with certain circumstances. Better to learn from other people's mistakes than your own and I reckoned many an aircrew had been lost by taking the wrong action or no action at all. In this case we wanted to know how much time he had to get out before the aircraft sank. It wasn't much. In what sequence did he clear himself of straps, harness and helmet cords ? The last answer was interesting. He took it off. That must have saved a second or two but didn't give his head any protection as he removed it before the ditching. Poor Bob must have been fated. A few weeks later he did another forced landing. This time they went down on a runway at a disused airfield and crashed into a barrier of oil barrels. The aircraft burst into flames and they didn't get out. I never could see the point of putting the barrels there.

Joining Triumph and picking up the routine was quite an experience for me. I'd had a quick look at Argus, Ark Royal and Illustrious but had never acclimatised to carriers as my sea time was so short. In any case Triumph was a Light Fleet Carrier and there were innovations that I'd never seen. It was a bit awkward being a C.P.O. and yet having to traverse the ship without appearing green on fundamentals. It didn't even start well. I'd been in charge of the new draft from the troopship and left them manhandling kit aboard from a lighter whilst I went to find the Master-at-Arms. So what did they do but leave one of my bags on the lighter and it finished up back on the quayside. The Jaunty didn't like that -obviously it had to be my fault. When he referred to the M.F.V. alongside I didn't know what he was talking about especially as it sounded like "enefbee". It's the same in any sphere. One just has to know the colloquial language and not be put off by terminology. Once explained, in no time it becomes second nature. The trouble I found in the Navy in earlier days was that no one ever explained. One was expected to know. I believe this was a studied technique amongst the old hands to reserve their position, and ensure that the new boys appeared suitably ignorant. "You'll learn it the hard way, like I had to."

The flying procedures were still basic but faster speeds and mechanical aids had quickened things up. Previously each aircraft landing on would have been struck down the lift as the next approached with perhaps a couple of minutes interval. Now, with barriers, it was only necessary to cross these to a forward deck park and the next could touch down. No messing about with flags to say who was next. (The hours we'd spent learning these and the codes that went with them !) Called in by radio a flight of four would fly down the starboard side of the ship into wind and in line astern. Then a peel-off one by one at 15 second intervals and a 180 degree turn brought one downwind at 30 second spacing. Another 180 degree turn as one came abreast of the round down and we were approaching the stern. As soon as the prior aircraft was moving forward off the wires we were under batsmans orders. The chap in the back could only view the beginning of this and then he lost sight of bats for the last few seconds before touch down. The view astern after touch down was really a bit nerve wracking. The chap behind seemed literally about to land on top of you. This was an illusion. Due to the ships forward speed one was retreating away from the next aircraft and so his relative approach speed was rather less. Even so there wasn't a lot of time to get across the barrier and see it rise before chummy behind touched down. We faced forward in the Firefly and weren't too worried about the early period when being unhooked. Not only weren't we looking, but knew that any delay at that point and bats would wave off the next aircraft. It was when we were getting out and did look back that we got concerned, if chummy behind didn't touch down and catch a wire. This was perhaps one of the most dangerous points in carrier operating and led eventually to the angled deck. We didn't have it then. Aboard Ocean, Nutty George had a near miss when another aircraft chewed up his tail and the prop stopped about a foot behind his head. On one occasion aboard Triumph I was just climbing out of the cockpit when I noticed an aircraft whose approach looked wrong. Sure enough he bounced and missed the wires and might easily have cleared the barrier. I could see him poised over the top of us like some huge bird of prey when incredibly his hook caught the second barrier. With no give from the barrier, something might well have broken but it didn't and he stopped suddenly right there behind us with me lying on the deck transfixed. After that I tried deserting the aircraft at the first opportunity, but nearly came unstuck. My pilot gave a burst of throttle as he was directed into place by the deck handlers. This caught my chartboard and I was nearly propelled into the barrier myself. So it became a case of sitting there and hoping. I did have to make myself scarce on yet another occasion when an aircraft cleared the barrier. This time two or three other aircraft had already come on behind us and we were in position and walking clear. I saw this aircraft coming way over the top of the barriers and jumped clear to a sponson. This carried a tarpaulin over the Bofors gun and I put a foot where no gun part existed underneath. A sprained ankle was a small price to pay for survival as this aircraft pushed a couple of others over the bows and we lost some men who were there at the front end of the deck.

We did a few navex's to prove our capability, but much of the flying was done as a flight or squadron or even as an Air Group. This was why the TAGs were still useful crews without needing navigational prowess. Wherever possible aircraft went as a pair giving safety cover to each other. This had stemmed from the earlier days of normal fighter practice. We flew finger formation. Why finger ? Look at your hand. The middle finger is leader with forefinger as his No.2. The third finger is another section leader with the little finger as his support or No.4. In formation it was a simple gesture for the leader to signal "open finger" or "close finger" by holding up the fingers accordingly.

Many of these carrier techniques were used by the squadrons in the Pacific operations, who adapted to lessons learned by the Americans. There was a further innovation whilst we were aboard Triumph. A change to American batting signals. These indicated aircraft position rather than what you should do and were therefore the reverse of the previous system. For example, arms held outstretched but below horizontal meant you are low rather than come down. The technique was also altered to cut engine at greater height and drop on rather than fly on. It had much to commend it. Less bother about rise and fall of round-down and less chance of float across the wires. One came down like a sack of spuds. It played havoc with undercarriages and the Seafires took a pounding. The Fireflies stood up to it but I believe a lot of aircraft had to be strengthened. It did mean commonality with the Americans and we could if necessary land on their ships. Of course this had happened during the war though only after our own batsmen had gone aboard. As already explained, we in the back lost sight of bats prior to touch down, but could see the ship's wake and then the deck and then the wires going by, so we well knew how successful a landing it was. The view from the back of a Firefly was very limited. The windows were flat with no bubbles so we couldn't look directly underneath. Nor ahead. Nor behind. Just above and sideways on about a 45 degree arc. This was helped if in a turn or by flattening one's nose against the window. However, the Firefly proved a very sound aircraft and stood the Navy in good stead over a long period. Developed from the Fulmar it moved through Night Fighter to Fighter Bomber to Reconnaissance and finally to anti-submarine aircraft. It should yet take a place alongside the Swordfish in posterity.

We practised with rocket fired flares. This was interesting. If only we'd had this form of illumination for tackling our wartime submarines. I believe they were under experiment during the war but came along too late to be used with great effect. I was sent off on one trip to record radar response on a submarine. Again this was interesting for me but disappointing. We did little better than we had done years before. It was now centimetre radar but pick-up ranges were at best 10 miles fully surfaced and when at schnorkel depths it was all I could do to get anything as close as 2 miles. If I hadn't known they were there the response would not have been seen. Our cooperating submarine dived and surfaced in various ways to aid the tests. Clearly there was a long way to go in radar techniques against submarines.

The ship carried out the usual peacetime activity of showing the flag and to my enjoyment we visited places that were enemy held on my previous Mediterranean excursion. The first visits were to Venice and Trieste. At Venice we did "Catherine Wheel" which meant turning the ship round by using the engines of all the aircraft ranged on deck, pointing outboard, and without help from tugs. By controlling on the radio which aircraft revved up, the turn could be set in motion and then checked. Then once more back to Malta and lots of squadron drill, rocket firing practice, and similar exercises, which did little to utilise our back-seat skills. Then back again to compass swinging. We found ourselves being used as the handling party. It really rubbed it in if the observer boobed and put the corrections in reverse such that it had to be done again. I felt it was time to draw attention to the fact that we were trained navigators and requested to see the Captain. That stirred it all up and I was hardly popular at higher levels. Even the Captain ticked me off, but it certainly caused a change. From that point on the three of us did all the compass swinging with a ground crew as handling party. Furthermore, we took on some of the duties that the observers normally did. I got the job of squadron radio and radar officer. Immediately the percentage of serviceability fell ! Not in fact, but in presentation. I found that it had been counted as a percentage of flights and if the radar had not been used it was counted as satisfactory. Everyone was misled into thinking all was well, not least the Air Group

Commander. So I had them all checked out and needless to say there were doubtful ones. We got them 100% before return to the ship. They wouldn't stay that way, but at least we stopped kidding ourselves that they were better than they really were. The reliability of that particular radar (A.S.H.) was never very good.

The summer cruise of 1948 took us to the Eastern Med.. For me it included a nostalgic look at Cyprus, though only from the air. Then we covered the final withdrawal of British troops from Palestine, including an unsuccessful search for some missing tanks! Flying exercises gave us a chance to do some individual navigation with

HMS Triumph at Venice, 1948

The 13th Carrier Air Group aboard HMS Triumph ranged for take off. Seafire XVIIs with Firefly 1s in the background

various searches and patrols. When the important one cropped up I muffed it, though not in the sense of getting lost. As is often the case with exercises the Fleet was split as Reds and Blues. We were the Red force and southeast of the Dodecanese heading west. The Blue force of Destroyers had set off from Malta to intercept us. The question was, would they take a course north or south of Crete ? I was detailed to search an area south of the island and extending nearly to its western end. My pilot thought they would be slipping round that end and wanted to extend our track and look round the corner. Before we got that far I had a radar echo to the south of track and turned towards. A small merchantman came into view and we turned away. I immediately got another echo to the west and turned towards that. Again a small ship. We turned to regain track. It was here I went wrong. I knew I should go right back to the point of our first turn off. If I did, there would be no time for our look round the corner, and my pilot who was skipper would be annoyed. The coast showed up clearly so I simply went north and left an 8 mile gap in the search. Well, of course you've guessed, that's where they were. Tucked right in to the coast. Well camouflaged and not distinguishable on the radar from the numerous rocky islands. In any case the radar chose that point to pack up. I was never carpeted for the mistake, but only because others were more at fault. My pilot got a rocket for extending the prescribed search. A follow up aircraft went right over the top of the destroyers without seeing them. This didn't surprise me. We had been briefed to fly at 8000 feet. This was far too high for the heat haze conditions. The two echoes I chased only came into sight at 3 miles. With the poor downward visibility from a Firefly they were nearly under our nose and we might have missed them without radar to tell us they were there. No wonder the other crew went over the top of the destroyers. Would we have done the same ? Perhaps initially. On the other hand, with the experience of the small ships, we deliberately reduced height and if I'd gone back to the first turn off point, with an approach from the south I think we would have seen them. We learn by mistakes and this was an old one in the sea search book. The lesson went home strongly for me.

We carried out many simulated strikes and coming back from this cruise we made dummy attacks on Malta. On the second of these I was leading a flight of four with an hours flying to get back to the ship. Our briefing had given us two possible positions for her. A signal would confirm the second of these. I headed for the midpoint. When no signal came this established the first position as the one required and I calculated the course change necessary. At that point I could not raise my pilot. After checking my gear I concluded his plug had come out. It immediately recalled the situation that day over Crete. This was a similar aircraft with a petrol tank between us. How do I attract his attention ? On these exercises one didn't transmit if it could be avoided and I held off. Yet now we were getting miles off course. In desperation I called our No.2 and asked him to come up and push my pilot round. Once he came up and signalled across, my pilot discovered the problem and all was soon sorted. I got ribbed a bit over this incident as apparently they could detect the concern in my voice on the radio.

Back at Hal Far we were sent off for a few days to a rest camp. Very nice too. In peace time they do take recognition of the pressures of carrier flying. On return we carried out some night flying exercises and in due course were off on another cruise. This time round Corsica and Sardinia where we took in Ajacio and Leghorn among the ports of call. The latter was in Italy and from there we were able to have a couple of days in Florence and visit Pisa on the way. Summer holiday cruise ? Almost.

On one of the exercises, my job was to shadow the Triumph whilst the fighters looked for us. Hide and seek in fact and good fun if you can get away with it. There was little low cloud and visibility was good. How were we to do it ? I had to play the radar game and try to come in under the beam. This is possible beyond the horizon but as one approaches a point is reached where radar pick-up is almost certain. I didn't want the fighters waiting to jump me then, so some miles out we climbed up and let them see us on radar on a positive approach course. Then we dived to get off their screen altered course and came in low on a quite different bearing. We played this game for some time without getting caught. I came in just close enough to sight the ship and then sheered off. A further part of the exercise was to send out course and speed reports on the W/T, just like our old wartime training had demanded from a shadowing aircraft. This keeps one rather busy in the back when doing all the jobs. It is also very difficult to decide on the course of an aircraft carrier when viewed from sea level at about 8 miles distance. It is just a shapeless blob. A number of times we saw the fighters heading towards where we'd been and knew the ruse was working. I had to keep ringing the changes to keep them guessing. Then at one point we had doubled back to such an extent that we actually came up behind the fighters looking for us. In any serious situation we would have got to hell out of it, but this was too good to miss. We climbed behind them and then cheated by listening on their frequency. It was quite funny to hear the Director in the ship saying they must see us we are right there, and the fighters denying any sight of us. Of course they twigged in the end and peeled round to bracket us but we'd had our little joke at their expense.

There followed a much more serious situation. A Lancaster was missing in our area. The weather had deteriorated atrociously. We were east of Sardinia and to the north there were gale force winds with low cloud and rain and visibility down to half-a-mile. The ship itself was on the edge of the storm in a clear area, though winds were high. We took off and headed into the worst of the storm spread out on a search pattern. After it closed round us I didn't see another aircraft. We did see two destroyers. We sort of burst upon them and nearly took away a mast. I don't think there was a hope of our seeing a downed aircraft. The met report said the wind was 40 knots. It wasn't true. I kept pushing up my estimate based on the state of the waves. I reckoned on 80 knots at the worst point. I feared the coast of Sardinia and altered course with each new estimate until my chart was all dog legs. I expect my pilot wondered where we were. When we broke clear on the return leg there was the ship ahead of us. Some aircraft had turned back, but two who battled it out as we did, appeared from downwind and they had been on tracks to the east of ours. I was rather pleased with this result, because otherwise the thrill of navigating had been rather a let-down. This time the radio was so full of static we could never have got a bearing and it was one occasion when dead-reckoning really mattered. Other times we were so well cossetted with radio aids that we couldn't get lost and at 180 knots a few miles of error can soon be made good. This was just not the same as looking for a ship in a Swordfish in which a ten mile square search could take half-an-hour.

The Lancaster we were looking for had unfortunately flown smack into the island of Elba. Unlucky perhaps, but in that storm understandable. A Triumph party picked up the crew and they were buried at sea.

Take-offs from the ship at this period were simply the basic method of flying off. On occasion we would use RATOG - rocket assisted take-off. This was intended to help when loaded or if wind speeds were low. When we used it, it was for exercise rather than necessity. No one liked RATOG. The two fixed rockets fired electrically and independently. There was too high a possibility of only one firing with dramatic results which could be disastrous. The aircraft would be slung over to one side and could easily stall and sideslip into the sea. We saw this happen once and a second time there was a very near miss.

After returning from the second summer cruise the Air Group flew to Tripoli where we participated in Army liaison activities including an attack on an old fort with live rockets. For me the crucial trip was on the way over. My rear hatch blew open - could I perhaps have failed to shut it properly ? I have shut such a hatch so many times both before and since that I can only believe it was a faulty catch. I never knew what to blame, but the effect was startling. Open cockpits up to the chest at 90 knots are one thing. Open to the seat at 180 knots I thought I was going to be sucked out. I couldn't shut it against the slipstream and had to suffer it for the rest of the journey.

We continued at Hal Far throughout November, and on one of the many flight drills staggered in formation up to 30,000 feet. It was the aircraft's ceiling and we wallowed drunkenly with the sun blazing down from a blackish sky. It must have been very difficult for some of the pilots who had to look towards the sun and eventually we almost fell out of the sky with the formation breaking up in disorder.

Early in December the U.S.6th Fleet exercised an attack on Malta. We in turn defended and our first job was to shadow the 6th Fleet. They made no attempt to intercept us and so we watched as they flew off a huge striking force from their two big carriers. They seemed to take a long time to get off and formed up. I don't know why they just ignored us. Then it was our turn. After a return for refuelling we assembled two groups. The first was a diversionary strike and this must have been effective because our main force got through to their ships unopposed. Their fighters only caught up with us when we were on the way home and they then made a head on attack in formation which was a bit frightening.

In January I was lent to the Ship's Flight and went to Tripoli in the Sea Otter. On the return we did a deck landing and it made a change to sit up there alongside the pilot and see the whole deck landing operation from the front. This heralded a general return to the ship and in the period during which pilots were refreshing themselves on deck landings there was a crop of barrier incidents, all of which I fortunately avoided.

We got in some more navex's and these were combined with strikes on the ship. The typical pattern was to lead a flight of 4 on a round sea tour for a couple of hours, and on return intercept the ship and come straight in with a dummy attack. If we were not the leader we did following navigation and this was more difficult as we had to monitor every course change on a drifting compass needle with the pilots endeavouring to maintain open formation. It was about this time that I decided to dispense with the cumbersome official chartboard. In its place I had a smaller board on which I could clip a piece of perspex and work with a chinagraph pencil and protractor. I would have done this long before, but was doubtful if it would be allowed. Then I saw an observer had done something similar so I went ahead. A number of others followed suit. There was no point in trying to work to close accuracy, as one could cover two or three miles in a simple turn. It was far more important to make a good estimate of the wind. The resulting board was much easier to handle.

The ship met an intense storm about this time and had to ride it out for 3 days outside Valetta harbour. (Should we have warned Gorbachev and Bush that this was likely ?) We soon found out that we'd been a fair weather ship. All sorts of things came adrift and I recall the suitcase shelf in the Chiefs' Mess acting like a launching ramp. With each roll of the ship during the night, yet another case would be catapulted across the mess. No one felt interested enough to get out of hammocks and do anything about it. Far too late we began lashing everything down.

Triumph's sister ship Ocean had been having a lot of trouble and was again in dock for engine overhaul. So it was thought expedient to operate her aircraft as well as our own aboard Triumph. This meant that for the first time we would have a deck park. Sharing accommodation was one big problem. A Light Fleet Carrier is not well off for space at the best of times. With the extra squadrons there was a considerable squeeze. It certainly livened things up on the Mess deck to have our opposite numbers aboard with a natural spirit of rivalry. More Aircrewmen had joined both ships from subsequent courses to ours and our regular Bridge table now took on the air of a tournament with Tommy Vaughan leading the Ocean challengers. When it came to squeezing up to fit in all the aircraft, the problem rose to a peak. One snag was that the aircraft were of different types. The same family, yes, but Oceans Firefly Vs and Seafire 47s did not match with Triumphs Firefly 1s and Seafire 17s. The different wing foldings and shapes made hard work of parking and operating a deck park was itself an innovation. The culmination came when an aircraft fell down the lift well. On a day when most of the aircraft had got airborne together, a point was reached when the deck park was full and aircraft were still coming aboard. Clearly some had to be struck down. This was undertaken, but flight deck communication went wrong and an aircraft was taxied forward whilst the lift was still down. It disappeared. Everyone held their breath. Then an intrepid man crept forward and looked over the edge. The Seafire was wedged on its nose partly upside down between another aircraft and the lift wall. There was no fire and every one got away with it. The photographs seen subsequently of the row of deck handlers each in grotesque stance trying to stop the aircraft taxying, was only paralleled by that marvellous cartoon of the row of dogs queueing for the solitary tree. It was evident that there had to be a set of rules, but it had been shown that a deck park was possible. The answer was to ensure that on any sortie the number of aircraft due to land must not exceed the size of the deck park.

After this we went off to fight the 'Spring War' with a reduced element of Oceans aircraft. For the purpose of the exercise Triumph would represent two carriers. The Home Fleet came out from England and took station at Gibraltar ; the Med. Fleet operated from Malta. I won't bore you with all the details of the objectives and limitations imposed by the umpires. Peacetime "wars" are always unrealistic. In principle some Cruisers belonging to the Med. force were in the Atlantic and had to get through the Gibraltar Straits. We would support by diversionary strikes. The glory rather rests with Earl Mountbatten who commanded the Cruisers and who publicised the main events. Due to his guile and that of his Warrant Tel. we knew that the opposing carriers had first come looking for us. Triumph took up a position north of the Balearic Islands (Majorca etc.) where it was hoped she would be difficult to find. We kept quiet and waited for their forces to come within range. They already had aircraft searching for us. Apart from having the strength of two Fleet carriers they had better aircraft types with greater range. When we did set off it was as both a search and a strike. The three flights were spaced on a broad front each with fighter escort. We kept low to avoid radar. Anyone sighting was to signal, when we would close on him for a combined attack. The C.O.s aircraft lifted now and then for a quick radar scan ahead. We didn't find them and reluctantly turned back. They cannot have been more than another twenty miles ahead and in a real situation we would probably have continued. However. peacetime operations demanded a reasonable safety margin and we couldn't eat into that petrol reserve. A pity as we would have caught them ranged on deck.

By now they had traced our ship's position and were preparing for a strike. With their greater speed they actually overhauled us on the run back - we weren't being followed and in fact they didn't see us. Yet on our return we had to hold off while they made their dummy strike, and so we needed our safety margin of fuel. For real we probably wouldn't have had a ship to land on.

After that there were no more cat and mouse tactics. Both sides put up strike after strike against each other. We made a dawn strike on Implacable the following day and another at midday. In the afternoon I was detailed to go and look for the opposing Battle Fleet which must be in the Atlantic west of Gibraltar. Another aircraft would shadow the Fleet Carriers and also act as radio link for me. To get to the Atlantic I first had to slip past these carriers. One aircraft caught by two fighters had to regard himself shot down. Such an aircraft would not be debriefed. To get past I used our old technique of coming in high and then suddenly diving and changing course. Keeping low we changed course a second time and squeezed our way by without being intercepted. The Spanish and Moroccan coasts were taboo to us and as the ships commanded the narrows there wasn't much choice.

We slipped through the Straits and out into the Atlantic and there we found a Battleship and four Cruisers with escorting destroyers. Surprisingly they had no air escort and we had the field to ourselves. I expect they saw us but it didn't seem to matter. We kept well out of range and for an hour we shadowed them and sent back our reports. Our link man must have had a busy time with his own reports to send as well. I must have been a bit tired and over casual on our return, for though we skirted round their Carriers, I didn't take any special action beyond keeping low. Maybe I thought we'd be ignored coming from the West. Anyway two Sea Furies found us. In fact we saw them first and they were on the wrong track but as they were between us and our ship there was no where else for us to go except towards their ships. If I did an about turn I wouldn't have enough fuel to get home. So when they swung towards us we knew we had to accept defeat. Meanwhile we would have a game of tag. They weren't very good. As they came in I kept my pilot posted and he turned inside them. Foolishly they stuck together. In avoiding one we avoided both. I could tell they wouldn't have hit us from my drogue days. I'd seen more dangerous attacks when we weren't the target. Then -bang,cough,splutter -our engine complained. This is a bit nerve shattering as the aircraft slows and falls. In the effort of evasion my pilot had forgotten to change petrol tanks, but soon we were running smoothly again. As my pilot sorted himself out our attackers had our mark. We waggled submission and turned home. Where ? What had we been doing in the last few minutes. I decided to ignore it and continued on the prior course. Whatever we'd done that should be our error. If I guessed some incorrect direction we might be wrong by twice as much. We reported being "shot down" and as it happened the ship appeared up ahead much as expected. I suppose our evasive turns had continued roughly along the original track. It was galling to be ignored on landing. One felt one had been a complete failure. I did see the plot showing the 'enemy' battlefleet correctly. 'Ops' caught my eye with a raised eyebrow and seemed happy with my brief nod.

At the end of the exercise the two fleets joined forces and all the aircraft took off to form one large group and make a combined mock attack on the Fleet. From three carriers there was quite an impressive force. At the grand debriefing many aspects were discussed. Much had taken place of which we were totally unaware. The Cruisers had very nearly squeezed through under cover of a neutral merchantman but for a smart searchlight operator. It was given an amusing touch when a certain Admiral was quite scathing about a radar report which said two major war vessels were approching Gibraltar when this was Triumph and her escorting destroyer. Lord Louis, as he will always popularly be known, reminded us that Triumph represented two carriers and suggested that the radar was more clever than the Admiral imagined.

We returned to Malta and on the way carried out further flying exercises. Triumph had now completed her commission and was to return to U.K..We were lucky to have joined her part way through. For us a short foreign commission indeed. A deck cargo was taken on board which meant we would do no flying on the way home. A much more comfortable homecoming than my earlier experience. We made our way to Greenock there to disembark and leave a very happy ship. So to Lee-on-Solent as usual and some leave.

What then ? I suppose it was inevitable. As Aircrewmen with current carrier experience, Robbie and I were sent to Seafield Park as instructors.

Seafield Park. A name to conjure with. Yes, it really was attractive. A mansion set in woods with a pathway down to the sea. A cricket pitch and tennis courts. What a shame that whilst we'd been with Triumph a fire had burned down the main hallway and the central part of the building. We had seen this on our previous visit and admired its wood panelling. Now only the two wings remained and these formed the basis of the school.

Several instructors were already there and these were presided over by one of the more senior TAGs in the business - Freddie Stewart. Like all newcomers to the instructing game there was much work to do establishing a set of notes and planning the sequence of each lecture to cover the syllabus of the subject. Necessarily brushing up to be 100% and able to answer any question. As a class, pupils can be very sharp and soon penetrate weaknesses. These would not be junior rates but TAGs on their conversion course. I was detailed to take the radio sphere but it was not exclusive. All instructors still had to fly in the Ansons which were flying classrooms, when we would be covering the practical side of the radar.

A great many TAGs have in their time been instructors. There were the schools at Worthy Down and Yarmouth in Canada. Also the Air Gunnery school at St.Merryn. As also the Observers schools at Arbroath and Piarco in Trinidad. Almost anyone coming back from a tour of operations was likely to be sent to one of these to pass on their knowledge from experience to the new generation. It was perhaps almost remarkable that I had gone so long before arriving at a school as an instructor. I'd spent much more time on the other side of the desk. Having said this I expect there will be a few TAGs who will be quick to tell me that they never got such a quiet number. Some unfortunates appeared destined to go from one operational squadron to another.

I'd been away from a morse key quite a bit. Could I manage to send an S.B.X.? Not to worry - it tripped along all right. In fact I later began to think it must be a habit like shaving, because sometimes I sent a few S.B.X.s with a hangover like a zombie, but nobody complained.

We took through Conversion courses 9 and 10. A final course No.11, was the last of the TAGs. Well nearly but not quite. There were still the chaps on the Reserve who came through once a year for a refresher. There was no point in training them as Aircrewmen so they remained TAGs. We had one such group through Seafield Park. I fear they found the old spirit had shifted a little. As aviators a few of the regulars were about to retire and so the Chiefs Mess was not exactly humming as it did in the past. There was yet another group similar to the reservists. These were the volunteer reservists (R.N.V.R.). A few such squadrons had formed and these also included

TAGs. They were the keen ones who gave up their week-ends to carry on flying and keep in touch. One particular TAG of this kind ,Eric Bond, eventually obtained a bar to his Long Service and Good Conduct Medal (RNVR).

Other courses came to the Air Signal School but most were of short duration and the main objective was to give familiarity with airborne communications. They included Naval Officers of various Commonwealth Navies, Petty Officer Telegraphists and even Wrens. Then a new intake was started. Once more the Navy was to train Observers. This was presumably also linked to the end of the Aircrewmen pupils. More observers were still needed and the training schools existed. With no more TAGs it was necessary to recruit directly. A group of Midshipmen appeared on the scene and these were to become a new No.1 Observer's Course. I was appointed W/T instructor. My old colleague from Crete days, Bomber Newman, was their Radar instructor. This was a little different. It meant instructing in morse, W/T procedure and everything else from scratch. A nice challenge. Instructor flying had to increase. We went with them on many more trips before they went on their own. The Ansons became truly flying classrooms. I took three such observer courses through training and each was rather longer than for the Aircrewmen. They were spared a knowledge of radio circuitry and their W/T knowledge was limited to block diagrams. As they probably barely touched a W/T set subsequently, I expect they wondered why even that had been necessary. The radar homings and RT instruction was worthwhile. Another ex-TAG, Roy Tolley, who had been commissioned, was their Course Officer. He had a favourite opening gambit. He would unroll a wall chart showing a complicated radio circuit diagram in all its detail. After the horrified gasps and groans had subsided he reversed the chart to display a family tree of organisation which was his real subject. I found all these chaps very keen and intelligent and it was a pleasure to instruct them. I hope my approach came across rather different to the manner in which much of the knowledge was thrust at me.

About this time yet another type of course was introduced. Telegraphists (Flying). You could have knocked us down with a feather. After all the efforts to turn TAGs into navigators, suddenly they wanted communicators again. So the wheel turned full circle and they went to the Fleet for trained Telegraphists and converted them to a flying role. How had this come about ? The story hinged on the requirement for anti-submarine aircraft. The Barracuda had been replaced by Firefly VIIs but this was not very satisfactory in this role and was only a stop gap. In fact they had to continue for some time with the Barracuda until eventually the Fairey Gannet came into operation. The point of it all was that these aircraft were three-seaters and the work load in the back cockpit fully occupied two men. For a while two Aircrewmen or an Observer and an Aircrewman carried out these roles, until finally a revival of the airborne Telegraphist

Avro Anson

took the third seat. This was not the only slot demanding such men. There was the communication role on the "bus routes" so long carried out by TAGs. Once again we saw the familiar badge of the Telegraphist, this time with a pair of wings on the cuff. Later the name of such courses was changed to Telegraphists (Air). When they came through Seafield Park they did not need much instruction - just familiarisation with airborne equipments. Several of these men were later to see action in Korea.

In November 1949 the Ansons disbanded as 783 Squadron at Lee-on-Solent, but the same aircraft then moved to Hamble as part of Air Services Training. and continued the same role from there. Hamble was a grass field which later became the centre from which many a civil airline pilot began his flying training. The move was a reflection on the Defence cuts, in which any Services support from cook to accountant which could be carried out by a civilian, was so switched to release all possible servicemen for direct activities afloat. The Anson aircraft were now flown by pilots in a civilian capacity.

Now came a change which had far reaching effects. Aircrewmen could become Branch Officers. It was an opening for promotion which had been closed since the end of the war for Air Gunners. It will be recalled that I have previously mentioned how a pre-war Telegraphist Air Gunner had to return to the Fleet and a ground role, if he wished to advance to Warrant Telegraphist. The Rating Observers were more fortunate, and a route to Warrant rank was open to them. They were tickled pink when the name chosen for them was Boatswain (O). The first of these appointments were in 1941 for Howard Payne and Ginger Donovan. The Air Gunners did achieve the break through during the war and a few became Warrant Officers (AG). This route had since terminated. Much to the chagrin of many senior Chief TAGs who, having achieved the necessary qualifications, were occupying a position on a shelved roster. This situation caused many to opt for the Aircraft Handler role when it commenced. Now, as aircrewmen were considered as Observers, a new role was made available. At the rate of three a year. This rather took the gilt off the gingerbread, as people calculated how long they might have to wait to even get on a course. In fact, for a reason I never understood, news of the AFO never circulated initially at Seafield Park. Yet that was where 6 keen men appeared for the first qualifying course. None failed, so that fulfilled the available posts for the first two years. It so happened that this introduction more or less coincided with the abolition of the old style Warrant ranks. Henceforth these men would have full commissions and so the new rank was described as Commissioned Observer.

I didn't think a great deal about it. Warrant Air Gunners of the past had almost always taken up administrative appointments. That didn't suit me - flying was my game. Fifteen months in the Signal School was beginning to pall and once again there was an urge to join a squadron. I requested a return to HMS Triumph of happy memories. The Captain casually approved with the comment that I could do with some more sea time !

Supermarine Sea Otter

CHAPTER 25

"Once More Unto The Breach..."

Though I had asked to join Triumph it appeared she was about to return from her foreign commission. HMS Theseus, a similar Light Fleet Carrier was preparing to relieve her. So I was sent to join Theseus. They didn't waste any time and this was the nearest I got to a pierhead jump. I went up the gangway in Portsmouth just before she sailed - and straight back down again. With a pilot I was en route for Lee-on-Solent to pick up the Sea Otter. This wasn't what I'd had in mind, but it would have to do. I had relieved Bobby Beynon who never thought he would make it off the ship. I gathered he was keen to take a Commissioned (O) course.

I had never hooked on an amphibian before but there's always a first time. A quick brief from the pilot and we took off. The ship was now out in the Solent. We made a water landing and out I went through the back hatch, after first putting out the water drogues. Then up through the engine hatch and I was ready. Mind you, every catch, handle, and foothold, had to be found on the way, but there's nothing like the deep end for learning to swim. Going through the middle of the hot engine nacelle with the engine still turning was quite an experience. We taxied round and down came the crane hook. I got hold of it all right but they didn't have enough free line to give it to me all the way. I was nearly left hanging on to it ! So round we went again and were successful second time. Then away with the handling lines and my job was done. We were lifted aboard, and only then did I appreciate that this performance was viewed by the larger part of the ship's company. It was just as well I was preoccupied - I might have had first night nerves. However, I did get an appreciative word from Commander (Air), who had also watched, and understood the quick decision to go round again when I wasn't given enough crane line.

Having got over the surprise of being drafted as Ship's HQ and not to the squadron, I came to terms with the idea. At least the Sea Otter pilot was keen to get airborne whenever possible and this was, after all, a new sphere for me, with some appealing

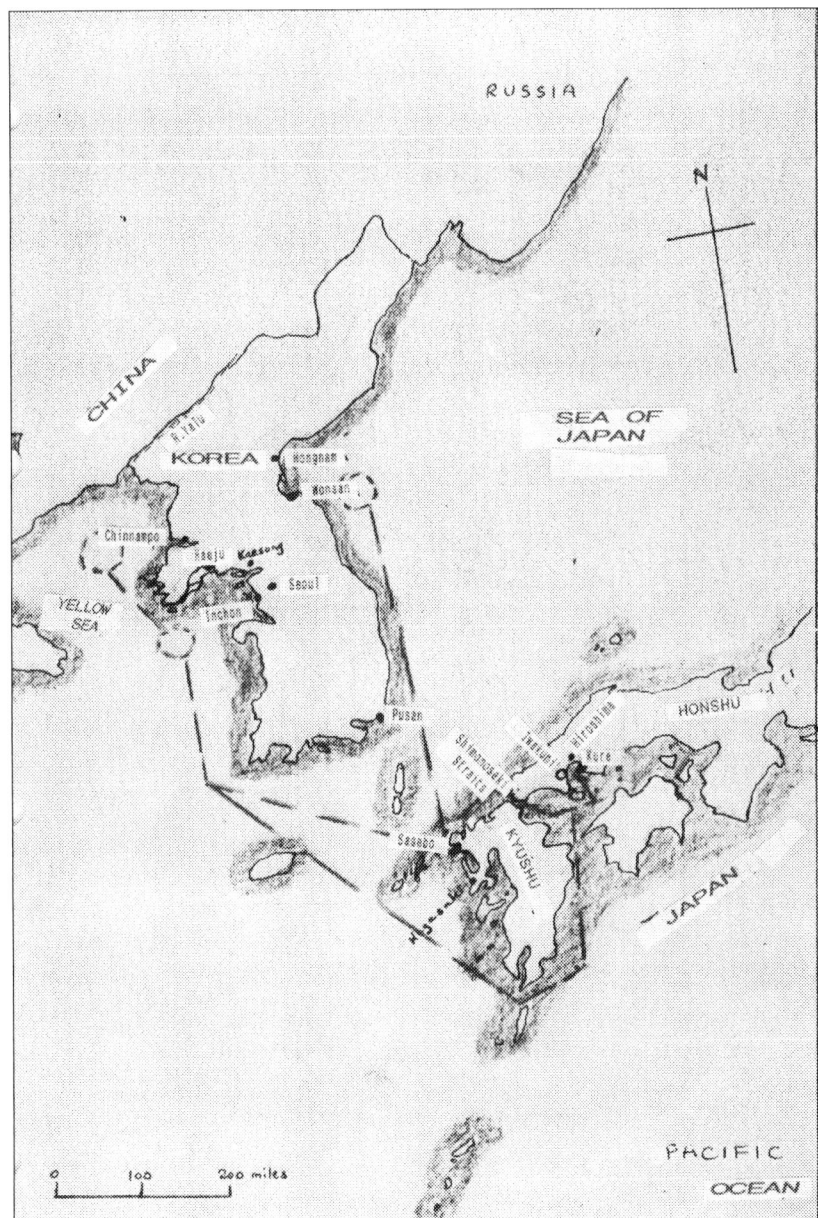

RUSSIA

N

CHINA

SEA OF JAPAN

R.Yalu

KOREA • Hongnam

Wonsan

Chinnampo

Haeju Kaesong

YELLOW SEA

Inchon

Seoul

Pusan

HONSHU

Shimonoseki Strait

Iwakuni Hiroshima

Kure

Sasebo

KYUSHU

JAPAN

PACIFIC OCEAN

0   100   200 miles

Marshalling yards in North Korea blasted by bombs from
Theseus aircraft

Bombing of the dock area at Chinnampo by aircraft from Theseus. A Firefly V is
seen in the upper right hand corner

variations. However, I made a point of going to meet all the lads in the squadron and let it be known that if any of them wanted a change I was their man.

Though the Light Fleet Carriers were all the same class of ship, internal messing arrangements varied widely. The dockyards could pull down and re-erect partitions upon request, and so produce a quite different appearance. Theseus had a set of bunks forward of the Air Chiefs Mess under the forecastle, and these were earmarked for the rating aircrew - a facility not present in Triumph. The Aircrewmen aboard Theseus were Charlie Beeton, Harry Griffin, Tug Wilson, Jimmy Loveys, Sam Ball and Paddy Shiel. There were also two Tels(F), King and Butler. In addition there were four Pilot IIIs who ranked as P.O.s. These latter were the result of a switch in Admiralty policy. Too many officers can be an embarrassment in the promotion stakes as time progresses and they all become senior. As it transpired, they had to revoke this rating pilot idea because it failed to attract enough suitable recruits. With so many aboard Theseus it was possible to establish a separate aircrew mess. As ship's staff rather than Air Group, I remained in the Air Chiefs Mess.

The ship was bound for the Far East. This we knew. There was trouble in Korea. It was possible we would be drawn into the conflict. In peacetime there are often flare-ups in various parts of the world and the Royal Navy may send ships. Some of these troubles can disappear overnight. This one, though, seemed a bit more serious. Triumph had already been involved, as Britain was implementing her commitment to the United Nations. Triumph, however, was still equipped with Firefly Is and Seafires and only to squadron strength of 12 of each. Theseus was planning to operate with a deck park, and had on board Firefly Vs and Sea Furies to a total of 36 aircraft. When it became clear that the Air Group was to form part of the United Nations Force all aircraft were painted with distinctive black and white stripes. On the way out through the Med. and down to Singapore the Air Group would be working up to achieve slickness in its mode of operation. With a deck park it would be necessary for all aircraft to use the booster. This was the steam catapult on the forward flight deck.

My main role was in the Operations Room. The Sea Otter was an Air-Sea-Rescue machine with only a stand-by responsibility. A Chief TAG or Aircrewman had become a tradition in HQ, but the jobs I found to do could have been carried out by almost anyone. Checking the aircraft off and on, and keeping tabs on where they were at any time. Updating all the codes and procedures and supplying standard information at briefings. At least in the Ops. Room we knew what was going on. I did man the ship's HF ground station during a few exercises on the way out - this way the exercise reports could more readily be passed for plotting on the large table in the Ops.Room. The position of this room was in the island directly under the bridge.

A morse key and a pair of earphones paralleled to the W/T room were a bit limiting. So I got a receiver put in direct, and then I could swing round the dial and find anyone off frequency in the normal way. W/T procedure was awkward. I knew as well as any other ex-TAG what would suit us best, but I was a product of the Naval Air Signal School and felt tied to the rather top-heavy arrangement as laid down in the manuals. I wondered if anyone would ever get the manual written to satisfy what the operators wanted to do. I do know that 7 or 8 aircraft sending half-a-dozen "for exercise" reports apiece within the hour, can tax a ground operator to the limits. All the addresses and times had to be repeated in the log and on the message form so I was writing a lot of stuff twice and the blighters were queueing up to get their messages across. I believe they were doing it on purpose. An old TAG wouldn't miss a chance to take a rise out of a colleague - it was part of the game.

At Malta the Sea Otter flew off the ship and landed at Halfar. Yes, it was still there and I had about lost count of the number of visits I made over the years, commencing with that dramatic day in January 1941. The following morning the ship sailed again from Valetta and we made another water landing and got hoisted aboard. It all went smoothly this time. By now I'd had a chat with the P.O. on the line and we had got our procedures straight. This hooking-on was centred on not letting the hook hit the airscrew. On the old Walrus they had a pusher prop..Therefore the TAG climbed out from the cockpit in front of the engine. The hook could be lowered right down to a suitable height for grabbing but it was necessary to pull it tight quickly before any of the apparatus fell back into the airscrew. Now with the Sea Otter the procedure was reversed. It was a conventional front airscrew. One climbed out of the back hatch and up through the engine. Now the problem was to judge the height to keep the hook above the blade tips - one could see it going round -well you were only two feet behind it. As the hook came overhead you reached up and got hold -now the line handler had to give you an extra two feet quickly before drifting past. There was no worry of what it would do behind.

The hook was known as a Thomas Grab and had been developed many years before. It was in two parts. The upper part was fixed to the main crane wire. The lower half was raised or lowered on a manual line. This was the part you got hold of and slipped under a shackle in the upper wing of the aircraft. Once hooked on, they would pull the two halves together until they mated. Then the crane could lift the aircraft. To guide the P.O. one showed the palm of the hand for up and the back of the hand for down. A clenched fist stopped everything. Handling lines were sent down attached to the hook. One released these and clipped them to further lines on the aircraft itself. There was some choice here. If using the two wing tips then once the plane rose above deck level the far line became useless as it was then draped across the aircraft. So we decided it was better to use a tail line instead of the far wing. They couldn't do much with it on the way up but when clear of the flight deck it came into its own. This was the point when cross-deck breezes could swing the aircraft round. When being lowered over the side to drop into the water it was all much simpler. They still needed lines but did not latch onto the aircraft's ones which were now housed in their clips. Instead a line was passed through wingtip handling grips and then merely pulled through to release. The Thomas Grab was in the mated condition with a pin holding the hook closed. For my part therefore I only had to pull the pin when on the water to unhook and taxy away.

Like so many similar operations they are dead simple when carried out correctly but how easily they can go wrong. I was embarrassed on one slip to find that someone inside had closed the rear hatch. It couldn't be opened from outside and we were taxying merrily away across the water. I had visions of it taking off with me outside. If he had opened the throttle I suppose I would have jumped off. Anyway I had to go back inside the engine where I could plug in my helmet and tell the pilot my problem. It was quite comical to see the look on the face of our passenger who had to open the hatch to let me in.

I have described all this in some detail because it was an activity well known to a great many TAGs even back in the 1930s and through to the early war years when amphibians were carried on all major vessels. Mostly these were Walrus but many seaplanes were operated with success. Seals, Seafoxes, Fairey IIIFs and Swordfish on boots. Eventually it was found too hazardous to try to operate these in the face of enemy action and they were something of a nuisance to ships at war, if carrier borne aircraft could offer the sighting information they usually provided. TAGs of the pre-war era can describe many variants of their operation, such as being fired off the cat-apult above the gun turrets and taxying up into nets trailed from the booms until the "step" caught and held them. It was almost remarkable that the flying boat and sea-plane techniques still held good in 1950.

We sailed through the Suez Canal and into the heat of the Red Sea. The canal gar-risons were then still in residence and turned out in their brown knees to watch us go through - white knees gleaming. We had their best wishes and someone on the way signalled "well you made it your chosen career". As the Japanese name for Korea was Chosen we grimaced at the double pun. The Air Group maintained its work-up across the Indian Ocean, and as we approached Singapore the Sea Otter took off to land at Sembawang. We had two or three days to have a quick look round, and then off for Hong Kong with the Sea Otter getting aboard with another water landing and hook-on. It was becoming routine now.

Shortly after we arrived at Hong Kong, Triumph came in. I think they'd been feel-ing the strain of operations at the end of a long commission, and it hadn't helped that the Americans looked with disdain at her paltry number of aircraft, and so were hard-ly cooperative. Triumph seemed more than glad to see us. We took immediate steps to get across and meet our colleagues. Aboard we found five aircrewmen with the squadron and Gil "Lofty" O'nion with the Sea Otter. My opposite number in the Ops.Room was Sid Craig. This was a surprise as I hadn't seen him since 1940. Sid had had a very near miss working right there in the Ops. Room - who said it was a quiet number ? An aircraft had gone into the barrier ; the prop had shattered and some pieces had come through the port, killing an officer who was stood there, and felling Sid who was stood behind. He was still recovering from the incident. Nibs Cottis was now transferred to Theseus to join the Air Group, having but recently come out as a relief.

They briefed us with the known situation and passed over maps and such like. Then we bade them farewell and set off for Japan. Triumph had put all they could into their effort but with limited aircraft did not match up to the American levels. It was now up to Theseus to show that the Royal Navy had learned a trick or two. We arrived at Sasebo which sat right at the Western end of Japan. It wasn't much of a port but had a tremendous natural harbour. The harbour was full of American ships, so we got a berth just inside the entrance. The last arrival might well expect this, but somehow it was also enough to make us feel we weren't particularly wanted. It took at least half-an-hour to get ashore by liberty boat. So there was a challenge to be met. The ship had to show its mettle.

We lost no time in getting the Sea Otter over the side and spent much of the day practising water take-offs and landings. We might need to do some air-sea-rescue work. Triumph's Otter with Lofty O'nion had carried out such a rescue successfully. Operating from water is in a way almost the opposite to operating from a runway. Landing is a very short affair. Once in the water the boat hull can stop nearly as quick-ly as by arrester wire. Take-off, however, is a prolonged and dicey affair. Unsticking from placid water can be very difficult. One likes a little chop. It is quite typical to have to bounce the machine into the air. The noise on the hull during this operation can shatter the uninitiated. During these practises, which took place whenever we were in harbour, it was usual to leave the aircraft tied to a buoy when we went to lunch. A boat would ferry us to and fro. Now some coxswains were skilled and under-standing, but not all. So at times it became a case of repelling boarders, as I climbed around the wings with a boathook trying to ensure the boat did not do us any damage.

Some of them seemed to think they were coming alongside a jetty. Shackling to the buoy could barely be achieved without getting the feet wet, as the bight we wanted was well down under the surface. Now the airman had to become a seaman. It all had a high element of fun.

Almost a boatload of American literature came aboard Theseus. Triumph said they did not get much information. They must have asked the wrong people. We were nearly swamped and burnt the midnight oil swotting up on every aspect of the Fleet organisation, the state of the battle, codes, authorisations, frequencies and the variations of ice cream available at American ship's soda fountains. Much of this paperwork appeared in the Ops.Room and the Army Liaison Section were equally inundated with maps of Korea. All very necessary and we could see we were in for a busy time.

The military situation was that the first onslaught from the North had overrun the South almost down to Pusan in the southern corner. Pushing back from there wasn't very helpful. So there had been a seaborne landing at Inchon halfway up the west coast. This had turned the tables and many North Koreans were cut off. This is where we came in. Now the United Nations forces were about to push up from Inchon into the North. Theseus was directed to the West Coast and our area of operations would be the bulge of the coast from Inchon up to the port of Chinnampo. Largely it was a case of looking for targets of opportunity as support in depth, though there were other specific tasks such as denying the enemy chance to mine or use any part of the coast.

We set off on the 8th October 1950 and began operations next day. I watched them take off with mixed feelings. An airman does not like to be left grounded, though few relish the prospect of operations. The flying procedures had been well established, and it only remained to improve the efficiences. Each take-off group would consist of some 15 aircraft. Two flights of Sea Furies and one flight of Fireflies - some 12 aircraft in all to form a strike, though often working independently. Two additional Furies would remain as Close Air Patrol (C.A.P.) and one Firefly on anti-submarine patrol. Notice how the numbers were limited to the amount that could be got on a deck park. A similar group would then be ranged with the two front Furies at immediate readiness by the booster should they be needed whilst the other work proceeded behind them. Sorties would be about two and a half hours duration, at which point the follow-up group would get airborne and the first group returning would land on. Though sometimes there were variations, this was the general pattern throughout the day. To begin with, the winter months limited daylight hours and most crews were doing two sorties a day. When this stretched out in the summer it lifted to three sorties a day.

I was kept busy enough dishing out maps, (I don't know what some of the crews did with them - they always wanted more), and chalking up all manner of information on the Briefing Room blackboards. The evening found me printing off sets of codes as these changed daily. It was routine but a supercharged one. On the second day a Fury was brought down in enemy territory. He was given cover from the air and an American helicopter plucked him out. It sounds simple, but was a two hour operation of considerable behind-the-scenes organisation. Before the campaign finished this was re-enacted many times, and our admiration of the helicopter crews knew no bounds. In fact it was clear that a helicopter was worth its weight in gold, and before long an American machine and crew were sent on loan to us. It henceforth operated continuously whenever flying was in progress, as it had a rescue function for take-offs and landings, apart from pick-ups ashore. The Sea Otter's usefulness as an air-sea-rescue machine dwindled correspondingly. However it still had a use in communications and on the 17th we were hoisted over the side and flew off to land at Kimpo. This was the airfield at Inchon, and there we took some passengers who needed to consult with people ashore. At this point the ship was being refuelled from a tanker, which is when the Otter showed its handiness as other aircraft could not operate. It was probably fortunate that the tanker was alongside on the port side and so not interfering with the crane. We brought the passengers back and were hoisted aboard.

HMS Theseus alongside at Kure, Japan, January 1951. In the opposite berth, on the right, is HMS Unicorn with replenishment aircraft. On the far right of the picture is HM Hospital ship Maine

An American S51 Helicopter, later christened 'The Thing', landing on the flight deck of HMS Theseus. USS Bataan steaming ahead

Fairey Firefly V

The operations continued until the 22nd - two weeks almost continuously and then we returned to Sasebo to rearm and provision. Within days we were back again and this time steamed right up into the Yellow Sea not far from the Chinese border. The advance ashore had been very fast and the troops were not far from the river Yalu. After a few days there was little more that the aircraft could do. The carrier's job was considered ended and she was directed back to Hong Kong.

On arrival, exercises were carried out with the defence garrison, and on one of these flights I managed to get in my first trip in a Firefly 5. The Sea Otter was on overhaul and could not operate.

Then it became evident that all was not over in Korea, and we were called back in some haste. The Chinese had decided to take a direct hand and had crossed the Yalu. The United Nations troops, consisted largely of South Koreans and Americans. During the advance many of these had moved up the eastern coast towards Manchuria. I can only assume that it was thought that the strongest backing for the North Koreans, and therefore the danger, came from the Russians along that border. Thus the strength of the forces approaching the Yalu had been much reduced. These forces had in any case outstripped their supplies, and the rate of advance therefore slowed. The Chinese troops were able to filter through these scattered troops over the very rugged country and now there was general confusion all round. Lines of communication had been cut and it was difficult to get a true picture of the position. No basic battle had occured, merely some skirmishes. There was an order to pull back to a more secure and defendable line. Many groups had not received this order, whilst others were not clear which route to take with the Chinese behind them.

Theseus' operations recommenced on the 5th December and the first activity was to find groups of these troops and to drop messages directing their movements. Now there was the added threat of enemy air activity. Previously it was understood that most of the North Korean aircraft had been neutralised. The Chinese might use their Migs.. In fact it was soon found that the Migs would not stray far from their bases. Over the Yalu they were immune from reprisal. A quick foray and a chase back by Sabres was all they'd undertake. No one knew when they might get bolder.

The ground picture began to unfold and stabilise. Pilots could attack targets north of a certain line when it was known they were clear of U.N. troops. At this stage the troops were very dependent on air support to hold up the enemy advance. Operations became more and more difficult as winter closed in. Korea was on the 38th parallel and the snow came down and lay heavy. Theseus was hit by frequent blizzards which swept across the flight deck and iced up the deck park. However, sorties continued. There was a brief break for refuelling. The prospect of Christmas in port in Japan came and went. (I could have told them that with my record of Service Christmases it wouldn't happen.) Finally after 3 weeks of constant effort the ship broke off and returned to rearm. This time she headed for Kure where there were several Australian Messes and Clubs. Off Sasebo on the morning of the 28th we took off in the Sea Otter and headed for

Iwakuni, the airfield in the bay opposite Kure. After refuelling we came back with the object of filming the ship passing through the Shimonoseki Straits. Unfortunately we had evidently been misinformed on the time this would occur or else the plan had changed. When we got there she had already gone through. However I got some good shots of her adjacent to other small islands with their unmistakeable Japanese topography. We had a near squeak flying down the Shimonoseki Straits when we suddenly came across and flew underneath a high tension cable that must have been about three hundred feet up. We landed back at Iwakuni and had an enlightening train journey to join the ship at Kure. Whilst we admired the scenery from the luxury of our 1st class compartment, the Japanese in other trains seemed intent on observing us. With their snub noses they are able to flatten quite close to a window and we would keep seeing seas of faces occupying every bit of window space in other trains. One wondered just how many other bodies were jammed behind them.

Our Christmas Day was celebrated aboard on the 31st December and after a short rest we were off again on the 5th January. We had to go back to Iwakuni to get the Otter but that was no problem. This time we were to work alternately with an American carrier of similar size. First the "Badoeng Straits" and later the "Bataan" This cut the operational period down to spells of 10 days with an overall time of 12 to 14 days at sea to get to and from the area. Such an arrangement lasted throughout the rest of the tour and eased the pressure of sustained operations.

It was about this time that the ship first made direct contact with the British Commonwealth Division, which had done much to hold the line north of Seoul. It consisted of a Canadian Brigade and a mixed Australian/British Brigade with elements of other Commonwealth troops. The Gloucesters asked Theseus to take photos of their positions. Sea Furies carried out a difficult sortie flying up a valley in a continuous banked fashion to produce a film overlay. The Glorious Gloucesters defence of that position has gone down in history.

On the next spell of rest, again at Kure, our Sea Otter was unserviceable so we borrowed one from Unicorn. This was the maintenance and supply carrier which came up periodically from Singapore with more aircraft. We carried out many trips from Unicorn practising water take-offs and landings. Hooking on to Unicorn was a little unusual in that we had to taxy towards the ship to get under its crane and that meant no safe chance of going round again. This was no real problem but they couldn't settle on an understood method for the handling lines. First I gave them port and starboard as red and green as one would expect relative to our aircraft. This apparently wasn't right for them and there was much swapping over by the handlers. Once aboard I had a long chat with their P.O. pointing out that it was usual to work left and right as seen from the aircraft. Not so aboard Unicorn the P.O.insisted, he had to deal with a flight deck party who saw it as port and starboard from their point of view. So next time I came alongside they got it their way as instructed, with the red tab on my starboard wingtip and green to port. Except that a new officer was in charge on deck and he had ordered them to change over. Now he was shouting at me to do the same. You can't win.

So back to the Yellow Sea for another spell. The ship would be fully blacked out at night and movement aboard other than through the lower central gangway was hazardous. Much of a Light Fleet's hanger deck outboard is a weather deck, and traversing that in the dark was guaranteed to bark shins and knees as one tripped over all manner of motors, pumps and other apparatus utilising these areas. The aircrews were finding that ground defence was building up. Mostly light machine guns but larger stuff here and there. A number of machines landed ashore damaged and we also had some losses. Deck-landing, though, was accident free. It is surprising what improvement constant practise achieves.

Next time in, at the end of February, we went in to Sasebo. Off went the Sea Otter again to Itazuki airfield. We were looking for a place from which we could operate without all the bother of hoisting aboard each night. Itazuki was OK for Kure but too far from Sasebo. So we looked all over the island of Kyushu. It was surprising. The maps were covered in landing grounds - they were war time issue. We found that airstrip after airstrip had become a village with huts and houses flanking the old runways and the rest of the field growing crops. I suppose our East Anglia must have been a bit similar with the airfields going back to farm country, but not like this with new villages. We couldn't find a usable landing ground anywhere. So we had to continue our Sea Otter work from Sasebo harbour - tying to a buoy midday, and being hoisted aboard in the evening. On one of these flights we went to have a look at Nagasaki. Nestling round the sides of the hills enclosing the harbour it was completely rebuilt, and from the air there was no obvious evidence that the Bomb had ever dropped there.

Now, suddenly, I was being asked if my request to join the Firefly squadron still held. One of the ex-TAGs who had been a P.O.W. felt he had had enough. Yes indeed, my offer still held. In no time I was allocated to a pilot, briefed with squadron information and ready to go. It was perhaps just as well I'd had the squadron experience aboard Triumph, and knew all the background information. It was almost routine to slip into flying kit, climb into a Firefly on deck and be ready for boosting. I think all I had to get hold of was a parachute and a set of maps. Off we went from Sasebo on the 5th March and the following day I took off on the first strike.

Enemy coast ahead. There is always a stomach twisting pull about such a situation if it is a new area and a first approach. No matter how sure one is of the briefing, it is as though opposition will begin at this point. In fact this is seldom ever the danger point. That comes much later, often when least expected. Doubtless the other crews were already immune to the implication of the coast. Later I came to feel the same. We ruled the air and these flights were regarded as routine.

The Fireflies carried an almost regular load of two 500lb bombs and four rockets. Targets for the bombs were often bridges. Such was our present target - a railway bridge north of Hwangu. A bridge sounds big enough to hit easily but it is still small in one dimension. Whether one comes down the line or across it accuracy is demanded. It is perhaps easier to hold the line of a dive and this is how we made most attacks. This time we missed the bridge and hit the tracks at one end. Other aircraft in the flight were successful though. One might wonder that the railway was still working or that bridges still existed. They were very determined adversaries. They ran the trains at night when we weren't around, and hid the rolling stock in tunnels during the day. All the major bridges were down, but minor bridges abounded. This was not the rainy season and most rivers were down to a trickle. Thus they could build earth ramparts across much of the river course and just have a small temporary bridge across the stretch of water remaining. All the major bridges were by-passed in this way. If they took away the temporary span in daylight one could easily fly past, see the gap and ignore the bridge as one that was already broken. We only wised up to this after studying photos and gaining experience.

On my early sorties I didn't contribute much and spent the time familiarising on the terrain and noting landmarks. Navigation to and from the ship was no bother over the short distance of 40 miles and in any case we followed the leader of the flight. Map reading was the big role, plus looking hard for targets of opportunity.

The second sortie was much more interesting. For some time we had wished to give more direct support to front line troops. Now we were acceptable for close air support known as C.A.S.. For this an Auster or similar light aircraft was flown up from the front line positions, with a controller who knew exactly what the ground situation was. He could direct strike aircraft onto precise enemy positions by firing a marker rocket. Then, by voice, he would explain exactly where, relative to the marker, he wanted you to attack. American jet aircraft were coming in all the time on this task and they had little fuel to hang about. We had endurance and could wait, so we frequently gave way to them. The jet aircraft's speed made precision attacks in steep sided ravines difficult. Even the Americans found it desirable to bring back squadrons of Mustang propeller driven aircraft. Our manoeuvreable, if slow, Fireflies were much appreciated.

We would report ourselves as 4 Fireflies with bombs, rockets and cannon, time over target one hour. It sounded impressive. This time the controller had just the target for us. A tank, he said, (very rare for the enemy) hidden in a small railway culvert. The C.O. put one bomb straight through the top of it and the smoke blew out each side. A perfect shot - a bit lucky of course - but reported with suitable nonchalance. The controller was delighted. Then he was at a loss what else to give us, but settled for a railway tunnel up which there was a train - he said. We tried to skip our bombs into the entrance but any such achievement was not obvious. We fired our rockets up the tunnel with greater success but no sign of results. Then further bombs blocked both entrances. We may not have hit the train but they would be kept busy getting it out. There was no doubt about the importance of the earlier culvert. The attacking aircraft had been hit with machine-gun fire and a bullet narrowly missed the Senior Observer.

Defended points usually indicated the presence of something important. The difficulty was knowing that it was defended. The terrain was so deceptively quiet that one might be excused for thinking nothing was there and come carelessly low. Tracerless fire in the daylight was almost undetectable until one was hit. There were lots of reports of ground fire and the flak map which I had laboriously kept up to date whilst in Ops. gradually extended to cover almost the entire area. To this the reaction had to be two-fold. First, expect fire from virtually anywhere, no matter how innocent it looked. Second, clean the flak map down to the areas which were repeatedly reported, so that we knew the real hot spots. As time progressed larger guns began to put in an appearance, usually only of the 20mm variety, but these were just around the few prime targets.

The following day we were again on Close Air Support and this time American tanks were seen advancing up a valley. Evidently there was opposition from a high ridge. The controller directed us to hit the top of it - and he said he meant the top. We obliged with fair accuracy - first bombs then rockets and cannon - though the ridge was a razor's edge and a narrow target. I actually saw men running down the far side of the hill so we certainly got close enough to winkle them out. Most often we saw little or nothing of the enemy both before and after our C.A.S. attacks and were entirely dependent on the controller to assure us that they were there. On a subsequent day at Hongchon we attacked through smoke and haze and could see very little at all. There was plenty going on down there but our only guide was a coloured smoke marker. Then we went back to railway bridges, this time to one north of Sariwon. We took a 1000lb delayed action bomb. Another aircraft hit and destroyed the bridge with direct action types. Because they were so quick at rigging temporary replacement spans we thought a few delayed action jobs would make it more difficult. We went back to have a look at this bridge on later sorties and were surprised to see big holes in the ground some distance off. Had our bombs really skipped that far ? Surely not. Could they possibly have dragged them there without trying to defuze ? The mind boggles at their audacity.

After each of these strikes we would carry out recces over specific areas looking for new activities and attacking targets of opportunity with rockets and cannon. These might be ox-carts. At first it seemed criminal to go for these apparent farm implements belonging, one supposed, to the peasants. When many of them blew up, confirming that they carried ammunition or such like, we became aware of how they were bringing up their support.

About every third day it would be our turn for the A/S patrol around the ship and its escorts. This vigilance was continued as there was no knowing if submarines would be thrown into the war. On one of these patrols we sank an oil drum with cannon fire. Just so that it would not be mistaken for a mine. One often saw junks fishing and we would always investigate these to make sure they were what they seemed. Earlier in the campaign sampans had been used to lay mines. At least one of these was caught and blown up. Photos that were taken clearly showed the mines aboard. It might seem primitive but was certainly effective and one could not ignore the most inocuous item. Sweeping low across the fields one day I was casually observing the numerous corn stooks, when I was surprised to see a face peering at us out of one of them. We came round for another look and three of the stooks upped and disappeared into the nearest ditch. It was evidence of the excellent camouflage they adopted and explained why we seldom saw anyone about.

We went back into Sasebo after our 10 day spell and I was promptly back doing water landings with the Sea Otter. It hadn't occurred to me that I wouldn't get out of that job. I still belonged to the ship and was only on loan to the squadron. Not that I minded the Otter. It was just that I didn't get a break. Even during our tours there could still be a call. On the following trip out I was sent for to go with the Otter to Suwon and back with some ground personnel. Suwon was the airfield near Seoul and anyone shot up was likely to be directed there rather than risk a damaged aircraft on a deck landing.

I have described some of the sorties in detail to give an impression of the type of attacks that took place. We continued in this vein. Attacks on bridges, close air support, targets of opportunity and much scrutiny of the ground looking for tell-tale signs of activity. Now and then we would be briefed for special targets. Intelligence sources would advise on the whereabouts of particular strongpoints. They were invariably right. Sites could look like sleepy villages. When we showed interest there was much retaliatory ground fire and things blew up when we hit them. Several were right little hornets nests.

We were back in Sasebo again on the 2nd April and off went the Sea Otter once more. After various take-offs and landings it was hoisted aboard Unicorn there to remain for an overhaul. For Theseus' next and final tour she went up the East coast of Korea. We operated in conjunction with "Bataan" and this made a change. The east coast had always appeared a more active region, judging from reports, and had been the hunting ground of the larger American carriers. They'd gone in for a rest and left us to keep up the pace. There was a biggish port there - Wonsan, and some larger towns. Certainly it was a new area to explore and we seemed to spot more activity. For instance we came across some hidden and camouflaged vehicles including what we thought were tanks. This was suspicious. We'd once seen a "tank" on the West coast. A second look showed it to be very much a mock affair and several guns opened up. What then about this little lot that we had found? It certainly wasn't a trap. There were some guns, yes, but not enough for us to be lured on to. After being circumspect and having a good look we gave the transport a pasting. We also found both a road and a railway bridge intact (how had the Americans missed these ?). Both were hit and demolished.

One of the Sea Furies was attacked by American aircraft. Obviously we hadn't been seen around there before and the man didn't know his silhouettes. Though a Fury was not unlike a Yak the latter had all been downed a long time since. Unfortunately this episode had a tragic sequel. While this plane was being nursed back to the ship, amidst much chatter on the air, another Fury was lost. His section leader suddenly missed his No.2. We heard him come up to report this and although there was much searching around, the missing plane could not be found. No one had heard any distress signal. Was it swamped in the general hubbub over the first plane ? The lost man happened to be a Pilot III and there was a subdued rating aircrew mess that night. At the time it was assumed the man had been killed but it is now known that he was a P.O.W..That couldn't have been pleasant.

One flight of Fireflies attacked some stores at Songjin and followed this with a recce up the coast to the northwards. During this excursion one Firefly came up with a distress message. Presumably he had been hit during the attack. I was with this flight and we watched the aircraft ditch not far off the coast. Unlike the West coast which had sandbanks and lots of shallow water, the water here was deep. The Aircrewman was Jimmy Loveys and we could see he'd got his dinghy working. The plane sank and the pilot didn't have his. So they both had to share the same one man dinghy. With the flight leader circling high to maintain communication, we had to keep an eye on the dinghy. This wasn't easy. An orbiting Firefly covers quite a wide area and several times I thought we'd lost them. Beyond a mile they were too small to be seen. It taught us how difficult it would be to spot a dinghy if on a rescue search. We didn't have a smoke float but dropped some sea markers. Soon there were umpteen planes over the top and the helicopter was on its way. We had to leave before it got there, but they were successfully rescued. Jimmy told us the water was bloody cold. As usual I taxed him on his technique. He said that as soon as he knew they were going to ditch he unfastened his chute, took off the dinghy on which we normally sat, and remained with it on his lap without the chute to interfere. Thus once in the water he merely slipped his straps and went over the side clutching the dinghy. The pilot had slipped his chute straps as well as the aircraft straps in getting out, and so his dinghy went down with the aircraft. I considered this approach but concluded that if I had to ditch I would go out with the chute and the dinghy complete.

Two days later another Fury went down. Our Firefly flight also happened to be in the area. So first of all we climbed as a flight to get good link communication with the ship. As ever with a downed machine everyone in the area gathers round to help and in no time there was a right circus with all manner of American planes besides our Furies and Fireflies. They pick up the distress calls and the requests for helicopters and collect around the spot. The Fury pilot was a Canadian and we understood he'd been seen to get out and was lying down beside the aircraft. It was in a field but in an adjacent field were some long huts. The purpose of the circus was to make sure no one got near the downed man while he waited for a helicopter. He would seem to have been a little unfortunate, and gone down near someone on the ground from whom he was hiding. Our ship was too far off and a helicopter was coming from some American destroyers. The radio was crackling with all manner of messages -everyone had something to say - suddenly over it boomed the unmistakable Canadian voice of the downed pilot - "get out of it-they're shooting at you". This to his colleagues who were orbiting low around him. No callsigns were needed. We all knew who it was. They were shooting at him too. This was going to be a tricky pick-up. The Furies started to give the huts a pounding and suddenly there were figures pouring out of them making for ditches and bushes. We appeared to have stumbled on a military camp. Finally the helicopter arrived and we all joined in. Dive after dive, anything that moved around the edge of the field, the huts, the ditches, the bushes. Everyone plastered the area to keep them occupied and get their heads down. At first, the helicopter coming in low, overshot, but he turned back and put himself beyond the Fury away from the huts. I don't think they even touched down. The pilot jumped aboard and they were away. We shot up and burnt the Fury, gave them one last burst and then the circus dispersed. All was not quite over. The helicopter had been delivering mail. With an extra man aboard she was heavily laden. They had to clear some hills and couldn't get the height. So the mail bags went over the side. They got him back all right. History doesn't record the comments of the destroyers crew about their mail.

We sailed round to the West Coast during the night and for the last two days roamed over the old area just to show they weren't forgotten. Another two railway bridges were hit and we fired rockets up a tunnel likely to have a train in it. If one wonders how we came to find such targets so late in the day, the answer is that these were all on a narrow gauge branch line. Previously they had been considered unimportant, but now there was evidence of it still being in use. So it was time to put a stop to that. They wouldn't fix the bridge in a hurry as it covered a wide expanse of water.

On April 20th it was back to Sasebo for the last time with Theseus. She would be returning home having broken many records. Perhaps the most important was over 1000 accident free deck landings. The 17th C.A.G. was awarded the Boyd trophy for the outstanding air feat of the year. Several decorations were awarded to the aircrews including DSMs for Charlie Beeton and Paddy Shiel. Two Commanders were promoted to Captain such that the ship had three Captains aboard. Most of the aircrew had logged over 40 sorties. On 23rd April HMS Glory arrived as relief and shortly after that HMS Theseus sailed for home. She was well loaded with gifts for the family bought in Japan and some wag christened her HMS "Teaset".

CHAPTER 26
"The Luck Still Holds..."

One pilot and myself were transferred to HMS Glory. It was thought we would be useful in imparting our knowledge and experience to the new Air Group. First of all I had to give a lecture on the use of all the codes and authentications. It was a bit shattering to face all the Ship's officers and the entire Air Group aircrews, but at least I knew my subject. When I came to hand round samples of the codes I just passed them to the nearest man in the front row. Catching the Captain's eye in the middle I knew at once I'd put up a black. I should have given them to him first. That was a bad start.

Glory wasn't too happy about this stint. They had been sent to Korea from a Mediterranean commission, and now had to follow a showpiece ship which had done very well. However they soon knuckled down and I found them a happier ship than Theseus. The Aircrewmen aboard were George Mortimer, George Wells and Des Jackson - a somewhat smaller contingent than Theseus. Thus there was no rating aircrew mess but we did have the use of the ready room which was fitted with bunks. Our mess was the Air Chiefs, and strangely different from Triumph or Theseus, this was situated central in the ship below the hangar. Although a bit stuffy it was much quieter. We didn't have that booster banging away over our heads as in Theseus. I put up a map of Korea on the wall but no one was interested. Most of them would never see the place so the names meant nothing. The Air Group was number 14 and the Firefly squadron No.812. Aircraft were the same as Theseus, Sea Furies and Firefly 5s.

We set off late in April 1951 for the West Coast area and our first two sorties on the 29th were both Close Air Support. I flew with the transferred pilot, and we led the earlier strikes as we knew our way around. Later we split up to share experience with the new crews and because I suspect that the new commanders felt that they should be at the front of things. From this point on I was tasked with taking photos of attack results. The standard hand held cameras were quite bulky affairs needing two hands, and not at all easy to manipulate in the back of a Firefly with its lack of visibility. One might easily get a good picture of the wing. It also meant doing a final run at quite low level after everyone had stirred up any ground opposition.

The front line was now stabilised some 10 miles north of Seoul, and though the same few hills changed hands many times C.A.S. was very much over the same familiar areas. Within three days a Fury was downed near Kaesong, and we acted as communication link while a helicopter went in and got him out. It was remarkable how quickly Glory's Air Group got into the routine of the operations. The techniques developed by Theseus for swift working with the deck park, and the many other little ideas must have been fed back and tried by Glory on her way East, because in no time she was operating as smoothly as if she'd been there for months. The only sphere in which they were still finding their way was in reading maps of the terrain. By now I knew the area like the back of my hand and only needed the map to identify obscure names. I had to pipe up now and then to offer assistance. We went through the first tour without undue trouble and came back into Sasebo on 12th May to refuel and rearm. On the last day of that tour for some reason I clicked for two A/S patrols. On one of these we had to go and search the Inchon area for a reported sub..It was a false alarm but it made a bit of a change for me to do some navigation.

Several of the Observers in 812 were from the No.1 Observers course of Midshipmen I had instructed at Seafield Park. I expect they were surprised to find me joining the squadron. In their eyes I was probably an old has-been war time aviator. Certainly here they weren't utilising any of the skills they had been obliged to master. A pair of eyes and ability to map read about summed up the needs.

Glory had taken over the American helicopter loaned to Theseus. By now we had become very chummy with its pilot CPO Fridley USN who was quite a character. Glory had managed to provide a complete mess deck for all the American ground and air crew, and though they seemed to enjoy the different approach of a British ship they doubtless missed their usual comforts. Aboard Theseus their machine had been boldly painted with the name "The Thing", after a pop tune of the day. Chief Fridley told us he'd held a USN commission as a Lieutenant during the war but had to drop to

HMS Glory, 1951

Glory replenishing at sea from Wave Premier which is also oiling an attendant destroyer

Chief to remain in as a regular. He even joined us on some of our runs ashore, so we certainly got to know him. He was airborne almost continuously alongside the ship during flying off and on. Glory didn't use a Sea Otter at all.

We set off on the second tour. Intelligence sources had been giving us excellent information and this enabled the Air Group to make successful strikes on many strongpoints. On the third day out and my fourth sortie of the tour we were attacking a village west of Haeju. Much earlier this area had been very quiet but there had been an enemy build-up, and following information received this spot was singled out for attention. The flight of Fireflies, including ourselves, gave it the usual hammering from bombs, rockets and cannon. Then we went down to photograph. I hadn't flown with this pilot before and I was aghast at his straight and level approach. I was actually calling to him "weave - weave", whilst sitting sideways holding the camera. There was a bang and my arm went numb and I knew I'd been hit. "I've been hit - head home". I wasn't mucking around with mock heroics - let's get out of there. Off the coast was an island held by South Koreans and it had a beach where one might force land. It was the nearest haven and I decided to head there first and follow on to the ship if all was well. It was pure instinct - the aircraft was still flying all right. I told the pilot my intention and gave him a course by guesswork. It was quite a struggle to get rid of the camera and turn the seat around as I only had one usable hand. The cockpit reeked of cordite and I was almost afraid to look at my left arm. When I did there seemed to be nothing wrong with it. Huh - as usual making a lot of fuss over nothing. Just then our No.2 piped up "white smoke coming from your engine". Well that was it. The coolant had been hit. We wouldn't last long. We were still over land and for a moment I considered heading for the sea. Instantly I realised this meant crossing some hills. In fact my guesswork course and choice of the island was the luckiest break because it took us straight across an inland waterway - a long inlet stretching up from the sea. With a splutter and one final bang the engine went dead. We had gained a bit of height and had got up to about 4000 feet. Diving down from this gave us enough speed to manoeuvre round for a dead stick ditching. The pilot made an excellent job of that. Just before he touched down I jettisoned the hood. I didn't want that jammimg if it was a hard impact. We splashed in and stopped. I followed my pre-determined plan. Out helmet plug. Off straps and over the side, complete with parachute and dinghy. Then nearly twisted my ankle on the bottom. We were in three feet of water. I'd fallen forward, so now I was soaking wet when I might have been comfortably dry. Thinking back I realise I should have known it wasn't deep in these inlets and in any case the way we plonked in with only one bounce and not two and then stayed on an even keel should have told me the score. I inflated the dinghy in case we needed to paddle away and somehow in the process I lost the chute which floated off and sank. I could see the other aircraft orbiting and knew they'd be calling up a rescue. We were still in enemy territory but there was no sign of life in the surrounding hills. Just the same I expect someone was watching us. I had a look at my arm. It was numb and awkward and wouldn't straighten. The wound was somewhere under the elbow and I couldn't see it. There was a fair amount of blood now, so I put on a tourniquet with a handkerchief and had to ask the pilot to tie it for me. Then the reaction set in. The shock was one thing -being soaking wet didn't help at all. I started shivering violently. My own cockpit was now full of water so I had to sit up front where it was still dry. I gave the pilot my codes but he couldn't manage to set light to them. We had no matches and the only cigarette lighter we had was very weak. I don't know if he succeeded. I was no help at all. I spent a very uncomfortable half-hour shivering all the time and not caring much what happened next. I was aware that a boat had come into sight down the loch. I guessed these would be friends as I knew from the intelligence reports that South Korean boats had a virtual monopoly of these waters despite the country itself being enemy held. Eventually the air cover let them come up to us and their leader showed his American pass. I suspect he thought I was the pilot because I was sitting in that seat. We didn't enlighten him. I came round a bit after that -having dried out somewhat. They even gave me their South Korean flag to use as a sling for my arm. At one point a flying boat crossed high overhead and I thought perhaps he would land to get us out. The circling Fireflies flashed a signal saying a helicopter was on its way and would arrive in half-an-hour or so. I had to ask the pilot to give them a Roger in semaphore as I couldn't hold out my left arm. Then they went on about the radio. We'd tried to use it but only got whistles. Obviously there was water in everything. For the life of me I can't remember why I didn't use the aldis to flash back. Perhaps I did try and it didn't work. With the back cockpit full of water the aldis socket would be under water and so was the aircraft accumulator. I know I wasn't thinking very clearly. A little ingenuity here and we could have tried drying out the radio socket. Or even pulled the battery out and put the aldis on it direct. I did ask the pilot to try and get at the radio to see if it was clear of water. He didn't seem to be able to get at it. I took photos of everything and then left the camera behind. After an interminable wait the helicopter appeared. The one from the ship. Obviously I went first. The pilot was skipper. I waved away the boat which had a tallish mast and went out on the opposite wing. Down came the sling. I got in - its just a loop round your armpits. I didn't go up as expected. The 'chopper was drifting and I was dragged across the aircraft and broke the aerial with my feet before we got clear. Then to my surprise we lifted up some 80 feet before the winchman reeled me in. I had expected a simple winch up a few feet, not to be dangled around in space. However once safely aboard I felt fine - at first. My old chum Chief Frindley was there at the controls with his aircrewman on the winch. "I'm going to put you down ashore -OK?" I hadn't bargained for this. "OK - how long will you be ?" "Only ten minutes or so while I get your pilot - we can't manage two at once". So picking a quiet bit of shore he came down. I jumped out and off they went. Now it can be very lonely on your own in such circumstances as I soon discovered. I'd loaded my revolver shortly after ditching and this felt comforting strapped to my leg. Apparently Frindley expected me to hide, as he told me later. I didn't read it that way. First I wanted to see if anyone approached and secondly I wanted friends to see me. If I was in trouble I could show them where it was coming from. Then again, Frindley had to find me when he came back. A Fury roared overhead and I gave him a wave. So I just kept walking up and down keeping my eyes peeled until the helicopter returned and landed. Then, on instructions, we all had to run around and pick up large stones to put into a hatch near the tail rotor. The 'chopper was an S51 and very nose heavy with four aboard. The stones helped to balance out a bit. We got in and leaned well back. She staggered rather down in the nose but finally lifted and we were on our way. As we looked back the Firefly burst into flames. The boys had finished it off. I suppose the flight back took some time. I don't recall it. The mere fact of being on the way was sufficient. Then "Glory" came into view. An exhilarating sight. I climbed out feeling on top of the world. Quite fit enough to walk below. They insisted I take to a stretcher - well, I ask you ? So down the lift we went and onto the bomb hoist. This apparently was the standard method of getting a casualty from the flight deck into the sick bay. Then the bomb hoist stuck - we weren't as heavy as its usual load. Being trapped in a lift is one thing. Trapped in a bomb hoist is less funny. Finally they got us shifted.

The doctors were very good. After thoroughly examining the situation they opened up my arm and pulled out all the bits that shouldn't be there, and they were well scattered. There was quite a matchbox full. Shrapnel, wadding and bits of aircraft. As far as I could judge it must have been a cannon shell which hit the aircraft. It carried through to burst inside. Hence the smell of cordite. I shudder to think of the consequences had my seat been facing forward as normal. I had been hit by the bits of shell and other pieces of metal. One bit had hit a cigarette tin in my pocket. The anaesthetic laid me low,

HMS Glory in the Yellow Sea, 1951. Clearing snow from the flight deck before ranging

Jackstay transfer. HMS Glory to USS Hannah

but I was happy to talk with a string of well wishers who looked in the following day. I now wish I had asked for the South Korean flag used as a sling. That would have made a good memento. I wonder if anyone kept it, or whether it was thrown away ?

At the end of the tour, I was sent off for a few weeks convalescence aboard the hospital ship "Maine". When they took the stitches out I found they'd opened up the whole of my arm to get at the bits. The only permanent damage was the loss of some gristle over the "funny bone" and lack of feeling in two fingers.

When I got back to the Glory she was still engaged on the same routine of operations. There had been rather a lot of casualties. George Wells and his pilot had been killed. Apparently they went straight in during an attacking dive. Another lost crew included the pilot from my particular encounter. A Pilot III had been killed - a man I had never met because we did not have a rating aircrew mess. We had also lost Observers whom I knew from No.1 course. George Mortimer had very rightly been relieved from operations. It must have been tough on him to know that one pal was dead and another in hospital. We were all aircrew of long standing and prior association.

Though back with the ship I was not fit to fly so made my way to the Air Intelligence Room. This part of the organisation was run by the Army Liaison section and was the area from which the background information of all briefings emanated. When I had come over from Theseus I had made aquaintance with the A.I.R. and its personnel. My prior knowledge had been useful at the commencement of their operations. Now they happily accepted me as an addition to the team and I got the job of recording photographs. It sounds a bit mundane, and I suppose it was, but a lot of photographs were being taken and it was desirable to file these in an accessible fashion. In the rush of debriefings and film development many of these arrived unidentified. With my knowledge of the area I could usually place them. We built up a considerable file of cross annotated prints and most often were able to produce a photograph of whatever target came up for consideration. It was also interesting to study photos of the same area taken at different periods. We often found evidence of the build-up of a strong point. Any signs of increased activity called for further investigation. It was work which an A.I.R. might be expected to do but only with a large staff. Here we were operating a "do-it-yourself" function. One of the Fury pilots was acting as photographic officer and if he was short of information, well he simply went off on a sortie and got it himself. He did a complete run of one of the river inlets, produced an overlay and delivered it to the destroyers as requested. It enabled them to sail upstream missing the sandbanks and bombard some enemy positions. I enjoyed working in the A.I.R.. Here we knew what was going on and I could follow the activities perhaps even more closely than when flying.

We kept a wall map which portrayed the entire front with all the forces marked and named. Nightly I would update this map as every piece of information came in. At any moment I knew almost exactly the dispositions of every unit taking part. We received enormous quantities of literature from the Americans on every conceivable aspect of the campaign. Much we would just ignore, but there were some regular secret intelligence reports which added a James Bond touch to the whole proceedings. Many were concerned with rescues of airmen from behind enemy lines and I would read them avidly. One account was particularly memorable. A Boston bomber had been hit and its crew baled out. The navigator was apparently a huge man of renowned strength. He was caught hiding in a ditch by a Chinese officer and two soldiers. The officer levelled a revolver at him but when the two soldiers approached to complete the capture the Navigator took them one in each hand by their necks and banged their heads together. Using one as a shield he then got out his own gun and shot the officer. Finally he escaped after meeting up with others of his crew and attracting a helicopter. The full details were so remarkable that it shamed any fictional story. There were other equally interesting accounts and one day I noted a report that a Mig had come down nearly as far as Chinnampo. In a duel with a Sabre the latters pilot reported the Mig as last seen heading seawards trailing smoke. This report was merely one of many, not all of which could possibly be read let alone remembered. Hardly anyone else appeared to read them.

A day or two later a Fury pilot reported at debriefing seeing an aircraft partly submerged on the coastal sands north of Chinnampo. Actually he mentioned some other small place so there was nothing to relate the two events. Something clicked in my mind and I went scurrying for the reports. Then I showed them to our Royal Marine Captain who became as convinced as I was. To his great credit he persevered with higher authority until he persuaded them that a MIG was lying on the sands just waiting to be retrieved. Furthermore, it was possible to do it because of adjacent deep water channels. Of course, meanwhile we had dug out all the relevant maps and photographs of the area. We hadn't captured a MIG at that time, so it could be important. Not all of this was immediately accepted. Further Fury flights were told to look more closely at the aircraft and bring back pictures. They confirmed our guesses. Much perusal of charts and photos supported our views on its recoverability. Eventually a special mission was raised and small boats went in, covered by our aircraft. The MIG was lifted and brought back. Unfortunately the enemy had already stripped and blown up part of it, but some was still useful for investigation and analysis.

I worked in the A.I.R. for three or four tours. The ship took to going back to Kure whenever possible, as it only added half a day or so on the time out, and the port facilities were much better for us without American dominance. On an early visit of this nature George and I had been allowed to stay at an Australian Sergeants Mess for a few days leave. From there we went on a visit to Hiroshima which was not far away. It had largely been rebuilt in the flimsy Japanese style. On our return next morning we were walking through the barracks to the mess when a Sergeant grinning all over his face said "Missed your ship". "Oh no", we replied, "we have come to stay for a day or two". "Yes I know",said he, "you've still missed your ship". We hastened to the end of the building where we could look across the bay to the jetty. Sure enough she had gone. She had sailed in a hurry and we had missed the recall. We had to catch her up via a destroyer and make a jackstay transfer. Many other men from various ships had also been away at rest camps and this destroyer had quite a few to round up. With the various casual rigs were all wearing, it began to look like a pirate ship when they were on deck.

At a subsequent revictualling period we were in Sasebo, when Les 'Stevie' Stevens joined us. He had been flown out to relieve George. He brought a real breath of freshness to the mess with his unbounding vitality. Like all the old crowd we had met him before. I was delighted to show him the sights ashore. These were not intended to include the main street sewer, an open ditch which ran through the middle of Sasebo, but he seemed determined to have a look at it. He promptly fell in. We fished him out but didn't reckon on his chances of a further run ashore on that visit. He had brought only one white suit. We underestimated our Stevie. He washed and ironed it and was ashore with us again on the following night.

In September, after I'd been off flying some three months, it seemed time to tell the doctors I felt fit. They appeared delighted with my progress and declared me 100%

again. Privately I was a bit embarrassed at leaving it so long but no one had suggested I should restart any sooner.

The first time off the deck was a shade disturbing - almost like defying the Fates. After that it was as though there had been no break. The routine had not changed but we were ranging further afield in search of targets and gave areas around Chinnampo a taste of our interest. I liked the way everyone was more circumspect of the unseen enemy. Get in and get out was the order of the day and don't go back hanging around low down. I got in enough sorties by counting those from Theseus to bring me up to the typical average from Glory of 60. There were more daylight hours than the winter spell that Theseus put in.

Glory came back to Kure after her final tour. She was to be relieved by the Australian carrier HMAS Sydney. The Royal Marine band was up on deck to welcome Sydney in. Apart from the obvious Waltzing Matilda the Bandmaster had confided to us that he was at a loss to think up something appropriate. He rose to the occasion. We heard the strains of a well known tune, for which there is an equally well known parody sung in the canteens. At first we didn't get the significance - it was "The Tattooed French Lady". As it progresses one comes to - "on the flip-flap of her kidney was a bird's eye view of Sydney". Everyone was tickled pink. Glory's ship's company started singing - sotto voce - such that it was impossible to identify who was singing. The combined effect however brought out the words quite clearly. I fear "Sydney" weren't appreciative.

Naturally we went across to see our opposite numbers who included Len Kenderdine, Nobby Clarke, Taff Morris, Les Bailey Phil Hancox and Taff Hughes. These chaps were TAGs who had joined the R.A.N. after the war. They took an Aircrewman's course and had been my pupils at Seafield Park. They were known as Observers and most of them later obtained commissions. It is always a little unfair for the newcomers facing unknown dangers to see the relief of those who have been through the mill. I suspect we overdid the casualness. With Sydney's HQ was Blood Reed on loan from the R.N.. We wished them happy landings, but to rub it in they knew we were off to Australia.

We steamed out of Kure and enjoyed a pleasure cruise south via Hong Kong and Singapore without a single flying operation on the way. We were joined by two more Aircrewmen, Bungy Edwards and Taffy Leigh.

We flew ashore to Nowra - the Australian Naval Air Station in N.S.W..It was quite some way from Sydney where the ship docked. Early on in the stay everyone was allowed three weeks leave and many Australians offered to put up members of the ship's company. Stevie, Bungy and I, went off to a sheep farm near Cooma. Bungy is a well known nickname for any Edwards and is pronounced with a soft g as in bung. Our hostess, the wife of the sheep farmer, was unhappy at this and insisted on calling him "Bungee" with a hard G. We had a free and easy happy three weeks.

On return we did a little flying at Nowra. Visibility over New South Wales was very poor. There always seemed to be bush fires and what with the smoke, the heat haze and the lack of land marks, map reading around the area was quite a task. There was a move round amongst the crews with some going home and others joining. Our newcomer was Alex Japp. Another was Geoff Gibbs who was now a Commissioned(O). This surprised me. It seemed that they were going to get flying appointments after all ! If so, I'd probably missed the boat. We stayed at Nowra for Christmas. Whatever happened to my Christmas jinx ? All too soon after that we re-embarked and were on our way north. We started more extensive flying to get back in the swing of things but at Singapore Des Jackson and I were told we would be sent back to the U.K.. I think we could have stayed if we'd pressed for it, but we were advised that it was thought we'd done enough. Glory herself was going back to relieve Sydney for another few months. At Singapore she picked up a Westland Dragonfly helicopter with Jimmy Glen in the crew. We bid farewell to another happy ship and squadron and made our way home by troopship.

Later the Ocean came out from U.K. to relieve Glory. Aboard Ocean were five Aircrewmen of the old school. Bungy Edwards transferred to Ocean from Glory and was then killed on a strike. Glory returned yet again to Korea with a change of Air Group but I think without Aircrewmen on this tour. However, Glory now aimed at sending up a record number of sorties during a single day of over a hundred, and to meet this challenge all available aircrew were put into action. This included Bill 'Gerry' Germon who was otherwise appointed as Assistant Ops..So again, an ex-TAG got into the act. Aircrewmen were also absent from the Air Group when Ocean went out again to relieve Glory. They did however have helicopters and on 16th December 1952, Taff Ripley was killed in a helicopter crash. Other helicopter crewmen during this period included two Tels(F), whilst Aircremen manned the traditional slots in H.Q.

Eventually that war was concluded with a truce.

All told in the Korean operation a large number of ex-TAGs had participated and several appear on the Roll of Honour.

De Havilland Sea Hornet

CHAPTER 27

"Where We Came In..."

I followed the further efforts of the chaps out East from the comfortable surroundings of Lee-on-Solent. In previous visits I had not been able to get out of the Barracks quick enough. Somehow it didn't seem so bad when one was an established member of the staff, and I had a cabin in the main Chief's Mess. When passing through we used to have sleeping quarters in a hutted camp and these were very frugal.

I had joined 771 squadron which was the F.R.U. for Lee-on-Solent. My first few flights were in a Sea Hornet in which we flew approach courses to calibrate a ship's radar. This was a beautiful aircraft only marred for the man in the back by the time it took to get out in a hurry. He had to stand, lift the seat, climb down a few steps, crawl to the hatch, open it and drop out. It sounds easy, but took about 12 seconds even with practise and this could be too long. However, Ted Dingley made it when two of these aircraft collided during a fly-past for President Tito. Ted's pilot got hung up on the tail of the aircraft and Ted himself still had a rough time. When dropping into the sea his parachute release jammed. A rescue boat got to him, but they couldn't pull him aboard against the tug of his chute, which drifted under the boat. Well intentioned helpers banged away at the release box and poor Ted suffered stomach injuries which persisted after the rescue.

My pilot in the Hornet was an American. Quite a lot of exchange tours took place, and this often meant that a visitor got more chance for a wide experience than our own pilots. So it was, that at this time, the American pilot was the only man on the squadron who could fly the Hornet. He might as easily have been English - our airborne conversation was so naturally normal, and I liked the way he trusted my navigation implicitly.

Another new introduction was a Firefly with drogue towing equipment. Once again I found myself carrying out this age-old duty. This time the winch was in a pod outside the aircraft and one felt so helpless. Just four buttons. IN-OUT-STOP and CUT. The machine simply cut the wire to slip the drogue. If it was shot off that was that. I wasn't satisfied and borrowed a boat hook from the Sea Otter. With a bit of fishing down the chute I could hook the wire in. I hoped to be able to tie on another drogue and continue. Unfortunately there wasn't enough wire to get hold of. So I tried pressing OUT. I should have stopped to think. Without a weight to pull the wire back it simply slipped wire off the drum and jammed in a right mess. The trouble was I couldn't see what was happening and learned the hard way that it wasn't on.

226

Yet another squadron job was Air Sea Rescue with the Sea Otter. Such helicopters as existed were going first to the Carriers, and the Sea Otter was still in demand along the South Coast. We had a regular week-end duty in which we took the Otter to Ford and stood by throughout the R.N.V.R. squadrons flying.

Supermarine Sea Otter

Within a month of my joining them 771 squadron disbanded, but its entire responsibilities were taken over by 781 squadron. This was the Communications squadron, and from now on it became in effect Lee-on-Solents Station Flight. I joined them with many other ex-771 personnel. This made it quite a sizeable group. 781 had the old faithful Dominie for many of its communication roles. These were augmented by Beechcraft Expeditors for the longer trips. Also a Sea Prince which was specifically the Admiral's Barge. The squadron also had a fair number of dual-control Fireflies, which were used to give refresher courses to pilots who had been out of touch for a period ; often after spells at sea gaining their watch-keeping certificates.

All told there was quite a range of duties which we might be called upon to perform. On top of that, remarkably enough, there were calls from Seafield Park to go across and act as Instructor in the Ansons. Their staff had been reduced and there were insufficient of them to man all the aircraft - they knew I had been there before. 781 were not exactly overstaffed with back seat men. There was one other Aircrewman - Sharky Ward of the red beard - and he was later relieved by Blood Reed, back from Australia. The rest of the chaps were Tels(F) including PO Ron Weaver. Sharky had his home in Gosport so I happily covered all late hour rescue stand-by's and all the week-ends at Ford. Late on the 8th September we had a scramble for a Meteor in the sea off Portland. The weather was atrocious. Very high winds, low cloud and driving rain. We struggled almost blind out to the scene. It was a little clearer out there but the seas ran high. If we'd had to go down it would have been a rough job. However the Meteor pilot had been picked up by a tanker and we thankfully turned for home. This was worse than coming out. I had visions of flying slap into the Needles. We had to keep low under the cloud. I was guessing very hard on the wind and was grateful to see the Needles slip by on the starboard side as we groped our way back in the murk. This was one of the more demanding trips. We had many other calls to go and look for things, usually missing yachts. Sometimes we would be successful but at no time did I have to land to pick anyone up. In due course helicopters from Gosport took over the rescue role from the Sea Otter.

The communication flights always gave us plenty to do. With NATO active on the Continent many officers required to be taken to conferences. We vied with each other for some of the more attractive trips. The whole of Europe was a possibility. Though 782 at Donibristle was an introduction to commercial operating, these flights were more the real thing. The W/T frequencies were a welter of continuous morse with dozens of aircraft trying to get through. We adopted little cheat moves like putting an F in front of our callsign when over France. They listened if they thought you were

French otherwise you might be ignored. In September I did a round trip through Valkenburg, Bremen and Kastrup and back. Over the following months there were trips across much of France, Holland and Spain. In between these were numerous visits to the various airfields in the U.K. to transport men and aircraft spares as required.

Then began a very special and unusual activity. Her Majesty the Queen was to come to Lee-on-Solent to review the Fleet Air Arm. A grand fly-past was proposed with squadrons coming from all the other Naval Air Stations. Not only was 781 the home squadron, they also had the slowest aircraft - the Firefly 1 Trainers. So 781 would lead the fly-past. We began a series of formation practises. As the squadron had no officer observers it fell to me to fly with the C.O..At first we just flew locally as a squadron. Then the route was decided. We would set off from Lee and go anti-clockwise round the Isle of Wight turning finally over Selsey Bill and so across Portsmouth and back to Lee. It sounded easy enough but had to take place with very close accuracy. We would be picking up other squadrons on the way and as some of these were of vastly different performance levels, they had to slot in as planned or we would arrive as a scattered heap. We were also expected to cross the airfield to the second - well give or take a few. This was a challenge. A short course but navigating in seconds. I went round once with the C.O. on our own and then again with three aircraft. This one was a fiasco. Visibility was poor and we crossed the north side of the airfield without recognising it. If we met those conditions it could be awkward. Just as well we found out soon. I drew a line on the map and took to studying every local landmark on the route in. Even half-a-mile of error was unacceptable. Soon I knew all the field shapes and felt happier about it. On every practise I was given the Met wind which was helpful. We hadn't time to go through any windfinding procedures. I started getting results within 5 seconds and one day was even spot on. We took the whole squadron round and then used them individually to represent other squadrons. As we went they tagged on behind from each pick-up point. There would never be a full scale rehearsal so we had to anticipate everyone's problems, and trust that in due course they could fit in. Came the day - 21 November 1952. All the other aircraft arrived, mostly overnight, and they were lined up right along the edge of one runway with the men in divisions in front of them. The aircrew formed a separate group at the end. There had been a slight drizzle and it was a little overcast but not bad. Various officers in ascending rank looked us over, and one decided we should split into two groups, with the ratings separate from the officers. Many of the other squadrons had brought selected ratings for the occasion. Hardly any were aircrew, but as they would fly directly back they were dressed in flying overalls and mustered with us. Two were detailed to hold umbrellas should these be necessary. Meanwhile the umbrellas were carefully hidden behind the rear rank. The Queen's car was approaching down the runway when yet another officer viewed the assembled party and decided to close the ranks into one group. The umbrellas were disclosed for all to see.

The Queen's red coat was an ideal contrast to the navy blue. After inspecting the aircrew and inevitably talking to the Wren who had been brought along, she moved on to a group of selected personnel representative of all trades. Then we were being dismissed and moving off to our aircraft for take-off. I hadn't realised it would be like this. What of my Met wind then ? There was no way I could get to a telephone and I don't suppose they had sent up a balloon anyway. So I wet my finger and had a guess. Off we went, formed up and set course. All went well. The various squadrons were there tagging on behind as planned. As we passed St.Catherines Point I got a fair confirmation that my wind was reasonable. Then we were approaching Selsey Bill and there waiting for us were the jets. Behind us were 8 squadrons of various marks of Fireflies. Some 200 aircraft all told. An unidentified voice piped up, "Cor, just like the Battle of Britain". I checked the time - "stand-by - turn". With that gaggle behind us it had to be gentle. Why hadn't I anticipated that ? - I'm going to lose 2 or 3 seconds in that turn. At this point our Admiral took station ahead in a Vampire jet. I studied the track. Oh,dear. Looks like there's an off shore breeze. We are a bit too far south. "Starboard,starboard,steady". That's better. A quick re-assessment. Pity - we shall be late - I can't make that up. Our Admiral had drifted off to port following the original course. Then he saw us and jinked back into position. We are losing height now as we cross Portsmouth. The helicopters take off from Gosport and preceed us across the airfield. Then we are there and roaring over. Seven seconds late. Ah,well, nothing disastrous but it should have been better.

After the special occasion we were back to the many communication runs. Flights to Dijon, Lyon, Istres, Eglinton and so forth. Who else were flying some of these trips but Ben Rice and Hooky Walker? Several ex-rating pilots are well remembered by various TAGs, but somehow it is Ben who is known by the vast majority. Not only does he count many TAGs as his friends but I reckon he must have carried

De Havilland Dominie

Avro Anson

Beechcraft Expediter

more TAGs than anyone else in his long career. Sitting placidly up front puffing at his pipe he ate up the flying hours. I flew with him in at least three different squadrons and he must be known to every Aircrewman.

In January 1953 the North Sea was hit by that terrible storm. Our East Coast and the North of Belgium and France were battered badly enough but for the Dutch it was utter disaster. The dykes broke and the country flooded. 705 squadron from Gosport sent their helicopters to the rescue. We had to take ground crews and special oil to keep the helicopters flying. This was followed up with all manner of relief supplies.

On the way over we would do our own spotting and on landing would report on groups we had seen that needed rescue. We shuttled from Lee to Holland for trip and trip in the Dominies and some of these were more than difficult. There was a great deal of mist around and the Dutch coast was unrecognisable. The helicopters were operating from Woensdrecht, which was little more than a landing strip. That meant no help from the ground and anyway the Dominie had no nav aids. So we groped our way in the old fashioned manner, but getting better as we became familiar with the odd landmark or two. Some of the stories from the helicopter crews, as relayed to us from the various ground crews, were quite macabre. Such as the small child at the upper window of a house surrounded by water. They thought they were rescuing the child but she took the sling inside the room. The crew were a bit worried by this and eventually pulled away. A bedridden woman - the child's mother -came out of the window like a cork out of a bottle - but was safely rescued.

As it happened I didn't actually see any of the helicopter crews. They were out on their search and rescue, whilst we dropped our supplies and returned home. Had I done so, I would have been surprised to find that one was my old pal Sid Craig, still actively flying. His involvement came to light at the end of it all, when he received not only a BEM, but a prized Dutch award, the Bronze Medal of the Order of Orange Nassau.

We kept up the continuous support for two weeks and then eased up. The aftermath of the requirement kept us going over to Holland right through February. Much of this was in bad weather and several times we had to make diversions. On one occasion they turned us away from Valkenburg and I was very glad of the experience of an earlier trip. They wanted us to return to England because the cloud base was down to the deck but we hadn't the petrol. Fortunately I knew that the military base at Gilze Rigen would talk us down and that's where we got out of that spot of trouble. The Dominie power supplies were awkward. The plane was now fitted with VHF but if that was in operation then we couldn't use our W/T generator. The aircraft supply had to be switched from one to the other. Thus when we latched on to Gilze Rigen by voice we naturally stayed with them. I couldn't tell the W/T controller what we were up to. I could hear him frantically calling us. We had to tell him by phone when we landed.

Through March I got in flights to Nice, Tousous-le-Noble, Bordeaux and Madrid carrying out W/T duties just as when we were TAGs. Almost a case of "this is where we came in." Until the day arrived when I was to report for demobilisation. The normal 12 years Service plus the initial 6 months under-age, had been extended as demanded by the Korean war and I had completed 14 years. My final discharge papers were endorsed by the Captain "would make an excellent Branch Officer". Yet no one came to encourage me to apply for such a consideration. My disappointment over the Upperyardmans course turned me against such a thought. Apart from which, at that time, Branch Officers usually retired without reaching the rank of Lieutenant. So I gave up the naval career and started a new one as a civilian.

What did the Aircrewmen do in subsequent years ? One big sphere of activities was with the Skyraiders or Guppies. These American machines were fitted with elaborate radar and several Aircrewmen went over to the States to learn about this. On return they joined 849 squadron at Eglinton. The Guppy had the capability of re-transmitting its radar picture back to the parent ship and therefore was the "over-the-horizon" eyes of the Fleet. There were many recriminations at the time of the Falklands affair to find that this ability had suffered the chop, along with other cut-backs politically forced upon the Fleet Air Arm in the late 60's.

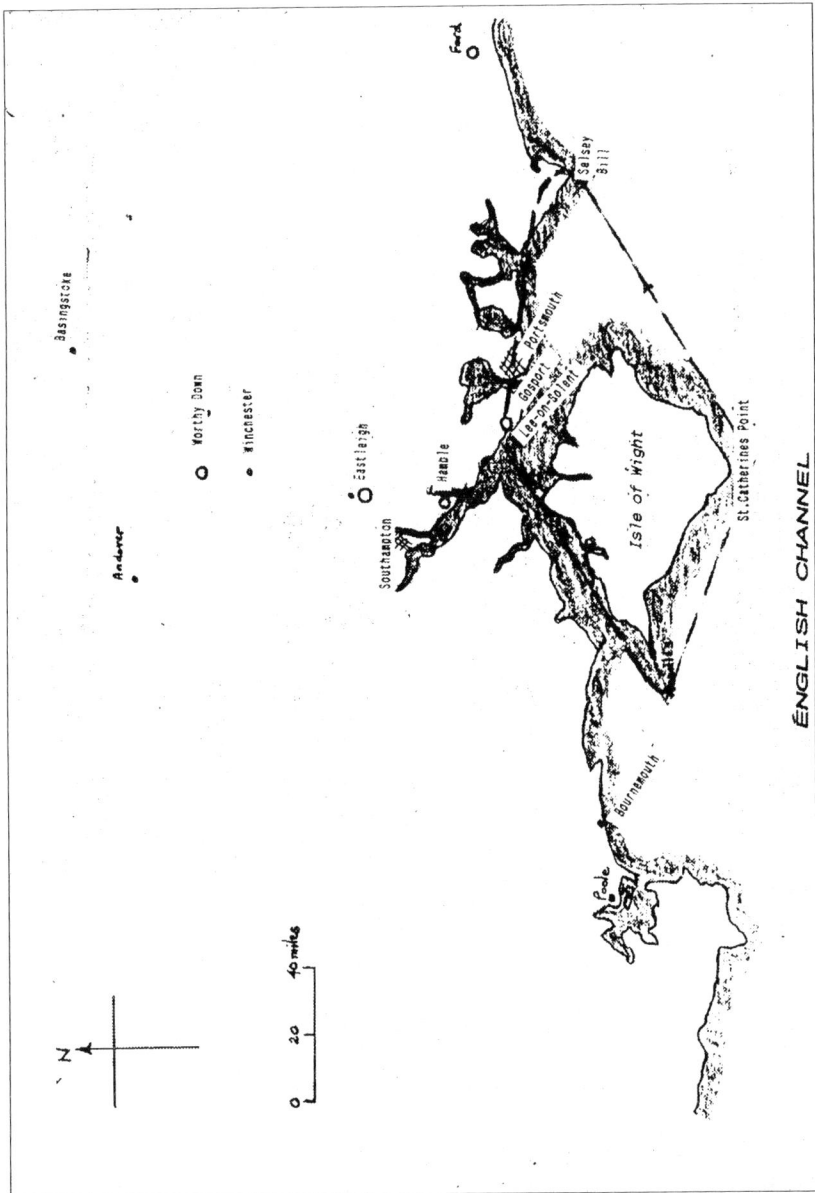

N

0   20   40 miles

Basingstoke

Andover

○ Worthy Down

● Winchester

○ Eastleigh

Southampton

Hamble

Poole

Bournemouth

Lee-on-Solent

Gosport

Portsmouth

Selsey Bill

Isle of Wight

St. Catherines Point

ENGLISH CHANNEL

Fairey Firefly 1

Up at Eglinton, other Aircrewmen flew in the Gannets or Avengers and even in a few old Barracudas. This was 815 Squadron and the A/S School. It represented the largest group of Aircrewmen still in squadron service. Another sphere involved the increasing use of helicopters by the Royal Navy. To begin with it was the Aircrewmen and Tels(A) who manned these machines and operated the rescue winch. Most of the Carriers on their way to and from Korea let their helicopters assist in various ways against the terrorists in Malaya. One Royal Navy helicopter was put on full loan to the RAF.Its Aircrewman, Taff Hayball was awarded a DFM for his part in several rescues from the jungle. This award is believed to be unique for a Navy man. Helicopters, though, also had nasty habits when they went wrong and Taff Leigh was killed when one crashed at Brawdy in 1955. In the end it was realised that simply operating the winch was a waste of a well trained navigator and radio operator, apart from which such men were getting old. For a while they were replaced simply by winch men who were recruited from the Aircraft Handlers branch on a short term basis. Then the idea was born that in rescue work it is often desirable for the rescuer to descend on the wire to assist those being rescued. Such ideas could not be augmented with the smaller S51s initially in use, but with the advent of Wessex and Sea Kings such was well possible. Now there were two crewmen in the back. One to go down with the wire and one on the winch. Almost at once it was also realised that the man on the wire might need to go under water to make his rescue and therefore needed to be an expert swimmer and diver. Such crewmen needed to be fully trained on a regular basis and not simply be part-timers. So began a whole new breed of aircrewmen who would replace the ex-TAG and wear the wings worn by that branch with such pride. Who should be in charge of the Training School set up for these men, but another old TAG now commissioned - Norman Lauchlan.

Slowly the numbers of serving ex-TAGs dwindled. Their flying jobs disappeared or were taken over by men in specialist roles. Two Chiefs lasted for a very long time. Jan Lock served in HQs in just about every post-war Aircraft Carrier that we had and after 30 years service was awarded the BEM. He was survived, if that is the word, by Angus 'Jock' Donaldson, who being two or three years junior to Jan, went on a bit longer to complete his 30 year stint. At the end he was recognised as the 'granddaddy' of all aircrewmen, having trained most of them.

There were two other TAGs who were still flying in their original aircrew colours. These were Eric Bond and Tom Mogford. In their case it was as members of the

R.N.V.R.. Eric also reached the milestone of a bar to his Long Service Medal, in his case mostly with the R.N.V.R..In fact they occupied the back seats of Firefly aircraft, much as their regular counterparts were doing. However, they were not granted the opportunity to qualify as navigators.

Though Jan and Angus were the last TAGs serving on the lower deck, they were actually out-lasted by one or two others who were commissioned as Branch Officers and so continued for some years as Observers in administrative appointments. Many of the ex-TAG Branch Officers retired in the cut-backs that occured in the 1960's when Aircraft Carriers as such were phased out. A few stayed on and when an enlightened Admiralty opened the way to higher promotion these men had risen to Lt.Cdr.. In one exceptional case there was a promotion to Commander.

However, those ex-TAGs who had been successful through an Upperyardmans course had even greater prospects than the Branch Officers. As several actually qualified as pilots if not observers then it was not always common knowledge that they had been TAGs. One is known to have reached the rank of Captain and at least two others are known to have become Commanders. In the Commonwealth navies some did even better. Nobby Clarke was a Commodore in the Royal Australian Navy and Laurie Farrington a Brigadier General in the Royal Canadian Navy.

We had been hoping for the day when an ex-TAG might become an Admiral but that does seem to have been a pipe dream.

T.A.G.A.

As the lads were being demobilised in 1945 and 1946, some thoughts were expressed that TAGs should form an Association to keep in touch and foster the old spirit. A couple of small groups met for a while, but it was yet another group who, on meeting together late in 1946, found when they compared notes that they were frequently bumping into old chums. Therefore it was thought that quite a crowd could be rounded up if they held a Dinner. Now this too could so easily have gone sour if it had not been for the drive and enthusiasm of the organisers. They held an inaugural meeting and with Dickie Davis as Secretary and Slats Dymond as Chairman and Treasurer they arranged a Dinner at The Cock Tavern. This proved a roaring success and the Telegraphist Air Gunners Association was duly set in motion.

The elected Chairman for the following year was Les 'Ginger' Sayer, a pre-war veteran who was held in high esteem as a Chief TAG who regarded his squadron TAGs as special. He also tackled the job of magazine editor and this did much to spread news of TAGA. As word got round, more and more joined, and it even attracted some of the regulars still serving who were pleased to meet up again with wartime chums. Shortly after the start, Ginger made a happy contact with the Chevrons Club in Dorset Square , and with this as a regular venue it did much to further the Association scope. These meeting places were necessarily in London, as that was where the majority of the ex-TAGs were finding their feet. Passing visitors knew that they could call in there on a regular day each month and be sure to meet a crowd of friends. So the TAGA flourished.

It is known that many a similar association was formed amongst servicemen after the war to keep alive their particular attachments. With the passing of the years most found it difficult to continue. The ones that kept going usually had some form of official backing or even gained public fame - the Kelly Association is a notable case. Oddly enough, now that it is 50 years on, many of the groups that foundered are trying to re-establish themselves.

T.A.G.A. makes no claim to be unique, but it does believe it is rare amongst those that survived with undiminished spirit to have achieved this with its own funds and organised and run by its own committee. The Association has held its 50th Anniversary year and is as popular as ever before. Whilst it may still claim to be independant it has won the recognition of Senior Officers of the Fleet Air Arm and enjoyed official support on the occasion of its Annual Memorial Service at Lee-on-Solent. Now HMS Daedalus has officially closed, we have been taken under the wing of HMS Sultan.

The Memorial on the sea front carries the names of 432 TAGs who lost their lives. Our unofficial count puts the figure even higher. It is therefore hardly surprising that those that are left wish to pay homage to their lost comrades. On a Sunday morning in May a service is held at which the Admiral (Flag Officer Naval Air) and the Captain and Officers of HMS Daedalus used to attend and representatives of the Fleet Air Arm Officers Association gave support. The Station band was in attendance together with a guard. There was also a wreath carrying party and a bugler to play the Last Post. TAGA are indebted to the Royal Navy for this recognition. One further and special action was always looked forward to at this function. The Historic Flight would put up a Fairey Swordfish for a fly-past. This would bring many a wet eye to those watching.

After the service the TAGs repaired to the lawn in front of the Wardroom, where a Fairey Swordfish was standing, and gathered in front of the aircraft for the annual photograph. Subsequently, as would be befitting for TAGs, they moved on to the Warrant Officer and Chief Petty Officers Mess where the bar was open and lunch was available. The use of their Mess was a marvellous gesture on the part of the Warrant Officers and Chiefs. When I was a member of that Mess I know how inconvenient it was to have our home taken over for the day by somebody else.

At the 50th Anniversary there was a special get-together at the Museum at Yeovilton, where the Historic Flight took many old TAGs up for one last nostalgic flight in the venerable Stringbag.

The Memorial Service is not the only function and as one would expect there is an Annual Dinner and other forms of get together are held monthly. The Dinner takes place at various venues around the country to give everyone a chance to attend. We haven't yet been up to Scotland but that may come one day if the support is there.

There is a flourishing Midlands Branch and an active Northern Branch which happily is able to meet in the Royal Naval Club at Liverpool. They have recently celebrated their 48th Anniversary, having begun only two years after the national group. TAGA still produce a regular magazine which is avidly read by members. Jack Bryant did a sterling stint as Editor and today Roy Gibbs carries this banner. How the stories are still dug out of the archives is amazing. This magazine helps us keep in touch with our members who are far flung. We have groups in Australia and Canada naturally and others scattered around the world. Yet we know that even now there are TAGs who don't know that we exist. If any happen to read this please get in touch.

The ties of the past bind us together and we are all still young in heart, yet you will find there is a healthy interest in the present. When the young men were called up for their National Service, just before the outbreak of war, the favourite expression of the Press, was that they came from all walks of life. Such a description could not have been directed at TAGs when they joined, as many came straight from school, or at least too early in life to have had a regular job. When they left, however, and went their various ways we find that they did indeed enter into all walks of life. We have

Publicans (naturally), Hoteliers, Policemen, Professional Cricketers and Footballers (well once they were), a Vicar, Farmers, Coastguards, Customs Officers, Company Directors, Shopkeepers, Photographers, Journalists, a Mayor, Councillors, Travel Agents, Engineers, Pilots, Salesmen, drunks (inevitably) and now-a-days most of these have become Gentlemen of Leisure. Whatever the calling I expect we have a kindred spirit.

Which reminds me. Up Spirits ! The Royal Navy may have stopped the practise but we haven't forgotten. As one settles back and lets the nostalgia take hold, the taste and the glow of the rum is readily remembered. The chatter of comrades is clearly heard and surely that steady roar is a Pegasus ! Dit - dit - dit - dah - dit. Yes, we still know the language, and we know that to have been a TAG was to have been something special.

CHAPTER 28

"T.A.G.'s Badges"

T.A.G.'s badges have varied over the years. Because the original TAGs were basically Telegraphists, they wore the Tel.'s badge on their right arm. Their Air Gunner insignia was an aeroplane badge worn on the right arm under the Telegraphist badge. This early aeroplane badge had square wing tips, typical of aircraft of that date. The non-substantive level of these men was determined by their status as Telegraphists and they would wear appropriate stars according to whether they were Trained Operators (one star as shown) or more as WT3s or WT2s. With the advent of the Fleet transfers and later the direct entries, such men were only known as Air Gunners, not having previously been Telegraphists, despite having training to enable them to operate the aircraft radios using morse transmission. These men, therefore, only wore the aeroplane badge on their right arm. This was the badge worn by the greater number of men in this book. By this time the badge had adopted a more modern appearance by the wings having rounded tips. It was never intended to represent any particular aircraft, though it has been likened to the Baffin. Non-substantive status was now related to the branch of AIR GUNNER and a 2nd Class AG wore one star above the aeroplane, while a 1st Class AG wore a star above and one below (as shown). These would usually be CPOs when the badge (in miniature) would be in duplicate on the lapels. With the overlap of TAGs and AG some anomalous situations resulted. Whereas previously a TAG who passed for higher status (such as P.O.Tel.WT2) would be returned to General Service and relinquish his flying activities, it was now possible for such men to remain in the branch.

They became AG2s or AG1s, and wore the aeroplane badge. To indicate their telegraphist origins, some would wear a miniature Tel.'s badge on the cuff. When some TAGs or AGs qualified to take an Observer's course they became known as Observer's Mates. The aeroplane badge was still worn but now it gained a crown above and a star below, as shown. It was not until 1942 that Air Gunner's wings were introduced. The wings were widely acclaimed as being more indicative of aircrew. The wings were worn on the left cuff and were additional to the aeroplane which was still worn on the right arm. These wings had followed the introduction of Observer's wings at a previous date. Observer's wings were surmounted by a crown and also had a fairly prominent 'O' around the anchor as indicated in the sketch. These features were absent in the AG's wings. It was shortly after the advent of the wings that it was decided to formally call all AGs 'Telegraphist Air Gunners' and so recognise their full responsibilities. Just after the end of the war there were a number of re-organisations in the supporting branches of the Fleet Air Arm, in particular the formation of an Aircraft Handlers branch. It was felt that the aeroplane was sufficiently distinctive to be used by many of the new branches now being formed and as the TAGs had their wings then they no longer needed the aeroplane. So the order went out and down came the aeroplane and the wings were transferred to the right arm, much to the annoyance of almost all concerned. Appropriate stars were now added to the wings and when these appeared in duplicate on a CPOs lapels it looked like anything but what it was meant to. The order was rescinded – in fact it was so short-lived that several were not aware that it had happened. There was a reversal to the aeroplane once more but now, because it was in use by other branches, the letters TG were added underneath. Initially, this did not seem unreasonable to get on a C.P.O.'s lapels, including two stars. Because it took some time for the badge makers to follow up the various trends, very few men actually caught up with these authorised changes. It was possible to see TAGs as a group wearing all the various combinations. There was considerable objection and criticism and even local instructions had to be thrashed out. The popular action was simply to dispense with the aeroplane (and hence any distinction about TAG2 or TAG1) and just wear the wings on the cuff. This situation was formalised with the advent of the Aircrewmen's course. Though effectively now Rating Observers, they were called Aircrewmen and put up a crown above the wings on the cuff. Note, however, that this did not include the distinctive central 'O' as worn by the officers. Those men who became Commissioned Observers did change to the Observers badge, It will be noticed that my sketches suggest a veriation in the shape of the actual wings. This is not an official variant and has crept in due to the vagaries of the badge maker. Early variations of both the Observer's and TAGs wings were of a rounded shape similar to that shown for the Observer. At a later date many badges appeared looking more like that drawn for the TAG and later for the Aircrewman. The badgemakers seem to have settled for this style. When TAGs made the change to Radio Mechanic or Aircraft

A.G. or T.A.G

AIRCREWMAN
1st or 2nd Class

handler they were allowed to continue to wear the wings in addition to the badge of their new trade. In this way they could continue to show pride in their early origins. When the Telegraphists(F) and (A) appeared on the scene they also wore the wings on the cuff in addition to the Tel.'s badge on their arm. Almost back to where we came in. We now find that the wings are the badge for the new breed of rating aircrew known as Aircrewmen, though these men are not quite the same as the ex-TAGs but are required to be expert swimmers and divers in order to meet the demands of air-sea rescue. This is a standard which our kind might have found somewhat strenuous.

Appendix A
List of Casualties in Date Order

Oliver, C.L.D., Carl Llewellyn Dewhurst, Kd. 6-5-25, (Karl) 440 '25, flying accident Malta crash 30-4-25 DOI 6-5-25

Burgess Kd.1926, ('Snowy') Tel '22, 'Press' night flight

Haddow, J.W., James William, L/Tel Kd. 6-9-26, ('Ginger') 421 Furious 25/26, Bison crashed in sea

Gibbs, R.W., Robert William, Tel Kd. 21-10-26, J81144, (Gibby) 423 '26, Bison crash off Malta

Burton, G.W., George William, L.Tel Kd. 18-1-27, J39729, George, 423 '27, at HalFar in Bison

Jackson, S., Stanley, Kd. 3-4-28, J77956, (Stan) 440 Hermes '28, off Hong Kong in IIIF

Carter, R.P., Reginald Percival, Kd. 12-5-28, J70337, (Nick) 446 '28, crashed at Farnborough

Grigson, Edmund George Bourke, Tel. Kd.6-9-28, J77760, (Ed) 422 Argus '28, Blackburn crash

McGowan, Donald O., LSTAG Kd. 19-3-30, (Don) 444 '30, Seagull Mk.III crashed whilst spotting

Armison, J.R., James Robert, Tel. Kd. 10-4-30, J111384, (Jim) Gunnery School, spun in Eastchurch

Goyns, W.F., William Frederick, L/Tel. Kd. 2-10-33, (Bill) 811 Fur '33, Ripon off Tarbat Ness

Hunter, John Adair, Tel. Kd. 7-1-36, JX112421, (John) 822 Fur '36, in Channel off IoW

Overal, B., Tel. Kd. 5-2-37, (Bert) 825 Glorious 36/37, Air collision off Alexandria

Currie, W.H.8., William H., Tel. Kd. 15-2-37, JX133704, (Bill) 821 '37, Shark K5619 ftr navex

Baxter, G., George, Tel. Kd. 11-5-37, JX125974, (Di) 821 '37, Thrown out of Shark at Fleet Review

Peerman, R.H., Robert Henry, L.Sig. Kd. 30-1-39, (Jos) 822 Glor '39, collision landing on

Goy, L.N., Leslie N., A.B.(AG) Kd. 20-5-39, JX138693, (Les) 712 Glasgow '39, Walrus overturned landing Gulf of St.Lawrence

Norman, W.H., William H., L.Air(AG3) Kd. 2-8-39, (Bill) 803 Ark '39, Skua accident

Frizzell, F., Frederick, N.Air(AG3) Kd. 11-9-39, FX76312, ('Ginger') 822 Cour '39, S'Fish failed to return from recce

McKay, G.V., George Vincent, P.O.(O) Kd. 14-9-39, FX76293, (George) 800 Ark '39, Skua failed to return after attacking U-boat

Simpson, J., James, P.O.(O) Kd. 14-9-39, F55041, ('Willie' 'Jock') 800 Ark '39, Skua attacking U-boat off Rockall Bank

Owen, B.J., Bernard John, P.O.(Obs) Kd. 17-9-39, F55127, (Taff) 811 Cour '39, Courageous sinking

Marsh, Alfred, Alfred, N.Air.Kd. 17-9-39, F55042, (Alfie) 811 Cour '39, Courageous sinking

Byrne, R.J., Reginald James.W, N.Air(AG3) Kd. 17-9-39, FX77487, (Reg) 811 Cour '39, Courageous sinking

Eason, R.E., Robert Edward, N.Air(AG3) Kd. 23-10-39, FX77463, (Bob) 803 Wick '39, Skua ftr patrol off Wick

Brown, W.H., William Harry, L.Air(AG3) Kd. 3-11-39, FX76411, (Bill) 711 Sussex '39, lost on recce flight shot down in Walrus by 3 ME's

Shayler, E.H., Edgar Henry, L.Air(AG3) Kd. 25-11-39, FX76307, ('Ted') 810 Ark '39, 2 S'fish collided in cloud S.Atlantic

McLoughlin, Michael, L.Air(AG3) Kd. 12-12-39, FX21495, (Mick) 754 Lee '39, collision with balloon cable Southampton died in Haslar

Uren, G.E., George Edward, L.Air(AG3) Kd. 11-1-40, FX77469, ('Ginger') 803 Merlin 39/40, forced landing Stronsay, Orkneys

Baxter, J., John, L.Air(AG3) Kd. 18-1-40, FX76321, (John), 0, forced landing Bishop Briggs, Glasgow

White, J.W., James Wilfred, N.Air(AG3) Kd. 3-3-40, FX76338, ('Knocker') 816 Fur '40 S'fish collided with stationary A/C on TO at Cambeltown

Riley, J.O., John Ormonde, N.Air(AG3) Kd. 12-3-40, FX77511, (John) 819 Glorious 39/40, S'Fish returning from night flying crashed at Hal Far

Burgess, T.G., Thomas George., N.Air(AG3) Kd. 9-4-40, DJX146721, (Tom) 803 Hats '40, Skua at Hatston A/C crashed when joining up for convoy work

Dale, R.F., Raymond Frederick, N.Air(AG3) Kd. 13-4-40, FX79417, (Ray) 818 Fur '40, S'fish shot down at Narvik

Barnard, A.A., Albert Alexander, P.O.(AG3) Kd. 14-4-40, FX76460, (Bert) 803 '40, Skua raid on Bergen (Konigsberg) A/C crashed in sea

Hall, M.M., Maurice M., P.O.(AG3) Kd. 20-4-40, FX76325, (Maurice) 800 39/40, Skua lost off Orkneys

Brown, K.A., Kenneth Admiral, N.Air(AG3) Kd. 22-4-40, FX77401, (Ken) 801 Glor 39/40, A/C crashed into sea

Cutler, T.G., Thomas George, L.Air(AG3) Kd. 22-4-40, FX77748, (Tom) 818 Fur 39/40, S'Fish shot down by AA fire Narvik

Adams, C.E., Charles Edwin, N.Air(AG3) Kd. 24-4-40, FX77476, (Ed) 700 Edinburgh '40, on A/S patrol in Walrus from Hatston in Fair Isle channel

Lloyd, L.M., Leslie Melville, P.O.(AG3) Kd. 25-4-40, FX76328, ('Taff) 810 Ark 39/40, ftr Vaernes

Baldwin, K.G., Kenneth George, P.O.(Obs) Kd. 26-4-40, FX78406, (Ken) 803 Glor '40, Skua shot down at Andalanes by 3 JU88s

Bax, S.G., Sidney George, L.Air(AG3) Kd. 16-5-40, SSX15409, (Sid) 814 Hermes '40, a/c hit water dummy attack on Hermes

Hill, W.H., William Henry, L.Air(AG3) Kd. 18-5-40, SS55056, ('Bunker') 700 Devonshire '40, Walrus.died of wounds after aerial combat

Parkinson, R., Roy, N.Air(AG3) Kd. 18-5-40, FX77481, (Roy) 823 Glorious '40, forced landing in sea

Chichester, C., Cyril, L.Air(AG3) Kd. 24-5-40, FX76379, ('Chi-chi') 825 Kestrel '40, S'fish Dunkirk cover.enemy action 5 miles off Calais

Burton, J.B., Jack Bryan, N.Air(AG3) Kd. 28-5-40, JX147764, (Jack) 806 '40, Skua from Manston bullet wound

Murrin, H.K., Herbert Kitchen, L.Air(AG3) Kd. 29-5-40, FX76383, (Bert) 825 Kestrel '40, S'fish from Detling Dunkirk cover

Gardner, L.P., Leonard Percy, L.Air(AG3) Kd. 29-5-40, FX76361, (Len) 825 Detling '40, enemy action France shot down near Albert Canal

Nicholson, G.R., George Robert, N.Air(AG3) Kd. 31-5-40, FX80148, (George) 801 Detling '40, Skua from Detling shot down in flames by ME's over France

Reid, N., Noel, P.O.(O) Kd. 31-5-40, FX76578, ('Blood') 801 Lee '40, Skua Dunkirk cover 5m N of Nieuport

Hill, W.H., William Henry, L.Air(AG3) Kd. 8-6-40, FX76375, (Bill) 823 Glorious 39/40, loss of Glorious

McLellan, P.M., Patrick McN, L.Air(AG2) Kd. 8-6-40, FX76382, (Pat) 823 Glorious 39/40, loss of Glorious

Heath, J., Joseph, L.Air(AG3) Kd. 9-6-40, FX77507, (Joe) 823 Glorious '40, loss of Glorious

Brett, B., Basil, L.Air(AG3) Kd. 9-6-40, FX82386, (Basil) 823 Glorious '40, loss of Glorious

Crichton, A.W., Alexander Williamson, L.Air(AG3) Kd. 9-6-40, FX79430, (Alex) 812 Glorious '40, loss of Glorious

Burns, W.H., William Herbert, N.Air(AG3) Kd. 9-6-40, FX79432, ('Ginger' 'Robbie') 823 Glorious '40, loss of Glorious

Puntis, E.H., Edward Harry, P.O.(TAG2) Kd. 9-6-40, F55054, ('Percy') 812 Glor '40, loss of Glorious

Houldsworth, J., Joseph, L.Air(AG3) Kd. 9-6-40, FX76362, (Joe) 823 Glorious '40, loss of Glorious

Morton, D.C., Donald Conrad, L.Air(AG3) Kd. 9-6-40, FX77512, (Don) 823 Glorious '40, loss of Glorious

Crawford, W., Wallace, P.O.(TAG3) Kd. 13-6-40, FX76537, ('Lofty' 'Stand on the box') 800 Ark '40, Skua attack on Trondheim

Tremeer, W.J., William James, L.Air(AG3) Kd. 13-6-40, FX77400, (Bill) 800 Ark '40, Skua shot down. Trondheim

Poole, R.G., Robert George, N.Air(AG3) Kd. 21-6-40, FX79428, (Bob) 826 Peregrine '40, Albacore attack on Texel, Netherlands. A/C shot down in flames

Hull, C.H., Charles Herbert, A. N.Air(AG3) Kd. 21-6-40, FX77524, (Bert) 823 Hatston '40, S'fish Scharnhorst attack Trondheim

Davis, F.W., Frederick Walter, P.O.(TAG3) Kd. 21-6-40, FX76376, (Fred) MID, ;823 Hats '40, forced landed in sea after attack on enemy cruiser

Berry, F., Frederick, N.Air(AG3) Kd. 22-6-40, FX82150, (Fred) 801 Vulture '40, Skua shot down in attack on guns at Cap Blanc near Calais

Burt, H.W.V., Harry William.V., L.Air(AG3) Kd. 2-7-40, FX80195, (Harry) 810 Kestrel '40, S'Fish shot down at Schipol

Chatterley, H.T., Horace T., N.Air(AG3) Kd. 3-7-40, FX77466, (Tom) 803 39/40, off Oran shot down

Jones, K.L., Kenneth Llewellyn, N.Air(AG3) Kd. 18-7-40, JX152768,(Ken) 806 Illust '40, Skua spun into sea on exercise attack on S'Fish

Wynn, R.J.W., Rowland John.W., P.O.(Obs) Kd. 21-7-40, F55068, ('Willie') 813 Eagle '40, died of wounds after raid on Tobruk

Bass, S.A., Sydney Alfred, N.Air(AG3) Kd. 26-7-40, FX77498, (Syd) 801 Hatston '40, Skua from Hatston collision during attack on Haugesund

Clarke, J., Jack, P.O.(TAG3)Kd, 1-8-40, FX76313, ('Nobby') 810 Ark 39/40, S'Fish crashed on TO to attack Cagliari

Snow, S.J., Sidney John, N.Air(AG3) Kd. 13-8-40, (John) 758 Raven '40, on course Proctor spun in

Pearson, R., Robert, AB(AG3) Kd. 13-8-40, JX145547, (Bob) 830 '40, Swordfish bombing attack Augusta, Sicily

Tyler, A.T., Alfred Thomas, P.O.(AG3) Kd. 14-8-40, FX76299, (Tom) MID, ;821 Ark 39/40, S'fish ran out of fuel on A/S patrol from Hatston

Cooke, B.A., Bernard Albert, L.Air(AG3) Kd. 16-8-40, FX76323, (Ben) died in Haslar multiple injuries Lee air attack

Gould, S.H., Samuel Howard, P.O.(TAG2) Kd. 24-8-40, F55139, ('Nat') MID, Fulmars, collided after fighter patrol in Med

Newton, H., Harry, N.Air(AG3) Kd. 24-8-40, JX151417, (Harry) 806 '40, 2 Fulmars collided in Gib waters

Derwent, G.E., Gordon Emmett, L.Air(AG3) Kd. 4-9-40, FX76649, ('Dickie') 813 Eagle 39/40, S'Fish.bombing Rhodes

Clayton, A.G., Alfred George, P.O.(AG3) Kd. 9-9-40, FX76535, ('Popeye') MID, 803 Hatston '40, enemy action nr Haugesund

Stevens, J.A., James Alexander, N.Air(AG3) Kd. 12-9-40, FX79426, (Steve) 826 B.Newton '40, Albacore forced to land in sea by enemy action

Maunder, J.R., John Richard, N.Air(AG3) Kd. 13-9-40, FX82141, ('Claude') 801 Hats '40, Skua attacking oil tanks near Bergen. enemy A/C

Gaynon, G.H., George Harry, N.Air(AG3) Kd. 22-9-40, FX80437, (George) 821 Hats '40, S'Fish forced to land in sea on A/S patrol

Webber, L.A., Leslie Arthur, L.Air(AG3) Kd. 22-9-40, ('Jan') 816 Fur '40, S'fish attack on Trondheim

Moore, F.C., Francis Cecil, N.Air(AG3) Kd. 24-9-40, FX80800, (Frank) 810 Ark '40, S'fish air battle off Dakar A/C crashed in sea

Bunnett, C.K., Colin Kenneth, POTel(TAG) Kd. 25-9-40, 17469, (Colin) 700 Australia '40, shot down in Walrus (Seagull V) over Dakar by Vichy French fighters

Howe, G.F.K., Grant Frederick.K., N.Air(AG3) Kd. 30-9-40, FX77340, (Grant) 826 Manston '40, Albacore failed to return from Rotterdam

Adlam, E.J., Eric James, N.Air(AG3) Kd. 2-10-40, FX77405, ('Dizzy') MID(p), 801 '40, Skua shot down in flames Bjorne Fjord

Brewster, B.F., Basil Fred, N.Air(AG3) Kd. 26-10-40, FX79418, (Basil) 821 Hatston '40, S'Fish crashed into sea on A/S patrol

Charnock, D.W., Dennis W., N.Air(AG3) Kd. 20-11-40, FX77516, (Dennis) 700 Manchester '40, Walrus at Sullom Voe enemy action A/C capsized

Garnham, J.C., James Charles, L.Air(AG3) Kd. 26-11-40, FX80213, (Jim) 819 Illust '40, S'Fish.raid on Leros

Noble, A.L., Alexander Laird, N.Air(AG3) Kd. 27-11-40, FX79397, ('Jerry') 808 Ark '40, Fulmar off coast Sardinia engaged enemy fighters

Clark, L.O., Leslie Oswald, L.Air(AG3) Kd. 12-12-40, FX76303, (Les) 818 Ark '40, S'Fish collision with another A/C. crashed in sea off Gib.

Sperry, W.E., William Ernest, N.Air(AG3) Kd. 21-12-40, FX80149, (Bill) 819 Illust '40, did not return from a search

Hurford, R.F., Ronald Frederick, P.O.(Obs) Kd. 1-1-41, FX76333, (Ron) 803 Formid 40/41, Fulmar failed to return from recce

Fitzpatrick, H., Harry, L.Air(TAG2) Kd. 10-1-41, F55059, (Harry) 819 Illust '40, bombing of Illustrious

Cray, F.T., Frank Thomas, L.Air(AG3) Kd. 10-1-41, LDX5393, (Frank) 806 Illust 40/41, bombing of Illust.

Allwright, K.G., Kenneth.G., L.Air(AG3) Kd. 10-1-41, L/DX4620, (Ken) 819 Illust 40/41, bombing of Illust.

Kensett, R.D., Robert Douglas, L.Air(AG3) Kd. 10-1-41, JX149022, (Bob) 806 Illust 40/41, Fulmar.shot down by enemy A/C

Tallack, N.E., Norman Edwin, P.O.(AG3) Kd. 10-1-41, FX77404, (Norman) 819 Illust 40/41, bombing of Illust.

Tapp-Smith, G., George, L.Air(AG3) Kd. 10-1-41, FX77502, ('Tappers') 819 Illust 40/41, bombing of Illustrious

Bushell, J.D., John Draper, P.O.(O) Kd. 11-1-41, FX55083, ('Scouse') 806 40/41, bombing of Illust 10-1-41 died of wounds 11-1-41

Frank, H.J.S., Harry James.S., N.Air(AG3) Kd. 14-1-41, FX79431, (Harry) 824 Eagle 40/41, S'Fish.lost on a search

Cooper, D.A., Denys Allan, L.Air(AG3) Kd. 17-1-41, FX77302, (Den) lost in Almeda Star

Harding, R.F., Ronald F., L.Air(AG3) Kd. 17-1-41, SFX410, Ron, lost in SS Almeda Star

Hoare, R.G., Richard George, L.Air(AG3) Kd. 17-1-41, FX77281, (Dick) lost in SS Almeda Star

Dicks, A.W., Alfred William, CPO(Obs) Kd. 17-1-41, FX55098, (Alfie) lost in "Almeda Star"

Kirk, A.A., Arthur Alvan, L.Air(AG3) Kd. 17-1-41, FX79452, (Arthur) lost in SS Almeda Star

Milner, C.H., Charles Henry, L.Air(AG3) Kd. 17-1-41, FX77298, (Charlie) lost in SS Almeda Star

Murray, A.M., Arthur Meldrum, L.Air(AG3) Kd. 17-1-41, SFX439, (Arthur) lost in SS Almeda Star

Naughton, J.E., John Elliot, L.Air(AG3) Kd. 17-1-41, FX78113, (John) lost in SS Almeda Star

Richmond, D.W., Douglas W., L.Air(AG3) Kd. 17-1-41, FX78377, (Doug) lost in SS Almeda Star

Scott, Robert Albert.G., N.Air(AG3) Kd. 17-1-41, FX78172, (Bob) lost in SS Almeda Star

Smailes, S.R., Stephen Ross, L.Air(AG2) Kd. 17-1-41, FX76546, (Steve, lost in SS Almeda Star

Elliott, L.D., Leslie D., L.Air.Kd. 17-1-41, (Les) to Obs(U/T), lost in SS Almeda Star

Halifax, G.W., George William, L.Air(AG3) Kd. 9-2-41, FX79391, (George) MID, 800 Ark 40/41, S'fish failed to return from bombing attack Leghorn

Ashby, A., Archibald, P.O.(AG3) Kd. 19-2-41, FX76332, (Archie) 801 40/41;801 40/41, Skua flew into Snowdon in fog

Burton, E.W.E., Eric William E., N.Air(AG3) Kd. 20-2-41, FX79506, (Eric) 755 Kestrel '41, on course Shark crashed at Keynsham nr Bristol

Mitchell, G., Gordon, L.Air(AG3) Kd. 5-3-41, FX77413, ('George') DSM, 700 Dorsetshire 40/41, A/C searching for Von Scheer killed Port Victoria, Seychelles

Stockman, D.R., Douglas Ronald, L.Air(AG3) Kd. 19-3-41, FX80745, ('Sprog') MID(p), 805 Maleme '41, Fulmar in action with CR42s over Suda Bay Crete

Howes, J.W., Joseph William.J, L.Air(AG3) Kd. 19-3-41, FX79427, 760 Yeovilton '41, Roc crashed on air firing practice Woolston, Somerset

Biggs, B.C., Barron Christopher, L.Air(AG3) Kd. 21-3-41, FX79416, (Barron) 818 Ark 40/41, killed from Ark Royal A/C accident

Blenkhorn, G.L., George Leslie, P.O.(AG3) Kd. 28-3-41, FX77411, DSM, 829 Formid 40/41, Albacore torpedo attack on enemy fleet Matapan

Evans, D.R., David Richard.B., N.Air(AG3) Kd. 28-4-41, FX77300, 810 Ark 40/41,

Welsh, W.G., William Gracie.T., P.O.(AG3) Kd. 7-5-41, FX76532, 830 Malta '41, S'fish raid on Tripoli 6-5-41 died as POW in hospital

Coston, F., Frank, P.O.(TAG2) Kd. 8-5-41, FX76320, (Frank) DSM, 803 Formid 40/41, Fulmar crashed in sea in engagement with enemy A/C

Norman, C.F., Clement Francis, L.Air(AG3) Kd. 8-5-41, LD/X5398, MID, 829 Formid 40/41, S'fish failed to return from search for enemy shipping

Thompson, C., Clifford.H., Clifford.H. L.Air(AG3) Kd. 10-5-41, JX154414, 806 Formid '41, Fulmar crashed over side of ship on TO

Rush, A.S., Alfred Samuel, (Alf) L.Air(AG3) Kd. 11-5-41, LD/X5370, MID, 806 Formid '41, Fulmar crashed in sea during engagement with enemy A/C

Collyer, E.G., Eric Gordon.E, L.Air(AG3) Kd. 22-5-41, FX77501, 785 Jackdaw '41, A/C spun into sea off Arbroath during air-firing practice

Grant, G.R., George Raymond, L.Air(AG3) Kd. 22-5-41, JX207052, 785 Jackdaw '41, firing practice off Arbroath spun into sea

Foster, C., Colin, L.Air(AG3) Kd. 22-5-41, FX77377, ('Feety') 700 Gloucester 40/41, loss of Gloucester

Day, C.A., Charles Arine, P.O.(TAG2) Kd. 22-5-41, FX77376, ('Happy') 700 Gloucester 40/41, lost with Gloucester

Clitheroe, P., Percy.W., L.Air(AG3) Kd. 26-5-41, FX79969, DSM, 825 Vic '41, S'fish forced landing in sea after recce

Savill, J.L., John Lawrence, L.Air(AG3) Kd. 29-5-41, FX77294, ('Jimmy') 700 Sheffield '41, Walrus crashed by Renowns quarterdeck dropping mail

Page, E.W., Edward William, O.Sea(AG3) Kd. 30-5-41, JX149955, 774 St. Merryn '41, S'fish on course hit overhead cable near Tintagel

Thurlow, Frederick, O.Tel(AG3) Kd. 30-5-41, JX205792, (Fred) 774 St Merryn '41, on course S'Fish hit overhead cable

Stevenson, S.R., Stuart Rex, N.Air(AG3) Kd. 31-5-41, JX151691, 803 Ark '41, Skua. Missing after attack on Trondheim 13-6-40, died in hospital Norway

Jarvis, T.E., Thomas Edward, L.Air(AG3) Kd. 1-6-41, FX78107, 805 Maleme '41, missing in Crete believe as ground defence party

Jary, W.G., William George, L.Air(AG3) Kd. 1-6-41, SR645, MID(p), 805 Maleme '41, missing in Crete believe as ground defence party

Atkin, A.J., Arthur J., P.O.(AG3) Kd. 3-6-41, FX77465, 816 40/41, in East Channel lost attacking enemy shipping

Pickering, H., Harold, L.Air(AG3) Kd. 9-6-41, FX79450, 803 Formid 40/41, from Grebe Fulmar on fighter patrol over ships

Blatchford, S., Stanley.G., P.O.(AG3) Kd. 17-6-41, FX76302, 775 Malabar '41, dummy attacks at sea

Smith, J.R., John Robert, L.Air(AG3) Kd. 25-6-41, FX77523, 830 Malta '41, attacking enemy shipping

Millington, H.D., Harry Donald, P.O.(AG3) Kd. 27-6-41, FX76606, ('Ginger') 700 Exeter '41, flying accident at sea

Miller, E.F., Edwin Francis, L.Air(AG3) Kd. 7-7-41, FX78923, 804 Pegasus '41, Fulmar to Aldergrove flew into hill S.end of Kintyre

Powell, L., Leslie, L.Air(AG3) Kd. 12-7-41, FX79197, 809 Vic '41, Fulmar flying accident at sea

Bavidge, F.B., Frederick B., L.Air(AG3) Kd. 14-7-41, FX80446, 821 '41, crash in fog at Ayr crash in fog at Ayr

Barnes, F.A., Frederick Allan, P.O.(O) Kd. 25-7-41, FX77002, (Freddie) MID(p), Fulmar air combat with Italians SW of Sardinia crashed into sea

McLeod, H., Hugh, L.Air(AG3) Kd. 25-7-41, FX79478, 807 Ark '41, Fulmars SW of Sardinia combat with Italian A/C crashed into sea

Ryalls, G., Grant, L.Air(AG3) Kd. 26-7-41, FX81925, , A/C accident E. of Shrewton Salisbury

Curwen, G., George, L.Air(AG3) Kd. 29-7-41, FX79481, 832 Landrail '41, Albacore.Navex W. of Kintyre

Beardsley, J., James, L.Air(AG3) Kd. 30-7-41, FX82598, ('Lofty') DSM, 800 Vic 40/41, Fulmar forced landed 6 miles off coast after action at Kirkenes

Beer, C.F., Cyril Francis, L.Air(AG3) Kd. 30-7-41, FX80778, ('Jan') 828 Vic 40/41, Kirkenes attack died in A/C crashed Russia buried 1990

Barrow, L.E., Leslie Ernest, L.Air(AG3) Kd. 30-7-41, FX78373,809 Vic '41, Ops in Norway picked up dead by enemy

Fabien, E.P., Ernest Percival, L.Air(AG3) Kd. 30-7-41, SR648, (Percy) MID(p), 827 Vic 40/41, Kirkenes.Dead on return to ship

Corner, D.W., Dennis William, L.Air(AG3) Kd. 30-7-41, FX80946, ('Boy') 828 Vic 40/41, at Kirkenes picked up dead by enemy

Sharples, F., Frank, L.Air(AG3) Kd. 30-7-41, SFX418, 827 Vic 40/41, Albacore hit cliff wall at Kirkenes

Wade, H.J.R., Harold John Robert, L.Air(AG3) Kd. 30-7-41, FX79403, 827 Vic '41, Albacore at Kirkenes picked up dead by enemy

Black, J.F., Joseph Foster, P.O.(O) Kd. 30-7-41, FX76311, 800 Fur '41, Fulmar missing following action off Petsamo

Fox, A., Alfred, L.Air(AG3) Kd. 30-7-41, FX79453, 828 Vic 40/41, at Kirkenes

Huxley, H.F., Harold Francis, L.Air(AG3) Kd. 1-8-41, SFX899, DSM, 810 Ark 40/41, flying accident aboard Ark

Shields, A.T., Archibald Tony, L.Air(AG3) Kd. 7-8-41, FX77305, 820 Ark '41, Albacore at Lee spun in during dummy torpedo drop

Sands, W., William, N.Air(AG3) Kd. 13-9-41, SFX2215, 756 Kestrel '41, on course killed at Stratford on Avon

Game, J.E., James Ernest.R., L.Air(AG3) Kd. 18-9-41, JX193189, (Jimmy) 754 Arbroath '41, , fell from Lysander

Pimlott, K., Kenneth, L.Air(AG3) Kd. 22-9-41, SFX392, 830 Malta '41, crashed from 500ft torpedo exploded died in Imtarfa hospital

Porter, L.P., Laurence Philip, L.Air(AG3) Kd. 27-9-41, SR16224, MID(p), ;826 WDesert 40/41, bullet in back attacking Bardia died of wounds

Johnson, H.C., Henry Charles, N.Air(AG3) Kd. 29-9-41, FX76314, 700 Nigeria 40/41, A/C accident

Stewart, J., Joseph, L.Air(AG3) Kd. 1-10-41, JX201416, ('Jock') 772 Landrail '41, accident at Craignish flew into mountain in cloud

Eastmant, M., Melbourne. S, L.Air(AG3) Kd. 6-10-41, FX78907, 809 Vic '41, Fulmar failed to return to ship after patrol

James, W.M., Walter Mallet, L.Air(AG3) Kd. 12-10-41, FX77170, 817 Vic '41, Albacore crashed into sea night deck landing training

Weldon, N., Norman, L.Air(AG3) Kd. 23-10-41, FX79502, 832 Vic '41, Albacore forced landing in sea engine failure during navex

Davis, A.G., Alfred George, N.Air(AG3) Kd. 27-10-41, SFX2207, on course killed at Upper Heyford, Oxford

Gilbert, A.G., Albert George, L.Air(AG3) Kd. 1-11-41, FX77486, 700 Newcastle '41, dive bombing exercise

Moulden, N.C., Norman Charles, L.Air(AG3) Kd. 1-11-41, FX77503, MID, 700 Newcastle 40/41, Bermuda bombing & air firing exercise

Griffiths, K.D., Kenneth D, L.Air(AG3) Kd. 12-11-41, FX77337, (Ken) 830 Malta '41, missing from search for enemy convoy crashed in Sicily

Abernethy, R., Roderick, Kd. 20-11-41, , 700 Sydney '41,

Fibbens, W.S., William Sidney, Tel(TAG) Kd. 20-11-41, 21652, (Bill) 700 Sydney '41, lost with HMAS Sydney

Carmichael, R.J., Ray John, L.Air(AG3) Kd. 13-12-41, SFX393, ('Lofty') 826 Formid/WDesert 40/41, hit Blenheim on take-off at El Adem

Hall, G.H., George Hedley, L.Air(AG3) Kd. 13-12-41, SFX2244, ('Wee Geordie') 771 Sparrowhawk '41, height finding exercise at sea

Kelly, J.B., James Birrel, L.Air(AG3) Kd. 15-12-41, JX234628, 772 Landrail '41, flying accident died of injuries Greenock

Kennelly, E., Edward, L.Air(AG3) Kd. 15-12-41, FX77277, Ted, MID, 826 WDesert '41, Albacore night ops bombing Derna

Hale, R.J., L.Air(AG3) Kd. 13-1-42, JX240811, 774 '42, drowned at Padstow

Rennick, A.E., Albert Edward, L.Air(AG3) Kd. 13-1-42, JX253206, 774 St Merryn '42, A/C in sea drowned off Boscastle, Cornwall

Tew, G.C., George Charles.G., L.Air(AG3) Kd. 28-1-42, FX77470, ('Bunker') 831 Indom 41/42, S'fish off Java A/S patrol ahead of ship in heavy storm

Davison, N., Norman, L.Air(AG3) Kd. 12-2-42, FX78099, 889 '42, Fulmar shot down whilst on patrol W Desert

Johnson, A.L., Ambrose Lawrence, P.O.(AG3) Kd. 12-2-42, FX82042, DSM MID(p), 825 '42, S'fish Channel attack on Scharnhorst & Gneisenau

Smith, W., William.G., L.Air(AG3) Kd. 12-2-42, FX79499, MID(p), 825 41/42, S'fish from Manston Channel attack

Tapping, E., Ernest, L.Air(AG3) Kd. 12-2-42, FX76365, ('Hoss') MID(2)(p), ;825 '42, S'fish from Manston Channel attack

Wheeler, H.T., Henry Thomas., L.Air(AG3) Kd. 12-2-42, JX189404, MID(p), 825 '42, S'fish Channel attack on Scharnhorst/Gneisnau

Clinton, W.J., William John, P.O.(AG3) Kd. 12-2-42, JX143258, ('Clints') MID(p), ;825 '42, S'fish Channel attack Scharnhorst & Gneisenau

Thomas, S.J., Samuel John, L.Air(AG3) Kd. 21-2-42, SFX1159, (Sam 'Taff') 818 Formid '42, Albacore missing from A/S search N Atlantic

Clark, C.H., Clive Hilary, L.Air(AG3) Kd. 23-2-42, FX77171, 817 Vic 41/42, lost in snow storm 30m east of Shetlands night search for enemy fleet

Hibbs, T.A., Thomas Albert, P.O.(TAG2) Kd. 23-2-42, FX76523, ('Lofty') 817 Vic 41/42, lost in snowstorm 30m E of Shetlands search for enemy fleet at night

Dryden, J.E., James Edward.W., P.O.(TAG2) Kd. 23-2-42, FX76550, 832 Vic 41/42, lost in snowstorm 30m E of Shetlands. night search for enemy fleet

Kerry, B.R., Brian Roland, L.Air(AG3) Kd. 24-2-42, FX87219, 755 Kestrel '42, on course Shark crashed making landing circuit

Leslie, N., Norman, L.Air(AG3) Kd. 5-3-42, FX79399, DSM, 826 40/42, Albacore 826 A/C shot down on way to Dekheila by JU88

Stuttle, E.W., Edward William, L.Air(AG2) Kd. 5-3-42, F55120, ('Ernie') 821 Grebe '42, Albacore passenger shot down at Fuka in 826 A/C on way to Dekheila by JU88

Sivewright, C.F., Charles F, L.Air(AG3) Kd. 9-3-42, SR16551, 817 Vic 41/42, Albacore torpedo attack on Tirpitz

Hollowood, S.G., Stanley George, L.Air(AG3) Kd. 9-3-42, JX203477, (Stan) 832 Vic 41/42, Albacore torpedo attack on Tirpitz

Clarke, T.H., Thomas Herbert, L.Air(AG3) Kd. 10-3-42, FX79447, MID, 813 Gib '42, collision with another S'Fish

Allen, R.A., Ronald Arthur.V., L.Air(AG3) Kd. 10-3-42, FX79444, ('Darby') 813 Eagle 41/42, collided with another S'Fish at Gib

Betts, W.H., William Howard, L.Air(AG3) Kd. 13-3-42, SFX828, 819 41/42, S'Fish failed to return from recce ex from Twatt

Tuttle, W.P., William Patrick, L.Air(AG3) Kd. 23-3-42, FX79518, (Bill) 828 Malta '42, Albacore attacking Rommels convoy

Beardwell, W.H., Walter H., L.Air(AG3) Kd. 24-3-42, JX237077, 817 Vic '42, Albacore went over side on take off DCs exploded

Loman, G., George, P.O.(AG3) Kd. 25-3-42, FX82145, ('Bluey') 829 Illust '42, S'Fish did not return from dusk patrol

Bolton, D.A., David Alec, L.Air(AG3) Kd. 5-4-42, FX79396, 788 China Bay '42, air raid on Colombo shot down

Edwards, F., Frederick.H., L.Air(AG3) Kd. 5-4-42, FX77173, 806 '42, air raid on Colombo shot down

Hall, J.R., John Rushworth, P.O.(AG2) Kd. 5-4-42, FX76569, 788 China Bay '42, S'fish shot down Jap attack on Colombo

Porter, K., Kenneth, L.Air(AG3) Kd. 5-4-42, SFX1147, (Ken) 827 Indom 41/42, Indian Ocean sighted Dorsetshire survivors but failed to return shot down

Price, A.E., Albert Ernest, P.O.(AG2) Kd. 5-4-42, FX79387, 700 Dorsetshire 41/42, lost with Dorsetshire

Skingley, G.E., George Edward, N.Air(AG3) Kd. 5-4-42, FX79400, 788 China Bay '42, shot down by Zeros over Ceylon died in hospital Colombo

Bristow, J.R., John Raymond, L.Air(AG3) Kd. 4-5-42, FX79404, 816 Avenger '42, S'Fish lost on recce in Atlantic

Dowling, P.F., Patrick Francis, L.Air(AG3) Kd. 4-5-42, JX246513, 803 Formid '42, accident at sea

Tarrant, C.J., Cyril John, L.Air(AG3) Kd. 4-5-42, FX82907, ('Eddie') 816 Avenger '42, S'fish ran out of fuel on recce landed in sea

Blacklin, A.D., Anthony D., L.Air(AG3) Kd. 6-5-42, FX82914, 833 Landrail '42, S'fish. ftr night navex W.of Mach.

Haddrell, F.J., Frederick J., L.Air(AG3) Kd. 6-5-42, JX217350, 829 Illust '42, S'Fish hit by AA fire over Madagascar crashed nr the barracks

Blakey, Il.G., Hugh Gordon, L.Air(AG3) Kd. 11-5-42, FX89586, 756 WDown '42, on course Proctor hit ground and house in cloud

Howe, N.E., Norman Ernest, L.Air(AG3) Kd. 16-5-42, JX287923, 756 Kestrel '42, Proctor on course crashed Abbotsbury Dorset.landed on minefield

Nuttall, H.W., Herbert William, P.O.(AG2) Kd. 18-5-42, FX76368, ('Betty', 807 Argus '42, A/C shot down at sea

Hetherington, W., W.H., L.Air(AG3) Kd. 20-5-42, JX259395, 817 Vic '42, A/C accident

Paxton, W., William, P.O.(A) Kd. 5-6-42, FX76322, Jock) 811 Landrail '42, S'Fish dived into ground at Langhorne, Dumfries

Lewis, E.T., Eric Thomas.G., L.Air(AG3) Kd. 6-6-42, FX76789, 814 Hermes 40/42, S'fish shot down by Norwegian MV Indra NE of Ceylon

Stapp, C., Cameron, L.Air(AG3) Kd. 6-6-42, FX86434, 772 Landrail '42, flying accident.died of injuries

Duncan, J.B., John Brown, L.Air(AG3) Kd. 14-6-42, SFX1370, ('Jock') 807 Ark/Argus 41/42, Fulmar.Malta convoy A/C did not return from patrol

Hughes, E.T., Ernest Thomas, L.Air(AG3) Kd. 17-6-42, FX82897, ('Blondie') 834 Archer '42, crash on deck

Orme, R.N., Ralph Newton, L.Air(AG3) Kd. 26-6-42, FX82144, MID, 808 40/42, 2 Fulmars collided at Stamford Lough, Co Down

Graham, W.R., William Ross, L.Air(AG3) Kd. 29-6-42, JX263527, 776 Woodvale '42, Roc forced landing in sand dunes Ainsdale

Newell, R.L., Raymond Leonard, L.Air(AG3) Kd. 7-7-42, FX91011, (Ray) 756 WDown '42, on course Proctor crashed at Abingdon

Jones, A.G., Alexander George, L.Air(AG3) Kd. 9-7-42, JX22991, 771 Tern 41/42, A/C accident

Atkin, A.E., Arthur Edward, L.Air(AG3) Kd. 10-7-42, FX79443, ('Tommy') 821 WDesert '42, shot up by ME's 5-7-42 died of wounds 64th Gen Hospital

Howard, G.W., George W., L.Air(AG3) Kd. 23-7-42, JX236066, 817 Vic '42, from Hatston flying accident North Sound, Orkney

Way, W.E., William Ernest, L.Air(AG3) Kd. 23-7-42, FX82909, ('Taff') 815 '42, S'fish A/S patrol between Alex and Mersa enemy coastline

Lowe, F.R., Frederick Ronald.R, L.Air(AG3) Kd. 24-7-42, FX79410, (Frank) DSM, 826 Formid/WDesert 40/42, Albacore night ops W.Desert

Elson, J.F., James Frederick, L.Air(AG3) Kd. 7-8-42, FX78368, 809 Vic '42, Fulmar stalled into sea waiting to land on

Stewart, John, L.Air. Kd. 12-8-42 FX77310 Fulmar Malta convoy failed to return from interception of enemy A/C

Regan, Walter Richard, L.Air(AG3) Kd. 12-8-42 JX228503 809 Vic '42 Fulmar Malta convoy failed to return interception enemy A/C

Brown, Frank Edward, L.Air(AG3) Kd. 17-8-42 JX236728 815 Gamil '42b S'Fish failed to return from A/S search believe shot down by enemy sub

Nicholas, Patrick J, P.O.(AG2) Kd. 20-8-42 FX76378 ('Nutty') 812 40/41,700 Daedalus '42 Walrus crash at Lee

Low, Bertram William, L.Air(AG3) Kd. 20-8-42 JX260816 700 Daedalus '42 Walrus crashed on roof of building in RN Depot

Fletcher, Alfred L, L.Air(AG3) Kd. 27-8-42 JX255011 771 Tern '42 Skua spun off turn Howton Head, Orkney

Hill, Robert Thomas, L.Air(AG3) Kd. 8-9-42 FX86431 766 Landrail '42 Albacore, crash at Shiskin, Isle of Arran night flying

Bassett, Benjamin, L.Air(AG3) Kd. 18-9-42 FX89048 771 Tern '42 killed at sea

Payne, Frederick John .P., L.Air. Kd. 24-9-42 FX78201 700 Sheffield '42 collided with another Walrus Pentland Firth

Penn-Simkin,s C, L.Air(AG3) Kd. 24-9-42 SFX825 700 Sheffield 41/42 collided with another Walrus Pentland Firth

Whitehead, Bernard T., L.Air(AG3) Kd. 10-10-42 JX237126 mining Le Havre. MPK 816 Thorney Island '42

Locke, George Ernest, L.Air(AG3) Kd. 27-10-42 JX234649 ('Jan') 812 Gib '42, 779 Gib '42 Fulmar collided with RAF Hurricane

McBride, Alexander, L.Air(AG3) Kd. 30-10-42 JX226976 821 W Desert '42 Albacore failed to return from night ops collision with a Wellington

Dixon, Gordon, L.Air(AG3) Kd. 8-11-42 JX153666 822 Fur '42b Albacore bombing MID(p) attack La Senia

Johnson, Raymond A, P.O.(TAG3) Kd. 15-11-421932 F55086 812 Glorious '33 loss of Avenger BEM 705 Repulse 36/38, E'gh '39 833 Avenger '42

Oldnall, Martin Harry, L.Air(AG3) Kd. 29-12-42 FX89132 825 Thorney Island '42c S'fish minelaying off French coast failed to return

Crowther, William T, L.Air(AG3) Kd. 1-1-43 /27 SFX2260 703 Fidelity '42 loss of Fidelity. sunk by U435

McEvoy, Patrick Joseph, L.Air(TAG3) Kd. 10-1-43 FX86555 (Pat) 832 Vic '43 (Norfolk) Norfolk Virginia ground accident in Avenger

Dawson, Thomas James, L.Air(AG3) Kd. 11-1-43 JX243176 (Tommy 'Speed') 813 Gib '42, 821 Malta '43 Albacore attack on enemy convoy shot down by night fighter S.of Cape Granitola

Chester, Bernard, P.O.(P) Kd. 25-1-43 FX82258 700 Cormorant 42/43 Walrus landing at Gib enginechecked & landed in sea wheels down

Harris, Kd.4-2-43 ('Maggs') 813 '43 lost at sea from Algiers not confirmed (shot down by American ship?)

Watts, Norman, L.Air(AG3) Kd. 6-2-43 FX82908 771 Hats '41, 832 '42a, 833 '42b, 833 Thorney Island '43 S'fish did not return minelayinga Le Havre

Willcock, R. N, L.Air(TAG3) Kd. 6-2-43 JX309030 766 Landrail '43a, 1700 '44 ex, Albacore crashed on night bombing

Hensman, Frederick Er, P.O.(AG2) Kd. 7-2-43 FX76519 803 39/40813 Cormorant 42/43 S'Fish missing flight Bone to Blida

Tilbury, Cyril Albert, L.Air(AG3) Kd. 15-2-43 FX80764814 Hermes 40/42a, 782 DoniB '43 overdue on flight Hatston to DoniB

Bayne, Allen Millar, C.P.O.(O) Kd. 17-2-43 say FX76845No.9 Obs Mates course 39/40, 754 Condor '43 Albacore spun into ground W of Edzell

Stubbs, Thomas, L.Air(TAG3) Kd. 24-2-43 JX314067 766 Landrail '43a S'Fish.night navex W. of Islay

Lovell, William Freder, L.Air(TAG3) Kd. 28-2-43 LD/X5299 (Willie)MID 700 Stornoway '40, 787 '41, 832 Vic 41/43 Avenger crash on deck   25th died 28th

George, Eric Raymond, L.Air(TAG3) Kd. 7-3-43 SFX2232 836 Thorney Is.'43 S'fish returning from minelaying ditched in sea off I of W

Forrest, Benjamin K, L.Air(AG3) Kd. 12-3-43 SFX2240 (Ben) 828 Malta '43 Albacore attack on enemy shipping off Palermo, Sicily

Faulkner, Ronald .H., O.Sea(AG3) Kd. 13-3-43 JX366668 on course kd.in RCAF Ventura crash

Stagg, John Kenneth, L.Air(TAG3) Kd. 16-3-43 FX86635 ('Roly') 766 Landrail '43a S'Fish night navex sent SOS giving position

McNiven, George Ander, L.Air(TAG3) Kd. 18-3-43 FX115035 off Tanga.Fulmar dived into sea 803 Kilele '43

Pell, Frederick, L.Air(TAG3) Kd. 27-3-43 JX193497 (Fred) 811 '42 6 AGI 42/43, 816 Dasher '43a Dasher blew up

Jackson, Henry Rensha, L.Air(TAG3) Kd. 27-3-43 FX87319 ('Joe') 816 Dasher '43 loss of Dasher

Moody, Joseph Henry, L.Air(TAG3) Kd. 27-3-43 FX89609 816 Dasher '43a blew up in Dasher

Dando, Edwin James, L.Air(AG3) Kd. 27-3-43 SFX2864 816 Dasher '43a loss of Dasher

Young, A. J., P.O.(TAG3) Kd. 27-3-43, 1928 F55142 ('Brigham') lost in Dasher 803 Eagle '33, 821 Cour 36/37, 816 Dasher '43

Murphy, Peter James, L.Air(TAG3) Kd. 31-3-43 FX91318 782 DoniB '43 flying accident

Callnon, Denis, L.Air(TAG3) Kd. 3-4-43 FX115107 820 Formid 42/43, 766 Landrail '43a, Albacore flew into sea at Ballure bombing range body washed ashore

Evett, Sydney, L.Air(TAG3) Kd. 5-4-43 FX82879 ('Butch') 800 '41b Albacore lost on A/S patrol bad visibility

Wakefield, Cyril, L.Air(TAG3) Kd. 19-4-43 say FX115036 710 Albatross '43 Walrus crashed during dummy dive bombing (combined ops ex. at South Crest Bombay)

Darke, Ronald Clayden, L.Air(AG3) Kd. 24-4-43 FX77178 (Ron) 801 '41a, 831 42/43a flying accident crashed in sea

Hartley, R., L.Air(TAG3) Kd. 27-4-43 say FX86655 770 Jackdaw '43 Chesapeake crashed into bus dummy dive bombing, Leith

Yates, George, L.Air(AG3) Kd. 30-4-43 SFX2261 ('Calio') 826 Algeria '43a flying accident at Hannibal

Pritchard, Peter, L.Air(AG3) Kd. 1-5-43 /31/33 FX115102 766 Landrail '43 S'Fish flew into sea at night A/S bombing ex (broke ankle baling out of Shark on course)

Astley, Glyn L., L.Air.(TAG3) Kd. 5-5-43 FX114989 796 Tanga '43 S'Fish local night ex found wrecked Kwale, Kenya

Marsden, George H, L.Air(TAG3) Kd. 12-5-43 FX115050 811 Biter '43 S'fish attacking U230 presumed shot down

Hatfield, Vernon V, L.Air(TAG3) Kd. 13-5-43 FX78549 790 Charlton Hor.'43 Fulmar at Queen Camel spun in making forced landing

Harris, Gerald, L.Air(TAG3) Kd. 10-6-43 FX115022 826 N.Africa '42, 826 Formid '43 Albacore forced landing in sea DCs exploded

Clifford, G.A., L.Air(TAG3) Kd. 25-6-43 FX86847 ('Gus') 755 WDown '43 on course Proctor spun in at Whitchurch, Hants

Ritchie, Dennis, L.Air(TAG3) Kd. 4-7-43 FX115075 889 '42, 846 Ravager '43 Avenger stalled on TO from deck Chesapeake Bay

Rowe, Frank Harry F., P.O.(TAG3) Kd. 14-7-43 FX115026 ('Tubby') 827 Jackdaw '43 Barra failed to pull out from dummy dive bombing attack

Tudge, Richard, P.O.(TAG3) Kd. 17-7-43 1940 SR8144 (Dick) 807 '40, 710 40/42, 783 Arbroath '43 Walrus sank during water landing

Taylor, Frederick John, N.Air. Kd. 10-8-43 FX79489 727 Cormorant '43 missing presumed killed off Algiers (target towing Naval Air.)

Grubb, Cecil Herbert, L.Air (TAG3) Kd. 10-8-43 JX344902 785 Crail '43 Albacore flew into hillside NW of Crail on night ex

Jenkins, Graham Neatby, L.Air(TAG3) Kd. 26-8-43 FX86772 816 Tracker '43bc S'Fish.went over side night D/L

Whiteside, Norman, L.Air(TAG3) Kd. 27-9-43/41 FX91886 831 Landrail '43b Barra failed to return from night navex

Thomson, William E, L.Air(TAG3) Kd. 3-10-43 FX77344 ('Bill') 830 Malta '41, 832 '43, 849 Saker '43 Avenger at Chesapeake Bay A/C struck sea during ALT

Morgan, Ralph, P.O.(TAG3) Kd. 7-10-43 FX82142 ('Ginger') 831 41/42, 827 '43a S'Fish forced landing in sea out of fuel 842 Fencer '43

Rough, Gavin, P.O.(TAG3) Kd. 9-10-43 /19 FX82878 ('Jock') 827 Indom 41c/42, 827 '43a, Stalker '43, Hunter '43 to UK 845 Hatston '43 Avenger off Old Man of Hoy spun into sea after collision with Seafire

Ward, William David, L.Air(TAG3) Kd. 22-10-43 FX115099 ('Widdy') 836 Empire MacAndrew '43 S'Fish lost convoy ran out of fuel

Freeman, Roy Hardy, L.Air(TAG3) Kd. 23-10-43 FX91320 766 Nightjar '43b Albacore crashed on take off died as result of injuries

Anderson, Frederick, L.Air-11-43/40 FX115136 ('Andy') 830 Fur '43 collision in Barra Fighter evasion ex Clyde area

Artlett, Frederick, J. P.O.(TAG3) Kd. 10-11-43 FX114981 810 Illust 42/43 lost overboard from boat deck off N Ireland

Bridges, Stanley D., L.Air(TAG3) Kd. 15-11-43 FX95744 ('Tony') 827 Fur '43 Barra collision Clyde area during fighter evasion ex

Beall, Lewis Henry, L.Air(TAG3) Kd. 17-11-43 FX86892 772 Landrail '43 Martinet off Greenock crashed in sea in flames astern of Argus

Murray, Walter Edward, L.Air(TAG3) Kd. 17-11-43 SFX3445 ('Lofty') 810 Mach/Illust '43 Barra from Landrail mid-air collision off Ailsa Craigb

Coles, James, L.Air(TAG3) Kd. 17-11-43 FX76534 ('Stalky') 822 Courageous '39 (survivor), 800 Ark 40/41, 785 Crail '42, 810 Mach 42/43 Barras collided near Ailsa Craig

Bensted, John Charles, L.Air(TAG3) Kd. 18-11-43 FX86815 836 Shrike '43 S'Fish crashed on beach at night Kintyre, Argyll

Williams, Thomas, Ch.L.Air(TAG3) Kd. 18-11-43 SFX1157 ('Fluter') 700 Trinidad 41/42, 772 42/43, 850 Saker '43 Avenger night flying A/C seen to bounce on water and dive into sea

Paige, Stanley Alfred, L.Air(TAG3) Kd. 6-12-43 FX86660 836 Shrike '43 S'Fish A/C dived into sea bombing ex Ballochantry, Kintyre

Afford, Donald Ernest, L.Air(TAG3) Kd. 7-12-43 FX96366 853 '43 Avenger struck sea and sank Plymouth Bay Mass

Kelly, Edward William, L.Air(TAG3) Kd. 9-12-43 FX86637 (Ted) 830 Fur '43 Barra Ranma Stacks Shetland dived into sea during live dive bombing ex

Elliott, John Trevor, L.Air(TAG3) Kd. 14-12-43 FX86851 829 Owl '43 Barra night navex Moray Firth failed to return

McEntee, Hugh, L.Air(TAG3) Kd. 18-12-43 FX86884 770 Jackdaw '43 Chesapeake ditched with engine trouble near Crail

Buttery, Dennis, L.Air(TAG3) Kd. 20-12-43 FX86846 747 Nightjar '43 Barra lost touch with formation night crash near Ambleside

Chadwick, Walter L., L.Air(TAG3) Kd. 4-1-44 FX86678 (Laurie 'Chad') 847 Illustrious 43/44 Barra in Atlantic forced landing in sea on TO DCs exploded

Martin, Arthur Charles, L.Air(TAG3) Kd. 7-1-44 FX86909 836 Mach '44 flying accident off Mull of Kintyre

Gates, Robin Frederick, L.Air(TAG3) Kd. 10-1-44 FX89594 846 Tracker '44a Avenger wing broke off in glide bombing ex on ship

Baelhauwer M. L/S Kd.11-1-44 860 Acavus '44 S'fish ditched bad weather

Cork, John Leslie, .N. L.Air(TAG3) Kd. 18-1-44 FX86818 829 Owl '44 Barra wing broke off practice attack nr Moray Buoy

Martin, John Millan, L.Air(TAG3) Kd. 18-1-44 say JX401581 ('Jock') 772 Landrail '44a A/C accident

Randall, Clifford M, L.Air(TAG3) Kd. 31-1-44 FX86871 836 Ancylus '44 lost from Ancylus

Nield, George Nowell, L.Air(TAG3) Kd. 5-2-44 FX115137 835 Nairana '44 S'Fish in Atlantic Ocean overdue from A/S search

Hughes, Sydney, L.Air(TAG3) Kd. 6-2-44 FX86950 836 Empire MacCallum '44 Empire MacCallum killed flying accident

Dennis, Norman Alfred, L.Air(TAG3) Kd. 11-2-44 FX87066 766 Inskip '44 S'Fish crashed in sea at night washed ashore Morecambe Bay

Burt, Albert Leslie, L.Air(TAG3) Kd. 12-2-44 FX91604 sinking of SS Khedive Ismael Indian Ocean

O'Brien, Desmond, L.Air(TAG3) Kd. 17-2-44 say FX86867 815 Owl 43b/44a Barra crased into sea during night ALT off Tarbat Ness

Martin, George Harry, L.Air(TAG3) Kd. 17-2-44 FX96799 ('Eric') 772 Landrail '44a Martinet off Iron Rock, SW Arran

Ferguson, William G., L.Air(TAG3) Kd. 4-3-44 NZ4383 835 Nairana '44 S'Fish A/C fell over stbd side in night ops

Webb, Harry Trevor, L.Air(TAG3) Kd. 7-3-44 FX86723 ('Shorty') 766 '43, 836 Empire MacMahon '44 S'fish drowned in flying accident

Absolon, Norman Henry, L.Air(TAG3) Kd. 10-3-44 FX96102 ('Lofty') 810 43/44a (Barracuda) off Illustrious Failed to pull out of A L T Bay of Bengal

Stone, John, L.Air(TAG3) Kd. 12-3-44 FX90683 20-6-44 825 Vindex 43b/44 MID(p) S'fish shot down by U-boat flak in Atlantic buried at sea

Seddon, Henry, L.Air(TAG3) Kd. 14-3-44 FX87099 855 Squantum '44 Avenger night A/S bombing ex Cape Cod USA did not return

Hall-Law, Henry B., L.Air(TAG3) Kd. 19-3-44 FX77270 Piarco 42/43 825 Vindex 43b/44 MID(p) S'fish lost at night in Atlantic

Scott, Michael Joseph, L.Air(TAG3) Kd. 24-3-44 FX87016 826 Jackdaw '44 Barra on ALT crashed into sea near Crail

Colwill, Colin James, L.Air(TAG3) Kd. 3-4-44 FX91933 789 Wingfield '43, 829 Vic '44 Barra crashed on take-off Tirpitz attack

Burns, George Joseph, L.Air(TAG3) Kd. 3-4-44 FX88966 ('Paddy') 830 Fur '44 Barra.Tirpitz attack

Plain Eric Henry L.Air(TAG3) Kd. 11-4-44 /31 FX115071 848 43/44a Avenger failed to return night navex N of Eglinton

Reed, John, L.Air(TAG3) Kd. 11-4-44/18A FX115143 848 '43, 848 Landrail '44a Avenger crashed in sea Carradale Point

Airey, Clifford D., L.Air.(TAG3) Kd. 14-4-44 FX86811 851 Shah 43/44 Anti-sub ex off Ceylon Avenger stalled into sea and caught fire

Gaston, Harry, L.Air(TAG3) Kd. 18-4-44 FX96031 747 Owl '44 Barra night ALT Moray Firth dived into sea in flames

White, Frederick Harry, L.Air(TAG3) Kd. 23-4-44 say FX91888 836 Emp. Macdermott '44 S'Fish off Little Cumbrae light probable DCs exploded

Murray, William, L.Air(TAG3) Kd. 26-4-44 FX87083 827 Fur '44 Barra dived into sea attacking ship off Norway

Read, Derrick, L.Air(TAG3) Kd. 26-4-44 say FX113680 771 Tern '44 Skua forced landing at sea Stromness

Grapes, Richard Crawford, P.O.(TAG3) Kd. 1-5-44 FX87259 (Dick) 776 '42, 785 Crail 43/44, 838 Crail '44 S'fish attack on German destroyer at (attached to 19 Group) night off French coast

Rockley, Albert, L.Air(TAG3) Kd. 1-5-44 FX86788, 838 Vulture '44 S'fish night ops attacking Elbing class destroyer Isle Vierge

Rowntree, Brian L., L.Air(TAG3) Kd. 1-5-44 FX87018 838 Vulture '44 S'fish night ops against Elbing class destroyer Isle Vierge

Boar, Alec Stewart, L.Air(TAG3) Kd. 1-5-44 FX86896 771 Tern '44 Skua dive bombing ex. Isle of Ronsay, Kirkwall

Jacques, Wilfred Harold, S.Lt. Kd. 2-5-44 FX90852 785 Jackdaw '44 pilot killed as pilot Barra dived into sea

Reynolds, William H., L.Air(TAG3) Kd. 6-5-44 FX608014 827 Fur '44 Barra attack on convoy off Kristiansand

Bussey, Bernard P., L.Air(TAG3) Kd. 6-5-44 /42 FX95666 830 Fur '44 Barra lost on recce washed ashore Kristi island (Tirpitz)

Mears, Albert William, P.O.(TAG3) Kd. 11-5-44 SFX2259 ('Mick') 825 Vindex 43/44 S'Fish went over side when landing. U-boat hunting Atlantic

Bream, George Gordon, L.Air(TAG3) Kd. 19-5-44 FX91295 848 '43 848 Manston '44a Avenger failed to return from patrol Flushing to Helde

Kemp, Donald Charles, L.Air(TAG3) Kd. 23-5-44 FX86773 ('Dog-watch') 816 Vulture '44 A/C accident

Terry, Alfred James W., L.Air(TAG3) Kd. 25-5-44 FX608016 826 Jackdaw 43b/44 Barra's wings broke on bombing range

Twining, Archie Dan, P.O.(TAG3) Kd. 26-5-44 FX77185 Piarco 42/43, 841 Owl '44 Barra port wing came adrift in dive on bombing range

Shotton, William S., P.O.(TAG3) Kd. 27-5-44 FX77299 (Willie) 818 Ark 40b/41 Empire MacCabe 818 Formid '42a, 820 Formid '42b, 766 '44 836 MacCabe '44 explosion on board

Sim, Alan Black, L.Air(TAG3) Kd. 28-5-44 FX87037 829 Vic '44 Barra left Mach for Hatson in 831 A/C wreck found 4 miles N.of Crieff

Winder, Alan Glenister, L.Air(TAG3) Kd. 28-5-44 FX86931 ('Ray') 852 Nabob/Landrail 43/44 Avenger flew into hillside NW of Carradae Mull of Kintyre

Watts, Leonard F., L.Air(TAG3) Kd. 30-5-44 FX113694 766 Nightjar '44 S'fish last seen in vicinity of Morecambe Bay

Sutcliffe, Norman, L.Air(TAG3) Kd. 30-5-44 FX95635 ('Angel') 836 Shrike '44 ftr patrol body recovered Halifax N S

Green, Leonard Charlesm L.Air(TAG3) Kd. 7-6-44 FX96769 854 Lee '44 Avenger from RAF Hawkinge.missing from patrol Pas de Calais

Sutton, Leslie John, L.Air(TAG3)Kd 7-6-44 FX96096 ('Chutney') 828 Owl '44 Barra collided with another A/C after ALT Tarbat Ness

Allison, Ernest W., L.Air.(TAG3) Kd. 7-6-44 FX96794 ('Lofty') 828 Owl '44 collided with another Barra returning from A L T Tarbat Ness

Rigby, Robinson, P.O.(TAG3) Kd. 11-6-44 FX86789 (Bob) 836 Coastal Command '42, 766 '43a, 756 '43 810 Illust '44a Barra crashed in sea after dummy torpedo attack off Sumatra

Pritchett, Stanley C., L.Air(TAG3) Kd. 16-6-44 FX113681 768 Argus '44 S'fish crashed into sea off ship

Mills, Arthur Derrick, L.Air(TAG3) Kd. 20-6-44 FX703508 821 Landrail '44 Barra dived into sea during ALT 3m S Cumbrae

Watkins, Victor W.,L.Air(TAG3) Kd. 21-6-44 FX97208 831 Vic '44a Barra broke up practice dive bombing crashed in sea

Kitley, Ivor Charles, L.Air(TAG3) Kd. 21-6-44 FX88989 829 Vic '44 Barra wing folded practice bombing attack crashed in sea

Upton, Ronald, Tel(TAG) Kd. 24-6-44 17428 Matafele '44 lost with HMAS Matafele

Gillison, Alan, L.Air(TAG3) Kd. 26-6-44 FX96222 836 Adula 44, S'Fish lost on flight off Newfoundland

Grossett, William A., L.Air(TAG3) Kd. 27-6-44 FX113994 770 Jackdaw '44a Chesapeake into spin on landing flames on impact died of injuries

Sargent, Eric George, L.Air(TAG3) Kd. 13-7-44 FX608015 812 Jackdaw '44 flying accident at Crail

Kimberley, Arthur H., P.O.(TAG3) Kd. 18-7-44 FX95538 827 Vic '44, MID 830 Fur '44 Barra failed to return from A/S patrol

Watson, John Bryan, L.Air(TAG3) Kd. 19-7-44 JX394477 (Bryan) 856 Landrail '44 Avenger A/S ex dived into sea E of Campbeltown

Elmer, Christopher F., P.O.(TAG3) Kd. 21-7-44 FX607659 744 Shrike '44 missing presumed killed at sea

Norman, Stanley W., L, Air(TAG3) Kd. 23-7-44 SFX2228 (Stan) 855 Hawkinge '44 from RAF Hawkinge patrol off French coast

Selby, Harold Cecil, P.O.(TAG3) Kd. 24-7-44 FX79495 ('Bash') 831 Indom 41/43a, 855 Lee '44 Avenger from Hawkinge patrol between Boulogne & Fecamp no trace

Blissett, Bernard K., P.O.(TAG3) Kd. 29-7-44 FX95691 852 Nabob 43/44 Avenger off W coast of Scotland took wave-off crashed in sea DCs exploded

Wilkinson, Henry R., P.O.(TAG2) Kd. 1-8-44 FX76556 820 '37, 813 Eagle 40/41, 822 '42b, 774 Vulture '44, S'Fish flames seen went into spin and crashed St Merryn (TAG2 refresher)

Camp, William Walter, P.O.(TAG2) Kd. 1-8-44 1935 FX76504 811 '36, 813 '37, 700 Resolution 41/43, 774 '44 S'Fish crash at St Merryn-flames under engine (TAG2 refresh)

Allen, William Arthur, P.O.(TAG3) Kd. 4-8-44 FX95770 831 Fur/Vic '44 Barra flying accident collision Trinco

Hunt, Frederick Henry, L.Air(TAG3) Kd. 4-8-44 FX87071 (Fred) 831 Vic '44b Barra mid-air collision after practice (at Trinco) attack on Fleet

Gillespie, John A., L.Air(TAG3) Kd. 5-8-44 FX91547 792 St Merryn '44 Defiant TT spun off turn with target streamed dived in sea inverted

Ashton, James Herbert, P.O.(TAG3) Kd. 10-8-44 FX91197 MID(p), 846 Tracker/Trumpeter '44 Avenger shot down AA fire Vigro, Norway crashed in sea

Griffiths, David R., L.Air(TAG3) Kd. 14-8-44 FX572773 771 Tern '44 aircraft accident

Mitchley, George E., L.Air(TAG3) Kd. 15-8-44/19 FX82875 772 42/43, 753 Condor '44 on Obs course Albacore on navex off Arbroath

Fryer, Gerald George, P.O.(TAG3) Kd. 22-8-44 FX95624 ('Jerry') 830 Fur '44 Barra preparing to land crashed into sea 40m off Norway

Atkinson, Philip W., L.Air(TAG3) Kd. 24-8-44 FX86809 822 Ukussa '44 near Ceylon Barra hit by A/C on fighter evasion ex and ditched

Evans, Geoffrey Jones, L.Air(TAG3) Kd. 24-8-44 FX90686 (Geoff) 815 Indom '44ab Barra after strike on Padang, Sumatra approached ship but rolled and crashed into sea

Mew, Derek Albert Thomas, L.Air(TAG3) Kd. 29-8-44 FX112438 769 Peewit '44 Barra crashed on TO at Maydown plane recovered May 1971

Stephenson, George A., P.O.(TAG3) Kd. 4-9-44 FX77482 855 Thorney Island '44 Avenger anti-shipping patrol attacking DD's off Dutch coast

Cox, Leslie Kenneth, P.O.(TAG3) Kd. 28-9-44 FX608008 842 Fencer 43/44 S'fish. ftr patrol from Benbecula

Douglas, James, P.O.(TAG3) Kd. 1-10-44 FX86988 828 Implac '44 accident at sea

McFee, James, P.O.(TAG3) Kd. 13-10-44 FX114987785 Jackdaw '44 from Crail.missing presumed killed

Jenner, Kenneth W., P.O.(TAG3) Kd. 17-10-44 FX90676 766 '43b, 733 '44, 756 '44, 815 Indom '44b Barra attack on Nicobar shot down by AA

Maitland, Philip W., P.O.(TAG3) Kd. 19-10-44 LD/X5350 Piarco 42/43, 841 Implac 43/44 A/C accident

Bennett, John Arnold, L.Air(TAG3) Kd. 20-10-44 FX606923 745 Yarmouth '44 Ansons collided on course Yarmouth

Stanier, Raymond E., L.Air(TAG3) Kd. 20-10-44 FX605203 745 Yarmouth '44 on course Yarmouth. Ansons collided

Brookes, Albert D., L.Air(TAG3) Kd. 20-10-44 FX605894 745 Yarmouth '44 Ansons collided on course Yarmouth

Taylor, Henry, L.Air(TAG3) Kd. 20-10-44 FX614771 745 Yarmouth '44 Ansons collided.on course Yarmouth

Bone, John William, P.O.(TAG3) Kd. 26-10-44 FX87060 (Jimmy) 828 Implac '44 Barra on strike take-off went over bows into sea

Cribb, Owen Llanwarne, L.Air(TAG3) Kd. 16-11-44 FX96196 848 Formid '44 accident at Dekheila

Hughes, Gordon Taylor, P.O.(TAG3) Kd. 25-11-44 FX114001 ('Don') 812 Owl '44 Barra collided with another Barra joining formation Cromarty

Balsam, Hubert Desmond, P.O. (TAG3) Kd. 25-11-44 FX86991 812 Fearn '44 collided with another Barra in formation Cromarty Firth

Davis, Reginald John, P.O.(TAG3) Kd. 28-11-44 FX86801 775 Grebe '44 Martinet engine cut on take-off crashed on beach NW of Dekheila

Neal, Guy William, P.O.(TAG3)Kd 30-11-44 FX95979 728 Takali '44 Beaufort Takali to Blida no trace found

Addison, Denys, L.Air(TAG3) Kd. 5-12-44 FX512249 710 '44 Ronaldsway Night A/S bombing ex Barra dived into sea

Westcott, Norman, L.Air(TAG3) Kd. 7-12-44 FX605264 763 Nightjar '44 Avenger night ALT flew into ship 'Glen Marson' which sank

Penny, Trevor William, L.Air(TAG3) Kd. 7-12-44 FX96625 (Joe) 814 Owl '44 Barra crashed in sea on approach for ALT

Waugh, Victor George W., L.Air(TAG3) Kd. 8-12-44 FX112408 785 Jackdaw '44 Barra in sea E of Leuchars dinghy empty

Moore, Reginald Frank, L.Air(TAG3) Kd. 8-12-44 FX582207 785 Crail '44 Barra overdue on search for lost A/C

Bennett, Michael Vivian M., S.Lt. Kd. 8-12-44 FX77268 773 '41, TAG to '42 pilot via U/Y 785 Jackdaw '44, Barra crashed in to sea nr Leuchars killed as pilot, (+TAG Waugh)

Battersby, John C., L.Air(TAG3) Kd. 12-12-44 FX112062 710 Urley '44 Port Sedrick Bay Barra went into sea at night after releasing bombs on A/S ex

Michie, William Ford, L.Air(TAG3) Kd. 12-12-44 FX564115 786 Jackdaw '44 Barra overdue on shadowing exercise

Maguire, Robert A., P.O.(TAG3) Kd. 15-12-44 FX77831 815 '42b 814 Owl '44 Barra crashed into hill on return from night navex

Rankin, John, P.O.(TAG3) Kd. 21-12-44 FX113684 831 Fur 43b/44a, 710 Urley '44 Barra night dive bombing ex wing broke off

Kennedy, William, L.Air(TAG3) Kd. 22-12-44 FX578007 786 Jackdaw '44 hit sea off Crail missing presumed killed

Gurden, Leslie William, P.O.(TAG3) Kd. 2-1-45 FX115084 815 43b/44, Wagtail '45 accident at Isle of Islay

Morgan, David Lewis, P.O.(TAG3) Kd. 2-1-45 FX81830 811 Biter '43, 781 Lee '45 Anson crash after take off from Toussus

Brooks, James Edward, L.Air(TAG3) Kd. 3-1-45 FX567668 785 Jackdaw '45 Barra hit target vessel on A L T near May Island

Pritchett, William, L.Air(TAG3) Kd. 6-1-45 FX611435 ('Roger') Wagtail '45, 814 '45 Barra on navex lost S of Mull of Kintyre

Cole, Lewis Edward, P.O.(TAG3) Kd. 13-1-45 FX87167 (Lewis) 820 Indefat 44b/45 dummy attack on Colombo

Mallorie, Philip Roy, L.Air(TAG3) Kd. 16-1-45 FX578011 763 Nightjar 44b/45 Avenger night navex spread on hill West Water, Cumberland

Jackson, Robert Joseph, L.Air(AG3) Kd. 18-1-45 FX79433 826 '40a Albacore shot down 22-6-40 Insel, head injury died as POW cancer of stomach

Harris, Clifford Louis, L.Air(TAG3) Kd. 24-1-45 FX87003 852 Nabob 43/44, 774 '44, 820 Indefat 44b/45 Avenger Palembang presumed crashed in sea

Morris, Walter, L.Air(TAG3) Kd. 24-1-45 JX421389 786 Jackdaw '45 Barra.on NALT crashed in sea

Duncan, David Henry, P.O.(TAG3) Kd. 24-1-45 FX87175 852 '43, 857 44/45 Avenger Palembang Jap fighter crashed in jungle caught fire

Whitford, Alan, P.O.(TAG3) Kd. 25-1-45 FX77269 814 Hermes 41/42, 752 Piarco 44/45 Reliant circled and dived into ground

Woodhead, Terence N., P.O.(TAG3) Kd. 27-1-45 FX95670 ('Nutty') 747 Urley '45 Barra homing ex steep dive and crashed in sea

Stollery, Henry George, CPO(TAG2) Kd. 29-1-45 FX79439 819 '40, 813 '43a, MID(2)(p) 854 Illust 44/45 Avenger balloons at Palembang

Elston, William, L.Air(TAG3) Kd. 29-1-45 FX115004 795 '43, 785 Jackdaw '45 Barra flew into Sicily '43 sea during ALT off May Island

Barber, Alwyn, N.Air(TAG3) Kd. 29-1-45 FX96751 854 Illust '45 lost in balloons at Palembang

Johnson, Frederick, P.O.(TAG3) Kd. 8-2-45 FX114955 788 '42 815 Gannet '45a Barra lost on Arbroath 44/45 operational flight from RAF Mullaghnore

Smee, Norman Frederick, L.Air(TAG3) Kd. 22-2-45 FX112219 821 Puncher '45 Barra Haugesund Fjord, Norway minelaying A/C hit water and exploded. died after being picked up

Brooks, Harold Joseph, L.Air(TAG3) Kd. 22-2-45 FX86817 821 Puncher '45 Barra. lost Haugesund Fjord, Norway

Graham, Vivian, P.O.(TAG3) Kd. 15-3-45 FX605365 837 Owl '45a Barra at Fearn spun in off steep turn on fighter evasion exercise

Brown, John, P.O.(TAG3) Kd. 26-3-45 SFX1328 818 42b/44, 854 Illust 44/45 Avenger at Sakishima Gunto

Sumner, Arthur George, P.O.(TAG3) Kd. 26-3-45 FX115100 ('Slash') 821 Puncher '45 Barra A/S patrol ahead of fleet Northern Waters R/T suddenly ceased

Firth, Percy Harold, P.O.(TAG3) Kd. 27-3-45/31 FX100702 818 42b/44, 854 Illust 44/45 Avenger Ishigaki hit by AA wing broke off on way back

McGregor, Peter G,. P.O.(TAG3) Kd. 28-3-45 FX113108 815 Landrail '45a Barra struck water after A/S bombing off Ballura Point, Argyll

Begley, Robert Osmond, P.O.(TAG3) Kd. 29-3-45 FX114962 (Bob) 832 Vic 41/43, 832 '44, 783 Arbroath '45 accident at Arbroath

Hewkin, Norman, L.Air(TAG3) Kd. 31-3-45 FX87191 756 '44 849 Vic '45 Avenger Ishigaki crashed on target burst into flames

Hamill, Victor Albert, P.O.(TAG3) Kd. 6-4-45 FX112752 812 Vengeance 44/45 Barra from Halfar night search no further trace

Claughan, Geoffrey, P L.Air(TAG3) Kd. 12-4-45 FX114037 756 '44, 849 Vic '45a at Matsushima (Formosa) Avenger crashed in target area

Ryan, William George, L.Air(TAG3) Kd. 16-4-45 FX611439837 Glory '45a Barra overdue on navex off Western Isles

Mellard, Leslie Arthur, P.O.(TAG3) Kd. 16-4-45 FX112662 857 Indom '45 Avenger hit by flak Sakishima

Irvine, Charles William, P.O.(TAG3) Kd. 17-4-45 FX86771 ('Chuck') 848 44b/45 Avenger Mijako Jima presumed shot down seen to crash in sea

Orsborn, John Peter, P.O.(TAG3) Kd. 21-4-45 FX114019 816 Owl '45a Barra dummy attack failed to pull out of turn crashed in sea

Allen, Mark, L.Air.(TAG3) Kd. 29-4-45 FX86978 (Pop) 832 44/45, 828 Implac '45 Avenger collided with Seafire glide bombing ex Indian Ocean

Kay, Thomas Dodson, P.O.(TAG3) Kd. 30-4-45 FX115081 776 '43, 819 '44a, 740 Landrail 44/45 accident at East Lochalsh Scotland

Mansfield, Peter Bern, L.Air(TAG3) Kd. 4-5-45 FX87081 846 Tracker/Trumpeter 44/45 Avenger raid on Norway-"Black Witch" & "Karl von Hering" shot down

Denton, Leonard R., P.O.(TAG3) Kd. 4-5-45 JX307816 ('Slim') 856 '44, 857 Indom '45 at Sakishima (airfield at Miyara)

Palmer ,Stanley Arthur, L.Air(TAG3) Kd. 12-5-45 FX673631 ('Toff') 763 Nightjar '45 Avenger flew into cliff on navex Port Soderick

Wilcox, Roy Langle,y L.Air(TAG3) Kd. 16-5-45 FX87042 827 Colossus '45 3 Barras collided off Alex

Thomson, James Syrett, L.Air(TAG3) Kd. 16-5-45 FX87104 827 Colossus '45 3 Barras collided after dive bombing ex at Alex

Randle, Eric Franklin, L.Air(TAG3) Kd. 18-5-45 FX113687 827 Colossus '45 A/C accident

Boyle, Kenneth Albert, L.Air(TAG3) Kd. 30-5-45 FX113671 827 '44, 827 Colossus '45 Barra failed to return from night bombing ex coast of E Africa

Smith, Harold Walter, P.O.(TAG3) Kd. 5-6-45 FX96071 851 '44, 817 Owl '45b Barra A/C dived into ground during dive bombing practice

Telford, William Robson, P.O.(TAG3) Kd. 7-6-45 FX86874 728 Takali '45 drowned at Malta

Wick, John Wordsworth, P.O.(TAG3) Kd. 18-6-45 SFX1163 (Johnny) DSM 819 41b/43a, 817 Owl '45b Barra.crashed in sea

Barker, Basil, L.Air(TAG3) Kd. 4-7-45 FX614751 786 Jackdaw '45 Kingsbarn bombing range Barra wing disintegrated crashed in sea in flames

Semple, William, P.O.(TAG3) Kd. 14-7-45 FX617536 786 '45, 818 Fearn '45 Barra on navex flew into hill north of Fearn in cloud

Rawlinson, Gordon C., P.O.(TAG3) Kd. 24-7-45 FX703022 ('Tiger') 848 Formid '45 Avenger Tokushima attack on airfield

Jones, Neville Mallin, L.Air(TAG3) Kd. 7-8-45 FX575500 816 '45a, 713 Urley '45 Barra crashed into sea bombing exercise Port Soderick

Huntingdon, Arthur, P.O.(TAG3) Kd. 8-8-45 FX614760 840 '43 (as non-TAG?), 744 Shrike '45a Barra stbd wing hit water A/C disintegrated

McRae, William James S., P.O.(TAG3) Kd. 15-8-45 FX96155 (Jim) shot down Palembang 29-1-45 766 Vic 44/45 executed by Japs at Changi

Barker, Ivor, P.O.(TAG3) Kd. 15-8-45/43 FX86731 849 Vic 44/45 lost at Palembang 29-1-45 executed by Japs at Changi

Williams, Robert F., P.O.(TAG3) Kd. 8-10-45 FX114047 820 '44a, 710 Urley '45 Barra night homing ex crashed in sea Douglas Head

Doherty, John, L.Air(TAG3) Kd. 15-10-45 FX703501 742 Sulur '45 Expeditor crashed Ratmalana landing in bad weather

Hook, Ronald Charles, L.Air(TAG3) Kd. 15-11-45 FX671256 786 Jackdaw '45 Barra stalled when joining formation Crail

Butterworth, Edmund, P.O.(TAG3) Kd. 31-1-46 FX79950 ('Beezel') MID 819 Illust '40, 815 WDesert 41/42a, 834 Battler '44, 744 '45 814 Venerable '45, 814 Schofields '46 flying accident at Lewisham NSW

Berry, Ernest, L.Air(TAG3) Kd. 8-2-46 JX558666 837 Glory 45b/46 flying accident at sea off Jarvis Bay NSW

Reynolds, George G., P.O.(TAG3) Kd. 11-2-46 FX77304 ('Lucky') DSM 816 Ark '40, 830 Malta 41/42, 851 Shah 43/45, Condor, mid-air collision Wimboldsley, Cheshire

Desborough, Ernest J., P.O.(TAG3) Kd. 1-3-46 FX523614 721 Kaitak '46 Vengeance at Nabcatcher pilot lost control in cloud sunk in bay

Clark, Harold John, C.P.O.(TAG2) Kd. 30-8-46 FX82398 832 43/44, 782 DoniB '46 Abbotsinch to Stretton Dominie ambulance A/C struck high ground in Cumberland

Thompson, Thomas D., P.O.(TAG3) Kd. 17-8-47 FX704904 795 Implac '47 Firefly hit island on landing crashed in sea

Shipley, Edward, Wt(AG) Kd. 15-6-47 FX77412 (Ted) 700 Trinidad 41/42, WDown '44 W/Os course '45, Gannet '47 motorcycle accident.N.Ireland

Lovatt, William, CPO(TAG2) Kd. 20-7-47 FX82396 (Bill) 800 Ark '40 (Norway), 810 Ark 40/41, 812 Theseus '47 Firefly collision with another A/C off Melbourne A/C seen to crash into sea

Dean, Frank Arthur, CPO(TAG2) Kd. 17-3-48 FX79420 ('Dixie') MID 824 Eagle 40bc/42a, 728 Malta 47/48 baled out of Firefly off Malta trapped in parachute drowned

Sharman, Robert Walter, Acmn1. Kd. 15-2-49 FX79385 (Bob) 817 '41, 794 '44, 771 44/45, 812 (14th CAG) 12 TAG1s '46 No.1 Acmns '47Ocean 48/49 Firefly forced landing into barrels on disused runway Krendi, Malta

Gibbons, Stanley William, AcmnII. Kd. 17-4-50 FX606406 (Stan) 771 48/49, No.7 Acmns '49, No.10 Acmns '49 827 Triumph '50 Firefly off Kure Japan collision with RAAF Mustang

Heather, Ian, Tel(A) Kd. 13-9-50 P/X712202 ('Ike') Martinet shot down & drowned target towing by Sea Fury off Trevose Head, Station Flight Vulture '50

McFadden, William Robert, Acmn1. Kd. 6-10-50 FX79388813 Eagle 40b/42a, 772 42/43, 856 44/45, No.6 Acmns 48/49 812 Hal Far '50 Firefly collided with Firefly crashed in sea

Cordwell, Victor Herbert M., Lt. Kd. 31-10-50, 1936 (Vic) Lieut, 820 Courageous 37/38, No.9 Rtg 'O' 39/40, 800 Ark '40, 728 '50 Mosquito crash in sea off HalFar

Sharpe, J G., Kd.1951 No.9 Acmns '49, 815 '50 Nowra, 816 20th CAG '51 Firefly to RAN failed to return from night flying

Wells, George Bertram, Acmn1. Kd. 28-6-51 FX82746 (George) DSM MID(2) 813 Eagle '41a, 824 Eagle '41, 782 '42, 846 Tracker/Trumpeter 44/45 No.7 Acmns '49, 812 Glory 49/51 Firefly in Korea from Glory shot down nr Chinnampo

Edwards, Leslie Mervyn, Acmn1. Kd. 19-5-52 FX79445 ('Bungy') 830 Malta 40/41, 794 '45, 814 Australia 46/47, No.3 Acmns '48 814 Vengeance '50, 812 Glory 51/52a 825 Ocean '52 Firefly in Korea from Ocean hit by flak exploded on impact nr Kaesong

Ripley, Ernest Raymond, Acmn11. Kd. 16-12-52 FX78910 ('Taff') 781 Lee '47, Glory '52, No.10 Acmns '49, 827 Triumph '50 ASR Lossie 50/51 Helicopter off Glory, S.Korea hit island on TO and crashed in sea

Tierney, Edward A S., Acmn1. Kd. 26-2-53 FX78433 (Ted 'Jack') Crail 43/44, 834 Battler '44, 756 44/45, No.9 Acmns '49, 815 '51, Gannet '53 Barra lost in sea NNE of Portrush

Charlesworth, Harry L., Tel(F). Kd. 15-9-53 JX581280 744 Eglinton '53 Dominie overdue Stretton/Eglinton wreckage found at Cushenden

Holmes, George Lincoln, Cmd'O'. Kd. 13-5-54 ('Jas') 841 '44, No.12 TAG1s '46, No.2 Acmns 47/48, Cmd 'O' 728 48/49, 750 Culdrose '54 Sea Prince crash Cornwall

Tomkins, Robert John P., L/Tel(A). Kd. 31-3-55 JX581974 Culdrose '55 Avenger crashed in sea off Lizard

Forbes, Malcolm, L/Tel(A) Kd. 9-5-55 JX581974 820 Eglinton '55 Gannet in sea off Magilligan Point

Self, Norman John, Tel(A)RAN. Kd. 10-11-55 817 Culdrose '55 Gannet A/S ex crashed in sea St Catherines Point

Ramplin, F C., P.O.Tel(A) Kd. 6-3-56 JX646362 824 Ark '56a Gannet flew into sea after night TO

Sutherland, Alistair, Tel(A). Kd. 19-2-57 814 Seahawk '57 Gannet crashed into sea off The Lizard

Llewellyn, Raymond K., L/Tel(A). Kd. 20-8-57 814 Eagle '57 Gannet accident from Eagle

Chivers, Frank J L., Tel(Air) Kd. 20-2-58 JX899532 (Frank) 824 Albion '56, 847 Falcon '58 Nicosia, Cyprus Gannet crashed on landings

Leigh, Thomas, Miall L., C.Acmn1. Kd. 20-2-58 FX97069 ('Taff') 813 Eagle '42, 725 Egl '44 Brawdy No.7 Acmns '49, 812 Glory 49/50 812 Glory '52, Station Flight Goldcrest '58 Eagle Helicopter crash

Fowler, Peter L.,Tel(A) Kd. 17-9-59 JX898688 814 57/58 814 Culdrose '59 Gannet crashed Winkleigh, Devon

Appendix B
Awards in Alphabetical Order

ADLAM Eric James FX77405 MID(p) 22-11-40 801 Sqdn Ark Royal over Norway

ARMSTRONG John Walter Lt.Cdr. SFX900 DSM 16-9-41 as L/Air 771 Sqdn Hatston seeking Bismarck - Bergen

ARMSTRONG Thomas FX79514 DSM 19-5-42 832 Sqdn Victorious ops N. of Norway

ASHTON James FX91197 MID(p) 29-11-44 846 Sqdn Trumpeter minelaying Norway

ASTBURY William Ronald SFX384 DSM 7-8-45 853 Sqdn Queen Kilbotn

ASTON Edward Fielding FX79485 MID 31-7-45 857 Sqdn Indomitable Sakishima

BACON Robert Cecil FX86844 MID 25-7-44 829 Sqdn Victorious shipping Norway

BALDWIN Charles Philip Hector FX76555 MID 30-9-41 824 Sqdn Eagle Italian destroyers Port Sudan

BARNES Frederick Allan FX77002 MID(p) 25-11-41 808 Sqdn Ark Royal Malta convoy air combat

BARRICK Leonard Francis FX76495 CGM 15-5-43 884 Sqdn Victorious Malta convoy Pedastal DSM 31-7-45 820 Sqdn Indefatigable Sakishima

BEARDSLEY James FX82598 DSM 1-1-41 800 Sqdn Ark Royal ops in Med

BECKETT Reuben Valentine LDX5378 MID 1-1-41 801 Sqdn Furious over Norway

BEECH John FX97197 DSM 30-5-44 816 Sqdn Chaser Russian convoy

BEETON Charles Frederick FX76496 DSM 23-2-52 810 Sqdn Theseus Korea, MID 30-9-41 813 Sqdn Eagle Port Sudan, MID* 2-1-45 817 Sqdn Indomitable Emmahaven

BLENKHORN George Leslie FX77411 DSM 29-7-41 829 Sqdn Formidable Matapan

BODDY Robert FX77515 DSM 28-4-42 815 Sqdn Grebe anti-sub ops in Med

BOOSEY Sidney Leonard S.Lt. LDX4595 DSM 2-12-41 815 Sqdn Grebe torpedo attacks Albania, MID 6-1-42 815 Sqdn Grebe sinking Chev Paul

BOOTH Owen James FX82146 MID 29-7-41 829 Sqdn Formidable Matapan

BOWDEN Daniel Mark MID 1-1-42 HMAS Perth

BOYLETT Leonard Frederick FX114921 MID 9-11-43 821 Sqdn sorties from Malta

BRAY William Frank FX76359 DSM 3-1-41 812 Sqdn S.Coast mining enemy coast

BREWER Reginald Thomas John LDX5004 MID 30-6-42 830 Sqdn ops from Malta

BROWN Albert Edward FX78127 MID 30-6-42 830 Sqdn ops from Malta

BROWN Arthur Grainger F55063 DSM 24-3-42 812 Sqdn Argus anti sub ops

BROWN Frank Ridley Lieut FX79413 MID 13-2-45 851 Sqdn Shah sinking U198

BUGDEN William Henry FX76461 DSM 17-3-42 826 Sqdn Grebe W.Desert ops/convoy

BUNCE Donald Arthur FX754011 CGM 3-3-42 825 Sqdn Manston Channel attack

BUTTERWORTH Edmund McKenzie FX79950 MID 1-1-41 815 Sqdn Illust ops in Med

CARLYLE Reginald FX76541 MID 29-7-41 808 Sqdn Ark Royal Malta convoy

CARR Andrew Edward DSM 30-5-44 830 Sqdn Furious Tirpitz

CARROLL Ernest FX96245 DSM 29-8-44 829 Sqdn Victorious Tirpitz

CARTMELL Thomas FX114980 MID 11-7-44 827 Sqdn Furious ops off Norway

CLARE Leslie David Lieut. F55096 DSM 25-6-40 806 Sqdn Hatston over Bergen, MID 25-6-40 806 Sqdn Hatston over Bergen

CLARKE Thomas Herbert FX79447 MID 1-1-42 830 Sqdn ops from Malta

CLAYTON Alfred George FX76535 MID 25-6-40 803 Sqdn Ark Royal over Norway

CLINTON William John JX143258 MID(p) 3-3-42 825 Sqdn Manston Channel attack

CLITHEROE Percy William FX79969 DSM 21-3-41 810 Sqdn Ark Royal Dakar

COLLINGS Alan Terence FX77179 MID 28-4-42 826 Sqdn Grebe night ops W.Desert

COOPER John Mardon FX95604 MID 11-12-45 836 Sqdn Shrike convoy protection

COSTON Frank FX76320 DSM 29-7-41 803 Sqdn Formidable Matapan

COTTERILL Christopher James F55040 MID 10-4-40 800 Sqdn ArkRoyal over Norway

COULBY John MID 5-9-44 830 Sqdn Furious ops off Norway

COWSILL Gordon Eric FX77492 DSM 31-7-45 848 Sqdn Formidable Sakishima

COX Derrick FX86647 DSM 1-5-45 854 Sqdn Illustrious Palembang, MID 1-1-45 819 Sqdn Coastal Command

CRAIG Sidney FX77747 BEM 1-6-53 705 Sqdn Gosport Dutch flood rescues, BrMOr 1-6-53 705 Sqdn Gosport Dutch award rescues

CREER Kenneth Alwyn FX77509 DSM 2-2-51 827 Sqdn Triumph Korea

CREESE Wilfred Rumsey FX96772 DSM 31-7-45 854 Sqdn Illustrious Sakishima

CRIDLAND Thomas Leslie FX79962 DSM 25-8-42 831 Sqdn Indomitable Diego Suarez, DSM* 30-5-44 829 Sqdn Victorious Tirpitz

CRONE W. J. MID 1-1-41 801 Sqdn Furious over Norway

CUNNINGHAM Howard Gresley Lt.Cdr. FX76292 DSM 9-5-40 800 Sqdn Ark Norway, MID 9-5-40 800 Sqdn Ark Royal Norway, MID* 25-6-40 800 Sqdn Ark Royal Norway, MID* 14-5-45 Ark Royal as POW

CUTTRISS William Edwin FX55045 DSM 25-11-41 808 Sqdn Ark Royal Malta convoy

DALE Michael Wyndham FX77285 BEM 16-5-41 710 Sqdn Albatross rescue survivors, MID 19-9-44 825 Sqdn Vindex sinking U765

DAVIS Frederick Walter FX76376 MID 17-5-40 823 Sqdn Glorious mining Norway

DAWSON Charles Frederick FX114973 DSM 10-11-42 809 Sqdn Victorious Malta convoy Pedastal

DEFRIAS Frederick John Leonard Lt.Cdr.FX80801 DSM 4-10-40 803 Sqdn Ark Royal fighter ops in Med

DEAN Frank Arthur FX79420 MID 1-1-42 824 Sqdn Eagle New year Hons.

DIXON Gordon FX77265 MID 1-1-43 827 Sqdn Indomitable escaped Zero attack

DIXON Gordon JX153666 MID(p) 16-3-43 822 Sqdn Furious N.African landings

DIXON Robert Arthur FX114875 DSM 1-1-45 826 Sqdn Grebe night ops W.Desert, DSM* 20-2-45 826 Sqdn Grebe night ops W.Desert

DODWELL George FX80210 DSM 4-5-43 815 Sqdn Grebe anti-sub ops

DOOLEY Frederick Percival FX79187 MID 10-4-40 803 Sqdn Ark Royal Norway

DOUET Paul Reilly Louis LDX5331 DSM 1-7-41 806 Sqdn Formid fighter patrols

DOYLE Alwyn Joseph FX87064 MID 20-11-45 848 Sqdn Formidable Sakishima/Japan

DRISCOLL Sidney FX84782 DSM 20-2-45 826 Sqdn Grebe night ops W.Desert

DUNN Samuel FX89335 DSM 16-1-45 820 Sqdn Indefatigable Tirpitz

DUNNING Harold FX608630 DSM 20-11-45 828 Sqdn Implacable ops Far East

DURRANT William Harry FX96601 MID 5-12-44 824 Sqdn Striker Russian convoys

EASOM Arthur George FX103617 DSM 1-1-45 854 Sqdn Illustrious Palembang

EDMONDSON William Denby FX76497 MID 14-1-41 819 Sqdn Illustrious Rhodes

ELLIS Arthur Stratton FX608728 MID 31-7-45 857 Sqdn Indomitable Sakishima

ELLIS John George FX76304 DSM 1-7-41 810 Sqdn Ark Royal ops in Med

EVANS Harry FX703017 DSM 11-9-45 820 Sqdn Indefatigable attack on Tokyo

FABIEN Ernest Percival SR648 MID(p) 21-10-41 827 Sqdn Victorious Kirkenes

FALLON John Redmond FX77301 MID 29-8-44 830 Sqdn Malta escaping from enemy

FIELDING Jack SFX434 MID 30-6-42 830 Sqdn Malta ops from Malta

FIRTH William Raymond FX86853 MID 25-7-44 829 Sqdn Vic shipping off Norway

FORD Alan C. MID 11-1-41 801 Sqdn Furious over Norway

FORD Phillip Percival FX80201 DSM 21-10-41 800 Sqdn Victorious Kirkenes

FRANKLIN Dennis George FX86803 DSM 30-5-44 816 Sqdn Chaser Russian convoy

GEORGE Reginald Edward FX76491 MID 20-3-45 835 Sqdn Nairana Arctic convoy

GIBBS Roy John William FX112185 MID 31-7-45 820 Sqdn Indefat Sakishima

GILL Derek Victor FX76522 BEM 1-1-45 824 Sqdn Striker Russian convoys

GODFREY Charles Henry FX97108 MID 31-7-45 857 Sqdn Indomitable Sakishima

GOLD Horace William SFX412 MID 20-1-42 830 Sqdn Malta ops from Malta

GOULD Samuel Howard F55139 MID 25-6-40 806 Sqdn Hatston over Bergen

GOWAN Ernest Archibald FX77499 MID 7-4-42 812 Sqdn Argus crashed A/C help, RHSBrMed 7-4-42 812 Sqdn Gib crashed aircrew assistance

GRAINGER Frank SFX387 DSM 31-7-45 820 Sqdn Indefatigable Sakishima

GREEN John Worsley FX87221 DSM 2-6-43 822 Sqdn Furious N.African ops

GREENFIELD John Lt.Cdr.FX115045 DSM 18-7-44 846 Sqdn Tracker Russian convoy

GROVES Robert James Kenneth FX77527 DSM 25-8-42 810 Sqdn Illust Diego Suarez

HALHEAD Thomas William FX77364 DSM 30-5-44 831 Sqdn Vic Tirpitz(Pedastal)

HALIFAX George William FX79391 MID 25-6-40 800 Sqdn Ark Royal over Norway

HALL-LAW Henry Basil FX77270 MID(p) 20-6-44 825 Sqdn Vindex attacks U-boats

HALL Maurice FX76325 MID 9-5-40 800 Sqdn Ark Royal over Norway

HARPER Angus Scott FX77345 DSM 12-1-43 826 Sqdn Grebe ops W.Desert

HARRIS Desmond Charles FX112476 DSM 5-12-44 824 Sqdn Striker Russian convoys

HART Reginald Frederick Lt.Cdr.FX76506 DSM 19-7-40 800 Sqdn Ark over Norway

HARTWELL Edward Francis FX89523 DSM 26-1-43 817 Sqdn Victorious sinking U517

HAYBALL James Jeremiah FX114950 DFM 31-5-55 848 Sqdn Sembawang ops in Malaya

HAZELDINE Frederick William FX77519 DSM 17-11-42 826 Sqdn Grebe ops W.Desert

HEARNSHAW Colin Lt.Cdr.JX152244 DSM 2-12-41 806 Sqdn Formid air patrols Med

HEDGER George Stanley JX198440 MID 1-1-43 828 Sqdn Malta ops from Malta

HOGG Robert William Lt.Cdr. SFX413 DSM 29-7-41 829 Sqdn Formidable Matapan

HOLMES Raymond Hugh FX794141 MID 30-5-44 834 Sqdn Battler ops Indian Ocean

HOLT Harold Spencer 849 44/45 FX90979 MID 31-7-45 849 Sqdn Vic Sakishima

HOMER C.J. FX79409 DSM 9-8-40 826 Sqdn combat with enemy A/C, BEM 1-1-57 728 Sqdn Hal Far New Year Hons.

HOPPER John Alexander FX88539 DSM 20-11-45 848 Sqdn Formidable ops Pacific

HOWARD Leslie Gordon FX76579 DSM 29-7-41 808 Sqdn Ark Royal Malta convoy

HOWATSON Robert Norman Scott FX86767 MID 18-9-45 851 Sqdn Emperor DUKEDOM shadow HAGURO

HOYTE Harold Edward FX86770 MID 5-9-44 830 Sqdn Furious ops off Norway

HUGHES Gordon Churchill Lieut. A40205 DSM 28-10-52 817 Sqdn Sydney Korea

HUNT George Harold Pusey Lt.Cdr. FX77398 BEM 26-9-40 Daedalus prepare airfield Lakselv

HUXLEY Harold Francis SX22866 DSM 16-9-41 810 Sqdn Ark Royal Bismark

JAMES Douglas Leslie FX86952 MID 18-7-44 819 Sqdn Activity Russian convoy

JARY William George SR645 MID(p) 8-1-42 805 Sqdn Maleme Crete

JOHNSON Ambrose Lawrence FX82042 825 '42 DSM 16-9-41 825 Sqdn Vic Bismarck, MID(p) 3-3-42 825 Sqdn Manston Channel attack

JONES William J.FX115116 DSM 28-9-43 811 Sqdn Biter A/S patrols Western App.

KAY Ian McKenzie FX90724 MID 18-7-44 819 Sqdn Activity Russian convoy

KENNELLY Edward FX77277 MID 28-4-42 826 Sqdn Grebe night ops W.Desert

KENNY John MID 31-7-45 854 Sqdn Illustrious Sakishima

KIMBERLEY Arthur Howard FX95538 MID 5-9-44 830 Sqdn Furious ops off Norway

KNIGHT Ronald Thomas FX86710 MID 2-1-45 831 Sqdn Victorious Emmahaven

LAMBERT Herbert John F55106 MBE 1-1-53 Campania atomic tests, DSM 21-10-41 827 Sqdn Indomitable Kirkenes, MID 25-8-42 827 Sqdn Indomitable Diego Suarez

LAMBERT William Gordon JX152946 DSM 1-5-45 820 Sqdn Indefatigable Palembang

LASSON Lionel Ernest FX76297 MID 30-9-41 814 Sqdn Hermes rescue Shaibah

LESLIE Norman FX79399 DSM 11-6-42 826 Sqdn Grebe night ops W.Desert

LINDLEY John William Gorbut Captain FX77303 MID 1-1-44 832 Sqdn Vic Tirpitz

LIVESAY Leo FX90759 MID 19-12-44 846 Sqdn Trumpeter minelaying Arumsund

LLOYD John Trevor FX88942 MID 26-6-45 845 Sqdn Khedive Sabang

LOCK Stuart William SFX23153 DSM 30-5-44 830 Sqdn Furious Tirpitz, BEM 10-6-61 Hermes Birthday Hons.

LOCKHART Frederick George JX307201 DSM 20-11-45 848 Sqdn Formidable Pacific

LONG Lewis George F55088 DSM 28-9-43 811 Sqdn Biter anti-sub attacks

LOVELL William Frederick LD/X5299 MID 19-5-42 832 Sqdn Victorious ops Norway

LOWE Frederick Ronald FX79410 DSM 11-6-42 826 Sqdn Grebe night ops.W.Desert

MACKECHNIE John Duncan Lt.Cdr FX77186 DSM 12-1-43 826 Sqdn Grebe W.Desert

MARSH Alfred Henry FX76331 DSM 14-1-41 813 Sqdn Eagle Bomba Bay attack

MATHEWS Robert Edward JX151327 DSM 12-11-40 826 Sqdn S.Coast ops off Calais

MCCOLL Robert Henry Lt.Cdr.FX76319 DSM 4-10-40 820 Sqdn Ark Royal ops in Med

MCCULLAGH Charles Patrick FX77282 DSM 19-5-53 825 Sqdn Ocean Korea

MILES Lionel William FX79822 DSM 5-7-40 801 Sqdn S.Coast over France

MILSOM Edwin Douglas FX79995 MID 21-6-40 821 Sqdn Hatston Scharnhorst

MITCHELL Gordon FX77413 Seychelles DSM 1-1-41 700 Sqdn Dorsetshire searches

MONTAGUE John Thomas DSM 29-7-41 829 Sqdn Formidable Matapan

MORRIS George Ronald FX76384 MID 29-7-41 829 Sqdn Formidable Matapan

MOULDEN Norman Charles FX77503 MID 14-1-41 700 Sqdn Newcastle good service

MURPHY Robert FX77521 DSM 1-5-45 849 Sqdn Victorious Palembang

MURPHY Thomas Steel FX112060 MID 20-11-45 849 Sqdn Vic attacks on Japan

MUSKETT George Alfred F55108 DSM 25-6-40 806 Sqdn Hatston over Bergen, MID 25-6-40 806 Sqdn Hatston over Bergen

NELSON Allan Lt.Cdr. FX79446 MBE post-1969, DSM 1-7-41 830 Sqdn Malta ops from Malta

NORMAN Clement Francis LD/X5398 MID 29-7-41 829 Sqdn Formidable Matapan

O'NION Gilbert Charles Edward FX77297 MID 2-2-51 Triumph Sea Otter rescue

OPPENHEIM Henry John SFX827 DSM 24-3-42 812 Sqdn Argus anti-sub ops

ORME Ralph Newton FX82144 MID 29-7-41 808 Sqdn Ark Royal Malta convoy

OWEN Iowerth Llewellyn SFX415 MID 30-6-42 830 Sqdn Malta ops from Malta

PACEY Maurice George FX76412 MID 29-7-41 700 Sqdn Warspite Matapan

PALMER Joseph James FX115112 MID 20-6-44 825 Sqdn Vindex attacks on U-boats

PARKER Stanley Edgar FX76360 DSM 16-9-41 825 Sqdn Victorious Bismarck

PEARCE Benjamin FX82913 MID 31-7-45 820 Sqdn Indefatigable Sakishima

PERRY John FX90977 DSM 18-7-44 819 Sqdn Activity Russian convoy U288

PERT Henry McKay FX78192 MID 1-1-44 832 Sqdn Victorious New Year Hons.

PICKLES Frederick FX76385 MID 1-7-41 830 Sqdn Malta ops from Malta

PIRIE William Taylor FX77836 DSM 31-7-45 857 Sqdn Indomitable Sakishima

POE John Charles FX86869 MID 11-12-45 836 Sqdn Shrike convoy protection

POOLE Donald Illingworth FX86629 MID 11-12-45 836 Sqdn Shrike convoy protect

POOLE Norman Alfred Frank FX86712 MID 11-7-44 827 Sqdn Furious ops Norway

PORTER Laurence Philip SR16224 MID(p) 7-4-42 826 Sqdn Grebe ops W.Desert

POTTER James Patrick FX704598 DSM 19-5-53 825 Sqdn Ocean Korea

REASON Philip Douglas Lee FX77517 DSM 24-3-42 812 Sqdn Argus anti-sub op, BEM 8-7-41 812 Sqdn Argus saving lives in a crash

REES Marquis FX608203 DSM 1-5-45 820 Sqdn Implacable Palembang

REID James B. FX82877 MID 1-1-45 819 Sqdn S.Coast Coastal Command

REYNOLDS George Geoffrey FX77304 DSM 30-6-42 830 Sqdn Malta ops from Malta

RICHARDSON Norman Edward FX115147 DSM 31-7-45 849 Sqdn Victorious Sakishima

ROLPH Richard Stephen FX76286 BEM 8-6-44 TAG Sch.Can.Birthday Hons., MID 19-7-40 800 Sqdn Ark Royal over Norway

RUSH Alfred Samuel LD/X5370 MID 1-1-41 806 Sqdn Illustrious fighter patrols, MID* 1-7-41 806 Sqdn Formidable fighters in Med

RUSSELL George Scott FX77464 DSM 10-4-40 803 Sqdn Ark Royal over Norway, MID 14-4-40 803 Sqdn Ark Royal over Norway

SALISBURY Norman Alfred FX77184 MID 30-6-42 830 Sqdn Malta ops from Malta

SAUNDERS Ronald Stratford SR16177 DSM 11-6-42 826 Sqdn W.Desert/Vittorio

SAYER Leslie Daniel FX76577 MBE New Year Hons.1997 Services to TAGA, DSM 16-9-41 825 Sqdn Victorious Bismarck

SEYMOUR Bryan M. Lieut FX76288 DSM date NK 800 Sqdn shot down Do18

SHERLOCK Edward Jutland Watts FX77496 DSM 10-7-45 851 Sqdn Emperor Haguro, MID 24-7-45 851 Sqdn Shah Car Nicobar

SHIEL Frederick Henry FX97073 DSM 23-2-52 810 Sqdn Theseus Korea

SHIRMER Frederick Christian FX115139 DSM 1-5-45 854 Sqdn Illustrious Palembang, MID 1-1-45 854 Sqdn S.Coast

SHOESMITH Eric A. DSM 23-2-40 718 Sqdn Exeter Battle of River Plate

SIMPSON Austin Alexander SFX2263 DSM 14-12-45 820 Sqdn Indefat ops Tokyo

SIMS Kenneth Laurence Joseph FX77278 DSM 2-12-41 815 Sqdn Grebe torpedo attacks Albania

SKEATS John Goldup JX140727 DSM 25-6-40 818 Sqdn Furious over Norway

SMEETON Frank FX87027 MID 19-9-44 825 Sqdn Vindex attack on U765

SMITH Laurence William Lt.Cdr. FX76351 DSM 2-12-41 815 Sqdn Grebe torpedo attacks Albania

SMITH William Granville FX79499 MID(p) 3-3-42 825 Sqdn Channel attack

SMYTH Victor FX86754 MID 5-9-44 831 Sqdn Victorious ops off Norway Lombard

SNOWDON Thomas William MID 20-3-45 Nairana Arctic convoy

SPENCER Thomas Charles Brackley FX95752 MID 17-10-44 849 Sqdn Victorious ops off Norway Lombard

SPOWART Oswald F55071 DSM 15-12-42 821 Sqdn Grebe ops W.Desert

STACEY Brian NZ7223 MID 11-12-45 836 Sqdn Shrike convoy protection

STOCKMAN Douglas Ronald FX80745 MID(p) 26-5-42 805 Sqdn Maleme Crete

STOLLERY Henry George FX79439 MID 1-1-45 854 Sqdn four ships in Channel, MID*(p) 15-6-48 854 Sqdn Illustrious belated Palembang

STONE John FX90683 MID(p) 20-6-44 825 Sqdn Vindex attack on U-boat

STURGES Alexander John FX76369 MID 19-5-42 817 Sqdn Victorious ops Norway

SUGGITT Arthur Edward Lieut F55136 DSM 1-1-41 818 Sqdn Ark Royal Ops, MID 9-8-40 818 Sqdn Ark Royal enemy A/C over Norway

SUTHERLAND Kenneth FX86562 DSM 11-12-45 842 Sqdn S.Coast ops

SWEENEY Dennis Eric Lt.Cdr. FX76517 DSM 1-1-41 826 Sqdn S.Coast ops

TAAFE Albert FX80196 MID 1-1-41 819 Sqdn Illustrious ops in Med, MID* 2-1-45 815 Sqdn Victorious Emmahaven

TAPPING Ernest FX76365 MID 25-6-40 818 Sqdn Furious over Norway, MID*(p) 3-3-42 825 Sqdn Manston S'fish.Channel attack

TAYLOR Alfred Newton FX89260 DSM 1-5-45 849 Sqdn Victorious Palembang

TAYLOR Stanley William FX95787 MID 31-7-45 849 Sqdn Victorious Sakishima

THOMAS Arnold FX86751 MID 18-9-45 851 Sqdn Emperor DUKEDOM shadow HAGURO

TOPLISS Cyril Lt.Cdr. FX76315 MBE 1-1-64 HalFar New Year Hons., DSM 25-7-44 827 Sqdn Victorious shipping off Norway

TRAVERSE Anthony Joseph S.Ldr. FX86720 DSM 10-7-45 851 Sqdn Emperor Haguro

TURNER Jeffrey George FX96080 DSM 20-11-45 849 Sqdn Vic attacks on Japan

TUTTON John Traviss FX89176 MID 11-12-45 836 Sqdn Shrike convoy protection

TYLER Alfred Thomas FX76299 MID 11-7-40 821 Sqdn Ark Royal

TYLER Kenneth Richard William FX91659 DSM 7-8-45 846 Sqdn Trumpeter Kilbotn

VINES Clifford Arthur FX115046 DSM 30-5-44 816 Sqdn Chaser Russian convoy

WARD Thomas Leonard FX79440 DSM 20-11-45 828 Sqdn Implacable ops Far East

WATSON Peter LDX5624 DSM 30-6-42 830 Sqdn Malta ops from Malta

WAYLES Jack FX76310 DSM 4-10-40 810 Sqdn Ark Royal ops in Med

WELLS Arthur George FX86880 MID 11-7-44 830 Sqdn Furious ops off Norway

WELLS George Bertram FX82746 DSM 19-12-44 846 Sqdn Trumpeter Arumsund, MID 18-7-44 846 Sqdn Tracker Arctic U355/U288 sunk, MID* 29-11-44 846 Sqdn Trumpeter minelaying

WHEELER Henry Thomas JX189404 MID(p) 3-3-42 825 Sqdn Manston Channel attack

WHYTE John FX115108 MID 11-7-44 830 Sqdn Furious ops off Norway

WIBROW Thomas Ernest FX76305 MID 27-3-45 Stalker invasion S.of France

WICK John Wordsworth SFX1163 DSM 13-7-43 819 Sqdn Archer sinking U752

WILLIAMS Christopher FX115059 MID 20-6-44 825 Sqdn Vindex attacks on U-boats

WILLS Norman Charles FX77510 DSM 1-1-42 824 Sqdn Eagle New Year Hons

WINFINDALE Samuel SFX1575 MID 31-7-45 820 Sqdn Indefatigable Sakishima

WOODLEY William Albert FX115065 MID 31-7-45 848 Sqdn Formidable Sakishima

WOODWARD Stanley Frederick FX96711 MID 20-11-45 848 Sqdn Formid ops Pacific

WOOLMER Thomas Arthur Lt.Cdr.FX78405 MID 15-8-44 845 Sqdn Illustrious Sabang/Sourabaya